Dear China

Dear China

Emigrant Letters and Remittances,
1820–1980

———

Gregor Benton and Hong Liu

UNIVERSITY OF CALIFORNIA PRESS

University of California Press, one of the most distinguished university presses in the United States, enriches lives around the world by advancing scholarship in the humanities, social sciences, and natural sciences. Its activities are supported by the UC Press Foundation and by philanthropic contributions from individuals and institutions. For more information, visit www.ucpress.edu.

University of California Press
Oakland, California

Library of Congress Cataloging-in-Publication Data

Names: Benton, Gregor, author. | Liu, Hong, 1962- author.
Title: Dear China : emigrant letters and remittances, 1820–1980 / Gregor Benton and Hong Liu.
Description: Oakland, California : University of California Press, [2018] | Includes bibliographical references and index. |
Identifiers: LCCN 2018000553 (print) | LCCN 2018006055 (ebook) | ISBN 9780520970540 (ebook) | ISBN 9780520298415 (cloth : alk. paper) | ISBN 9780520298439 (pbk. : alk. paper)
Subjects: LCSH: Emigrant remittances—China—19th century. | Emigrant remittances—China—20th century. | Chinese—Foreign countries—Correspondence. | Chinese—Foreign countries—History. | China—Economic conditions.
Classification: LCC HG3978 (ebook) | LCC HG3978 .B46 2018 (print) | DDC 332/.04246095109034—dc23
LC record available at https://lccn.loc.gov/2018000553

17   26   25   24   23   22   21   20   19   18
10   9   8   7   6   5   4   3   2   1

CONTENTS

MAPS AND TABLES

MAPS

TABLES

FOREWORD

It gives me great pleasure to welcome this comprehensive history of an institution that affected the lives of tens of thousands of overseas Chinese for over two hundred years. These Chinese were known to have regularly sent remittances home to their families in the two southern provinces of Guangdong and Fujian. What was less well-known was that they also sent letters together with the remittances. That was common practice among people who wanted their relatives to know how they were doing abroad and who also sought news of conditions at home. While this was mentioned in early studies of the *Huaqiao* (overseas Chinese), no institution sought to collect such letters, and this major source of social data about the lives of sojourning Chinese and their connections with China has long been neglected. In recent years, however, there have been systematic efforts to remedy this by local scholars in the two provinces, especially in the Chaoshan *qiaoxiang* of eastern Guangdong and those of Jiangmen-Wuyi west of the Pearl River delta. I began to meet scholars who were collecting all the letters they could find. They began to present their findings at national and international meetings to emphasize how these letters that accompanied remittances yielded remarkable stories of social, economic, and cultural changes in remote villages otherwise cut off from the tide of modernization sweeping the country.

   Greg Benton and Hong Liu have done us a great service by examining the collections and the materials in Chinese published so far about the remittance letters and by analyzing afresh their significance in the history of overseas Chinese dispersion and settlement. By so doing, they show how much the system of remittances helped to modernize key areas in local society and economy. They have persuasively argued that the institution of *qiaopi* and *piju* was wedded to local cultural values and, while the system evolved to take advantage of technical advances in modern banking and postal services, they remained rooted in traditional practices. By so doing, the authors have illuminated a key feature of Chinese adaptability, the capacity to utilize the latest methods of transport and transmission without losing the benefits for which the local system was devised.

During the first half of my life, the *qiaopi* culture was still alive. This book has triggered memories of bits of the system that were still relevant to *Huaqiao* lives. I was conscious of it when growing up in the 1930s and remember what still survived in the 1950s when, not least because of the policy changes made by the new government in China, the system began to wind down. I was struck by the system's resilience in the face of major political and economic transformations.

My most vivid memory comes from the late 1930s when I was a primary schoolboy. I remember the groups of letter writers sitting under trees in my home town of Ipoh in the Malay state of Perak, which was at the time a British protectorate. They were talking in Cantonese to customers about what to include in the letters that accompanied the remittances they were making. My family comes from a different region of China, and I knew that my mother sent her monthly remittances home through the local bank and wrote her own letters. The lesson for me was that I must learn to read and write so that I would never have to depend on someone else to write for me.

At that time, war with Japan had inspired patriotic meetings to raise money to support the government in Chongqing. Large sums were collected, and I understood that the money was sent via the Singapore branch of China's national bank. I still remember the day when my mother told my father how her friends suspected that some of that money had fallen into the hands of irresponsible officials who did not account for the sums received. Her friends had expressed the view that the *qiaopi* workers who served ordinary people were more trustworthy than Chinese officials.

Many years later, the subject of remittances came up in my economics course at the University of Malaya. That was in 1951, when my professor, Thomas Silcock, began to teach us about Chinese entrepreneurship in Southeast Asia and referred to remittances contributing to the development of South China. We were looking at estimates based on official figures used by Chinese governments. Professor Silcock focused on Chinese ingenuity in meeting practical needs and how they had devised a unique system that worked. I cannot recall how much he knew about the methods the Chinese used. What struck me was his undisguised admiration for how the Chinese competed wherever they could see a profit and how often they suffered from what he called "an excess of entrepreneurship." Looking back, I note there was no mention of the letters home that best displayed the cultural roots sustaining their practices.

When I began in the 1960s to write on the overseas Chinese in Southeast Asia, no one referred to remittance letters and there were but a few mentions in the extant literature. By that time, I understood that moneys were sent by regular post or through banks. It was not until I read this book that I learned that parts of the system were still operative at the time and continued to provide a valuable backup whenever there were breakdowns in communication or when new obstacles made connections in China inefficient or unreliable.

During my early visits to Xiamen University in the 1970s, I was reminded how important the *qiaopi* system had been to *qiaoxiang* life. Professor Lin Jinzhi told me of the remittance letters in Fujian that he and his colleagues had collected in the 1950s for the university and how they were lost or destroyed during the Cultural Revolution. He stressed how much the letters made a difference to the lives of Hokkien families connected with the Nanyang and why he regretted that there was nothing left of that collection.

Interest in *qiaoxiang* studies began to grow after the economic reforms that opened China to the world. By the 1990s, scholars at Jinan and Zhongshan Universities in Guangzhou used the *qiaokan* newsletters that local libraries had collected to draw attention to their links with remittances and the family correspondence that came with them. When I came to Singapore in 1996, I heard my colleagues working on the Teochew and Hakka communities speak eloquently about the *qiaopi* system and also learned about the systematic collection of *qiaoxiang* letters made in the Jiangmen-Wuyi Cantonese districts.

But there was still no analytical history of the system from its origins through more than a century of expansion and adaptations until it was gradually phased out a few decades ago. The painstaking efforts of Greg Benton and Hong Liu have given us one at last. They examined closely the latest collections and the work of *qiaoxiang* scholars and have not only drawn a full picture of the phenomenon in South China and its subtle links with charity and philanthropy but also provided illuminating comparisons with other migrant experiences elsewhere. For the first time, we can see the system in a global perspective and realize how extraordinary it was. In addition, and perhaps deserving the closest attention, the authors have shown us why studies of Chinese institutions today neglect at their peril the deep cultural roots that ensured their resilience and effectiveness.

Wang Gungwu
National University of Singapore
29 September 2017

ACKNOWLEDGMENTS

The idea of this book was born in April 2013, when its authors were invited to give papers at the International Symposium on Chinese *Qiaopi* and the UNESCO Memory of the World Program in Beijing, organized by the State Archives Administration of China, Guangdong Provincial Government, and Fujian Provincial Government. Two months later, *qiaopi* (emigrant letters accompanied by a family remittance) entered UNESCO's Memory of the World Register. We were impressed by the huge number of *qiaopi* collected and the rich data they contain. At the time, there were virtually no English-language publications on *qiaopi* and their global significance. Soon after the Beijing symposium, we decided to write a comprehensive comparative history of *qiaopi* and the *qiaopi* trade.

Many organizations and individuals have helped us in this research, undertaken in Southeast Asia, China, Europe, North America, and Australia. The Singapore Ministry of Education awarded us an AcRf Tier-1 research grant titled "*Qiaopi* and Changing Memories of the Homeland: Emigrants' Letters, Family Ties, and Transnational Chinese Networks" (M4011208), and Nanyang Technological University (NTU) provided start-up funding (M4081020 and M4081392). NTU's School of Humanities and Social Sciences (now the School of Humanities and the School of Social Sciences) also supported the project, including by hosting Gregor Benton as a visiting professor.

The *Qiaopi* Museum in Shantou, Guangdong Provincial Archives, libraries of Wuyi University and Xiamen University, National Library of Singapore, Chinese Heritage Centre Library, National University of Singapore Chinese Library, City of Vancouver Archives, University of British Columbia Library, and Museum of the Chinese in America provided access to data and, where appropriate, allowed us to reprint material from their collections. We owe all these institutions a deep debt of gratitude.

As a doyen of the study of China and Chinese overseas, Wang Gungwu has been an intellectual inspiration for our research, and we are grateful for his preface. We would also like to thank Zhang Huimei for her capable assistance in researching this book. Many other individuals have helped the project in various ways: Alan Chan Kam Leung, Chen Chunsheng, Kenneth Dean, Els van Dongen, John Fitzgerald, Takeshi Hamashita, Jia Junying, Michael Khor, Kua Bak Lim, Liu Jin, K. K. Luke, Glen Peterson, Shen Huifen, Akita Shigeru, Tomoko Shiroyama, Jing Tsu, Yow Cheun Hoe, and Min Zhou. We are grateful to them all.

The manuscript benefited from reviewers' comments. Our editors at the University of California Press, Reed Malcolm and Bradley Depew, helped prepare the book for publication and improved it in the process. Again, we thank them.

Needless to say, the authors are solely responsible for the views, interpretations, and any remaining errors in the book.

Gregor Benton and Hong Liu

Introduction

From one of the world's largest diasporas, Chinese migrants and their descendants have maintained close ties with their families and their ancestral homeland. Scholars have documented various forms of linkages, including investment, voluntary associations and other social institutions, charity, and political nationalism. However, little is known outside China about the role of *qiaopi* (letters sent together with a remittance) in the sociocultural and political history of China and the Chinese diaspora over the last century and a half (1820–1980). This book is one of a small handful of English-language studies, and the first book-length one, on the characteristics and transformations of *qiaopi*, including their forms, contents, and role in connecting Chinese migrants and descendants and their non-migrant families. It argues that such institutionalized and cross-national mechanisms not only helped sustain the ties of families separated by oceans and political regimes, but also contributed to the sending regions' economic development. Beyond that, they played an important role in the making of a transnational China characterized by extensive flows of people, capital, ideas, and social practices across different sociopolitical and cultural domains in East Asia.

CHINESE INTERNATIONAL MIGRATION IN SPATIAL AND TEMPORAL PERSPECTIVE

Three distinctive phases of international migration out of China can be identified in modern times. In the hundred years between 1850 and 1950, large numbers of southern Chinese (predominantly laborers) went overseas, mainly to Southeast Asia.[1] Until the end of the Second World War and beyond, most still saw themselves

1

as *Huaqiao* ("sojourners" or "overseas Chinese") or *qiaobao* ("overseas compatri-ots"), whose political and cultural orientation was toward the ancestral homeland. During the second period, from 1950 to 1980, two big changes came about: new ethnic-Chinese identities emerged, and the geography of Chinese emigration both in China and abroad widened and diversified. Most Chinese living overseas belonged by then to second or third generations; the outflow of new migrants from China had been put on hold after the founding of the People's Republic in 1949. Some *Huaqiao* continued to identify with China, but most became *Huaren* ("ethnic Chinese") by adopting local citizenship and identifying with their coun-tries of birth and residence. Observers have fixed on two traditional Chinese idi-oms to encapsulate the difference: *luoye guigen* ("fallen leaves return to their roots") refers to those who stayed loyal to their native places in China and wished (usually in vain) to return to them; *luodi shenggen* ("falling to the ground and tak-ing root") refers to those who considered themselves permanently settled outside China and renounced their Chinese citizenship (which did not exclude privately preserving a Chinese lifestyle and cultural values). Beyond these two groups, Hong Kong and Taiwan added new sources of Chinese emigration to the mix, joined by "re-migrants" from Southeast Asia, who also began spreading across the world. Unlike Chinese migrants of previous times, the great majority ended up in the migrant countries of North America and Australia and in Western Europe.[2] In the third and most recent period (1980 to the present), new migrants from main-land China (the so-called *xin yimin*) have begun to form an ever greater propor-tion of overall Chinese emigration, while the trends evident in the second phase have continued. It is now estimated that more than fifty million ethnic and migrant Chinese live outside China, and that Chinese live in almost every corner of the earth.[3]

A variety of mechanisms linked the Chinese diaspora with the homeland, including voluntary associations, investment, trade and business networks, par-ticipation in Chinese politics, and remittances.[4] Studies on these forms of modern Chinese transnationalism have contributed to our understanding of global Chi-nese migration and its roles in both homeland and host lands. However, we know relatively little about how family ties were constructed and maintained in the trans-national social and cultural spaces under different political systems. This question concerns not just Chinese international migration, which generally led to families' physical separation by geography, but modern Chinese history as a whole. In his study on American-Chinese family connections, Haiming Liu points out that "family and home are one word, *jia*, in the Chinese language. Family can be apart, home relocated, but *jia* remains intact, as it signifies a system of mutual obligations and a set of cultural values."[5] In modern China, family was intimately linked to another key unit of Chinese society, the village, which the anthropologist Fei Xiao-tong called "the basic unit of Chinese rural society," built in turn on family and kinship.[6] Hence the sociologist Siu-lun Wong declared that "the essence of Chinese economic organization is familism."[7]

Given the importance of family to Chinese international migration, some recent studies have focused on transnational family strategies and linkages in the age of globalization and the internet, especially the business family.[8] However, with some major exceptions, few studies have appeared in English on the linkages between Chinese international migrants (especially in Southeast Asia, where more than 85 percent of Chinese migrants lived until recently), the family, and the sending places before the advances in transportation and communication technology in the second half of the twentieth century, when most Chinese diasporic attachments switched from China to the country of birth or settlement.[9]

This book looks at the life and times of the *qiaopi*, a crucial link between Chinese migrants and their families and home villages. *Qiaopi* is one of the names (there are several, depending on locality) given in China to letters written home by Chinese emigrants in the 150 years since the 1820s. *Huipi* are the replies.

Around 160,000 *qiaopi* are known to have survived in private collections and public archives in China.[10] They are drawn from China's major regions of outmigration and of settlement overseas, in Southeast Asia, the Americas, and the Pacific. Far fewer *huipi* have survived, given their wider scattering and the greater mobility of their recipients and the recipients' descendants. These materials cover a crucial, defining period in China's modern history and the history of global migration, itself a driving force in global social and economic development.

In June 2013, an archival venture officially designated as the *Qiaopi* Project was formally registered under UNESCO's Memory of the World program, set up in 1992 because of "a growing awareness of the parlous state of preservation of documentary heritage" in the world.[11] The registration of the *Qiaopi* Project followed, and was inspired by, UNESCO's 2007 listing as a World Heritage Site of the Kaiping Village Conservation and Development Project, a project also linked to the history of emigration out of southern China.[12] The Memory of the World program is designed, in part, to bring into the historical record the documentary heritage of groups commonly excluded from it. Chinese migrants, whose documented lives have hitherto served chiefly as material for study by outsiders, are proclaimed by the *Qiaopi* Project's sponsors as a prime example of such a group.

The defining characteristic of a *qiaopi* or *zhengpi* ("main *pi*") was that it comprised both a letter and a remittance (*qiaohui*), usually of money, whereas the *huipi* served in the first instance as a receipt intended for the remitter.[13] This is a key difference between *qiaopi* and most non-Chinese emigrants' letters, which do not by definition include money. Scholars have noted the importance of remittances for China as a crucial factor in its economic growth and in the ideology and practice of its emigration. A main focus of this study is on the letters (and their sociocultural meaning), neglected by comparison with the better-known remittances.

However, letters and remittances were closely related and are not easily separated analytically. They traveled along identical logistical networks as part of a single transaction and simultaneously reinforced the families' transnational sentiment. The study, therefore, also examines the remittances, and the institutions through which letters and remittances reached China and through which the *huipi* reached the remitters.

The study aims to paint a broad picture of the *qiaopi* collection and of the historical and institutional context within which the *qiaopi* phenomenon emerged; the evolution of its institutions; the letters' themes, styles, types, and purposes; the range of the various recipients of remittances; the management and delivery of *qiaopi*; their role in maintaining ties of kinship and native place; and the moral world they helped sustain and at whose heart they lay. It will also explore differences in the *qiaopi* trade between Chinese provinces and parts of provinces; differences in letters' themes, depending on their writers' geographic origin in China or their destination (say, North America or Southeast Asia); and changes in the *qiaopi* trade over time, ending eventually in its demise. The study is based in part on archival materials collected in China and elsewhere, but it also draws on ideas and references from scores of essays and monographs written by *qiaopi* scholars in Guangdong, Fujian, and other places, as well as primary materials collected in Southeast Asia, North America, and Australia.

As the first monograph in English on *qiaopi*, this book is concerned not just with *qiaopi* themselves but with broader related issues that add to our understanding of modern China and the Chinese diaspora. The letters home served as an important link between China and Chinese overseas, who were tied emotionally, socially, and economically with a China that was in the middle of a process of radical change toward a modern society and state. The remittances sent home by Chinese migrants not only served to lift the migrants' families out of poverty but were a wellspring of China's economic modernization. Partly as a result of the *qiaopi* trade, modern mechanisms and institutions of finance and communication such as banks and post offices became a cornerstone of the modern Chinese state, from the late Qing and the Republic to the People's Republic. The study argues that *qiaopi* served as an indispensable mechanism linking Chinese migrants, their families, their hometowns, and China. This, in turn, has acted as a key foundation for the emergence and evolution of modern Chinese transnationalism, a dimension of Chineseness often ignored in the existing literature.[14]

So *qiaopi* provide a unique window into modern China. They illuminate our understanding of external China (the Chinese diaspora) and its impact upon and connections with a changing Chinese homeland, and they show China from new angles on its margins and at its lower levels. The immigrants were, on the whole, poor peasants without any formal education. Most were from Guangdong and Fujian, provinces that, until the reform era beginning in the late 1970s, were relatively peripheral to modern Chinese history and politics. Their voice, as heard in these letters, is a record of a China quite different from that described in writings of the Chinese elite in Beijing, Nanjing, and Shanghai. They are the big diaspora—not the tiny diaspora of students, diplomats, and established businesspeople that previously monopolized the attention of observers—the true voice of a transnational China whose formation can be traced back to the beginning of the nineteenth century, when the whole of Asia was swept up into the vortex of globalization.

This study aims to contribute to an understanding of modern and contemporary China from a transnational perspective. Since John Fairbank, scholars have paid much attention to how external environments and forces shaped China's domestic evolution from the point of view of trade, diplomacy, commercial culture, and diaspora.[15] Scholars have also begun to examine China from a transnational perspective. The anthropologist Mayfair Mei-hui Yang, for example, defines "transnational China" as geographically comprising "mainland China, Taiwan, Hong Kong, and overseas Chinese communities all over the world." She further argues:

> I would like to adopt the term *transnational China* to capture the spatial and geographical extension of Chinese culture across national and political boundaries and take into account the persistent interconnectedness among these cultural offshoots with each other and with the "Motherland." This interconnectedness can be seen in terms of both the flows of people, goods, and culture across these boundaries as well as the maintenance of a "Chinese identity," still defined as singular even though it is distinctively differentiated according to place. The fact that transnational China can be seen as a very loosely organized entity (more a network than a social organism) in the world today is due both to its being the product of an inherited cultural heritage as well as to the ongoing maintenance, renewal, and reinvention of cultural connections and a Chinese identity through cultural and materials flows across political borders.[16]

Existing studies on transnational China have been written primarily from a cultural studies perspective, with a focus on contemporary China at the time of globalization and technological advancement.[17] But it is important to understand transnational China historically and from an institutional perspective, examining the intersecting flows of people, culture, ideas, and capital. By analyzing both the material and the spiritual dimensions of this transnational connectedness, this study on the role played by *qiaopi* and the *qiaopi* trade in making China transnational cuts across different domains and approaches them from the perspective of *qiaopi* and their senders and recipients as well as associated agents, thus adding to the debate a hitherto neglected but equally important dimension of the matter.

This study on *qiaopi* in historical and comparative perspective will also contribute to an understanding of the continuing importance of remittance in developing countries. The World Bank estimated officially recorded remittances to developing countries at \$401 billion in 2012. Remittances remain a crucial resource flow, one that far exceeds official development assistance as well as private debt and portfolio equity in volume. China received US\$51 billion of remittances in 2010, second only to India, which received US\$55 billion.[18] China was again the second-largest recipient in 2015, with an inflow of \$63.9 billion.[19] While the means of communication have changed beyond recognition, with the telephone, social media, and the internet replacing handwritten letters mailed home through remittance houses, the substance of the remittance (linking immigrants with the family and homeland) and its various modes (formal and informal) remain a key feature of contemporary migration and overseas settlement.[20] Remittance has also continued to influence the political economy and social and cultural behavior of post-reform China.[21]

QIAOPI

Qiaopi as a specialist trade in the remitting of letters accompanied by money grew out of a rudimentary system that started, at the latest, in the eighteenth century, when migrants communicated with their families by way of returning kinsmen who took back an oral or written message, with or without cash. Some studies date the origins of the practice even earlier, to the Ming's Jiajing reign (1522–66), when two Fujianese brothers in the Philippines are said, in local records, to have regularly sent home remittances "on which the whole family relied," and when other overseas traders sent back "silver and letters."[22] Others claim that the first *qiaopi* were sent from Thailand even before the Ming.[23] As early as 1810, Chinese in the Dutch East Indies (today's Indonesia) are said to have remitted the equivalent of 1.7 million yuan to China.[24] However, early remittances are hard to trace, given that they were, for most of the time, illegal from the point of view of the Chinese authorities and did not usually figure in official records. The *qiaopi* traffic grew massively after the Beijing Convention of 1860, concluded between the Qing Court and Great Britain, France, and Russia. This treaty decreed the protection of Chinese emigrants, who had previously been unprotected. (The decree did not, in the event, prevent continuing discrimination against Chinese in many, if not most, migrant destinations.)[25] As for the *qiaopi* trade's eventual demise, some date it to in 1973, when a state directive put it under the direct control of the People's Bank of China, but most date it to 1979, when *qiaopi* personnel were incorporated into local state-owned banks and control of the remittance trade was put in the hands of the banks.[26] This study takes 1820 as the starting point of *qiaopi* as a distinctive mechanism combining letters and remittance joining China and the Chinese in diaspora, and 1980 as the equally rough, unofficial date of its final demise.

The defining feature of the *qiaopi* was, as we have seen, that it comprised a letter (*pixin*) and silver (*pikuan*, i.e., "money") in one envelope. The remitter usually recorded the amount remitted on the envelope, employing complex variants of numerals designed to prevent their fraudulent alteration, and again on the enclosed letter. As well as letter and money, the envelope might also contain bills, invoices, and other official documents recording the transaction.[27] Besides the amount, the envelope registered the name of the sender and the name and address (often just the village) of the intended recipient (often rendered simply as "father," "grand-mother," etc.).[28] Many remittance houses stamped the envelope with promotional slogans, Confucian homilies, or—during the war—calls for a boycott of imperial-ist Japan and defense of the Chinese motherland. The arrival of a *qiaopi* in the village was the equivalent for most recipients of a visit from a loved one, a form of intense psychological consolation.

Not all *qiaopi* conformed to the definition of money plus letter. In the case of death notices, a letter alone could be expected, but a so-called *baixin* (a letter with-out money) was otherwise unlikely; at the very least, a couple of dollars would be attached as a token of regard and a promise for the future. Nor was there always a letter, as we explain later, though its absence usually had a special explanation. So the saying "If there's a letter, there's bound to be money; if there's money, there's bound to be a letter" did not always apply.[29]

There were several forms of remittance. The three most common were *xinhui* ("mail transfer"), *piaohui* ("draft remittance"), and *dianhui* ("telegraphic transfer"). In the case of mail transfer, the amount (usually small) was generally recorded on the left-hand side of the envelope (and therefore also known as *waifu*, "handed over externally"). Mail transfers and *waifu* remittances had to be delivered personally, so they were relatively expensive. Draft remittances were money orders designed or sold by the *piju* and placed inside the envelope (hence *neifu*, "handed over inter-nally"). They were cheaper because they could be cashed by the payee at the *piju*, either on sight or a few days later, or by a third party (say, the owner of a local store). Telegraphic transfer was quickest (in fact, practically instantaneous), but it was also dearest and was typically used only in emergencies.[30]

After the consolidation of a modern banking and postal system in the region, *piju* in Southeast Asia began dealing with letter and money separately, although the two items belonged nominally to a single transaction. The letter was usually sent by post to the *piju*'s branch or agent in China, whereas the money was turned into a money order that could be exchanged in Hong Kong (the entrepôt for nearly all the *qiaopi* trade). Alternatively, it was either posted to an intermediary in Hong Kong who then turned it into currency that could be used in the Chinese interior or posted directly to the *piju*'s branch or agent in China, where it could be sold to a local bank or *qianzhuang*.

In her study on the role of Hong Kong in the Chinese diaspora, Elizabeth Sinn argues that "for Chinese migrants, two of the most meaningful ways of maintain-ing ties with their native homes were sending money and arranging while still alive to have their bones sent home for reburial."[31] She concludes that Hong Kong "occupied a special place in the consciousness of emigrants. For many emigrants leaving China, Hong Kong was their first stop outside China, and paradoxically, also their first stop in China on their return home. . . . The comfort zone that Hong Kong offered might have contributed to its reputation as the second home of overseas Chinese."[32]

In the interlude between receipt and delivery, the *qiaopi* sometimes underwent several currency conversions, starting with the initial conversion on receipt. Each conversion usually benefited the *piju*, which was more interested in charting a favorable course and devising appropriate strategies on the exchange market than in charging the remitter a fee for the remittance, which was therefore sometimes delivered at no cost.[33]

The remittance office issued a counterfoil on receipt of the *qiaopi* and put a serial number (*bianhao*) on the counterfoil, the envelope, and the envelope provided for the reply (the *huipi*). This serial, sometimes starting with a *huama*, one of the indigenous "positional" numerals traditionally used in Chinese markets, was typically prefaced in Thailand and associated countries and in Malaya by a *liezi* ("list character"), usually drawn from the *Qian zi jing* ("Thousand character classic"), and in Singapore and the Philippines by a character rotated from the name of the remittance company or from an auspicious phrase.[34] By consulting the list character, it was easy to distinguish which company had handled the remittance. The serial was supplemented by the *banghao* ("shipment number"), in Roman or (less often) Arabic numerals, based on the *bang* or *chuanbang* ("shipment"), through which it was possible to identify the place at which the *qiaopi* had initially been collected. Thus, the simple numbering of remittances practiced by *shuike* developed over the years into a complex indicator.[35]

The *bianhao* or *banghao* connected the entire process of remittance, each stage of which was tracked by the remittance office and its representatives. The shipping documents associated with a delivery were in some cases dispatched twice, on successive sailings, in case the first dispatch was for some reason lost or mislaid. An essential moment in the system was *xiaohao* ("cancelling the number"). This happened three times: on delivery to the recipient, in the port through which the reply (*huipi*) was dispatched, and on the reply's arrival at the original remittance place. An uncollected, uncashed remittance was usually kept by an office for a maximum of ten years, whereafter it expired.[36]

Migrants usually sent their first *qiaopi*, together with a token sum of a dollar or two commonly advanced by the clan association or a kin-based remittance house, from the port of disembarkation to let the family know they had arrived. This initial *qiaopi* was known, for obvious reasons, as the *ping'an pi* ("safe-and-sound *pi*").[37]

From a financial point of view, most *qiaopi* were designed to perform two main functions—to support the family and pay off debts, including debts incurred in the process of migrating.[38] They were used to pay for food and clothes, education, and building or repairing houses; lending to kin; paying local taxes; and funding weddings, funerals, and other family events.[39] Most letters, apart from general expressions of well-wishing, therefore contained a sentence along these lines: "Your son abroad herewith has a small benefit for you; naturally it should be more."[40] Instructions for distributing the remittance to blood relatives, affines, and (occasionally) friends were nearly always set out in strict order of seniority and kinship proximity.[41]

Big remittances were often done on credit and then paid on proof of receipt in China.[42] At times, huge amounts were remitted under the *qiaopi* system. In 1941, for example, under the special circumstances of the war, one *qiaopi* included a remittance of $10 million (in Nationalist currency) and another of $600,000.[43]

Qiaopi were nearly always addressed to the head of the family and members of senior generations, and the accompanying messages were cast in exaggeratedly polite language expressing humble salutations and as if the writer were kneeling in reverence. Around two in three recipients were the writer's grandparents or parents, and they were mostly male; the writer's sons were likelier recipients even than the writer's mother. Of five hundred *qiaopi* analysed in one study, only ten were addressed to the wife, and even fewer female in-laws.[44] Female recipients were likely to be senior: grandmother rather than mother, mother rather than wife.

Being in essence an appendage to a remittance, most letters were cursory, abrupt, and incommunicative, save for a stereotyped filial (husbandly, fatherly, etc.) salutation and a word or two about how to distribute the money. Space was in any case often limited by the size of the sheet of paper provided by the remittance house, which was usually skimpy and much smaller than normal letter paper.[45] Only a minority of letters went into detail.

Most remitters were illiterate or semiliterate, able to do little more than fill in the amount and date, so their *qiaopi* were often composed with the help of someone else, by professional scribes, or—in some *piju*—by an assistant, for free.[46] In Singapore, letter writers sat at roadside stalls "consisting of a small rude table, a little bundle of paper, a brush, some China ink, and a stool on which the operator sits." These stalls were situated on public verandas, under trees, or in the shadow of walls. The letter writers charged between three and six cents a letter, depending on the amount of writing done.[47] One paid letter-writer explained in a memoir the difficulties of rendering messages and even names and addresses given in outlandish dialects, and how what he wrote was sometimes based on guesswork.[48]

Some letters had a strong local linguistic flavor, full of dialect expressions; others were in semiclassical Chinese. Many were standard letters preprinted by the office as a convenience to remitters who feared that if they wrote the letters themselves and failed to observe conventions, they would be laughed at in the villages when their letters were read aloud by the postman. For the literate, a space was left on preprinted forms for private comments.[49]

The handwriting in the letters was often clumsy and done in a jumble of styles with a large number of miswritten characters.[50] However, some letters displayed considerable calligraphic skill, executed in the early years with the traditional brush.[51] Because the paper provided was generally not just flimsy but tiny, to keep the overall weight and therefore cost to a minimum, most letter writers opted for the *xingshu* ("running script") or *kaishu* ("regular script") style of writing, both of which are relatively regular and compact, allowing a larger number of characters to be fitted into a small space.[52]

Calligraphy had an elevated status in old China and was prized and revered above other artistic genres. In previous times it was associated exclusively with the educated elite, principally the literati, as an emblem of the ruling class and its authority.[53] In the twentieth century, however, it became a popular art form (known as *minjian shufa*, "people's calligraphy") practiced as a hobby and a means of self-expression by Chinese of all classes and circles. *Qiaopi* calligraphy was part of this artistic revolution. Calligraphy was an integral part of the curriculum of the primary schools set up in and after 1898 in China's towns and villages, and many of the migrants who went abroad from Guangdong and Fujian took with them a basic grounding in it. Migrants' children born overseas or taken abroad at an early age would also have been exposed to it at the Chinese-language schools set up in Chinatown, for such schools usually followed the same curriculum as those in China. Over the last twenty years, people's calligraphy has become more and more an object of study in China, and some scholars have written about its *qiaopi* variant.

Unlike elite calligraphy, a high art form, *qiaopi* calligraphy was typically simple and unadorned. The brush work was often clumsily executed, irregular, and slapdash, and the characters did not conform to accepted rules of structure and composition. For the educated elite, calligraphy was an object of intense study and constant practice, whereas for *qiaopi* writers it had a practical rather than an aesthetic purpose and was usually performed on inferior paper with poor-quality ink and brushes, or even with fountain pens and ballpoint pens. Yet the *qiaopi* writers' very lack of training in the finer points of brushmanship often lent their writing a special vigour and vitality, infused with an element of improvisation and naïve creativity.[54]

As later chapters show, the relationship between the remitter and the courier or entrepreneur who executed the transaction was based on trust, but that did not mean that remitters were unskeptical. Most remitters, especially the illiterate ones, were keenly aware of the chance of being rooked and fleeced. There are many folk stories about illiterate remitters using prearranged codes (e.g., drawings of dogs and temples to represent numbers) to outwit potential cheats.[55]

Not all *qiaopi* followed the "silver plus letter" formula. Some remitters sent goods as well or instead. From Singapore, Stamford Raffles reported in 1817 that Chinese remitted birds' nests, camphor, sea cucumbers, tin, opium, pepper, hides, indigo, and precious metals.[56] A typical later consignment consisted of cloth, a belt, a pen, a sweatshirt, headache remedies, and soap.[57] Medicines and health remedies like Tiger Balm were a staple item, and in the 1950s, especially during famines, people sent grain, flour, pig fat, and chemical fertilizer in crates or steel containers.[58]

Sometimes in the early years of the trade, before its professionalization, or during wars or to evade prying authorities, the remittance was accompanied by a *koupi* or "oral *pi*," a message transmitted by word of mouth rather than in writing. During the Sino-Japanese War of 1937–45, for example, sums were entrusted viva voce to a reliable deliverer, who memorized the amount and address and took back at most a bare signature to prove receipt. Some deliverers memorized dozens or hundreds of such messages for crowds of clients.[59]

The communication's principal aim was often to convey precise instructions on how to distribute the money sent. Other common topics included children's education, matters concerning children's or other relatives' emigration, children's marriage plans, the maintenance of good neighborly relations, and other family or communal business. The emigration policies of foreign countries, and tactics to deal with them, often figured in the correspondence.[60] Because of the Chinese Exclusion Act (which was signed into law in 1882), the letters that flowed either way between China and North America were particularly likely to focus on immigration, how to deal with interrogation (on arrival), and how to get work.[61]

One set of letters shows how a family used kinship ties to construct a migration network across the Pacific, North America, and Southeast Asia that provided family members with the information and resources (birth certificates, application forms, depositions, witness statements) necessary to circumvent the ban.[62] One lineage, the Guan, from Wuyi in Guangdong, used letters to create a Guan diaspora several thousand strong with branches and outposts across much of the United States, Canada, and Cuba.[63]

Some letters rose above the level of platitudes and clichés to deal with weightier issues, including the state of the world, China, and the writer's native place or place of settlement and proposals for radical reform.[64] Most migrants focused exclusively on hard work as the hoped-for way out of poverty, but some not only sympathized with these new viewpoints but proselytized for them in letters home. There are numerous instances of such proselytizing of family and friends in the *qiaopi* collections, just as there is evidence of migrants' and dependents' politicization in the inscriptions painted on the houses built in China by *qiaojuan* and *guiqiao*. At every important political juncture in the history of modern China and the Chinese diaspora, letters home and, in some cases, letters from China to abroad (the *huipi*), as well as intra-diasporic correspondence that followed *qiaopi* circuits, reflected the changes and discussed how to respond to them. This was particularly true during the Hundred Days Reform of 1898, the Emperor-Protection movement, the reformers' Business Revitalization campaign, the anti-Japanese movement, the National Salvation movement, the Sino-Japanese War, the Korean War, the Cultural Revolution, and the fall of the "Gang of Four" after Mao's death. Occasionally, correspondents described foreign customs, viewpoints, and institutions, providing a grass-roots perspective on the world often quite different from that reported by university students and diplomats in their correspondence and dispatches.[65]

Most letter writers spoke only sparingly, if at all, about themselves, and far more copiously about those left behind at home.[66] Only a small minority conveyed strongly personal or emotional messages, and love letters were exceedingly rare (though not entirely lacking).[67] Most of the more substantial letters remained relentlessly fixated on the ancestral place—its land and fields, gods and spirits, natural environment, and ecology—and, of course, on their own ancestors, whose souls demanded reverence and ritual attention.[68]

A rich popular culture grew up around *qiaopi*, both in China and overseas. Tales, anecdotes, and legends lionized well-known couriers (*shuike*), deliverers (*pijiao*), and remittance shops.[69] Praising stalwarts of the *qiaopi* trade continued after 1949, when stories about *qiaopi* heroes became a staple of Communist propaganda in migrant regions, designed to boost remittances and thus the wider economy, and when *pijiao* were feted, Stakhanovite-style, at conferences.[70]

Qiaopi songs and poems abounded in the *qiaoxiang*, China's regions of out-migration, and included "going-abroad ballads," "thinking-of-home laments," "returning-home melodies," and "reporting-home songs." They came in many styles—literary and elegant, vulgar and demotic—and took the form of folk songs, ballads, Hakka mountain songs, ditties, free-verse poems, and classical poems ranging from *lüshi* to *ci* and *lian*. Many of the songs were in dialect. Initially, they were anonymous. Later, however, authorship was claimed—by migrants, dependents, popular singers, professional singers, scholars, luminaries, and after 1949, "cultural cadres."[71]

HUIPI

The *huipi* were originally devised by the remittance houses as a way of setting at rest the minds of remitters, for whom they were proof of delivery. *Qiaopi* traders realized that families in remote areas could not easily come by paper and envelopes, so the traders started gluing a small *huipi* envelope to the bigger *qiaopi* envelope, containing a slip of flimsy paper at most two or three inches wide and three or four inches long—even smaller and less substantial than the paper provided for the letter accompanying the *qiaopi*. (Where this *huipi* sheet was not included, the office at the port of arrival in China might insert one.) The *huipi* envelope bore the same serial number as the original *qiaopi*. Often, recipients were required to sign two *huipi* stubs, one meant for the remitter and the other for the company. Some companies stamped the *qiaopi* with an instruction to recipients to "reply promptly on receipt [of this] in order to spare worry on the remitter's part" and not "to write at length." The post office, which at a certain point in the history of the *qiaopi* trade came to supervise its middle section (between initial receipt of the *qiaopi* or *huipi* and its final delivery), joined in the bullying, stressing that only one sheet might be used and that including others' letters in one's own envelope would incur a fine.[72]

In cases where *qiaopi* were dispensed by the *piju* on credit, receipt of the *huipi* triggered the remitter's repayment of the loan. It is not known when this system of advances first developed as part of the *qiaopi* trade, but it may have started with the *shuike*, especially after they became associated with stores and other businesses whose owners used loans to attract custom. Eventually, the system of advances became widespread in the trade, particularly in the Philippines,[73] and traders developed a system to check the creditworthiness of would-be recipients of advances. However, unlike modern banks, which also loaned money, there was usually no requirement of a guarantor.[74]

The *huipi* was originally a creative innovation by the Chaoshan branch of the *qiaopi* trade, but it spread across mainland and maritime Southeast Asia and in many places became an essential moment in the remittance process.[75] In the Americas and Australasia, where few Chaoshanese lived, the process of delivery and receipt was less sophisticated. There and in Wuyi, the main sending area for these two continents, few companies provided *huipi* envelopes, and *huipi* were often sent not to individual addressees but to Chinese stores, which displayed them in racks in the store window for collection by the migrant.[76]

Typical *huipi* themes included requests for money to meet family needs, complaints about missing remittances, and reasons why the addressee should return home (the wife's hard life, the father's yearning for his son, the father's or brothers' business plans, children's worries about their father's health, etc.). A mother would urge her son to come home and marry; parents would enjoin thrift and hard work on him. Others would inquire of the relative abroad about how to emigrate.[77]

Few recipients of *qiaopi* could read or write, so the courier or *pijiao* often wrote the reply on their behalf. The *huipi* were then bundled together and sent off, although some recipients mailed their own. After 1949, under the People's Republic, writing *huipi* became the job of specialist teams whose members wrote thousands of letters and, in the course of their work, reunited hundreds of lost relatives. This job required tact, knowledge, and guile. The bare mention of the export of money became taboo in some destination countries after 1949, when the authorities in some places banned *qiaopi* altogether. However, in the early years of the People's Republic, remittances were crucial for China's economic development, so the lines along which they flowed had to be kept open.[78] As a result, secret codes were used to enable remitters to evade the bans. At the same time, wives were urged to become literate so that they could solicit remittances and thus benefit both themselves and the state.[79]

Far fewer *huipi* than *qiaopi* have survived into the present. This is because most early Chinese emigrants lived makeshift lives and moved often. However, without the replies the record will remain one-sided and incomplete, for the majority of those left behind in the villages were women.[80] Chinese scholars in China and overseas therefore emphasize the need to track down and preserve them wherever possible.

QIAOPI TERMS

The *qiaopi* trade became a major force in the economies of the *qiaoxiang* and of Chinese communities abroad, and it enriched the Chinese language with dozens of terms, either newly coined or adapted from old usages. This terminology was complex and wide-ranging in itself, and it varied greatly by dialect and place and over time.

Overseas migrants were collectively known under various names, including the standard *Huaqiao* ("Chinese sojourner"). They were also known in southeastern China as *xinke* ("new guest") or *xintang* ("new Tang person"), *Tangren* ("Tang person") being a name applicable to both Cantonese and Fujianese. The term *Huaqiao* dates back to the nineteenth century, but it was not until 1918 that it was incorporated into the official nomenclature by the State Council of the then-warlord government in Beijing, which in 1922 elevated the Overseas Chinese Office to a bureau. However, the bureau existed mainly in name only. In 1927–8, the new Republican government in Nanjing set up institutions that had real power and influence, which deepened in following years.[81]

As for *Huaqiao* destinations, Southeast Asia was known in China as the Nanyang or Southern Ocean, also referred to as *fan* ("foreign, barbarian"), hence *fanke* ("overseas migrant") and *fanyin* ("foreign silver," i.e., "remittance"). Western regions of North America were known as *jinshan* ("gold mountain"), later renamed *jiu jinshan* ("old gold mountain," used today to designate San Francisco) after gold was discovered in Australia (*xin jinshan*, "new gold mountain").[82] Chinese laborers in North America were known as *jinshanke* or *jinshanbo* ("gold mountain guest/uncle"), their wives as *jinshanpo* ("gold mountain woman"), and their children as *jinshanshao* ("gold mountain youngster").[83]

The couriers who started taking remittances to China in the early days, on a largely individual basis before the institutionalization of the *qiaopi* trade, were known as *shuike* ("water guests") and less commonly as *nanyangke* ("Southern Ocean guests"), *zoushui* ("water goers"), or *yangshuike* ("foreign water guests").[84] The term *shuike* dates back to the Western Jin (265–316) or Tang (618–907), when it referred to boatmen and fishermen; later, it came to mean petty itinerant traveler, before acquiring its modern sense of "courier."[85] In some places, a distinction was made between *chidanshui* ("freshwater eaters"), couriers at the domestic end of the chain, and the *liucushui* ("saltwater skaters") who connected China and the world.[86] In Guangdong's Guangfu region, domestic couriers were called *xunchengma* ("town-patrolling horses") or, if they specialized in carrying goods, *zoudanbang* ("lone travelers"). Couriers who simultaneously (or exclusively) escorted migrants to and from places overseas, after assembling them in the nearest port, were known as *ketou* ("guest chiefs," often written as *kheh-tau* and translated as crimps, or "coolie brokers"[87]) or *datou* ("[guest] senders").[88] The premises couriers lived in overseas were called *hangguan* ("trade building") or *piguan* ("*pi* building"), and the hostels or barracoons the migrants lodged in were called *kezhan* ("guest hostels") or *kejian* ("guest spaces").[89]

The term *qiaopi* itself is a compound of *qiao*, "to sojourn abroad," and *pi*, where *qiao* is short for *Huaqiao*. Strictly speaking, *qiao* only applies to those living outside China who are Chinese nationals, not to the *Huaren* ("ethnic Chinese") whose tie to China is only of descent and ethnicity, and who came to account for an ever-growing proportion of remitters as the generations deepened. This was especially so after 1955, when dual nationality was abolished and Chinese outside China were required to choose between citizenship of China and of their country of residence.[90] It is inapplicable, for the same reason, to Chinese in Taiwan, Hong Kong, and Macao, who also remitted in large numbers. However, the term *qiaopi* endured in administration and scholarship, despite its terminological inaccuracy in some cases.[91]

As for the word *pi*, it has been the subject of intense debate among *qiaopi* scholars, especially between scholars from the *qiaoxiang* in Chaoshan and southern Fujian, where languages belonging to two major dialect groups are spoken. Some scholars explain the term by the fact that in southern Fujian *pi* means "letter," but others dispute this theory. Some believe that *pi* is a Chaoshan word unconnected with the Fujianese usage and means not letter but, in Chaoshan dialect, a note to record the sending or receiving of money, or even the remittance itself, the "silver." In fact, this usage has been firmly embedded in Chinese since Tang times (in the form of *pizi*, subsequently elided in the Chao dialect to *pi*). In this view, the Chaoshan term prevailed partly because Chaoshan people played a dominant role in Chinese migration overseas (and in establishing the *qiaopi* trade) and partly because speakers of Fujian dialects confused the Chaoshan meaning with their own.[92]

The Chaoshan scholar Zeng Xubo, in an analysis of linguistic evidence contained in letters and on remittance envelopes, cites a Qing envelope on which the term *yinpi* ("silver *pi*") clearly refers, exclusively, to the "silver" accompanying an item delivered by an official postal station, a domestic transaction originating in that case in the Lianghuai region of northern Jiangsu and unconnected with the dispatch of remittances from abroad. From this evidence, he concludes that this use of the term *pi*, which survived prominently in Chaoshan dialect and among Chaoshanese overseas, can be found in documents from other parts of China.

To reinforce his argument that *pi* does not mean letter but refers to the remittance or note of remittance, Zeng points out that many *qiaopi* were not actually accompanied by a letter or even by a brief note—not surprising, given that the great majority of migrant remitters were illiterate or semiliterate. While some illiterate remitters wrote letters with the help of friends, remittance-shop employees, or professional letter writers, this was often impossible, especially in the case of the remittances collected in scores or hundreds by representatives of the remittance shops who toured the mines, farms, factories, and jungle clearance sites where many of the migrants worked. These remittance touts were usually in a hurry to avoid missing the next sailing, and they could hardly write letters for all their clients. Most clients simply registered the amount and address of their remittances unless there was something urgent that needed saying. Zeng concludes that letterless remittances were far more common than most scholars assume, but that the evidence for them was—for obvious reasons—also far less likely to survive than those accompanied by letters. As a result, the phenomenon has been minimized or overlooked.[93]

The word *pi* can also mean "batch" in standard Chinese, which has led other scholars to believe that it connotes the shipments in which letters reached Chinese ports.[94] However, Zeng Xubo points out that the measure word *pi*, meaning "batch," is not usual in the dialects of either Chaoshan or Minnan (southern Fujian), both of which use the word *bang* to convey this meaning.[95]

Whatever its origin and precise meaning, it seems that Chaoshanese first used the term *pi* in its new context, referring to *qiaohui*, in Singapore sometime between 1829 and 1835, whence it spread to nearby Hakka-speaking Meixian in Guangdong.[96] Other names used to denote *qiaopi* include *fanpi* ("foreign [or barbarian] *pi*") and, in Guangfu, *yinxin* ("silver letter") or *xinyin*, short for *shuxin yinliang*. A variant form of *qiaopi* was the aforementioned *koupi* or *kouxin* ("oral *pi* or letter"), sent by mouth in the early days of the trade or in wartime; *anpi* ("secret *pi*") were remittances sent in code to evade overseas government bans, especially after 1945 and 1949. In the Guangfu region, the source of most of the Chinese emigrants in North America, the terms *yinxin* and *jinshan xin* ("gold mountain letter") were usual.[97] The term *qiaopi* must, of course, be distinguished from *qiaohui* ("emigrant remittance"), which has a broader meaning.

The word *qiaopi*, one name among many for a phenomenon that took regional forms and had regional names, became standard, at least in official parlance at the national level, in the years between 1928 and 1931, after successive government rulings. At first, the authorities in Nanjing rejected the *pi* element in the compound on the grounds that it was not linguistically "standard" (*dian*) and instead favored the term *qiaohui* ("remittance"). In most regions, however, the name *qiaopi* endured. Then, in 1931 a changed ruling gave official sanction to the popular term, though without the prefix *Hua* ("Chinese").[98]

There are at least a dozen names for the companies that ran the *qiaopi* trade, including *qiaopiju* ("*qiaopi* office"), *pixinju* ("remittance-letter office"), *yinxinju* ("*yinxin* office"), *xinju* ("letter office"), and *huidui zhuang* ("remittance shop"). Some names had regional associations. In southern Fujian, the companies were known as *minxinju* ("people's letter office") or *piju* ("*pi* office"), in the Chaoshan region of eastern Guangdong as *piguan* ("*pi* shop"), and in Guangfu as *huiduiju* ("remittance offices").[99] Different names were used in Thailand (*yinxinju*) and French Indochina (*pixinju*), although the trade in mainland (as opposed to maritime) Southeast Asia came in time to form a single system. The term *minxinju*, as we shall see, originally applied to native-style domestic post offices and was the usual name for remittance houses in Fujian, even those with overseas ties, during the Qing dynasty and in some places right through until the 1950s. In Chaoshan, on the other hand, the names *piju* and *piguan* prevailed.[100] Officially, the term *qiaopiju* was favored, after a meeting of businesspeople in 1931 argued that names like *pixinju* could lead to confusion with domestic postal services since they lacked the *qiao* prefix.[101] In this study, we stick to *piju*, to mark up their special function and because it is the shortest name. After 1949, the terms *qiaohuiye* ("remittance trade") and *qiaohui zhuang* ("remittance shop") were officially used, and employees in the *qiaopi* trade were known as *pigong* ("*pi* workers").[102]

Qiaopi deliveries were at first largely random and opportunist, but later they became more regular. The person (usually a man) who delivered the letters and money to the villages was known, variously, as *pijiao* ("*pi* feet"), *daipiren* ("*pi* deliverer"), or *piban* ("*pi* companion"), and his or her sack as the *pibao* or *pidai*. A substantial remittance was a *dapi* ("big *pi*"). The distribution of remittance letters around the houses was known as *fenpi* ("distributing *pi*"). The reply, or *huipi* ("return *pi*"), was written on a *pizai* ("*pi* child"), the tiny sheet of paper glued to the back of the *qiaopi* envelope by the *piju* for the recipient's convenience. In some places, the *huipi* were gathered together in the village store to save the *pijiao* time, a process called *shoupi* ("gathering the *pi*"). *Panpi* ("hoping for *pi*") and *kaopi* ("relying on *pi*") expressed the sense of *pi* as a lifeline. In the Sino-Japanese War, when the trade was disastrously interrupted in some places, a fateful new term entered the language: *piduan*, "the breaking off of *pi*".[103]

The complex and diverse terms used with reference to *qiaopi* highlight three key themes that are centrally relevant both to *qiaopi* studies themselves and to the history of the Chinese diaspora in the context of a transnational China. First, systemic mechanisms linked both the Chinese in diaspora and their respective hometowns and a China that, at the time, was emerging as a nation state. While the *qiaopi* sources and destinations changed across the 160 years covered by this book, an abiding set of linkages and modes of operation lies at the heart of this study.

Second, the variation in the terms used in the *qiaopi* trade reflected the diversity of the connections associated with localities, dialects, associations, and different political regimes in China and the diasporic hostlands. This study focuses on this diversity and its implications for an understanding of transnational China. Third, the interactions of *qiaopi* and their external sociopolitical environment shaped the nature and characteristics of *qiaopi*, also a key subject of our analysis.

The Genealogy of *Qiaopi* Studies

In recent years, histories of migration and overseas settlement have been increasingly written, in part, from migrants' correspondence. Edited collections of migrants' letters have appeared, particularly in the United States and Australia. However, this has been conspicuously less the case for some ethnic groups—in particular, non-white groups—than for others. Most of the better-known anthologies and studies written from letters concern richer, better-educated white emigrants.[1]

In China, however, curators have collected far more migrants' letters, absolutely and proportionately, than anywhere else in the world, generally dwarfing the efforts of their non-Chinese counterparts, including in the European countries that have fed global white migration for the last few hundred years. This achievement is all the more surprising given that China was, until recently, very poor and is still a developing country. We know of no other developing nation that has assembled an archive anywhere near as big as China's, even proportionately.

Why are the collections of white emigrants' letters smaller, less representative, and less comprehensive than the Chinese archive? The difference is partly due to the efforts of Chinese archivists in collecting and preserving these materials, and to the fact that the outflow of migrants from China dwarfed that from most other countries throughout much of modern history.[2] However, there are several other facilitating circumstances for China's lead that are worth exploring as hypotheses in a comparative, cross-cultural perspective that may shed more general light on special features of Chinese social science and data collection. The hypotheses are as follows.

One hypothesis is that overseas Chinese seem, in certain periods, to have written home more often than other emigrants. From 1947 to 1949, Shantou alone received more than five million letters, including 140,000 in December 1947.[3] In 1955, at the height of China's isolation, officials estimated that half a million letters per month passed between families in South China and Chinese overseas, about the same volume, proportionately, as some comparable documented groups, but greater than many.[4] This is an unexpected finding, since a far greater proportion of Chinese migrants than those of other nations were laborers, overwhelmingly without writing skills or the letter-writing habit.[5] One obvious reason for the large number of letters to China is that the Chinese homeland tie remained more vibrant than that of emigrants who were less subject than Chinese to discriminatory treatment and exclusionary laws overseas, with their letters as its measure. This was especially true of the Chinese in North America, who, as Madeline Hsu noted, "eagerly returned the gaze of their *qiaoxiang* compatriots, in part because they faced such severe rejection in their lives overseas."[6] Studies of other emigrant groups suggest that those who wrote home were likely "to have a higher than average propensity to return," while those who sank roots overseas wrote less often or stopped writing.[7] Overseas Chinese, too, nativized abroad, but at a slower rate than other groups, chiefly because fewer Chinese women emigrated than women of other nationalities.

Another hypothesis is that the kin of Chinese emigrants have done more to preserve the letters because of the special value placed in China on the written word. This sacred regard for characters on paper was magnified by the families' honoring of those engaged in enterprises of communal value, including going abroad on behalf of those left behind, and their keeping the tie documented.

Moreover, China's dense kinship institutions and clan associations and its relatively intrusive system of local government in recent times are good at mobilizing the resources necessary for realizing a scheme like the *Qiaopi* Project. Chinese officials at the local level are also driven to do so by Marxist ideology, which favors "mass history." The campaign to persuade families to make their *qiaopi* over to the authorities and to coax collectors into donating or copying them is waged in the local press and by researchers descending on the village to do "field work."[8] Emigrants' families, the letters' owners, are easier to identify in China than elsewhere. Today emigrants hail from all over China, but in the past most came from a handful of counties that specialized in emigration, whereas in metropolitan countries they were drawn from a wider spread of places. The emigrants' communities in China are more rooted than elsewhere, and family papers are more likely to survive than in more mobile societies. In the People's Republic, family members of overseas migrants and one-time migrants who return to China have a collective official status, that of "domestic Overseas Chinese," which is registered in their personal files and makes them easier to trace.[9] So their geographic concentration and higher visibility is another reason why letter caches have been easier to find in China.

Finally, a factor special to China is the revival in popularity of stamp collecting since Mao died in 1976. Today, China has twenty million philatelists, more than a third of the world's total, and fifty thousand government-sponsored philatelic societies.[10] Philatelists have held exhibitions both in China and abroad, where the price of *qiaopi* has shot up at auctions.[11] Philatelists collect not just stamps but "covers" (franked addressed envelopes) and the correspondence they contain. The *qiaoxiang* are a treasure house of historic covers and their collectors an unusual ally of archivists seeking to hunt down emigrants' correspondence. This development can be seen as a special application of the Chinese Communist tradition of "mass-based" investigation, a legacy of one of the "native" branches of China's official historiography employed in the drive to collect *qiaopi*, whereby officials of local bureaus for overseas-Chinese affairs and village elders are mobilized to visit families and to put pressure on philatelists to make their finds publicly available to appropriate archives.[12]

Without the combination of market forces and official propaganda, it is doubtful whether *qiaopi* would have survived as a substantial historical resource. In the past, before they became saleable, not everyone accorded them equal respect. Some *qiaopi* were allowed to rot or crumble or to become food for grubs and termites. While few emigrants' direct dependents or descendants would treat the *qiaopi* impiously, generational depth is a relative concept, more relevant in some classes and families than in others. Despite the adages about "brooks without a source" and pride in ancestry, Chinese families (as opposed to lineages) rarely tend to revere ancestors more than four generations above the living head.[13] Over the years, millions of *qiaopi* were received in China, but only a small fraction survives. The rest, one must surmise, were thrown out after the sender's death, probably during a New Year spring-clean. There are even reports of *qiaopi* being used for kindling during the famine of 1959–61, when firewood was in short supply.[14]

QIAOPI STUDIES AND THE RISE OF SOCIAL AND REGIONAL HISTORY IN CHINA BEFORE 2013

The growing interest in the *qiaopi* collection reflects changing trends in scholarship in recent years, particularly in China but also in parts of Southeast Asia. The focus of the collection, on emigrant communities in the diaspora, at home and overseas, is a welcome confirmation of the turn in Chinese historiography and social studies since the 1970s away from the rigid class approach that once ruled these disciplines, as well as a turn toward a scholarship based on evidence rather than employed to illustrate general principles.

The *Qiaopi* Project mirrors major changes in attitudes in China and its *qiaoxiang* over the past years. Between 1949 and the 1980s, few Chinese worked on ethnic and migrant Chinese communities abroad or their reciprocators in the sending regions, partly because of the stigmatization, climaxing in the Cultural Revolution, of social groups with "foreign" ties. For a long time, most of the research on Chinese communities overseas was done by non-Chinese nationals (including some of Chinese descent), and for many years it was far smaller in volume than the worldwide research on the "white" role in the great migrations.[15]

The rise of Overseas Chinese studies in China after the 1970s was a major factor in the global transformation of this scholarship. This happened because China-based researchers paid greater attention to ties to the *qiaoxiang*, which they studied less from the top down than from the bottom up, from the grass-roots point of view of local associations and local families. This approach was in part a legacy of Communist China's tradition of mass-based, "on-the-spot" investigation.[16] Chinese scholars had better access than foreign researchers to local records in China, as well as the language skills necessary for reading them. Whereas non-Chinese scholars looked in on Chinese communities from the outside, as objects of research, studies by Chinese scholars had the potential to become subject-centered and to show empathy with emigrants, an exercise in "native anthropology" whereby researchers study communities with which they share ties, interests, and languages. All these factors combined to focus attention, largely for the first time, on the Chinese emigrant community's own output, ranging from the publications and records of clan associations to correspondence from diaspora to hometown and back.

As the restrictions on scholarship in China fell away in the 1980s, new methods of study and new attitudes were popularized. Scholarship became not only more diverse but more local as monolithic models weakened in all spheres. This localism interacted with the strengthening of regional identities as the Chinese economy also "localized." Economic growth in the *qiaoxiang* and the strengthening of contacts with overseas Chinese created a material base for the funding of new regional studies in which the overseas Chinese role was often paramount. This paved the way to a new approach to migration studies in China that looked beyond class to the mentalities that drive emigrants. It also helped shift the attention of students of migration from the nation-state and the provinces, which had long been the dominant framework of its construction, to its deepest and most fundamental level, in villages, lineages, and families.[17]

These trends coincided with the emergence of new directions in Western ethnic and migrant studies. In the 1970s scholars increasingly rejected the view of ethnicity as a closed and static property reflecting cultural inheritance, and identified it instead as an outcome of the interplay of context and ethnic interaction, in which migrants and natives use the contrasts that arise in the course of everyday interethnic contact as markers of their own ethnic self-identification. Identity came to be viewed not as static but as protean, ethnic boundaries not given but constructed. So the emphasis switched from culture to identity, engendering a new interest in the active agency of the creative subject with its narratives and imaginings. In the

1990s transnational studies emerged, with its focus not on the emigrant group in isolation but on its interactions with the diaspora and the homeland.[18] These new trends were imported to China by Chinese returning from abroad and by the non-Chinese researchers that began arriving in China in ever greater numbers in the 1980s and 1990s. Both trends jibed with the switch in China to a radically new view of ethnic and migrant Chinese, not as inert things or a descriptive category but as makers of their own history.

This new Chinese research not only brings new and previously unexplored issues into focus but will enrich the voluminous literature that has emerged in the West since the 1990s on transnational Chinese migration. Most of this literature lacks an international and comparative angle, as do the studies that have appeared in China written from Chinese archives. Many Western studies on Chinese emigration and overseas settlement are based on statistical data, chiefly economic and demographic, derived from official sources and viewing emigrants from an etic perspective—from the outside and above. The new Chinese research is into history from below, an emic perspective on the "people without history," and its focus on transnational as well as domestic networks goes beyond the conventional nation-state paradigm and helps further a new approach to ethnic and migration studies based on the idea of "inbetweenness"—the realization that migrant identities are created and livelihoods pursued on multiple sites. *Qiaopi* studies are an exemplary model of this approach. Only a handful of studies have appeared in non-Chinese languages on *qiaopi*, which are barely known outside China, except in parts of Southeast Asia.[19] One aim of this study is therefore to bring the existence of the *qiaopi* archives and (in the course of critical analysis of them) the new Chinese research findings to the attention of non-Chinese scholars working in this field.

Jao Tsung-i played an instrumental role in the emergence of *qiaopi* studies as a field of research.[20] A historian from Chaoan in Guangdong, he stressed the importance of studying *qiaopi* in a lecture given at the Center for the Study of Chaoshan History and Culture in November 2000. (Chaoshan was a major site of the *qiaopi* trade and has by far the biggest *qiaopi* archive,[21] comprising some two hundred thousand *qiaopi* in the hands of official and private collectors as well as a substantial collection of associated materials.[22]) In his lecture, Jao explained the importance of *qiaopi* as historical documents and pointed out their value as a supplement to official documents. Jao is also credited with founding Chaozhou (Teochew) studies, which have been the subject of many international symposia in recent years and have a base in Shantou University funded by Li Ka-shing, a prominent Chaozhounese entrepreneur based in Hong Kong.[23] This connection illustrates the close link between the rise of regional or area studies in China and the shift away from a single focus on class analysis. Other scholars who, like Jao, approach China from a regional perspective include David Faure and Helen Siu (1995) and, in Guangzhou, Hong Kong, and Xiamen, Chen Chunsheng, Liu Zhiwei, May-bo

Ching, Choi Chi-cheung, and Zheng Zhenman. The latter group collaborates on South China studies (*Huanan yanjiu*), which combine interdisciplinary explorations of Guangdong and Fujian with fieldwork and archival research (including on *qiaopi*).

There is exceedingly little documentation on the *qiaopi* trade before the mid- to late nineteenth century and practically none in China, where it was ignored and went unrecorded by officials for whom emigration was for centuries a crime or a peripheral matter of marginal importance. It was not until 1860 that the Chinese authorities lifted restrictions on emigration, gradually began to recognize the need to protect Chinese overseas (though not, at first, to much effect), and started officially recording overseas trade, including remittances.[24]

Chinese remittances first attracted attention from politicians, government officials, and scholars not in China but overseas, particularly in North America, where they featured in state reports, political debate, journalism, and scholarship in the late nineteenth and early twentieth century.[25] In the interwar years, Japanese investigators collected a large amount of data on remittances.[26] In China perhaps the first public notice of the phenomenon was by Xie Xueying, whose *Shantou zhinan* ("Shantou guide"), which appeared in 1934, included a description of the *qiaopi* trade. In 1937 the Chinese version of *Emigrant Communities in South China*, by Chen Ta, divided the remittance industry into five regional groups (based in Fujian, Guangdong, Chaoshan, the Hakka counties, and Hainan); similar work by him followed later.[27] In 1943 Yao Zengyin published a study on the remittance trade in Guangdong, and in 1947 Zheng Linkuan (Cheng Lin K'uan, 1947) published a book on remittance in Fujian. Also in 1947, Jao Tsung-i compiled *Chaozhou zhi* ("Chaozhou gazetteer"), a pioneering work that analyzed the *qiaopi* trade alongside transport and foreign trade.[28]

In the first three decades of the People's Republic, *qiaopi* studies reached their nadir. They only started to pick up in the late 1980s, when Shantou was declared a Special Economic Zone and new work began appearing, especially by the 1990s, some of it done by philatelists. Deng Xiaoping's new policy of reform and opening up led, in the *qiaoxiang*, to exchanges between *qiaopi* scholars in China and the diaspora as well as the start of systematic study and the formation of specialist institutions, inspired by the scholarly and patriotic vision of Jao Tsung-i. In 2003 Jao called for the setting up of a *qiaopi* museum, which came into being in 2004. In 2010 the Chaoshan *Qiaopi* Archive was announced, and it was quickly followed by *qiaopi*-related museums in Meizhou and Jiangmen in Guangdong and Fujian.[29]

The earliest study on *qiaopi* under the Communists appeared in 1965. None followed between 1965 (the eve of the Cultural Revolution) and 1990, but since 1990 well over one hundred articles have been published on the subject in academic and other journals, including ninety-seven between 2003 and 2012. As the research field matured, an increasing number of multidisciplinary and multiauthored studies came out, and a core cadre of researchers formed.[30] *Qiaopi* scholars in China have discussed at length the special features and potential uses of these materials, at several conferences (in China and abroad) and in copious publications including specialist journals and anthologies. Historians praise *qiaopi* as an "encyclopedia" of local society, rich and varied in content, and archivists have published dozens of volumes of *qiaopi* facsimiles, as well as digitizing letters, setting up museums, and staging exhibitions.[31] In the drive to establish *qiaopi* studies as a special branch of research, scholars and local luminaries have defined them as a "constituent element" of numerous disciplines and special fields, including migration studies, communication studies, economics, architecture (due to the building styles favored by overseas Chinese remitters, dependents, returners, and investors), international politics, telecommunications, banking and remittance studies, modern cultural studies, and cultural exchange studies, and they have tied them to local and regional studies.[32] However, most of the studies that have appeared up to now focus on historical research; culture, customs, and the social impact of the *qiaopi* trade have been relatively neglected.[33]

QIAOPI STUDIES IN CHINA AND GLOBAL SCHOLARSHIP SINCE 2013

Since the inclusion of *qiaopi* in the UNESCO Memory of the World Register in 2013, interest in *qiaopi*, both as an object of collection and as a subject of research, has increased substantially. This has been reflected in an increased number of publications on *qiaopi* (including collections of letters, monographs, and conference proceedings) and in the development of institutions and projects devoted to collecting and studying *qiaopi*.

The past few years have seen a mushrooming of new publications devoted to *qiaopi* studies. A keyword search of the China National Knowledge Infrastructure (CNKI) database, which includes all journal publications in China since 1915, shows that of 225 articles on *qiaopi*, 103 (or 46 percent) were published between 2013 and 2016 (the rest were published between 1965 and 2012). Two recent studies merit special attention. Yuan, Chen, and Zhong focus on the Republican government's changing policy on remittances between 1929 and 1949, placing remittances in the context of the state-society relations.[34] Huang Qinghai provides a useful overview of the *qiaopi* trade against the background of Chinese international migration and financial networks.[35]

The compilation of *qiaopi* letters started from 2000 and several multivolume collections that have been published since 2013. For example, the third set of *Collections of Chaoshan Qiaopi* was published in 2015.[36] Like the previous two sets, it comprises 36 volumes, and it covers some twenty thousand *qiaopi* from Chaozhou and Shantou districts between the 1930s and the 1980s. *Collections of Minnan*

Qiaopi (15 volumes)[37] includes more than six thousand *qiaopi*, *huipi*, *huipiao*, and remittance receipts from southern Fujian in the period 1884 to 1992. Other *qiaopi* collections are dedicated specifically to different historical periods (e.g., the late Qing and the Anti-Japanese War) as well as to individual families, demonstrating the richness and multiformity of *qiaopi* across different times and spaces.[38]

Admission to the UNESCO Memory of the World Register has boosted institutional support and funding for *qiaopi* collections and studies. The Guangdong *Qiaoxiang* Studies Center at Wuyi University has played a pivotal role in this development, not only because 50,000 of the 160,000 *qiaopi* submitted as part of the UNESCO application came from Jiangmen, where Wuyi University is located, but also because it has undertaken a number of ambitious projects in the field. These include compiling a seventy-volume collection of *qiaopi* from Jiangmen and Wuyi and organizing a number of international conferences on *qiaopi* that have yielded bi-lingual publications.[39] Led by Zhang Guoxiong, Vice President of the University, the Center published the inaugural issue of *Zhongguo qiaoxiang yanjiu* (*China Qiaoxiang Studies*) in 2014.[40] In the preface, Zhang urged that "'qiaoxiang' be transformed into a new research area" and that it be elevated from a local to a national and transnational level.[41]

The institutional development of *qiaopi* studies has been supported by generous funding from local governments. In 2013 Guangdong provincial government laid plans to compile a series of multivolume studies on the history of overseas Chinese originating from Guangdong, including some on *qiaopi*, with Zhu Xiaodan, Guangdong's then-governor, as the chairman of the compilation committee and funding to the tune of fifty million yuan.

Qiaopi scholarship outside China is much more limited in scope and quantity. Among the handful of English-language scholarly articles on the subject, one looks at cultural beliefs underlying the *qiaopi* trade and another at the role played by the state and modern postal services in the *piju* system.[42]

We mentioned earlier that Japanese imperial organizations (especially the South Manchurian Railway Company) collected a wealth of data about overseas Chinese remittances from Southeast Asia, with the primary aim of cutting ties between Chinese migrants and China.[43] More recently, Japanese scholars have begun to look at modern China from the point of view of transnational networks and modern transformations within Asia. For example, Yamagishi Takeshi examines the role of remittances in post-reform China, especially in the Fujian *qiaoxiang*.[44] Since the 1980s, Takeshi Hamashita has been at the forefront of this endeavor. Hamashita argues that Chinese remittance networks constitute an integral part of modern Asian trading networks. His exploration of Chinese networks and their changing interactions with dominant regional orders over the past two centuries (tributary trade, colonial-imperial, nation-state and international relations, international relations during the Cold War, and globalization) have deepened our understanding of *qiaopi* and the role played by the *qiaopi* trade in the making of modern China and East Asia.[45]

The evolution of *qiaopi* scholarship over the past couple of decades cannot be understood outside the context of China's economic rise and growing self-confidence. *Qiaopi* scholarship has been increasingly globalized in terms of researchers, publications, and institutional setups, a process inevitably speeded by the successful inclusion of *qiaopi* in the Memory of the World Register. So, *qiaopi* studies are not simply about *qiaopi* as historical but part of a far wider cultural and political context.

DECODING *QIAOPI*: SOME METHODOLOGICAL CONSIDERATIONS

Scholars in the field of *qiaopi* studies have called for openness to new ideas, and for a scientific approach and systematic methodology in regard to cataloging, collating, preserving, and digitizing, where experience gained in mature fields like document studies can be used as a point of reference. Many issues of concern are noted, of which the most important is the ascertaining of a letter's date. Collectors of *qiaopi* must be instructed to preserve both cover and contents, including any insertions (for example, replies). To avoid mistakes, knowledgeable local people, ethnographers, historians, and philatelists must be consulted, and evidence in the form of chops stamped on the envelope by the remitting agency and the bank or post office and routes followed must be carefully researched. Forged dates and chops are not uncommon, given the market value of covers issued by important remittance houses; these too must, where possible, be spotted and clarified.

The rise of philately in China has been a mixed blessing for *qiaopi* scholars. While they can thank philatelists for having brought the *qiaopi* to public and official notice and in many cases for preserving them intact, the philately craze has led many families to focus only on the saleability of the stamps and to disregard the letters, which thus come adrift not only from their envelope but also from their context, or are torn or lost for good. *Qiaopi* collectors among the philatelists have been mobilized to take digital photos of their collections and to make the photos available to *qiaopi* archivists and scholars.

A big problem facing curators and researchers of *qiaopi* is that of accurately dating them. This is harder than it might at first seem, given the resort to three different calendars: solar, lunar, and Buddhist.[46] When dates are missing from letters and envelopes, which they often are, they can sometimes be ascertained by checking the Chinese character drawn from the *Thousand Character Classic*, used by the remittance house to code successive batches. Assuming an average of one batch per week, the one thousand characters it contained would have taken just over nineteen years to exhaust, thus allowing the date each represented to be roughly calculated counting from the year in which the company started up in business.[47]

Different regions and, within regions, different *qiaopi* traders or groups of traders used different dating systems on *qiaopi* envelopes, partly as a reflection of different regional cultures. For example, early Chaoshan *qiaopi* traders tended to use the old Sexagenary Cycle (*ganzhi*) based on the Ten Heavenly Stems and Twelve Earthly Branches, whose sixty terms were traditionally used to record a fixed cycle of sixty years (after which the cycle starts again). In a few instances, the dates indicated by this system can be unclear, for since the cycle repeats, exact years cannot be specified without additional information and must sometimes be guessed. In such cases, however, additional information is usually to hand, especially where the name of the remitted currency is recorded. (The currency changed frequently over time.) Other clues can often be found in the contents of appended letters. To add to the confusion, some *qiaopi* recorded the Heavenly Stem but not the Earthly Branch. *Qiaopi* from other regions, again due to cultural influences, specified years by reign names (*nianhao*), whose corresponding years in the Gregorian calendar are unmistakable, or by a mixture of the two systems, or by the Western system of year-numbering. However, many recorded only the day and the month and not the year, which again had to be guessed or reconstructed, where possible, from the contents of the *qiaopi* or from other available information.[48]

Another major difficulty is the failure of some envelopes and their contents to match up, as a result of recipients' actions or owners' carelessness in storing them; another is letters without envelopes and envelopes without letters. In some if not many cases, letters may be absent from the remittance envelope because they were never present in the first place, a possibility some scholars seem to ignore.[49]

Another possibility is that recipients removed or destroyed letters before cashing the *qiaopi* at the bank or store in order to stop private information, including addresses, being divulged to third parties. In the late twentieth century, when people realized there was a market for *qiaopi*, some deliberately separated letters from envelopes so that they could sell each separately and make twice the profit. Wisely, the general approach among archivists would seem to be that disparities and discrepancies should be left to deal with at a later date, especially after the digitization of *qiaopi* collections, which will make the matching of materials much easier.

Digitization is particularly urgent in regard to *qiaopi* and *huipi*, which are mostly written on machine-produced twentieth-century paper (unlike the high-quality Xuan paper used for official documents in the past) and are therefore liable to deteriorate. For decades they have sat in drawers or boxes, where they can become mildewed, especially in the sea-climate of some *qiaoxiang*, or food for paper-eating insects. As a result, many have crumbled or rotted, and the information they contain has been lost.

Digitization would solve many existing problems in *qiaopi* research and create opportunities for new advances in it. Undigitized papers can only be consulted physically, adding to the wear and tear on them. Digitization not only protects the *qiaopi* from excessive handling but facilitates their storing and their swift and accurate transmission, duplication, and searching according to sender, recipient, place of sending, place of receipt, date, and the amount remitted. This digital analysis paves the way to their classification by household, which in turn enables researchers to check and confirm obscure passages and details.

So a lot of thought has gone into how best to digitize the *qiaopi* and to overcome the many problems, foreseen and unforeseen, that this work has thrown up. Much of the thinking has had to do with the problem of standards—the need to ensure that different archives adopt a uniform approach to cataloging and conservation. A problem that in the past would have occurred to no one in China is the issue of privacy and confidentiality. China lacks clear legislation regarding a person's right to privacy in relation to correspondence, including a law stipulating when the right to such privacy might expire. So this too is potentially a problem for archivists planning to put families' private letters online.[50]

The view among *qiaopi* scholars is that collecting *qiaopi* should be treated with the same veneration as "gathering rare and scattered [classical] writings" (*jiyi*): they are precious relics that must "be treasured as archives of historical documents of village scholars" (*xiangxian*).[51] The same obligation is said to apply to the paraphernalia of the remittance houses. These include the signboards used to call attention to the shop, the tools of the trade (chops, stamps, ledgers), and letter-carriers' sacks, baskets, long-handled umbrellas, and scales (for weighing gold and coins in the days before standardization), together with photos of *piju* and *piju* staff, advertisements and notices for remittance services, company shares, and contracts. In this connection, interviews with surviving employees and shop premises have, where possible, been videoed or tape-recorded.[52]

The new focus on *qiaopi* studies coincided with a deepening interest in Chinese scholarship on oral history. Oral history has always featured in Chinese Communist historiography, but it was used principally to illustrate or prove general Marxist theories, and it lags greatly behind oral history in the West. However, source books on Chinese communities outside China have been compiled in recent decades using oral-history methods, and the same approach is increasingly gaining ground in China.[53] Its affinity with *qiaopi* studies is immediately obvious, for both fields focus on the lives of ordinary people. Oral history complements *qiaopi* studies by repairing its gaps and deficiencies. Most *qiaopi* correspondence lacks the relative detail, fullness, transparency, and dialogic quality of the high "epistolary genre" used by mainstream historians as evidence. Sequences of *qiaopi* are usually incomplete, and the content is far more likely to be obscure or unintelligible than that of literary letters. Oral historians can help to restore the record to completeness by consulting writers, recipients, descendants, and local experts.[54]

Scholars have likened the *qiaopi* archive to two other major local archives in Dunhuang[55] and Huizhou,[56] which, like *qiaopi*, are *minjian* ("of the common people," "non-governmental") and regional in character and which grew by natural accretion. In many respects, they therefore differ fundamentally from other well-known Chinese archives, which are primarily official in character. The Huizhou sources consist of private family records, numbering around twenty thousand documents passed from generation to generation across seven centuries (but mainly in the Ming and Qing) and dealing with the business not of officials but of ordinary people and their lives and institutions. The Dunhuang collections (there are several) are the world's largest early archive, comprising tens of thousands of manuscripts, printed texts, and art objects illustrating religious themes and aspects of everyday life, economy, and institutions.

Scholars point out that the *qiaopi*, too, cover a relatively lengthy period of time (though far shorter than that covered by the Dunhuang and Huizhou materials), are comparably full and systematic, are even more numerous, and deal with a similarly broad spread of topics, ranging from the "cellular" level of the family to the state and dealing with economic, political, and cultural issues as well as private and intimate domestic business. Unlike official documents, which usually have a broader and more abstract scope, they are detailed and specific, characterized by a richness of themes and a variety of human relations. They also have an additional dimension: their intrinsically overseas and transnational connection. They not only are temporally complete (potentially documenting family ties over several decades and even generations) but have a greater spatial breadth than the other two collections.[57] In other words, they are "encyclopedic."[58]

Qiaopi have also been compared, as a historical resource, with two other sources: *difang zhi* ("local gazetteers") and *wenshi ziliao* ("reminiscences on local history and culture"), which are often cited by economic, social, and political historians of China. In the past, *difang zhi* provided information about local history, geography, society, and economy and were designed to aid local government and promote local identity. They had less to say about local markets and financial and entrepreneurial activity than about financial institutions, currency circulation, and government financial administration, and the information they contain tends to be sketchy or synoptic; before the Republican period, many carried no financial reporting.[59] The *wenshi ziliao* series, published by the Communists since the late 1950s mainly at provincial, county, and city levels (and originally for domestic rather than international circulation), and based in large part on oral histories and firsthand accounts collected since 1949, are a useful source of detailed information about local society and economy. They are sometimes excessively guarded or skewed, for political reasons, but they nevertheless illuminate angles that other sources miss. As for statistical reporting by higher official bodies, while it is an essential source for analyzing China's finance and economy, reporting at regional and local levels was generally deficient in the period of the *qiaopi* trade, given that modern statistical institutions did not form at local levels until the 1920s and the 1930s and were laid lame by war and crisis in the late 1930s and the 1940s.

By comparison with these sources, *qiaopi* have various advantages and strengths in regard to China's financial history. Unlike typical migrant or other correspondence, they are intrinsically financial in nature. They are available in huge numbers and cover more than a century of time. They are more reliable than other sources because they usually had nothing to hide (except during wars and crises) and little reason to exaggerate. They are incomparably specific. They provide firsthand, unedited accounts, largely free of falseness and deception. They contain information about family finance as well as financial markets and institutions below county level unavailable in other sources. But they also convey information about inter-regional, international, and transnational financial dealings, networks, currencies, and exchange rates. So, in many respects *qiaopi* are a unique source of concentrated information on the synchronic and diachronic circumstances of the finance and economy of China's southeastern coastal region, at both the micro and the international level.[60]

Qiaopi studies are liveliest in Guangdong and Fujian, the two provinces of greatest overseas migration, although they are also represented in other places of lesser migration, notably Hainan (part of Guangdong at the time of the *qiaopi* trade) and Rongxian (Guangxi).[61] The mainland concentration can be explained by the massive collections of *qiaopi* available for study in China, whereas the return correspondence (the *huipi*) in overseas sites is more widely scattered and more easily lost. Overseas, *qiaopi* scholarship has promoted root-seeking among ethnic Chinese in Southeast Asia and led to an upsurge of interest in collecting both the *qiaopi* and the associated paraphernalia.[62] Outside China, most research has up to now been in Thailand, a fact that can be explained by the greater size, historically and now, of Thailand's ethnic-Chinese population and its richer documentation, partly as a result of Thai government restrictions and thus surveillance.[63] Needless to say, our understanding of the effect of migration on sending communities and the nature of diasporic networks would be all the greater if substantial caches of *huipi* were to be unearthed by Chinese researchers overseas.[64]

Qiaopi are by nature intensely local in character, and they are scattered across archives in different parts of Guangdong, Fujian, and Hainan, which makes coordinated projects difficult to realize. However, *qiaopi* scholars recognize the need for a holistic and comparative approach to the field of study and point to the successful registration of the *Qiaopi* Project under UNESCO's Memory of the World

Register as evidence of its potential value.[65] Digitization will partly resolve this problem by making materials from all three provinces universally available.

This chapter has surveyed the genealogy of *qiaopi* studies over the past eighty years or so and the changing sociopolitical contexts within which they have been pursued. We have observed a growing interest in the subject in China since the start of the present century, reflected in the large number of Chinese-language publications on it—and, in stark contrast, a virtual absence of English-language scholarship on *qiaopi*, with one or two notable exceptions. This suggests the need for *qiaopi* scholars in China to begin a constructive dialogue with colleagues working on Chinese migration and diaspora through the medium of English.

The focus of existing Chinese-language studies on the subject has been primarily on the role remittances play in the Chinese economy and in wider *qiaoxiang* development. This book, too, looks at *qiaopi* in economic, financial, and material terms, but at the same time it considers them a means of integrating and consolidating emotional and spiritual ties in families, clans, and local communities. In this sense, it hopes to contribute new insights to the emerging global scholarship on *qiaopi*.

Combining extensive study of *qiaopi* letters collected in China, Southeast Asia, and North America with a critical analysis of the findings of ongoing research in China, this study examines *qiaopi* as a key element in upholding China's linkages with the world and in the making of a transnational China based on extensive flows of capital, trade, people, ideas, and sociocultural practices across diverse sociopolitical and cultural domains. It therefore contributes to our understanding of modern and contemporary China from a global perspective and of its transnational history, a subject that has come increasingly to the fore in the past two decades.[66]

Our study also differs from most previous work on the subject in that it examines the *qiaopi* phenomenon from a comparative angle. Remittance and letter-writing by immigrants are part and parcel of migration and diaspora formation throughout the world. We compare and contrast the Chinese migrant experience in this regard with that of European migrant groups to help shed further light on the role played by *qiaopi* letters in the migration process, both in the sending and receiving places.

The Structure of the *Qiaopi* Trade and Transnational Networks

The *qiaopi* trade went through several stages, though these stages did not necessarily take an irreversibly forward direction. The trade started with *shuike* ("couriers") in the eighteenth and nineteenth centuries. The next stage was marked by the rise of the *piju* ("remittance shop") following Western intrusion, the opening in China of the treaty ports (port cities opened to foreigners under the unequal treaties of 1842 and 1860), and the rise of steam navigation. The final stage began with the establishment of telegraphic and modern postal institutions and a modern banking system in China, starting in the late nineteenth century and reaching its acme in the first half of the twentieth century. The origins of the *piju* can be studied from both an evolutionary and a functional angle. Both approaches are followed in this chapter, starting with an analysis of the *shuike* phenomenon, from which the *piju* sprang and the tie to which it never lost.

SHUIKE AND THE EARLY PHASE OF THE *QIAOPI* TRADE

In the early stages of migration, before the emergence of specialist institutions to suit the new global age, methods of remitting developed fairly randomly, more or less as opportunities arose. Couriering was the main method. Almost from the start, it took several forms along a continuum ranging from the improvised to the specialized. If someone was going home, he might take back money and messages for kinsmen.[1] Opportunistic couriering of this sort continued even after the later professionalization of the trade.[2] In some places and periods, many Chinese practiced temporary seasonal migration to coincide with harvest time in Southeast

Asia, and on returning to China might take back messages and money on behalf of others in longer-term employment overseas. After the strengthening of Chinese commerce in Southeast Asia, traders hired couriers to carry funds to China several times a year, an arrangement designed to benefit both the traders themselves and their employees. Other *shuike* initially worked as petty transnational traders between China and abroad, dealing in local products from both places or as boatmen, and gradually switched from taking *qiaopi* as a sideline to doing so as a principal occupation.[3]

Shuike were nearly always first-generation emigrants whose links with the sending places were still vibrant and who had a tie of kinship or native place with the remitter, or knew someone who did have such a tie and could vouch for them.[4] For trust, this tie was essential: initially at least, few *shuike* dared set their own or their clan's reputation at risk by misbehaving or defaulting.[5] Business was conducted exclusively in dialect. In all these respects, the *shuike* resembled another group of early domestic messengers, the *xinke* ("letter couriers"), who transmitted written or oral messages between relatively nearby places within China, usually for a small annual fee, a service largely terminated by government decree in the early twentieth century after the birth of a postal culture.[6]

Shuike in all their forms operated, at first, in nearly all the main Chinese migrant destinations—Southeast Asia, the Americas, and Oceania.[7] According to an account from 1847, letters and money "were either entrusted to a comrade from the same part of China, who, fortunate enough to have accumulated a small competency, is about to revisit his native land; or they are delivered to a passenger with whom the remitters may be acquainted; or, lastly, they are confided to one of those men, to be found in almost every junk, who make it a regular business to take charge of such remittances."[8] In the days before couriering became a profession, ship's captains were a favorite conduit, for they were usually economically secure and traceable, should things go wrong. Ship's crew were also used, a method that survived into the twentieth century. In Britain, for example, the small pool of seafarers stationed permanently in Liverpool got shipmates on the China lines to take back remittances and stuff their pockets with accompanying messages.[9] Couriering was "strongly feudal" in character: routes, clients, and connections passed down from father to son and from older to younger brother.[10]

The *shuike*'s appeal was his intimacy and multiple ties, of family, kinship, friendship, and place, to remitters. Some *shuike* issued and collected receipts that were mailed back to the remitter, and some even appointed guarantors. However, missions were usually based on trust, and the transaction was, at most, recorded in a ledger. *Shuike* were not just couriers of letters and remittances but intermediaries who took and fetched back news and gossip. Given the need for trust, most were seen as men of integrity, honest and reputable brokers, who would keep their word and displayed no obvious vices. They were also better educated; more cultured, knowledgeable, and assertive; and more capable in most respects than their fellow migrants, for they had to be literate and numerate, silver-tongued, entrepreneurial, and good at languages. They also needed trusted networks along which to travel, and to be good at creating confidence, ties of friendship, and personal and group relations. If they had spotless reputations and a compelling manner, they might even win the custom of non-clan outsiders.[11]

In circumstances where distance, lack of a sufficient pool of potential couriers, or lack of opportunity made remitting through kith and kin difficult, other trusted channels were sometimes used. In New Zealand, a white missionary known to and trusted by local Chinese acted as courier for them.[12] In Britain after the decline in visits by Chinese ships, one-third of the Shanghainese hired as shore-gang workers by Alfred Holt & Co. were happy to have their remittances wired home by the company, with which they had developed a collective tie based on trust.[13]

The *shuike* trade is thought to have started in Southeast Asia in the seventeenth century, to have persisted throughout the eighteenth century, and to have peaked in the Qing's Guangxu reign (1875–1908), when more than twelve hundred *shuike* and *ketou* ("head courier") operated in Xiamen and another eight hundred in Shantou alone.[14] However, some scholars claim that in Siam the trade predated the Ming, that hundreds of early *shuike* plied the route between Fuzhou and Saigon, and that remittances also entered China from the Philippines in pre-Ming days.[15] The earliest known explicit reference to *shuike* in the modern sense dates from 1786 in records of the Chinese association in Batavia (now Jakarta).[16] In North America the trade died out in the nineteenth century because of America's distance from China and the rise of modern banking, but it remained vigorous and ineradicable elsewhere, despite competition.[17] Singapore was the trade's main early modern center, with a steady flow of remittances as early as the 1830s.[18] In 1849, Singapore alone had some two hundred *shuike*. By the mid-nineteenth century, more than one thousand *shuike* were active in southern Fujian, and in the late nineteenth century, Shantou had eight hundred *shuike* and Hong Kong two hundred. (The contemporary claim that "tens of thousands" of *shuike* were operating around Chaoshan in the 1920s must have been an exaggeration.)[19] Similar numbers continued to operate into the 1930s, when the amount of money transferred by *shuike* was put at twenty million yuan a year, equal to 5.2 percent of China's total remittances.[20]

In the earliest days, *shuike* were a free-floating part of the general migrant population, without fixed premises. Once couriering became an established trade rather than a random or spontaneous practice, *shuike* paid regular visits to the mines, farms, and plantations where Chinese worked, touring the poorest settlements in the remote countryside in search of commissions. In time, to gain credence and impress potential customers with the intimation of stability, some sought association with a small store or business.[21] Stories about *shuike* losing or absconding with remittances were rife, and a connection with a business or shop increased the confidence of potential clients.[22] In Malaya, *shuike* were known to hold court at appointed times, which were advertised to the community. This happened in grocery stores, restaurants, gold shops, medicine shops, and other places.[23] Other *shuike* received clients or their representatives (usually kin) on shipboard or in migrant hostels.[24] At peak times, for example before the Spring Festival, huge numbers of Chinese would flock to town to entrust their annual letters to the *shuike*.[25]

Trust was often assumed, especially in the early days, but in time safeguards evolved. Shops and businesses were roped in as backers.[26] In eighteenth-century Batavia, the remitter could request a *hantar* (Malay "deliverer," in this context "guarantor," rendered in Chinese as *anda*) as well as a receipt, and could if necessary challenge the *shuike* before a tribunal of the local Chinese association, with or without a *hantar*.[27]

Some early *shuike* couriered for free to oblige family or friends, but such volunteers were not always seen as punctual and reliable, and financial reward soon became fairly standard.[28] Initially, commission was paid in the form of a variable tip, but this payment later became a fixed fee ranging from 10 percent, the traditional tithe, to as high as 20 percent.[29] However, large numbers were drawn into the trade by the high level of reward, and this later drove the rate down to around 3 percent, though charges varied according to the remittance's size and the distance to be travelled by the courier.[30] Some *shuike* profited by speculating on exchange rates, a sometimes risky business. Others used the remittances to buy goods overseas and sell them in China, using the takings to pay out to recipients and then using the profits to buy goods in China to export abroad.[31] Such people, known as "commercial *shuike*," did not necessarily exact commission.[32]

Many early remittances were in the form of bullion bars or coins tied around the *shuike*'s body or stitched into his clothing.[33] *Shuike* either changed small amounts of bullion or currency directly into Chinese or Hong Kong dollars or delivered them as received. In later years, however, many *shuike* changed their takings into money orders in the banks or the post office, and bigger sums were nearly always sent through banks.[34]

At first, the *shuike* made their deliveries in person. Some returned to China irregularly, once a year or once every several years. Once the trade got into its swing, most *shuike* from Malaya, Singapore, and Indonesia returned between two and four times a year, or, in the case of the Philippines, five or six times on average. Gradually, the deliveries became seasonal to coincide with important festivals when remittances were particularly needed and awaited.[35] So the recipients would know, through networks, when to expect them, and they would know where and when to gather to receive them.[36]

Delivering and receiving *pi* was fraught with high emotion and anxious waiting: beneficiaries wept on the *shuike*'s arrival and sometimes embraced him, and there was often a communal celebration.[37] The big year's-end remittance, usually scheduled for the tenth lunar month, leading up to the Spring Festival could spark even greater celebrations, with temple visits, red lanterns, firecrackers, opera performances, tomb visits, and much drinking of alcohol. Those dependents passed over in the distribution looked on with envy, wondering why they had been passed over and fearing the worst.[38] The *shuike* would stop to chat, find out what was going on in the village, and pass on news from abroad—and help write the *huipi*.[39] Later, the process of delivery became more complicated. Some *shuike* required recipients to collect the *qiaopi* from a convenient spot, or "saltwater skaters" would delegate their delivery to "freshwater eaters" or "town-patrolling horses."[40]

The early *shuike* tended to be solitary individuals, more likely to avoid one another than to cooperate.[41] Later, however, *shuike* working from abroad came in many cases to depend on networks of domestic collaborators. They also cooperated where necessary with the banks and the remittance houses, and used the post office where convenient. In 1933 *shuike* in the Chaoshan and Meizhou regions united in a federation, the *Nanyang shuike lianhehui* ("Federation of Southeast Asian *shuike*"), which had nearly one thousand members (most of them Hakkas; the two groups from Chaoshan and Meizhou spoke mutually unintelligible dialects, so how they communicated is unclear).[42]

The role of the *shuike* in the remittance process and their relationship with established *qiaopi* traders differed from that of ordinary *piju* employees and of the *pijiao* who delivered *qiaopi* to the door. Some *shuike* were part of the staff of a *piju*, but others were independent couriers who struck deals with and acted on behalf of the *piju*. Independent entrepreneurs in their own right, they used their associations to fend off officialdom. They may also have used them where necessary to negotiate their relationship with the *piju*, but that is a question that requires further study.

Over time, the *shuike* figure gradually became more complex, professional, and specialized. A differentiation arose in many places between domestic and overseas couriers, and a transition occurred from just *shuike* to *shuike* and *ketou*, the two ever harder to distinguish from one another.[43] The *shuike*'s three main functions were transporting remittances, goods, and people, but the third function tended to become separate as *shuike* began to cash in, in ever more diverse ways, on their knowledge of routes, languages, and procedures. The *ketou* who escorted people into and out of China also delivered letters and things.

The name *ketou* derived from this escorting function—at first of migrants to their destinations abroad, but later of migrants' children, the *Huayi*, from their parents' place of settlement overseas to the residence of their grandparents or kin in China, as well as of *guiqiao*, returned and returning migrants. The practice may have seemed new, but in fact it was old, stretching back in Guangdong and Fujian to the Ming. *Shuike* and *ketou* also took migrants back to find wives, helped them buy land and property in China, visited their relatives on their behalf, checked their fields, and ritually swept their ancestors' graves for them; these practices were said to be particularly prevalent in Hakka counties.[44] The business-minded *shuike* spotted a new business opportunity in the would-be but penurious migrant and offered to escort him for a fee or on a credit-ticket, gathering groups of migrants in a portside hostel to await a sailing.[45] Once overseas, the *ketou* helped track down his charges' migrant kin, introduced his charges to new friends, helped find them work commensurate with their skills, and in many cases provided them with a financial cushion until payday, a process known as *zuoke* ("being the guest").[46] The trade grew rapidly, and *ketou* began advertising their services in the overseas-Chinese press. In the Guangxu years, there were around one thousand *ketou* in southern Fujian alone, and these people were said to control important arteries of the regional economy.[47]

Couriering was profitable but risky. Numerous dangers beset the *shuike* on his travels. During the Ming and Qing, up until its final lifting after the second Opium War, China's "sea ban" meant that emigration, and the *shuike*'s job, was a capital offense, punishable "up to nine generations."[48] In the modern period, restrictions imposed on the trade by Chinese and foreign governments laid *shuike* open to interference, extortion, blackmail, prohibitions, fines, police raids, confiscations, expropriation, and arrest. *Shuike* also came under unofficial pressure to donate to charitable and not-so-charitable causes in the *qiaoxiang*, a form of extortion.[49] Travelling was in itself arduous and potentially perilous. This was particularly true of the long sea journey to and from China, when some *shuike* died and were thrown overboard, and others were robbed by pirates.[50] Seen as a trading venture, the *qiaopi* trade was vulnerable to fluctuations in exchange rates and the market prices of the goods *shuike* dealt in; this too was a risk the *shuike* had to take.[51] Finally, the *shuike*'s cargo of remittances, including bullion and exotic goods, was a magnet for thieves and bandits. That is why many *shuike* practiced martial arts and took with them on their travels a sturdy oil-paper sun-rain umbrella, not just to stay dry or cool but to ward off attackers (as well as dogs and, according to superstition, evil spirits).[52]

The *shuike* phenomenon was far from uniform, chiefly for reasons of geography and economics. Hainan, an island across the Gulf of Tonkin from Vietnam, had far fewer *shuike* than elsewhere, mainly because its migrants tended to return home across the water once every few years and, in any case, earned less than others.[53] The Hakkas of the Meizhou region of northeastern Guangdong, by contrast, inhabited remote mountain areas that were hard to reach and acquired banks and post offices later than other places. They had more *shuike* than other regions and kept them longer.[54]

Shuike featured prominently in *qiaopi* folklore as heroic figures. Song Zhi of Yongchun in southern Fujian was celebrated in song and written into local annals. According to legend, he was cast onto a desert island in a storm but loyally persevered after his rescue in delivering his *qiaopi*. (Yongchun was said to have had thirty famous *shuike*.) Guo Youpin (1853–1901), whose story is told below, was also shipwrecked and lost the *qiaopi* he was taking to China. One of a handful of survivors, he eventually made his way home and sold his family's land to pay out the *qiaopi*, on the basis of a list he had carried separately in his pocket. He went on to found the famous Tianyi firm, which dominated the *qiaopi* trade for decades.[55]

The *shuike* system had numerous faults that led eventually to the rise of the *piju*, or remittance shop, which represented a higher stage of development of the *qiaopi* trade. However, the *shuike* were not supplanted but supplemented by the *piju* system, which built massively on *shuike* antecedents, as we shall see. Rather than devise new ways, the new system merely separated out the totality of tasks previously performed by the *shuike* and delegated them to specialists in a relatively complex division of labor.

One problem was that many *shuike* took too long to deliver *qiaopi*, usually more than a month or even several months, because of their habit of using them to engage in trade, a practice that could go wrong. They returned to China too infrequently and irregularly for the likes of many remitters, especially after the practice got into full swing.[56] Because of their lack of scale, the *shuike*'s services were dear, usually costing between a tenth and a fifth of the remittance. And not all *shuike* were equally honest. Although the *shuike* business rested on reputation, the temptation to abscond with the takings was great, especially after the *qiaopi* boom brought undesirables into the business.[57] The erosion of trust was in part a result of the boom in migration and thus of remittances, which put the *shuike* system under extreme pressure and eventually undermined the personal connection.[58]

Several factors speeded the transition to *piju*. One was the *shuike* customers' perception of chaos, malpractice, and unreliability on the part of couriers. Another was the trend among *shuike* themselves to get organized, partly to defend themselves against the authorities' demand that they register but also to put their own house in order and promote cooperation. As the trade grew in sophistication, it came to rely more and more on networks formed by "twisted roots and gnarled branches, crisscrossing one another, scattered like stars across the firmament, ... not inferior in any single respect from the networks of the modern postal services."[59] These networks of agents and collaborators emerged as early as the eighteenth century in Batavia, where the *shuike* trade was moreover constrained by the local Chinese association's legal system. *Shuike* also networked in China with the domestic *minxinju* ("people's letter offices"), which preceded the modern post office. *Shuike* federations eventually emerged, signaling the transition to a more organized form of the trade.[60] Some *piju* arose because of the entrepreneurial flair of individual *shuike* who formed businesses and imported relatives to staff them. (One such, set up by a one-time seafarer in 1898, ended up in the 1930s handling remittances from the Philippines worth a million silver dollars per year.[61]) The *shuike* carried an ever greater volume of *qiaopi* and operated at an ever greater speed; by the early twentieth century, professional *shuike* could deliver to China in a month with the help of modern transport and communications.[62] These and other developments paved the way for the rise of the *piju*, although in some periods and places the *shuike* remained in robust health and continued to dominate the *qiaopi* trade.

PIJU AND THE INSTITUTIONALIZATION OF THE *QIAOPI* TRADE

According to some studies, the *qiaopi* trade, in the sense of an institution rather than a loose collection of lone individuals, was born in Malacca in 1757, when Chen Chenliu set up a trading company to handle remittances. Chen was followed in 1778 by Li Kan, who formed a company in Singapore.[63] Others say that *piju* in the modern sense first formed in the early to mid-nineteenth century in Zhangzhou (1827), Chaoshan (1829), Singapore (1829), and Bangkok (1861).[64] They emerged as a result of the explosive growth of Chinese emigration, starting in the 1830s and especially in the 1850s, when the Qing abandoned its controls on foreign travel, and after the Beijing Convention of 1860, which pledged to protect migrants (although the pledge was, for a long time, honored as much in the breach as in the observance). The explosion, which the *shuike* trade was ill-equipped to handle, was further fueled by the opening of eighty new treaty ports in China and the start of steam shipping between China and the world. Steam favored the *piju* because steam was more regular and dependable than sailing and thus promoted a more professional and large-scale style of business. Singapore was served by a regular mail boat, steam-driven, as early as 1845, and Shantou got its first steamship in 1867, after which the region's old red-bow junks sank into slow decline.[65]

Seen from another angle, the transition from *shuike* to *piju* was the result of a natural evolution within the industry, although one that happened unevenly. Couriering became less and less a solitary trade as routes became more settled and institutions arose specifically to serve them. *Shuike* had a longstanding association with stores, which gave them at least the appearance of collateral, and with hostels, where they stayed and, in the case of those engaged primarily in escorting people, accommodated their charges.

The association with stores, known as *warung* in Indonesia, *sari-sari* in the Philippines, *guanzai* in Vietnam, etc., benefited the storekeeper in several different ways.[66] The *shuike*'s customers bought goods at the same time as remitting.[67] Apart from extracting fees from *shuike* and their clients, shopkeepers could also dip into the capital flowing through their businesses, thus killing two birds with one stone.[68] The storekeeper might, in time, use his entrepreneurial skills to take over the collecting of *qiaopi*, perhaps in tandem with the *shuike*, and eventually take charge of the remitting by way of companies in the China ports.[69] Thus, the store became a *piju*, usually as a sideline. This is one reason why many later *piju* owners and managers doubled as traders in other spheres. Fields into which *piju* might diversify included currency exchange, the rice trade, tea, the gold and silver trade, hostels, the travel industry, and import and export.[70]

Of fifty-two *piju* studied in Singapore, only twenty-one dealt solely in remittances, whereas the rest were also general stores, medicine shops, bike shops, etc., or engaged in other forms of business including mining, shipping, and rubber. Another study found that more than 90 percent of Chaoshan *piju* dealt in things other than just *qiaopi*. The patterns were quite complex. Some firms put most of their effort into a trade other than remitting, some were half and half, some were mainly in remitting, and a few were exclusively in remitting.[71] Some started as remittance shops and later diversified, either to maximize profit margins in a highly competitive industry or to make better use of the capital represented by the accumulation of remittances before their dispatch.[72] As for the customers, they knew and trusted the storekeeper, swapped gossip in his or her shop, and went there for help and advice. For the customers, the store was also a bank, safe and convenient, where they could deposit savings and remit them in whole or in part once they had accumulated to a certain level.[73] They could also borrow money when necessary. Where cash was remitted in the form of an advance, the *piju* took back the advance on presentation of the receipt.[74]

The *piju* were diverse in their transnational as well as in their local operations. They delivered goods as well as remittances and can therefore be said to have engaged in a form of primary foreign trade. They worked as messengers, conveying information as well as money. In the words of one study, they were "multifunctional folk (*minjian*) financial institutions."[75]

The main reason for diversification was the fierce competition in the remittance trade and the resulting narrow profit margins. Diversification also gave the *piju* an advantage over the post office. In one sense, diversification was a continuation of *shuike* practices, which had also depended on a multipronged approach to trading. But at the same time, it solved a modern problem: how to provide an ever more intrusive government with guarantees of solvency and evidence of collateral.[76]

The hostels followed a similar pattern, except that they were mostly founded by *shuike* and *ketou*. To solve the problem of their own accommodation in the ports while awaiting embarkation, *shuike* typically clubbed together to set up a *hangguan*, or "trade house," known as a *zhan* ("hostel"), where they congregated and put up their "new chum" charges, recruited from among kin or fellow villagers and fellow dialect-speakers.[77] By the start of the twentieth century, there were 184 such hostels in Xiamen and 60 in Shantou.[78] The hostel organized the new chum's boat ticket and other procedures, and if necessary lent him money, paid back from his earnings at a slightly higher than average rate of interest.[79] Hostels that originally specialized in the export of people diversified into managing *qiaopi* starting in the 1890s.[80] The *shuike* then encouraged customers to visit the hostels to save themselves the trouble of drumming up custom on the streets and in the villages, a switch to "fixed-point collection [of *qiaopi*] and dispensing [of *huipi*]."[81] Known internationally as boardinghouses, run by boarding-masters that in many cases simultaneously crimped Chinese seafarers for the shipping companies, the hostels often had links with the shipping lines that dealt in emigration to Southeast Asia.[82] Many evolved into *piju*.

Like the *shuike* that preceded them, the *piju* were deeply rooted in kinship and locality. They prided themselves on a service that was humanized and individualized, and they had the additional attraction of financial security and fixed working premises.[83] The main feature of the *qiaopi* trade was its system of networks, in China and overseas. The chains of agencies and sub-offices and the links with other offices forged between the *qiaoxiang* and the foreign ports were complex and extensive, but they were nearly always formed on the basis of lineage, surname, dialect, or locality. Owners, customers, and workers were nearly always either related to one another and from the same place or at least speakers of the same dialect. For example, the Zhenshengxing *piju* in Thailand and Shantou was owned by a Zeng from a village in Chenghai, and all its workers were Zengs; Singapore's Zhicheng *piju*, associated with another village in Chenghai, was owned and staffed by members of the Huang lineage.[84] In some cases, there was a generational as well as a lineage tie, with managers of the different branches of a *piju* drawn from the same generation.[85]

Piju formed both overseas, in major port cities, and in China, in the ports and villages. Given their kinship origins, village-based *piju* were closely linked with kinship institutions—for example *citang* ("ancestral halls"), from which some initially ran their businesses.[86] Some overseas *piju* were branches of domestic *piju*, and vice versa.[87] However, in all but a few cases the overseas office had the upper hand. Only three Fujianese *piju* commanded branches in Southeast Asia.[88]

Many clients welcomed the switch from individual couriering to enterprises run from established premises, for such firms were more reliable and cheaper (because of better management and economies of scale), and more reputable and trust-inspiring, since the client had a fixed place, under a shop-sign, where he could make inquiries and the business could less easily decamp.[89] These considerations mattered more as the amounts remitted grew.[90] The *piju* had other advantages, too. Their operations were broader in geographic scope and function than those of their *shuike* counterparts. Although the *shuike* were also multifunctional, they lacked the *piju*'s range of contacts, institutionalized networks, and professionalism, as well as their orderly management not just of remittances but of currency exchange, savings, credit, etc.

However, *shuike* continued to ply their trade well into the 1960s, mainly in regions lacking modern roads and institutions.[91] In some circumstances, they could provide a better service than the *piju*. They were more personal and intimate; they were steeped in local geography, culture, and community (both over-seas and in China); and they performed a wider range of functions beyond those of collection and delivery. Their coexistence with the *piju* afforded customers flex-ibility and choice in a market that had to cater to widely differing and constantly changing needs, regulations, and pockets.[92]

Two other points of origin of the *piju* institution were the *minxinju*, private firms that delivered letters and goods in China, and the *yinzhuang*, or traditional bank. Both employed methods and had access to networks that suited *piju* opera-tions, and the *yinzhuang* had capital, both for investment and as a guarantee of solvency.[93] The emergence of the *piju* was inseparable from these two institutions.[94]

Chinese historians like to claim that China's traditional private letter service, the *minxinju*, had antecedents in China's remote past, as far back as the Shang dynasty (sixteenth to eleventh century BC) and the Han (when the *yi* postal sys-tem was founded). The antecedents certainly included the Song dynasty's *shili youting* ("courier stations") and the Tang's *feiqian* ("flying money") system.[95] These early postal systems were state-run and mainly delivered official docu-ments, proclamations, orders, and military correspondence. A postal system for private letters is said by many to have started around 1400, in the Ming's Yongle reign (1360–1424) at a time when China's economy was beginning to grow strongly. The system spread along the rivers and the coast, particularly in south-eastern China, where it became associated with the powerful Ningbo merchant clique. It handled private material ineligible for carriage by the imperial relay system of *youyi* ("postal stations"). By the late Qing, the *youyi* system had become increasingly corrupt and the *minxinju*, considered more trustworthy and reliable, had spread across the whole of China, after first becoming established in the Jiangnan region in the late seventeenth century.[96] However, as Harris points out, in some ways it is better to understand the *minxinju* as an invention of modern times that barely predated the West's intrusion, despite its sketchy earlier anteced-ents.[97] Like the *qiaopi* system, the *minxinju* had a close association with the tradi-tional banks (the *qianzhuang* and *piaohao*). They too carried (domestic) remit-tances and escorted travelers, networked among themselves, and similarly profited from the arrival of the river and coastal steamers used to transport let-ters, goods, and currency.[98]

The *minxinju* used a network of compradors on the post-boats or river steam-ers, and it could reach nearly all of China's cities and county seats. Most carried remittances as well as letters and parcels and took a commission of 1 to 3 percent, not unlike the *piju*. Like the *ketou*, they also escorted travelers. Founders of the *piju* overseas seem to have consciously copied this model, adapting it (for example, by inventing the "list character") to their new needs and circumstances.[99]

The *minxinju* peaked in the second quarter of the nineteenth century, when there were several thousand of them, including some with ties to Asia and the

Pacific.[100] They declined after the rise of China's post office, especially after 1933, when an official distinction was made between them and the *piju*, which the authorities policed less aggressively.[101] However, most *minxinju*, especially in Fujian, had already made at least a partial transition, perhaps as early as the Daoguang reign (1821–50), to carrying *qiaopi*, given the importance of international migration in the southeast, and either competed or cooperated with the *shuike*. (This is perhaps one reason why Fujianese remittance houses continued to be known as *minxinju*, despite the use of *piju* and associated terms in eastern Guangdong.)[102]

The similarities between the internal organization of the *piju* and the somewhat older *minxinju* were as striking as those between their external modes of operation. The *minxinju* had just a handful of staff working under the owner-cum-manager and some couriers, and were also likely to be run as partnerships. Larger firms had several assistants, including an old-style bookkeeper, receptionists, porters, a cook, an odd-job man, and couriers. Like the *piju*, they prioritized customer service. They organized late collections and provided insurance and guarantees.[103]

These similarities were not accidental but arose from a shared environment and functions, so much so that the post office at first tried to ban the two types of organization simultaneously, under the same ordinance. Where the one was not the direct predecessor of the other, domestic and overseas entrepreneurs in the overseas remittance trade closely copied the *minxinju* model and adapted it to their new needs.[104] Even employees of the imperial relay system were said to have joined the *qiaopi* trade, for example in Fuzhou (Fujian's capital, and the site of its oldest *youyi*), where they put their old skills to a new use.[105]

Traditional banks, variously called *yinzhuang*, *qianzhuang*, *yinhao*, *piaohao*, and *qiandian*, were particularly numerous in Fujian and Guangdong, mainly as a result of the remittance trade. Quanzhou alone had several hundred such banks. Migrants' families used them to cash remittances, exchange currency, and deposit savings.[106] Many of these small private banks took advantage of the transition from *shuike* to *piju* to diversify into the *qiaopi* trade, where they applied their numerous connections and financial resources, while scores of others arose as a direct result of the *qiaopi* trade, particularly in the remoter Hakka areas in the years before the arrival of modern banking there.[107] The *yinhao* and the *piju* often worked in tandem, with the former supporting the latter whenever trade slackened off.[108] In Wuyi and Guangfu in particular, many migrants' dependents and returned migrants invested in stores (selling rice, sugar, oil, salt, medicine, and other daily necessities), which sometimes doubled as exchange shops and depositories for savings. Some subsequently became *yinhao* (the preferred term in Guangfu), and started specializing in finance by looping into migrant networks and expanding into joint-stock companies.[109] Many such banks acted as *piju*, as either a sideline or a main line.[110] Again, the similarities between the *piju* and the *yinhao* and *piaohao* were not accidental.[111]

Piju faced stiff competition from banks and the post office in the twentieth century, so how did they survive? Partly because of their long history, stretching back to the *minxinju* and traditional banks from which many sprang, but also because they could in many respects offer a better service. They had a longer reach, both in China and overseas. They were open practically all hours, even on rest days—this was the so-called "door market" (*menshi*) trade—and some left a night watchman to receive late *qiaopi*. By practicing a minute division of labor at all stages of the transaction, most *piju* were able to ensure that their procedures were swift and simple. Their staff spoke dialect and wrote and read the correspondence for illiterate customers, both in China and overseas. They responded flexibly to their customers' emergencies and predicaments, offering loans and advances.[112] The banks and post office, in contrast, covered far fewer places (mostly urban); their staff did not necessarily know the appropriate dialect; their procedures were bafflingly complicated; they had set and, from a worker's or petty trader's point of view, inconvenient hours; their delivery was relatively slow; and they lacked the personal touch, exemplified in the writing and reading service.[113]

The *piju* were also cheap and often worked on the narrowest of profit margins. All sorts of measures were taken to keep costs to a minimum so that fees could be either held down or dispensed with altogether (in which case the profit came from speculation on exchange rates). *Piju* staff, owners included, commonly practiced an extreme form of self-exploitation, using every possible opportunity to make a profit, however small, and working deep into the night or even through the night when necessary. Relations between different levels of the *piju* trade were fine-tuned to achieve the greatest possible economy. The size of the staff was kept to an absolute minimum, and owners and staff members switched constantly between different sectors of the business, which usually included forms of trade other than just *qiaopi*. Ideally, no one was ever unoccupied, even for a moment. To meet changing demand, temporary workers were recruited and paid by the day, usually at a pittance, and were sometimes shared between two or more collaborating or even competing *piju*. Here, the difference with the post office, where postmen sat around chatting and drinking tea at slack times, was striking.[114]

The *piju* also economized on materials. For example, the *huipi* appendages that became *de rigueur* in the *qiaopi* trade were kept tiny—twenty-five were said to weigh the same as one normal letter—and many *piju* dispensed with envelopes and provided writing paper only, to lessen the overall weight and thus the costs of the sacks and baskets they were carried in, directing *pijiao* to stuff as many *huipi* as possible into a single envelope. After the authorities' introduction of a ban on bundles of *qiaopi* in Singapore in 1923 and a new regulation requiring each envelope to be stamped individually, where possible *piju* staff bribed postal workers to understate the overall weight or number of *qiaopi*, again to keep costs to a minimum, and similarly bribed customs officials in the Chinese ports. They also smuggled sackfuls of *qiaopi* through the Chinese receiving stations to evade ever-increasing postal charges. Ingenuity and cunning were essential in the cut-throat world of the *qiaopi* trade.[115]

The *piju* collared "fresh off the boat (fob)" emigrants with the help of the *ketou*, signed them up, and assigned them a number to match their name, job, and addresses, in China and abroad, and perhaps lent them a little money to tide them over until their first payday. This was an important moment that, for the most part, tied the remitter for the foreseeable future to the *piju*, which kept his details for future reference and was thus able to handle his correspondence swiftly and efficiently. A copy of his details was sent to the appropriate *piju* in his port of origin. On remitting, all he then needed to provide was the recipient's name.[116]

Whereas the banks, for many years, turned up their noses at the paltry sums often remitted, *piju* managers rarely, if ever, turned down a commission. This is because they kept their eye on the long term. Although each individual remittance was often tiny, "family-maintenance" *qiaopi* were, by definition, for the most part regular and sustained, and could, over the years, add up to a massive financial transfer, especially in the case of those emigrants that set up successful stores or businesses.

The *piju* played on fellow-feeling (*ganqing*) to cement the economic tie.[117] The trust displayed was extraordinary. *Qiaopi* traders commonly took money from poor remitters only when the *huipi* was received. One claimed in a memoir that no one ever failed to pay up on the loan; even if the remitter died, someone would do so on his or her behalf.[118]

In the early years, many emigrants lived scattered across the countryside, or on mountains or in jungles. To get their *qiaopi*, *piju* employees followed paths first blazed by the *shuike*, tramping round the mines, farms, and factories whenever a ship was about to set sail for China. Later, a simpler and less labor-intensive method of soliciting business evolved: the *piju* got local storekeepers to act as agents, or it paid mine, factory, or plantation managers to hand out registration forms.[119]

The remittance process sped up greatly after the start of steam navigation. In the days of junk navigation, the round trip between remittance and receipt of the recipient's acknowledgment could take months and even two or three years according to some accounts, chiefly because there were so few sailings.[120] In 1851, the journey to and from Luzon in the Philippines could take more than twenty days, and one or two months or more when typhoons struck.[121] In the 1910s, the *qiaopi-huipi* process between Singapore and Shantou took around forty days, but by the 1930s the time had halved, scarcely longer than modern airmail, and it reduced to just a week to ten days after the beginning of telecommunications.[122] Some people started remitting not just monthly but even weekly under the new conditions.[123]

The *piju*'s organizational culture was strongly paternalistic. Its core personnel was recruited on kinship grounds, and each *piju* was presided over by a *jiazhang* ("head of household"), who acted as the financial administrator and counter-chief and whose job was to sort the *qiaopi* into routes, check the amounts, and hand a day's-worth of remittances to each runner.[124] To retain staff members' loyalty and incentivize them, *piju* owners paid commission and subsidies and handed out gifts at appropriate times of the year. Some *piju* practiced profit sharing—70 percent for the owners; 20 percent for the manager; and 10 percent for the postmen, the cook, and other menial staff. Some set up compensation schemes for postmen, whose families might receive a given sum (also divided into three grades) if a postman died in the course of his duties or was incapacitated.[125]

Trade unions throughout the world have usually had little success in organizing postal workers. In Britain, agitators started recruiting members of the postal staff in the mid-nineteenth century, and in China Lu Jingshi set up the Postal Workers' Union in the early 1930s.[126] But despite low wages and poor working conditions, most postal unions have, historically, never acquired the bargaining power of the better-organized industrial unions. Although usually among the largest work-forces sharing a single employer, they were too scattered and their functions too diverse to unite and cohere. *Qiaopi* workers were even less likely to become class conscious and to fight for their separate interests as a class. Lowly workers had little security and earned a pittance, but even if they developed a sense of political grievance and a class identity, there was no way they could give it form and expression. They too were usually embedded in kinship networks from which it was it was nearly impossible to break.

The typical *piju* was rather small, with an average of around ten employees. The building that housed it had a room in which to sort the *qiaopi*, a room to live in, and one or more dormitories. The bigger *piju* had a score of workers, others just three or four. Few had much capital, and they relied mainly on the cash-flow resulting from remittances.[127] Their needs were minimal: food, perhaps bikes, a phone, and a table.[128]

The *piju*'s "internal" workers were close relatives or friends of the owner, for in their case trust was most essential. Trust mattered scarcely less in the case of the "external" workers that served the villages: even they were highly unlikely to be outsiders. Internal employees were usually paid more than the average worker to encourage a good attitude and ensure their honesty and loyalty. One *piju* paid them eighteen yuan a month, plus 0.1 percent of every thousand yuan of remittance.[129] Another paid the manager (the owner's partner) thirty yuan and the bookkeeper and the couriers twenty-four yuan. External workers were mainly peasants, although some were itinerant hawkers. They worked whenever the ship docked, and otherwise resumed farming or petty trading. They either took a fixed wage or worked as casual laborers (*duangong*), typically receiving one yuan a day.[130] In some periods, firms even charged external workers 1 percent of the *qiaopi*, so they had no choice other than to pester recipients for "tips."[131]

Only a small minority of *piju* were run by a single individual. Most were jointly owned by two or more people. In Fujian, 82 percent of *piju* were partnerships. The same was true of Hainan. (Partnerships enjoyed greater consumer confidence than one-person outfits, whose owners were more likely to go bankrupt or abscond.) Most were relatively poorly capitalized. In 1933 the average amount of capital held by Shantou's fifty-five *piju* was twenty thousand yuan. Smaller *piju* in the interior had an average capital of around 870 yuan in the early 1930s.[132]

The commission charged on remittances varied according to the amount remitted, the distance between remitter and recipient, and the exchange rate in the port of entry, as well as the nature of the remittance—whether it was in cash, on credit, or drawn on savings. At first, *shuike* and some *piju* owners shied away from the word "fee," which suggested an undesirably impersonal and commercial relationship, and talked instead of "tea money," the amount of which was often specified by the remitter.[133] Where competition was intense and the float (the money available in the interval between receipt and delivery of the remittance) could be put to profitable use, some *piju* charged nothing and even paid remitters. Manipulating the conversion rate was another source of income. Where a fee was charged, it was generally calculated as a percentage of the remittance, payable either on remittance or on receipt of evidence (in the form of a *huipi*) of the remittance's delivery. The size of the fee varied according to the overall or local economic climate, the remitter's relationship with the company, and other factors.[134] In time, some firms got together to standardize fees. As the trade became ever greater and more lucrative, many local merchants and powerholders, themselves senior kin of the remitters and recipients, used their status to squeeze their poorer and less connected relatives, who had limited ways of resisting.[135]

The operational model of the *qiaopi* trade was known as the *sanpan* ("three coils"). It comprised three stages: (1) receiving, stamping, handling, and registering the *qiaopi*, and (2) transmitting it (usually along with thousands of others) to an office in a Chinese port, where it was (3) sorted, and whence it was collected by an employee or representative of an office in a village or county town, which delivered it and collected the receipt. By the 1920s and 1930s, the final stage of delivery was supposed to happen within around five days, or a week in the case of deliveries to remoter places. These three stages corresponded to the first, second, and third coils. The reply-cum-receipt (*huipi*) followed the same route in reverse.[136]

There were two main sorts of *piju*. The larger ones were household names in the community and even across the diaspora, with registered branches or agents in China. The smaller ones had no transnational connections, sometimes passed on their *qiaopi* to the big ones, and were not always busy, unlike the bigger *piju*. For many of the smaller traders—between 80 and 90 percent of them, according to a 1914 study commissioned by the Bank of Taiwan—*qiaopi* were, as we have already noted, a sideline.[137] Some even worked from roadside tables in Chinatown.[138]

A handful of *piju*, bigger and better capitalized than the generality of *qiaopi* firms, controlled all three stages of the remittance process, from receipt to delivery, through a vertical hierarchy of corporate command known as the "single-whip" (*yi tiao bian*) system. In Xiamen, it was said to have been employed by just two firms. Most firms operated not corporately but through a system of parallel agencies. The vertically organized, self-sufficient firms ran sub-branches answerable to a general or "mother" office and took the whole profit, but they required a lot of capital and, being both resource-rich and conspicuous, were vulnerable to official predation, especially in places where they lacked sufficient local knowledge and connections. They were also more liable to internal corruption, although their verticality made them more profitable and efficient.[139]

Only around 10 percent of Southeast Asian *piju* had their own offices in China. The other 90 percent of less capitalized firms carried out the China end of their operations with the help of chains (*lianhao*) of independent agents. The relationship between agent and *piju* took one of three possible forms: some agents, a minority, shared profits on a yearly basis; others handled remittances for a commission of between 0.2 and 0.4 percent in cases where the agents bore the inland costs of delivery; or, in other circumstances, agents took between 1 and 1.7 percent. Where *qiaopi* went missing, the agent was deemed responsible.[140] The agents' role was crucial, and the relationship was usually based, like the rest of the trade, on consanguinity or native-place ties.[141] In 1948, 70 *piju* in Shantou acted for 441 *piju* in Hong Kong and overseas and for 141 *piju* elsewhere in China, an arrangement reinforced by a 1934 Chinese Government restriction on the China-side operations of overseas-based *piju*.[142] The serving structure radiated out from the ports to the inland towns and villages, across the plains and up the mountains, forming a complex and powerful system.[143] The *yinhao* or traditional banks also established networks overseas. In Thailand, Chaozhou *yinhao* even opened branches in some villages, where they continued operating for more than one hundred years.[144]

Piju belonging to the second and third coils were involved in complex relationships both with one another and with *piju* in the first coil. Some in the first coil accepted commissions from *piju* abroad, chiefly in Southeast Asia, in which sense they performed a second-coil role. Some first-coil *piju* even performed third- and second-coil functions over and above their first-coil function and were known as *touju* ("all-round *piju*"). Second-coil *piju* that also did third-coil work (i.e., delivery to recipients) were known as *ersanju* ("second and third *piju*").[145]

There were three categories of third-coil *piju*, those responsible for final delivery. The first sort, known as Class A, often set up by second- or first-coil offices in rural areas, maintained direct ties to upper-level *piju* in Southeast Asia. The second sort, Class B, served a narrower area than Class A and had no overseas ties: they received their *qiaopi* exclusively from *piju* in the second coil. The third sort were not delivery offices as such but were made up of self-employed *pijiao* loosely associated with one or more first- or second-coil *piju*. These *pijiao* delivered on average once a week and otherwise worked in agriculture or as urban laborers or petty traders.

Piju were distinguished by size as well as by function. Large-scale *piju* dealt on average with around five thousand *qiaopi* a month, rising to more than ten thousand at peak times of the year. (See the description of the Tianyi *piju* in the next section.) Middle-sized *piju* handled between one and four thousand *qiaopi* a month and were relatively numerous. Small independent *piju*, which served a restricted area and were often run as sideline businesses, were of three different sorts: type (a), located in the *qiaoxiang*, collected *qiaopi* and handed them to other *piju* for further dispatch or sent them on to Chaoshan; type (b), located in Hong Kong or a city in mainland China, had a purely intermediary function; type (c), usually located in a small town near the manager's hometown or village, only delivered *qiaopi*. These small independent *piju* were quite numerous, but their overall share of the trade was not great (most handled fewer than one thousand *qiaopi* a month), and most folded within ten or twenty years.[146]

In some places and periods, *piju* set up systems of distribution routes served by salaried postmen. This approach saved money and was generally said to work well. The postmen profited in more ways than one. They could solicit tips or commissions from recipients. They could also make money by manipulating the rate at which they changed silver dollars into fractional units for distribution to the villagers. The system of "postal routes" caught on in some areas, and even the Xiamen branch of the Bank of China started copying it in 1930.[147]

Why did most *piju* choose to act through agents rather than set out to control the entire process with their own resources? Naturally the single-whip system was potentially more lucrative, but it also required more capital than most *piju* could muster, and it demanded competencies that were beyond their usually parochial horizon. Few managers and owners were confident enough to risk operating in areas where they lacked personal relations and local intelligence. The main problem was how to deal with local officials, especially in a period of social unrest verging on and sometimes descending into civil war.[148]

Piju played a key role in both the migrant and the regional and national economy. Taking Chaoshan as an example, in the last quarter of the nineteenth century, 1.51 million emigrants left Shantou for Southeast Asia; today, millions of Chaoshanese and their descendants live overseas.[149] At their height, Chaoshan's *piju* handled 80 percent of overseas remittances, amounting to more than two million *qiaopi* a year.[150] In 1919, each ship arriving in Shantou carried around sixty thousand *qiaopi*. Before 1921, Chaoshan remittances amounted to tens of millions of yuan a year, and after 1921 to more than one hundred and even two hundred million yuan.[151] Chaoshan received 1.99 million *qiaopi* in 1947, valued at nearly 120 million Hong Kong dollars.[152] The remittances fed into the local and regional economy both by way of dependents' spending and through the exploitation by *piju* of the cash-flow leverage of float. The specialist *piju* might use it to speculate on currency markets, the nonspecialists to issue loans or to invest in or buy and sell goods in their other lines of business (land, property, import-export, etc.).[153]

Piju were deeply embedded not just in migrant-sending regions but in the business and social communities that formed in the foreign ports and towns. *Piju* were family or lineage-based firms, just as the *shuike* from which they sprang worked almost exclusively along lines of geosanguinity or dialect. In 1936 nearly 70 percent of Shantou's *piju* were family firms, and an even greater number had particularistic ties of other sorts, based mainly on native place.[154] *Piju* in all areas and eras were similarly rooted in family or wider kinship networks.

Because of the *qiaopi* trade's rural and lineage roots and clientele, the *piju* calendar exactly mirrored the calendar of Chinese rural society, with its festivals and associated rhythms. In the early days of the trade, the deliveries were seasonal, tied to big and small annual festivals: deliveries in or leading up to the first, fifth, and ninth lunar months (corresponding to the Spring Festival, the Duanwu or Dragon Boat Festival, and the Chongyang or Double-Ninth Festival respectively), were known as *zou dabang* ("big batch"), and those in the second, seventh, and tenth as *zou xiaobang* ("small batch").[155] In the run-up to the Spring Festival, the volume of remittance drew to a peak and then ebbed until the next surge. This pattern of activity continued even after the consolidation of the trade in the early twentieth century. It is illustrated by the fluctuating volume of *qiaopi* money handled by Shantou's Zhenshengxing *piju* in 1946: 100,000 silver dollars in the "slack months" (January–March); 150,000 in the "average months" (April–September); and 300,000 in the "peak months" (October–December).[156] The *piju* were perfectly suited to this constantly changing pace and rhythm, for unlike the more regular institutions of the formal sector of the economy, they were used to elastically adjusting their workforce and work rate.

Apart from kinship, lineage, and native-place ties, trade relations were an important thread in many of these networks. Because most *piju* engaged in other trades besides *qiaopi*, they developed trust relations with other traders that were not necessarily based on consanguineous or geographic ties. Where appropriate, they could lean on these people for support or use them as *qiaopi* agents.[157]

This style of ownership and management was economical, flexible, and profitable. However, because it depended primarily on trust, it lacked effective impersonal and systematic mechanisms of supervision and control. The threshold (in the sense of the amount of capital required) at the gate into the *qiaopi* trade was low, for the trade's main cost was labor, and the returns were high, so large numbers of newcomers flocked to join, not all of them equally honest. Corruption became rife in sections of the trade at all levels, including at the top. In 1929 Tianyi collapsed as a result of irresponsible and opportunistic speculation, sparking a general crisis in the *qiaopi* sector. (This crisis is described in the following section on Tianyi.)

The same happened again, on an even greater scale, in the late 1940s, when galloping inflation in China and official harassment overseas forced much of the trade to stick to illegal or underground conduits. Currency speculation, an essential moment in the remittance process and a main source of the trade's profit, sometimes got out of hand, with remittances gambled away by *qiaopi* traders. This corruption led at times to a loss of public confidence in the trade.[158]

In a lawless and chaotic age, the *qiaopi* trade was vulnerable to thieves and particularly pirates. In 1923, for example, pirates boarded a steamer near Xiamen and stole remittance checks worth half a million yuan from the Tianyi *piju*.[159] Local and national authorities were keen to get their hands on the profits, as were local strongmen and gentry leaders, who demanded "donations" from the traders.[160] Although firms like Tianyi were rich enough to make good on losses resulting from robberies and extortion, poorer *piju* were not.

The loss of trust that resulted from such practices and incidents led to a partial exodus by customers from the *piju*, in some places greater than others, and to a greater reliance for a while on the post office and the banks. However, the flight was never enough to overturn the preponderance of the *piju* system in the remittance trade. This is partly because *piju* remained better adapted to remitters' needs than modern institutions did, but mainly because the latter were unable to meet customers' needs during the postwar financial crisis in China, when inflation made going by the book a game you were far likelier to lose than win (see chapter 5).

Lawlessness in the warlord years and in the Sino-Japanese War and the civil war led many *piju* to adopt a special form of partnership in areas subject to bandit or official predations. *Piju* owners and managers vied to recruit local luminaries and powerholders (*shilipai*) to become their paid nominal "partners," and through the link they were able to recover large amounts of remittance money stolen by criminals or pocketed by local bullies (*tuhao*) or corrupt officials. To the same aim, other officials were invited to become shareholders. Banditry and lawlessness in some of the more isolated mountainous *qiaoxiang* became so endemic after the collapse of the Qing in 1911 that some *piju* stopped operating in them for several years. Eventually, rather than risk sending cash, most *piju* in such areas started sending coupons or credit notes known as *shanpiao* ("mountain notes"), *xiaopiao* ("small notes"), or *shandan* ("mountain units"), cashable either at the remittance shop or at a local store. A similar system developed in eastern Fujian near Fuzhou, where *qianzhuang* ran a system known as *taifu* tickets. *Shanpiao* quickly became an alternative currency, available in several denominations from one to fifty dollars. It was supposed to be secure, governed by a system of secret daily codes transmitted to the recipient. If stolen, a *shanpiao* could be reported and made good by the guarantor whose guarantee it carried, even if it had passed through several hands. However, the system was not properly controlled and sometimes got out of hand. Some *piju* owners saw it as a license to print money, and every now and then fake coupons flooded the market.[161] One *piju* in Jin'an with a capital of just two thousand yuan issued *shanpiao* worth one hundred thousand.[162] If the dispensing office went bankrupt or its owners defaulted, dependents were likely to lose their entire savings.[163] Between 1920 and 1936, twenty-four *piju* closed down or reorganized because of the reckless issuance of *shanpiao* and other notes. The biggest defaulter was Tianyi, which ended up owing dependents five hundred thousand yuan.[164]

The *qiaopi* system is not unique to China, though some of its features probably are. Migrants of other nations and cultures have also developed indigenous remittance systems. The best-known example is the *hawala* system, also known as *hundi*, used predominantly in and by migrants from the Middle East and South Asia. In its historical origins, operational features, and modern-day links with the formal sector, the *hawala* system (which still thrives) bears a strong resemblance to the now defunct Chinese model. It had its roots in the period before conventional banking became widespread. It is quick, cheap, and accessible at all hours; it is culturally consonant with local institutions and values; it is versatile; it engages in "batch processing"; and unlike banks, it serves even the worst-connected villages. Conducted outside the formal system, its transactions normally escape taxation. It can also be conducted anonymously, hence its strong contemporary association in the eyes of authorities with crime, including money-laundering and terrorism (the subject of the overwhelming majority of the large number of books on it). It depends heavily on trust, cemented by family networks or connections among the *hawaladar*, the brokers or couriers that run the trade. Like the *qiaopi* system, the amount remitted is often paid to the *hawaladar* only on confirmation of receipt.[165] The main difference with *qiaopi* is that letters do not seem to be an expected part of the *hawala* system. However, letters are sometimes forwarded to the payee, who confirms receipt in the form of an answer to the letter (called *jawabee hundi*, *jawabee* meaning "reply").[166]

THE TIANYI *PIJU*

Of the thousands of *piju* set up over the years, few have been studied in much detail, despite their importance in China's national and regional economies and in international trade. Apart from a few memoirs, little or nothing has been published about the great majority of them. The paucity of studies on *qiaopi* institutions contrasts strongly with the large number of studies on the Chinese banking system, including works on individual banks.[167]

A main exception to this pattern of neglect is Tianyi, China's biggest, best-connected, most extensive, most innovative, most influential, and longest-lasting remittance company, about which several studies have appeared.[168] Tianyi played a major role in the development of China's postal and financial services. It passed through, and indeed embodied, all three of the main stages of the *qiaopi* trade—individual couriering (*shuike*), the inauguratory remittance shop (*piju*), and the eventual transition to a full-blown specialist global business chain. Tianyi has featured in the work of several *qiaopi* historians, principally Jia Junying, Guo Boling, and Chen Xunxian. In this section, we borrow findings from the research of these three scholars to illustrate the nature of the *qiaopi* trade at its top end, including its strengths and weaknesses and Tianyi's dramatic demise in 1928.[169]

Tianyi was founded in 1880 by the legendary Guo Youpin, a former *shuike*. Guo started taking *qiaopi* back to China in 1874, working the route between China and the Philippines, along which he travelled back and forth several times a year.[170] He initially delivered the *qiaopi* in person, but later he started employing couriers to do so. He set up his own *piju* (using the term *piguan*) in 1880. Originally tiny, it later expanded enormously, with its main office (which Guo personally managed) in Guo's native village of Liuchuan in Longxi county in southern Fujian and with branches in Xiamen and Manila.

Guo Youpin employed only kith and kin in his company and ruled it in the patriarchal manner, with a rod of iron, keeping it largely clean and free from corruption. When he died in 1901, the firm passed into the hands of his eldest son, Yongzhong, also a spirited and innovating leader. The leaders of all Tianyi's main branches were sons of Guo or affines of the Guo lineage, tied together in a thick web of blood and marriage.

In 1892 Guo Youpin set up an office in Xiamen and another in Jinjiang near Quanzhou, and later expanded into Hong Kong. His company bundled *qiaopi* in Manila and cashed them in Xiamen, before distributing and delivering them to the villages. The *huipi* were similarly bundled in Xiamen. In the late 1890s, the post office tried to interfere with this arrangement but tacitly accepted it, at least in part because of its own shortage of experienced staff and poor geographic coverage in China.

Guo Youpin pioneered many of the measures devised in the late nineteenth century to modernize the *qiaopi* trade. He regularized procedures, strengthened his administration, introduced strict checks, produced standardized ledgers, and set up an intricate system of interlinking divisions (the *sanpan*) that knitted the whole process of collection, transmission, distribution, and delivery into a seamless whole, thus creating a template for the higher end of the *qiaopi* trade. He also established a scale of charges, set predictable exchange rates, hired reliable and trustworthy couriers, paid his couriers properly, forbade the extortion of "tea money," and forbade his *pijiao* and couriers to write *huipi* on customers' behalf, since doing so would give them the chance to cheat. (It is unclear how effective the ban was.) In the early days of steamship delivery, he prepared teams of rowers that stood ready for the steamer's arrival and rowed out to collect the mail. By streamlining procedures, he sped up delivery, its speed being a main customer concern. In 1920 Tianyi purchased three small steamers to carry *qiaopi* from Xiamen to ports close to the *qiaoxiang*, further slashing delivery time. He and his successors at Tianyi thought up various ways to make remitting easier and more convenient. For example, they hit on the idea of hoisting the Tianyi flag whenever a new shipment of *qiaopi* arrived at the main office in Liuchuan, and they provided a place to sleep for payees arriving in Liuchuan from remote villages. By 1901 nearly half of all the letters that reached Xiamen passed through Tianyi, which by 1911 had twenty-eight branches in China and abroad. The company became increasingly professional, and it diversified into credit as well as remittances. When rival *piju* and opportunistic newcomers to the trade tried to use Tianyi's trademark name, the company took action against them.

In its heyday, after 1911, Tianyi had thirty-three branches, including twenty-four in China and the rest in seven other countries.[171] It had 556 employees, 393 of them overseas, and had become a model for the industry. It was truly transnational in scope, with branches throughout Southeast Asia (see map 1). Between 1920 and 1926, it was responsible for remitting an estimated ten to fifteen million silver dollars per year.

Jia Junying analyzes Tianyi in terms of the transition through different sorts of trust—personal (*in personam*), relational (i.e., *guanxi*-based), and system-based (*in rem*)—although the transition between them was neither unilinear nor unidirectional. Guo Youpin won trust at the start of his career as a *shuike* by his personality and manner, which spoke sincerity and honesty and thus bolstered his company's credibility and reputation, and by his resolute insistence on paying out remittances lost during his legendary shipwreck by selling off family assets. Other companies responded to similar crises and disasters by declaring themselves bankrupt and leaving remitters with no remedy, a difference noted by migrant investors, among whom Guo's reputation soared.[172]

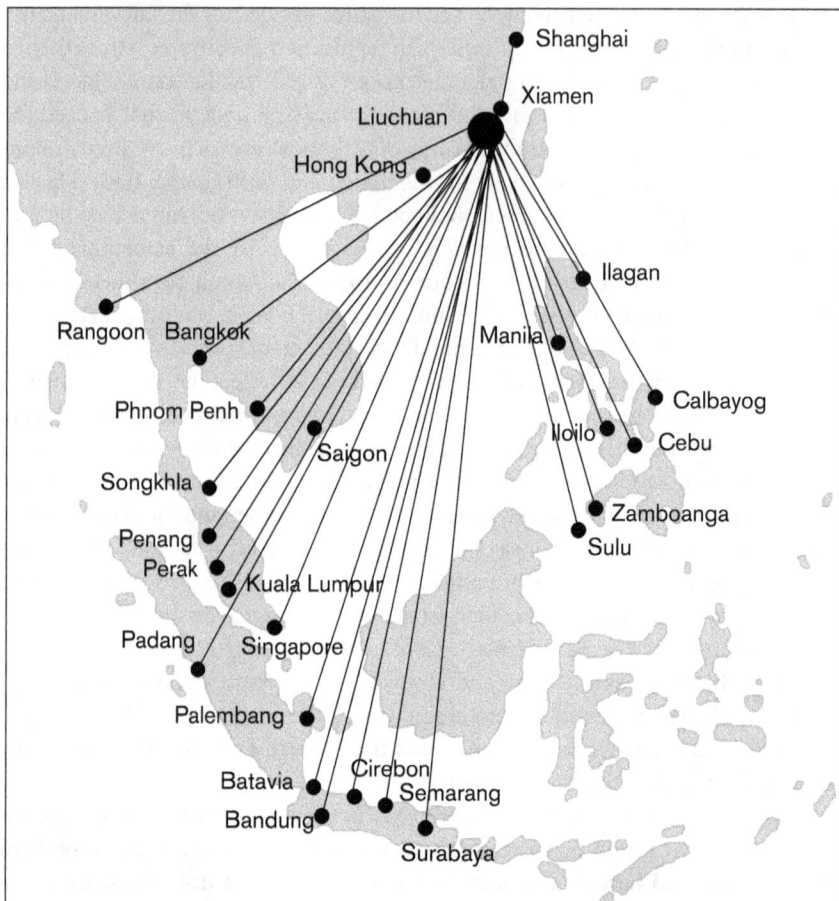

MAP 1. Headquarters and Branches of the Tianyi *Piju* in China and Southeast Asia. Source: Huang Qinghai. 2016. *Haiyang yimin, maoyi yu jingrong wangluo: Yi qiaopi ye wei zhongxin* ("Maritime Migration, Trade and Financial Network: A Case Study of *Qiaopi*"). Beijing: Shehui kexue wenxian chuban she, 126.

Tianyi was founded on blood and native-place relations of the sort associated with chain migration before the emergence of trust-producing systems. Guo Youpin personally took responsibility for all the remittances that passed through his company. The transition to system-based trust came with the elaboration of stamps, chops, ledgers, and procedures. This transition coincided with changes during the early twentieth century in the broader overseas-Chinese economy, which diversified in all directions and became increasingly prosperous. It also coincided with the rise, in China and overseas, of modern banking and postal services, which Tianyi saw as a threat but even more so as an opportunity.

Tianyi rode high on Southeast Asia's transition to greater prosperity before and during World War I and radiated out across the entire region, including China, investing in everything from shipping to rubber. While avoiding modern methods of management, scrutiny, and accountability and sticking to the family-firm model, under which all its ties and operations were strictly controlled by Guos, Tianyi cut transaction costs, ran simple and effective administrations, and swiftly accumulated capital. In time, however, corrupt practices crept in, and the model of "harmonious and tacit understanding" was not up to dealing with them, thus becoming a bane rather than a boon. Internal supervision was inadequately exercised in Tianyi and other such firms. In time, some became breeding grounds for embezzlement, reckless speculation, and competition between different branches of each individual company. In 1929 speculation led to a run on Tianyi's funds and to its closure, owing half a million yuan. The crisis was exacerbated by its timing: it coincided with the run-up to the Spring Festival, when liquidity was in short supply due to customer withdrawals from the financial system, which was unable to provide a sufficient volume of loans and temporary transfers to save Tianyi. Tianyi's closure was followed by the closing down of twenty-four other *piju*, unleashing a wave of panic across the region.

Tianyi's closing down was the endpoint of several years of the trade's general decline between 1921 and 1928, caused by inflation in the wider economy, growing competition among *piju*, growing competition from China's banking and postal system, and state measures in China and abroad to restrict *piju* activities, partly in response to malpractice and bankruptcies in the trade. Political turmoil in Fujian and Guangdong in the 1920s and warlord depredations, including in and around the *qiaoxiang*, led to even greater instability and chaos.

Tianyi's demise is sometimes portrayed as bankruptcy, but it can be better described as a result of the firm's having decided on its own initiative to go out of business. This decision was made in response to losses due to growing competition and the effects on the *qiaopi* trade of China's political and military instability, in addition to Tianyi's terminal internal crisis. However, the panic was relatively short-lived and the trade in general was restored to good health after the 1929 economic crash by a drop in the price of silver, resulting in a steep rise in the volume of remittances to China.

Guo Youpin was not only an outstanding entrepreneur but the *qiaopi* trade's most prominent educational philanthropist. He and his sons, who took over his roles as company leader and philanthropic donor, are an excellent example of the link between *qiaopi* and charity. Guo Youpin's charity was deeply rooted in Confucian thinking. He took the name Tianyi from a maxim of the Han philosopher

Dong Zhongshu (179–104 BCE), "the way of heaven (*tian*) and the human world are one (*yi*)," an assertion of his Confucian commitment and his belief that morality is an essential support of social order. His charitable activities are described in greater detail in chapter 6.

PIJIAO AS THE FINAL LINK IN THE *QIAOPI* TRADE

In the days of the *piju*, the *pijiao*, or runner, was the final link in the chain of remittance delivery. He was a direct descendant, as his name suggests, of the *minxinju*'s letter carriers, known as *jiaofu*, bearers (literally "feet men"), and did some of the same work as the *shuike*, at least in terms of the domestic delivery of *qiaopi*, though not in their collection.[173] Most *pijiao* were peasants, though a few were townspeople. As *duangong*, they usually did one delivery a week. In the *piju* system, the *pijiao* toiled hardest, rising at the crack of dawn, braving all weathers, and often not arriving home until late at night or the following day. They required alertness, high intelligence, physical strength and stamina, and fearlessness on lonely roads, through territory plagued by bandits, predatory militias, and warlord forces. A typical round was one hundred *li*, about thirty miles, following small paths to remote villages and isolated farmhouses. The *pijiao*'s load was designed to be deliverable within a day, but sometimes they were unable to finish it on time and ended up staying in someone's house in a village along the way. Some rounds lasted two to three days, especially in busy periods.[174] After 1949 some *pijiao* carried out their deliveries by bike.[175]

A typical *pijiao* earned one yuan a day, equal to two pounds of husked rice, plus a few cents for food and expenses supplemented by the occasional tip.[176] He—all but a tiny handful were men—wore a special outfit equipped with many pockets, carried a sturdy umbrella against the sun and rain and for defense, and wore straw sandals. He transported the *qiaopi* in cloth sacks or a tubular bamboo basket with a protective bamboo lid, attached to his back by high straps.[177] In the early years of the trade, he often delivered *qiaopi* in the form of silver bars or coins, which weighed heavily. In peak periods, for example before important festivals, he was expected to deliver more than one hundred *qiaopi* per day, valued at one to two thousand yuan. This consisted of many smaller sums; large amounts were usually transmitted through the banks. During the runaway inflation of the late 1940s, his sacks and baskets bulged with huge piles of paper money weighing many pounds.[178] One remittance of two hundred million yuan was said to have required a wheelbarrow.[179]

The *pijiao* was invariably a local person, intimately familiar with his patch. Because of his close association with villagers, he could deliver even to the sketchiest addresses, in villages without street names, and to recipients addressed by a milk name, an honorific, or simply "mum and dad."[180] Even the village name was not necessarily fixed or constant; letter writers used different names, elegant or colloquial, for their ancestral places.[181] The *pijiao* was expected to be familiar with the affairs, whereabouts, and genealogies of clients at both ends of the migration chain, in China and overseas. Where he did not know the identity of a recipient or the location of an address, he could inquire locally.[182] The job (like that of the *shuike*) tended to be inherited (three generations of *pijiao* in one family was not uncommon), and it was usually for life.[183]

Magnifying the sense of feudalism, the *pijiao* trade was subdivided into the *tou* or *chaitou* ("boss," "messenger boss"), who fetched the *qiaopi* from the *piju*, and the *zai* ("youngster"), who received them from the *tou*.[184] Some *piju* employed *chaitou* only for regular routes and expected them to recruit and pay their own *xinchai* ("letter couriers") for lesser routes.[185]

In the early days, many *pijiao* were not paid by their employers and worked instead for tips and fees that ranged from around half a percent to between 10 and 20 percent of the remittance. However, this practice was later abandoned by *piju* owners anxious to avoid alienating potential customers.[186] The *pijiao* became a popular and welcome figure in the villages, and he joined in the festivities his deliveries sparked off.[187] Even when the tipping stopped, he was often rewarded with a bowl of soup or eggs.[188]

Like the *shuike*, the *pijiao* was better educated and more capable than other villagers. He had to be numerate, so as to be able to check the money and make calculations, and literate, to read the addresses and pen replies for illiterate customers. In a lawless society, even a modicum of wealth could attract unwelcome attention, so recipients often buried their remittances. This is why it was essential that the *pijiao*, like the *shuike*, was judged to be honest and discreet, able to keep his customers' secrets and respect their privacy.[189]

After the *qiaopi* trade fell under stricter regulation, *pijiao* usually forbade recipients to seal the envelope containing the reply, to stop them enclosing correspondence from more than one family—a practice that could incur a fine on the *piju*. In cases where illiterate recipients nominated someone else to write the *huipi*, the *pijiao* was expected to track that person down and ensure that the *huipi* was written as arranged. When all the *huipi* had been gathered, the *pijiao* took them to the *piju*, where they were sent abroad singly or in packets. In cases where no *huipi* had been provided by the recipient, a stub served as the receipt; if the *huipi* was late and had to be sent separately, the recipient family had to pay the extra postage.[190]

Stories about *pijiao* reuniting family members that had lost touch are rife in *qiaopi* lore and legend.[191] One *pijiao* in the 1960s helped a Chinese immigrant in Penang, Malaysia, find his mother in China after a seventeen-year separation. The same man was famous for scouring the villages to track down payees, and he used to help migrants by banking money on behalf of those planning to retire to China.

He was also praised in 1963 for persuading migrants to remit a sum in excess of HK$74,000, a feat described as "patriotic" because it was a contribution, however small, to China's economic progress. As a reward for his efforts, he was invited to attend a national conference on *qiaopi*.[192]

In the warlord years and during the Sino-Japanese War and the civil war of the late 1940s, some *pijiao* were killed while delivering *qiaopi*.[193] In the Guomindang period, local communities mobilized to defeat bandits in the *qiaoxiang*, and the authorities, bowing to pressure from migrants and their families, agreed not to prosecute when bandits were caught and killed, and pledged to investigate robberies. Leaders of the *baojia* system of collective responsibility imposed on the villages by the Nationalists linked up with local clans to protect the *pijiao*. Under the *baojia* system, the robbers' village had to pay compensation to the injured party and risked being denied *qiaopi* deliveries for six months. *Piju* associations offered rewards for information about robbers and promised to take to hospital *pijiao* hurt in attacks and anyone injured helping them, and to pay a substantial sum to the families of *pijiao* who died while out delivering. These law-and-order measures were said to have been strictly enforced, so that although there was much unrest in the *qiaoxiang* and some violence against *pijiao*, *piju*, and the stores that served dependent families, robberies were not a serious problem for the *qiaopi* trade as a result of this combination of popular sentiment, social control, self-organization, and official shield.[194]

The *pijiao* was kept honest not only by his ingrained sense of duty but also by public opinion and the local moral economy. The potential employment of ostracism and even extreme physical measures against those who betrayed local trust was a risk few dared take.

QIAOPI NETWORKS AND NETWORK-BASED ASSOCIATIONS

The *qiaopi* trade was based on networks rather than on market ties and legally defined commercial arrangements. Networks were, and remain, a basic feature of transnational and chain migration and the essential tie along which Chinese migration flows, together with the information and resources upon which it depends. Because of networks, neighbors and kin concentrate in given destinations overseas, which become extensions of the sending place, at least for the migrant generation.

Networks based on kinship (family or lineage, and in some cases generation), common provenance (village or region), surname, and dialect engendered feelings of trust between clients and *qiaopi* entrepreneurs and among the latter in the forming of their partnerships. This trust was a check on corruption and dishonesty in a society in which agreements were not necessarily enforceable under law. In the eighteenth and nineteenth centuries and the early twentieth century, few Chinese migrants enjoyed the protection of embassies or consulates, and in many places they were singled out for ill treatment and abuse against which they had little remedy. Even the Nationalists' declaration in 1924 that they would support overseas Chinese and their dependents made scant difference in practice, either in China or overseas.[195] In such circumstances, ties of kinship or provenance provided the possibility of mutual aid and at least a modicum of protection.

Networks also explain the speed and ease of the delivery of *qiaopi*, an essential requirement of the trade, for networks were flexible, rooted in the masses, generally secure, accurately informed about circumstances at each end of the migration chain, and available everywhere they were needed, so they could spring into action automatically and at once, with the bare minimum of time-consuming checks. From the point of view of *qiaopi* entrepreneurs, mobilizing ties of blood, tongue, or place was the surest way of keeping ahead of the competition.

The dialect groups that gathered in their own overseas enclaves were known as *bang*. In Singapore, the Fujian *bang* preponderated and was subdivided into four main systems centred on Xiamen, Fuzhou, Xinghua, and Longyan. By 1937 there were forty-two Fujian-based remittance houses in Singapore. The Chaozhou *bang* was slightly smaller, though it controlled a similar number of *piju*. Both groups outnumbered the Hainanese, who in their turn outnumbered the Hakkas (divided into two systems, based on Meixian and Dabu) and the even smaller Guangdong *bang*.[196]

The networking principle suffused the entire *qiaopi* world. The complex relationship between the *piju* or its general office, usually overseas, and the sub-offices or agents in China was nearly always based on particularistic ties. So was the *piju*'s link to other agents or to offices belonging to other owners.[197] Networks not only tied China to the world but operated across countries other than China. For example, the *qiaopi* trade in Thailand was closely linked, along particularistic ties, to that of Vietnam, Cambodia, and Laos.[198] Singapore was an even more important hub, handling nearly 18 percent of all *qiaopi* in the late 1940s. Almost from the start, it acted as a staging post for the wider region, including Borneo and Indonesia, mainly to avoid the excessive charges levied by post offices in places other than Singapore.[199] Ties of trust governed not just the trade's upper management but its lowest reaches, right down to the *pijiao* who made the final delivery and collected the receipt. He too was, in nearly all cases, kith or kin of the migrant and his family.

Somewhat fewer networks were based on trade and business ties that had become close enough over time to warrant trust. Other networks were based on friendship.[200] Although *piju* serving the same place-based clientele were in competition, they cooperated where necessary. On receiving a commission to deliver to a place where they lacked a branch or agent, they might send it through a rival firm, acting together in a sort of informal postal union.[201] Such transactions usually involved a small fee, equivalent to 1 or 2 percent of the remittance.[202]

Networks were sometimes fixed and regular, at other times temporary or makeshift. They differed in size and extent; some were huge, others tiny. They also differed in duration; some were long-lived and seemingly indestructible, others episodic and transient. The many forms these networks took were an expression of their flexibility and adaptability.[203]

Although every *piju* was based, either wholly or mostly, on ties of geoconsanguinity, the networks they spanned and joined, taken together, covered huge numbers of villages and large distances. For example, the Chaoshan *piju* (which at one point numbered more than a thousand) covered all the villages in the region, including the 4,488 not served by the post office, and their imbricate and intersecting networks reached towns and villages along practically the entire littoral zone of the South China Sea as well as the big and small communities formed by Chinese migrants overseas.[204]

For the remitter and his family, trust relations of this sort were often the sole guarantee of the cash remitted or the savings migrants deposited, and they were also the *piju* owner's guarantee in the case of loans and advances. This relationship loomed largest when a *piju* went bankrupt. Those with close ties had first call at the settling of debts; others remained stuck at the back of the queue.[205]

At a later stage in the development of the *qiaopi* trade, ties based not on blood or place but on common purpose also developed. This happened much earlier than is sometimes assumed, a circumstance that bears heavily on how to understand the *qiaopi* phenomenon. In Batavia, for example, as we have already shown, *shuike* were held to common account as early as the eighteenth century by the local Chinese association. On the whole, however, holding the trade to a common political or professional purpose was a twentieth-century development.

The push for consolidation of the trade came from two directions. Internally, *qiaopi* agents were impelled on economic grounds to act together to find ways to minimize harmful competition and set common standards of conduct in order to win the confidence of an understandably often doubting clientele. Externally, hostile actions of the Chinese and other state authorities required a unified response.

In China, the first trade association, the Nanyang Qiaopi Ye Gongsuo (Nanyang *Qiaopi* Trade Association) was set up in Shantou in the middle years of the Guangxu Reign (1875–1908).[206] Other similar associations followed in Jieyang and Chaoyang, but the Shantou one led the trade, formulating safeguards and investigative procedures.[207]

Abroad, parts of the trade came together in 1876 to protest the Singapore Government's decision to set up a Chinese sub-post office, a step designed by officials to muscle in on the lucrative remittance trade and rid it of what the colonial government saw as corrupt and inefficient practices. The protest movement, which led to severe rioting and a shop strike, seems to have been restricted to members of the Chaoshan group in Singapore.[208] In Thailand, on the other hand, a government-decreed "Eighth Post Office," set up specifically to handle *qiaopi* and staffed by officials who spoke Chaozhou dialect, was a great success.[209]

In Thailand, a *qiaopi* federation is said to have started sometime between 1907 and 1912. The Overseas-Chinese Remittance Office Association (*yinxinju gongsuo*) was formally established in 1932 when the government tried to impose restrictions on the trade, but there is evidence that it was already in existence in 1926. The name of the association implied a trade-wide identity, but other federations (of Hakkas and Hainanese) continued to exist, and it has been suggested that the association was in fact controlled by Chaoshanese. Whatever the case, a common body did finally emerge, bearing the same name, in response to pressures brought to bear on the trade in the late 1940s.[210]

In the Philippines, the *qiaopi* trade was said to be more cohesive and united than elsewhere in Southeast Asia, perhaps because of its greater geographic compactness.[211] On China's National Day in 1931, several dozen *piju* in the Philippines formed the Manila Huaqiao Qiaoxinju Lianhehui (Overseas Chinese Federation of Remittance Offices in Manila) under the auspices of the Chinese Chamber of Commerce. Its aim was to unite against external pressures and protect common interests.[212]

The trade united on several other occasions in different places, in response to interference by the Chinese government. In 1918 protests erupted in Shantou against government plans to abolish both the *minxinju* and the *piju*. The protests spread to Beijing, where the government backed down, though only in the case of the *qiaopi* trade. In 1923, 1928, 1934, and 1946, the trade again united, both in China and abroad and with varying degrees of success, against further attempts to rein it in, chiefly regarding the two issues of "clubbed packages" (the bulk delivery of bundled batches of *qiaopi*) and licensing. These movements embraced not just the *qiaopi* trade but overseas-Chinese communities and chambers of commerce as a whole, as well as business interests in China with overseas-Chinese connections and overseas-Chinese associations in the Chinese capital.[213]

Another issue around which *qiaopi* traders sought to unite before China's currency reform in 1935 was the unit of remittance. In the late Qing years, the great variety of silver coinage in circulation and its variable size and quality meant that remittances from different foreign ports were not necessarily uniform, which created problems of accounting and distribution. Managers of Singapore's Chaozhou *piju* therefore proposed using foreign silver dollars (*yangyin*), which led to a greater degree of standardization.[214]

Singapore was the main site of this professional organizing, probably as a result of its geographic centrality to much of the *qiaopi* trade, and because it was (and remains) the most solidly ethnic-Chinese city outside China (with Hong Kong) and

Taiwan.[215] In May 1929, the city's Chinese Chamber of Commerce started a campaign in support of *qiaopi*, directly addressing Chiang Kai-shek and the Nanjing Government and Southeast Asian colonial governments. The campaign broadened to encompass issues other than *qiaopi*, and created new sinews of transnational organization across the Chinese diaspora. Before the first wave had subsided, a new campaign sprang up in 1930 to oppose a rise in the price of postage. Again, great masses of supporters rallied around the movement, representing forces in both China and the diaspora. Finally, in 1935 the Chinese government made important concessions to the overseas-Chinese pressure.[216]

Even after these two movements, each of the three main *bang* in Singapore (Fujianese, Chaoshanese, and Hainanese) retained its own separate association (*gonghui*), but in March 1946, a broadly based Nanyang Chinese Exchange and Remittance Association was formed under the leadership of Lim Soo Gan (Lin Shuyan), in principle serving the entire Malay Peninsula.[217] The occasion was the Singapore government's attempt to impose new controls on the trade. The association's three main aims were to increase solidarity among the various *bang*, promote the industry, and carry out necessary innovations and reforms. It claimed to represent *piju* workers as well as managers and owners, and it organized welfare and educational activities.[218] However, the proposed controls were relaxed after negotiations between the colonial government and the new body.[219] Again, Singapore's deeply Chinese culture and demography perhaps explains its Chinese population's exceptional degree of cohesion.[220]

The *qiaopi* mobilizations in Singapore and Thailand were part of a national and transnational awakening of Chinese migrants. Although they were in the first place economic, they also had great political potential as well as the deeply emotional connotation of keeping alive the tie to hearth and home. They not only reinforced the migrants' national identity but created a new sense of diasporic unity by fixing on an issue that Chinese migrants everywhere jointly faced. They were matched in vigor and extent only by the anti-Japanese mobilizations of Chinese in Southeast Asia in 1937. Moreover, the transnational ties and identity they created were a basis and template for the anti-Japanese transnational movements that took off among Chinese across Southeast Asia in the 1930s and 1940s.[221]

This chapter has provided a detailed account of the evolution, structure, and personnel of the *qiaopi* trade, which enabled financial transactions (remittances) and the exchange of family letters across national boundaries. It looks at the institutionalization of the *qiaopi* trade and the role played by the *piju* in this institutionalization of transnational Chinese social and business networks on the basis of primordial ties of locality, dialect, and kinship. Transnational *qiaopi* networks played a key role not only in supporting the social and economic development of

South China but in sustaining families separated physically by oceans. These networks predated, and coexisted with, emerging nation-states based on institutions such as a modern post office and other regulatory regimes in both hostlands and homeland. It was, however, an uneven and uneasy coexistence. Competition between *qiaopi* institutions and modern organizations such as the post office, modern banks, and ultimately, the ever more powerful nation-state eventually led to the demise of the *qiaopi* trade in the late 1970s.

3
___

The *Qiaopi* Trade as a Distinctive Form of Chinese Capitalism

This chapter asks how one should define the *qiaopi* trade in light of its distinctive features. Was it a modern form of "transnational capitalism" that depended on trust in a system of impersonal rules, as some argue, or a distinctive early form of a specifically Chinese capitalism dependent on cultural or familial affinities? We take the latter view. In stating our case, we thought it would be helpful to engage with the work of Lane J. Harris, which adopts the former position.[1] We make our argument as part of a broader approach shared by scholars both in China and elsewhere interested in identifying alternatives to modern capitalism. These alternatives are, at once, robustly cosmopolitan and expressions of a modernity that is multiple rather than modular.

THE *QIAOPI* TRADE AND ITS BUSINESS MODEL

Ethnicity and identity matter greatly in diasporic Chinese business culture as a source of entrepreneurial resilience and creativity. This is particularly so in the early stages of diaspora formation, before the rise to power in the management of enterprises of locally born descendant generations without direct personal and cultural ties to China.[2] Far from forming an obstacle to economic growth and technological innovation, business familism, social networks, and their associated cultural values can be shown, at least in some periods and contexts, to have greatly assisted economic development in Chinese societies at home and abroad by enabling social mobility, furthering family interests, building partnerships, facilitating contracts, and promoting other practices proper to a modern market economy.

The business culture that supported the *qiaopi* trade rested on forms of common sub-ethnicity rather than on generalized Chinese ethnicity.[3] It conformed to local ethnic attachments corresponding to deep intra-ethnic cleavages imported from China along migration chains. It only rarely assumed a pan-Chinese form, except during wars and political crises. Even the trade associations founded to repel state interference supplemented rather than supplanted "dialect"-based associations or acted as fronts for them. In our opinion, Harris overstates the extent of their restructuring on non-"traditional" lines, although he does concede that their internal organization "continued to show some signs of fragmentation along native-place lines."

Harris recognizes the uniqueness of the *qiaopi* trade and, commendably, repudiates its essentialist reduction. He rejects its description as "traditional Chinese," which he sees as an error belonging to a larger Orientalist discourse, arguing that although the overseas Chinese *piju* were initially based on mutual trust and "geo-consanguineous ties," by the 1870s they had changed as a result of new means of communications and transportation, and new banking facilities, and had turned into a modern business model (which he calls "colonial modern").[4] This model, according to Harris, represents the melding of culturalist business practices with capitalist profit-making strategies, and it is able to thrive in the interstitial gaps between nation-states, colonies, and empires.

Harris' definition of the *qiaopi* trade as a *sui generis* type of modern capitalism is, in our view, questionable on several grounds. We particularly question his identification of a rupture that came about in the trade in the 1870s as a result of new communications and transportation means and new banking facilities, from which a qualitatively new business model emerged.

From a methodological point of view, Harris' assertion would seem to imply that modern technology is incompatible with "traditional" structures and values. This argument gives primacy to technological development, which supposedly drives and determines change in social and economic structures. But technological determinism is no less essentialist than the cultural determinism Harris rejects.

To support his theory of a rupture, Harris draws a line between the "circumambulating overseas agents" (*shuike*) that handled remittances in the early years and the later, better organized and more sophisticated *piju*. However, the distinction between these two forms of the trade was not categorical or qualitative, contrary to what this argument implies. There was no qualitative leap from *shuike* to *piju*, no sudden revolution. The passage from one to the other was gradual and cumulative, and it was not just a forward movement but bidirectional. Problems of trust and distrust played a big part in the transition from *shuike* to *piju*, but *shuike* were aware of their customers' apprehensions and did their best to allay them. In Batavia, *shuike* were held to account under the local *hantar* system by Chinese associations in the colony that policed the trade on behalf of its customers.[5] (Most of the cases brought before the Batavia tribunal concerned lost *qiaopi*.) Many *shuike* issued receipts even before the appearance of the *piju*, and Huang Ting's study of documents of Batavia's Chinese association shows that the *qiaopi* trade was already quite mature in the years between 1787 and 1846, when it was still based mainly on *shuike*. In fact, most of the methods used by *piju*—collecting *qiaopi*; networking; making use of agents, substations, and even post offices; issuing receipts; simultaneously engaging in the delivery of *qiaopi* and in other forms of trade and finance; and manipulating foreign-exchange levels—were old practices inherited from the *shuike*.[6]

Moreover, the transition from *shuike* to *piju* was never completed, temporally or geographically. Instead, there was a marked continuity across the decades. In more remote places, *shuike* remained central to the *qiaopi* trade from its start to its finish, and during the war years they made a striking comeback in regions where they had lost ground in the 1930s, when Chinese and Southeast Asian authorities managed to assert a greater degree of authority than previously and subsequently.[7] The *shuike* and their clients relied on traditional (*in personam*) means of trust rather than applying a system-based (*in rem*) approach, at a time when systemic trust and the protection of private property had not yet been properly established among Chinese immigrant communities in Southeast Asia and elsewhere in the diaspora. The *pijiao* hired by *piju* to take the letters and remittances to the villages played a role similar to that played by the *shuike* and were an even more enduring and integral part of the trade, which they continued to ply even after 1949. When the *piju* did emerge as institutions, they copied and perpetuated practices devised earlier by the *shuike*. The procedures Harris calls "culturalist customer services" were no "tinge" or embellishment on an enterprise otherwise modern in essence, but ones that lay at its very heart. *Piju* owners and managers ran their shops and offices on "traditional" lines, by exclusively employing their own kin and others linked to them by native-place or dialect ties. Their relations with their customers also continued to be based, even after the technological modernization of their enterprises, on consanguinity and provenance. So did their relations with other *piju* and with their agents and employees in China or overseas, except in rare cases where these relations were based on trade ties. However, even trade ties usually assumed a particularistic form. This is why we doubt that the line between tradition and modernity was as clear-cut as Harris seems to assume, and why we hold that the two modes can, instead, be said to coexist and intersect.

In fact, the *piju* never killed off the *shuike*. *Piju* and *shuike* lasted equally long, until the Communists put an end to both after 1949 (Taiwan's Jinmen shop lasted a bit longer). *Shuike* continued to ply their trade, though mainly in regions lacking modern roads and institutions.[8] Their advantages over the *piju* were that they were more personal and intimate, they were true local experts (both overseas and in China), and they performed a wider range of functions.

Just as there was no impenetrable barrier between *shuike* and *piju*, so too the different sorts of *piju*, representing different levels of complexity and technological sophistication, ranged along a continuum. The relatively rare vertically organized and seemingly more modern *piju* that controlled all three stages of *qiaopi* dispatch (receipt overseas, transfer to China, and receipt in China—the so-called *sanpan* system) grew out of the simpler sort based on horizontal ties, but again the development was not one-way. Big *piju* could fragment or shrink back into small ones after fizzing brilliantly for a while, and revert back again into big ones, depending on circumstances. The smaller and more "traditional" *piju* formed a dense network of shops linked by ties of kinship, native place, and dialect.

Did the transnationalization of the remittance trade lead to the overriding of "cultural characteristics" by "instrumental economic practices," as Harris argues?[9] This line of reasoning implies that transnational organization cannot be based on "mutual affinities." However, China's early premodern domestic *hang* and *huiguan* ("guilds") were capable of horizontal and even transnational organization, not least in response to actions by the Chinese state and (later) foreigners; in this respect, the trade associations set up by the *piju* starting in the early twentieth century trod a well-worn path.[10] Although "traditional" in nearly all regards, these horizontally and transnationally organized guilds were at the same time complex and multifunctional, and they could be based on trade rather than on native place.[11] These early examples of horizontal and transnational organization undermine the thesis that the organization of the *piju* in formal trade associations necessarily disqualified them as "traditional."

The *qiaopi* trade was highly adaptable and resilient, so why did it eventually collapse? Harris has no convincing answer to this question, implying instead that the trade's "flexible, decentralized, rhizomatically organized network" and its "frontier attitude and celebration of transnational laissez-faire capitalism" enabled it to face down state and colonial attempts to bring it under regulation and engineer its downfall. He goes on to ascribe its shrinking and eventual disappearance after 1949 to political causes—the measures by Southeast Asian colonial and independent regimes to isolate China and the chaos of China's Cultural Revolution in the late 1960s and the early 1970s.

However, the trade was highly vulnerable to attempts by the Chinese and various colonial and other states in the region to assume its functions by way of the post office and the banks, especially in the 1930s. The main reason was that it was unable to compete with organizations and corporations, capitalist or state capitalist, chartered, supported, or controlled by the Chinese state and other states. The Sino-Japanese War, and the postwar inflation, saved the trade for a while, for *shuike* and *piju* both made a comeback in the late 1930s and early 1940s in association with modern (chiefly foreign) banks. The inflation was particularly important, for it made going through official channels hugely disadvantageous to the recipient and remitter. But despite this surge, the trade eventually fizzled out after 1949, not just on the Chinese mainland, where it succumbed to a strong state and changes in the *qiaoxiang* and the general overseas-Chinese economy, but also on Jinmen Island in Taiwan, where it was defeated by modern banks and postal services. The root cause of the inevitable clash between *piju* and the Bank of China and the post office lay in the traditionalist and fundamentally transnational orientation of the former and the fact that the latter were modern institutions operating within a capitalist framework and within the confines of a nation-state.

THE *QIAOPI* TRADE AND THE *QIAOKAN* PHENOMENON

The relationship between the *qiaopi* trade and modern capitalism is clarified by an analysis of the *qiaokan* ("overseas Chinese magazines") phenomenon, a concomitant if not a product of *qiaopi* culture that peaked between 1910 and the early 1930s. Two concepts bear centrally on the discussion.

Postal culture is a term coined by Gabriella Romani in her book on letters in post-unification Italy to describe the communicative practices supported by the nineteenth-century letter, which reshaped the lives and broadened the horizons of the masses and brought literacy to the villages. It created "a new geography of national identity, based on . . . an enhanced sense of belonging to a group [and] . . . an idealistic extension of the individual experience."

Naturally, this new culture was also the result of the migrant's passage from being a villager, usually a peasant, with narrowly bounded horizons to inhabiting a wider world and, in nearly all cases, to assuming a new social role as a petty trader or a worker in urban industry or commerce, in a mine, or on a plantation. Overseas, he—less often, she—was exposed to new social practices and political viewpoints. In the Chinese case, for example, the systemic racism of colonial society in Southeast Asia, of the white settler societies of North America and Australasia, and of industrial Europe predisposed migrants to be even more sympathetic to the new nationalist and republican politics that found their readiest audiences in Chinatown.

According to Romani, postal culture had a strong political edge: its primary role was to keep friends and relatives in touch, but it also created an information network that eroded distance, enhanced the sense of interconnectedness, and exposed people "to new ideas and customs [and] a world much larger than the one they inhabited."[12] The term "postal culture" was later extended to the United States by David Henkin, who argued that Americans became ever more aware of their participation in a network of communication that embraced the nation.[13] However, it has been less widely used in other national contexts. Lane Harris briefly mentions the term in his study on the post office and state formation in modern China between 1896 and 1949, but he does not analyze it in any detail, probably because his main focus is on the post office's contribution to forming the modern Chinese state, as opposed to its political role in broader society.[14]

Print culture, an idea first developed by Benedict Anderson, is a better-known idea and has been more widely explored and applied. We know from Anderson's work and from research inspired by it that the rise of nationalism and national identity is intimately connected with the rise of print and print-capitalism, triggered by the industrial revolution.[15]

The two cultures, postal and print, are clearly connected, and both are illuminated by Tocqueville's definition of modern postal services as that "great link between minds," a mainstay of the modern communications revolution and at the heart of modern institutional, ideological, economic, social, cultural, and political change in probably every country.[16] Modern postal systems reach places and classes of people previously barely touched by the central state and the mainstream economy, penetrating more deeply into society than any other branch of government except the military. As a result, they, together with newspapers, have played a greater role than most institutions "in shaping the pattern of everyday life," bringing "a steady flow of information on public affairs" to the towns and villages, and enabling ordinary people to "participate in national politics."[17]

Both a postal culture and a print culture thrived in the *qiaoxiang* in the context of migration and the *qiaopi* system. However, they differed in nature from those theorized by Romani and Anderson, and they fell short of the models of social practice the two authors put forward.

Regarding postal culture, the *qiaopi* trade's role in safeguarding affective family links led to greater literacy among the lower classes and to greater participation in the affairs of local society and the state by migrants and their dependents, including the women who stayed behind when the men migrated. In that sense, it fulfilled the conditions for a postal culture as set out by Romani and others. However, the *qiaopi* trade lacked essential features of a modern mail system, which in most countries forms a state monopoly and is internationally regulated, coordinated, and run according to uniform principles. In fact, it was quite the opposite of such a system; it was nearly always private, largely unregulated, and variform. The post office did try to muscle into the *qiaopi* trade, but it usually failed, and efforts at domestic regulation of postal services were intermittent and restricted. The *qiaopi* trade was, all along, demarcated, in China and without, by "dialect" and region, and it was further differentiated at sub-regional and sub-dialect levels. *Qiaopi* traders not only failed as a profession to develop a national dimension, but they actively (and, for the most part, successfully) resisted nationalization—i.e., the transformation of the remittance business into a monopolistic arm of the bureaucratic state, both Chinese and non-Chinese. That does not mean that the *qiaopi* trade was without national relevance, politically and—even more so—economically, or that it was not swept up in the great political mobilizations of the late nineteenth and twentieth centuries, but it did not spawn a postal culture in the usual sense of the term. Nor, despite their commonality of political and economic interest, did the *qiaopi* traders ever fully overcome their deep segmentation along sub-ethnic lines, and achieve lasting unity as a profession.

Regarding print culture, the *qiaoxiang* experience throws up interesting questions for Anderson's theory. Partha Chatterjee has faulted the theory for implying that Europe and America are history's only true subjects and that even the imaginings of colonial peoples "must remain forever colonized."[18] Radhika Desai added to the criticism: colonial and semicolonial (hereafter, Third World) countries need no sociology of nationalism because they were merely imitating, or "pirating," prefabricated Western models of nationhood, or (in a later version of the thesis) for arguing that "the immediate genealogy [of these models] should be traced to the imaginings of the colonial state." Either way, Anderson's theory is said to have rendered the study of Third World nationalism Eurocentric, and a Western construct.[19]

It is important to note, in light of this debate, that an indigenous print culture thrived in the *qiaoxiang* in the context of migration and the *qiaopi* system. Migrant and community leaders in the villages and counties of the *qiaoxiang* produced a great quantity of *qiaokan* and mailed them to expatriates all over the world to keep them informed about events at home and to encourage them to donate to local causes.[20] Wuyi in Guangdong was the main center of *qiaokan* publishing, though *qiaokan* also appeared in other *qiaoxiang*.[21] Before 1949, more than two hundred different *qiaokan* were published in Wuyi alone. Many were monthly, and some were fortnightly and even weekly. Nearly all were migrant funded.[22]

These *qiaokan* included "newsletters, newspapers and magazines published by individuals, clans, schools, villages and government offices" in the *qiaoxiang*. According to an early report, four out of five were sent abroad.[23] The first such, *Xinning zazhi* (*Xinning Magazine*), appeared in Taishan in Guangdong in 1908. It was designed to meet the needs of migrants and their families and communities by sustaining or reestablishing contact and exchanging information, particularly about Taishan—its problems, developments, general news, and history (specified as "customs and traditions"). The *qiaokan* phenomenon peaked between 1910 and the early 1930s. In the late 1930s, new, more expressly political *qiaokan* arose to support the anti-Japanese movement and solicit donations to support national defense. Starting in 1945, most *qiaokan* resumed publication after a wartime gap. Only a minority survived the transition to the Communist government in 1949. Those that survived played a role in attracting homeward-bound donations of food and materials and foreign currency remittances in the 1950s and early 1960s, before disappearing during the Cultural Revolution. They started reviving in 1978, when millions of copies were printed annually, but the government's hand was clear in the revival and the emphasis was, by then, on attracting capital investment.[24]

The *qiaokan* were evidence of a vibrant local print culture in the *qiaoxiang* that strongly complemented the regional postal culture set going by the *qiaopi* trade. *Qiaokan* were a public counterpart to *qiaopi*, not private but communal, and have been called "collective family letters" by Chinese overseas.[25] Indeed, *qiaopi* and other correspondence made up much of the contents of the *qiaokan* and village newsletters.[26] The *qiaokan* had a local or regional focus. Most served townships or lineages, although a few (like *Xinning zazhi*) appeared at county level. However, during political crises they transcended particularism and made propaganda for the nation. So there is no clear dividing line between *qiaokan* and *qiaopi* culture on the one hand and a national orientation on the other.

Qiaopi traders backed the *qiaokan* financially through donations and advertisements. Some 70 percent of advertisements in *Xinning zazhi* were placed by *piju* and other remittance firms.[27] *Yinhao, piju, shanghao* and other businesses active in the *qiaopi* trade handled the overseas dispatch of *qiaokan* and acted as agents for the publishers.[28]

Were these *qiaokan* evidence of a Chinese copying in the *qiaoxiang* of Western print-culture, like the modern-style newspapers that started to proliferate in China and Chinatown in the nineteenth century? Almost certainly they were not. Unlike the newspapers, which were distributed publicly and regularly, most *qiaokan* were brought out privately and occasionally. A much likelier model for them was the centuries-old Chinese habit of producing local and genealogical records, the so-called *jiapu* ("family records"), *zupu* ("lineage records"), and *zongpu* ("clan records"), as well as the *difang zhi* ("local gazetteers") that provided information at county level and above about local history, geography, society, and economy and were designed to aid local government and promote local identity.[29] The *qiaokan* replicated the same divisions as these compilations among kinship organizations and between them and the county. Traditionally, most genealogies were produced by the wealthiest sector of society, one able to defray the costs of printing. They displayed and symbolized membership of a powerful family or kinship group, and their appearance often signaled the revival of formal kinship organization after a period of decrease. In some cases, the production of a genealogy "created the organized kinship group, rather than vice versa." Genealogies were exclusively private: their role was to transmit family or lineage history, household or lineage instructions, and standards of moral propriety to future generations and to record glorious episodes in family or clan affairs. Urbanization and internal migration, far from weakening genealogy-making, strengthened it.[30]

The analogy between *qiaokan* on the one hand and *jiapu, zupu,* and *fangzhi* on the other has obvious limits. *Jiapu* and *zupu* were controlled, by definition, by single clans or branches of them, while many *fangzhi* were published by groups associated with local government or the broader community. These publications were not, in all cases, financed and produced in the same way as *qiaokan*, nor did they necessarily perform the same functions. However, the *qiaokan* phenomenon was multiform. *Qiaokan* operated at several levels in the *qiaoxiang*, from the county down to the village and the lineage, and some of its divisions corresponded to those of the older, kinship-based forms of local publication.

The link and commonality, and the partial equivalence, is reflected in the terminology used to describe some of the older migrant-linked publications. Names that reveal their role and provenance include *xiangkan* ("village publication"), *zukan* ("lineage publication"), and *xiangxun* ("village bulletin"), as well as names that combined two variants, one "modern" and the other "traditional" (e.g., *xiangkan xiangxun* and *qiaokan xiangxun*).[31]

Contributors to *qiaokan* also recognized the affinity between *qiaokan* on the one hand and *qiaopi* and *zupu* on the other. We have already noted that *qiaokan* were sometimes pictured as "collective family letters." A poem published in the inaugural issue of *Yingchuan yuekan* (*Yingchuan Monthly*) in 1926 explicitly likened the *qiaokan* to a *jiashu* ("family letter") or a *zupu*, in a metaphor.[32] The two publishing traditions were therefore not only related but were experienced as such by practitioners, and they continue to be seen as related by Chinese historians and experts on the *qiaopi* phenomenon.

To understand this relationship, it is helpful to recall that premodern Chinese society richly documented its laws and institutions, and that this tradition sank deep into the villages.[33] Local communities recorded their activities and organizational statutes in genealogies and gazetteers. Local society along China's southeastern coast has, for centuries, been marked by its history of maritime trade and overseas migration. Local dependence on remittances shaped the local migrant culture. Although *qiaokan* differed in some respects from genealogies and *fangzhi*, they nevertheless remained part of local culture and society. The genealogies recorded the origins, ranking, branching, and famous people of a family or a lineage, and the history of its spread and development. Local gazetteers chronicled and recorded the history and circumstances of local communities, including local politics, the local economy, and local society and culture. The *qiaopi* that emigrants sent home created and nurtured an integrated transnational field that encompassed both emigrants and their kin in China, and helped preserve traditional ways in the daily lives of both groups. Compiling genealogies and local histories was, by tradition, the work of members of the local gentry, who had the requisite skills and financial and social resources to do this work. In the *qiaoxiang*, transnational migrant entrepreneurs often played the same role, in many respects, as the traditional gentry in previous periods in conducting local affairs and public administration, either by remote control from overseas or after remigrating.[34] They also contributed to compiling and publishing *qiaokan* to give textual expression to the social affairs of the diaspora and its home communities. Some *qiaokan* (like *Xinning zazhi*) were published in China, while others were published overseas.[35] Principally, they reported on Chinese social, political, and cultural affairs at either end of the migration chain, conceived as a single field. *Qiaopi* reflected family and lineage affairs, including house-buying or house-building, weddings and marriages, and lineage financial and other interests; *qiaokan* reflected local and national affairs, including changes in the political situation and state decrees. Like genealogies and gazetteers, *qiaokan* reflected the relationship in traditional Chinese local society between the state, the locality, the lineage, and the family. Because of emigration, local society in the southeastern coastal region was transnational: it straddled the *qiaoxiang* and regions of Chinese settlement overseas, so its cultural traditions were reflected both in *qiaopi* and *qiaokan* and in genealogies and gazetteers. For example, the *Chaozhou zhi*, a gazetteer compiled by Jao Tsung-i, contained a special section on the *qiaopi* trade.[36] Most genealogies in the *qiaoxiang* listed the names of family or lineage members overseas. The second son of Singapore's famous Chaoshan trader Lim Nee Soon was born in Singapore but is described in detail in the lineage genealogy of his ancestral home in Chenghai.[37]

In the *qiaoxiang*, ordinary people's everyday affairs extended overseas but remained rooted in native places. The overseas segment and the nonmigrant segment existed, for the migrant generation and its dependents, as two parts of an indivisible whole. Together, they continued (at least for a while) to maintain the original social order and tradition, a dynamic in which *qiaopi* and *qiaokan* played a key role. *Qiaopi* cemented the tie between family and lineage, and they ensured the preservation of kinship institutions and local community. (Even after the males emigrated, they continued to exercise their patriarchal rights, precisely by means of remittances, which enabled them to perform familial and lineage tasks and to participate in directing kinship institutions). *Qiaokan*, on the other hand, helped preserve state institutions and local authority, and their contents reflected national or local political, economic, and social matters. By means of *qiaokan*, emigrants stayed in close touch with the situation in China, both local and national, and were able to participate in the construction and maintenance of the social order in China and in their native places.

Chinese researchers wanting to explore the transnational society that straddled the *qiaoxiang* and the emigrant community therefore resort to a variety of sources and publications. Many, in studying migrant families and lineages, use *zupu* and *qiaokan* as complementary sources, to obtain a rounded picture of the kinship system.[38] Family genealogies, lineage genealogies, local gazetteers, *qiaopi*, and *qiaokan* were all products of a similar set of social and historical circumstances. When exploring the tie between diaspora and native place and its attendant publications, it is impossible to draw a clear line between "traditional" and "modern."

So the emergence of *qiaokan* in the early twentieth century is entirely consonant with existing traditions of local publishing. To produce a *qiaokan* signaled a family's or lineage's achievement of wealth and power, under the special circumstances of emigration, or the elevation of the status of a *qiaoxiang* county as a result of emigration and remittance. Like the old-style genealogies, *qiaokan* could signal or speed the further incorporation of an agnatic group newly enriched, in this case by *qiaopi*. They were distributed free, by mail in the case of overseas subscribers, to anyone qualified to receive them.[39] They were a response to emigration and a mechanism to prevent the severing of the link between migrants and the local society they had left behind. Just like the *qiaopi* trade, the emergence of *qiaokan* in the early twentieth century represented a creative adaptation to new circumstances overseas of an indigenous tradition.

Abroad, the *qiaopi* trade had close connections with the new-style, modern press that grew up alongside it as one of the "three pillars" of overseas-Chinese society, the others being associations and schools. Between 1815, when a Chinese newspaper is said to have appeared for the first time outside China (in Malacca), and 1996, at least four thousand Chinese periodicals were published in Chinese or in a combination of Chinese and other languages in fifty-two countries and territories, alongside at least another two hundred published by Chinese in languages other than Chinese.[40] In Thailand, the first Chinese-language daily was founded in 1903, and in later years sixty-five others followed. This press developed more or less hand in hand with the *piju* system in its heyday, and each played a huge role in promoting the other, largely through advertisements placed by *piju* owners out to recruit customers and reports on the trade by journalists. The owners used the press to announce their removal to new premises (which happened frequently, as a result of expansion and shop fires), special offers, new regulations imposed either by the Chinese or Thai authorities, new currency arrangements, closures, and openings. During the early years of the war against Japan, they used the newspapers to warn Chinese about Japanese attempts to gain control of the lucrative remittance trade.[41]

Some *qiaokan*, like *Xinning zazhi*, started out in the late nineteenth and early twentieth centuries as a response to China's humiliating military defeat by Japan in 1895 and the failure of the reform movement of 1898. They subscribed, at first, to a common national discourse, and in that sense confirmed the thesis of "print capitalism," at least in certain phases. During political crises, the *qiaokan* transcended particularism and made propaganda for the nation. So there was no clear and permanent dividing line between *qiaokan* and *qiaopi* culture on the one hand and a national orientation on the other. However, the journals' main purpose was to meet the needs of migrants and their families and communities by sustaining contact and exchanging local information. They enabled migrants, returned migrants, and the homebound to swap news "as they had when they attended the same marketplaces" back in China.[42]

In her study on *qiaokan*, Madeline Hsu mentions Anderson's idea of "print capitalism" and notes, in a footnote, that his comments about "the role of 'print capitalism' in making it 'possible to "think" the nation' shed light on the role of *qiaokan* in the dispersed community of Taishan." However, there are clear limits to the analogy, which her study illustrates. Whereas Anderson sees nations in the Third World as prefabricated copies of Western models, Hsu concludes that the "imagined community" supposedly constructed by the printing press is harder to nurture than one founded on existing allegiances, "as in the case of communities defined by native-place."[43] Most *qiaokan* were parochial publications with a local or regional focus. The main concern of *Xinning zazhi*, for example, was to build a "better Taishan." Although this aim did not conflict with the wish to build a better China, national politics were not the *raison d'être* of the genre or even its abiding focus.

Xinning zazhi, which started out more committed than most *qiaokan* to the idea of building a stronger China, "lost its overt political orientation" after the fall of the Qing and was absorbed into county politics. It continued for a while as a sort of "village newspaper," until its later co-option into state politics by the Guomindang, which forced *qiaokan* to publicize its policies and plans. This political bullying alienated American Taishanese, who (according to Hsu) chose "loyalty to their county over the Guomindang's calls for nationalism." Only the looming threat of a Japanese invasion of China revived their attention to national politics. In the late 1930s, new, more expressly political *qiaokan* arose to support the anti-Japanese movement and solicit donations to support national defense. However, migrants' attention to China's national affairs eventually waned yet again as the focus of them and their descendants switched overseas. With the further passage of time and the changes wrought by war, even the native-place ties frayed.[44]

QIAOPI AND MARITIME (OR OCEANIC) CULTURE

Harris views the *qiaopi* trade not as "a distinctive form of Chinese capitalism" but as a form of "transnational laissez-faire capitalism." As such, it engaged in capitalist profit-making strategies, but at the same time it pioneered "a host of new cultural customer services" that its state-run rivals found impossible to replicate. According to Harris, the trade depended more on a system of impersonal rules than on cultural or familial affinities, and *qiaopi* traders used instrumental economic practices to transnationalize their businesses.[45]

Qiaopi historians in Fujian and Guangdong, on the other hand, have a different understanding of the nature and special features of the trade. Harking back to older theories about the relationship between their own region and the rest of China, they view it within the context of the commercial economy that grew up in China's southeastern littoral zone starting mainly in the Tang dynasty (618–907) alongside and in tandem with the growth of seaborne emigration out of the region. This contemporary revival of the case for Fujianese and Cantonese exceptionalism supports an explanation for the rise of the *qiaopi* trade other than that of its capture or lateral assimilation into the orbit of modern capitalism as a result of technological developments. Instead, its roots and strength lay in centuries of Chinese enterprise in Southeast Asia and the Pacific, where migrant traders and, in some cases, their locally born descendants mobilized cultural capital and their cultural and familial affinities in China to run businesses. Despite its apparent "traditionalism," the *qiaopi* phenomenon enabled Chinese entrepreneurs to compete successfully for more than a century with modern state-run banks and postal services both in China and overseas.

China's political culture and economic system are no longer as rigidly centralized as they once were, and they were never as centralized as in the Soviet Union. Regional differences and political cultures were never entirely wiped out in China by the revolution, and some new ones formed as a result of it, particularly in the southeastern provinces, which had their own revolutionary factions and traditions.[46] Since the post-Mao reforms, regional differentiation has deepened in China, as power in the national economy and political system has increasingly devolved. Local and regional fortes can now be pridefully declared rather than hidden. Different regions excel in different ways, and a strong suit of the southeast is its history of emigration. This is a particularly useful distinction in an age when China is expanding into ever more overseas markets, a distinction that provincial leaders can use to strengthen their hand in the country's national and regional councils. The emergence of *qiaopi* studies since the early 1990s must be understood in the context of this regionalization of historiography as well as of politics and economics.

Historians of the *qiaoxiang* of Guangdong and Fujian are proud of the special character that they claim centuries of overseas navigation and emigration have stamped on the two provinces. Like other regions and nations worldwide from which large numbers of people have left to go overseas, the tradition of venturing abroad to make a living has, according to their analysis, made sectors of the Cantonese and Fujianese population outward looking rather than narrowly focused on the landside. *Qiaopi* historians have resurrected from Hegel (a philosopher with whom they are probably familiar through Karl Marx) the separation of the world into the potamic (rivers), the thalassic (inland seas), and the oceanic (categories Hegel borrowed from the philosophical geography of Carl Schmitt), corresponding to Asia, Europe, and England and America (or to ancient, middle, and modern). According to Hegel, nations (like China) that shun navigation do not know freedom and sink into stagnation and superstition, whereas sea peoples are creative and industrious and without limits, like the ocean, a "free element."[47] They are wise, brave, and transcendent rather than closed and conservative. *Qiaopi* historians have extended this division into coastal and non-coastal cultures to China. In response to Hegel, who dismissed China as "the realm of theocratic despotism," they argue that China too had its "oceanic" culture (a term taken directly from Hegel's writings) in the past and must now reclaim it, and that sea-facing regions never lost it.[48] One study describes

China's southern peoples as "an ethnic group with oceanic characteristics," imbued with "oceanic civilization."[49] In applying these labels, historians implicitly assert the superiority over other parts of the country of the seaward southeast, especially Fujian, locked off until recently from the Chinese hinterland by high mountains with few passes, and Guangdong, furthest away from the stagnant and corrupting culture of China's landlocked heartland.

According to the newly revived regional lore, the southern Fujianese are courageous and heroic, a disposition that led Fujian's Han pioneers hundreds of years ago to climb into the region across perilous peaks. Their spirit is "daring and adventurous . . . and thick with sea culture."[50] The Chinese of southern Fujian are sometimes called the "Jews of China" or of Asia, a moniker scholars of the region accept with pride.[51] As for the *qiaopi* managers, they were "Robinson Crusoe-style ocean heroes."[52] This focus on enterprise and expansion chimes with China's current efforts to establish a "new silk road" to the West, but whereas Beijing's main official emphasis is on reviving the northern route across Central Asia, strategists in the southeast talk about reviving the "maritime silk road" or "silk road on water," of which the *qiaopi* trade was an essential part.[53]

However, these historians also argue that the oceanic tradition of Fujian and Guangdong is no mere replica of foreign models but (like Deng Xiaoping's socialism) has Chinese characteristics. It is a synthesis of China's Central Plains culture, which the pioneers brought south, Fujian's pre-Han indigenous culture, and oceanic culture. The impulse to sail the world and form communities abroad broke a major taboo of Chinese culture, that one must on no account "go roaming while one's parents are alive." However, it did not lead in China to a severing of the homeland tie. In that regard, China's heroes were quite unlike the "British ocean hero." They fulfilled humanity's "eternal wish" to conquer nature, but at the same time they recognized their responsibility to their ancestors and kith and kin. Indeed, it was attachment to the family that led them to go overseas in the first place, as the family's representatives. Foreign exploration strengthened rather than weakened the tie because of the lineage system, Chinese people's native-place orientation, and the control of emigration by senior kin, who kept the womenfolk at home. The *qiaopi* was the strongest link in this chain.[54]

The oceanic attribution is based on the unusual history of the southeastern provinces, whose inhabitants are known to have been trading and settling overseas since Tang times, and even more so after the southward refocusing of the Chinese economy in the Southern Song (1127–1279).[55] Maritime activity was prohibited under the *haijin* ("sea bans") during much of the Ming and Qing to curb piracy and prevent the emergence of self-sufficient regional economies. Coastal trade and shipping were declared illegal, and coastal populations were forcibly relocated inland. Although traders and emigrants did send back remittances to their families, returning to China during the bans was illegal and dangerous. Remittances were confiscated if detected, and their potential recipients were liable to severe penalties. However, during some of the Ming and Qing, ports in southern Fujian and eastern Guangdong were officially thrown open to trade, private and public, particularly with the Philippines and Thailand. Local merchants sailed around the whole of Southeast Asia and covered it with an ever growing and ever more diverse network of transnational operations.[56] When "sea bans" were imposed, they flouted them, and "the four oceans became their home."[57] The "oceanic economy" thrived most, in the premodern period, in the thirteenth to eighteenth centuries, when Chinese merchants competed successfully with European traders in Southeast Asia, even in periods when the Chinese court "disowned" them. However, Chinese thinkers in the southeastern provinces argue that this economy continued to influence the culture of southern China through into modern times.[58]

Today, the world is said to have up to ten million migrants or descendants of migrants from eastern Guangdong (chiefly Chaoshan),[59] and an even greater number from southern Fujian, put at twelve million by Fujian authorities, or forty million people if China itself is included.[60] More than six million overseas and ethnic Chinese are said to be migrants or the descendants of migrants from Quanzhou, where more than three million returned migrants or migrants' dependents and descendants live.[61] Migrants and the descendants of migrants from the two provinces have established communities in all continents and most countries, and they are an important economic motor in the new global age.

Historians of the *qiaopi* trade claim that the region's seaward gaze and the extent of private trade in the southeast led to the creation of a culture that did not relegate merchants to the despised fourth class in the traditional division of society into scholars, farmers, artisans, and merchants usually observed in China, but even held them up for emulation.[62] Jao Tsung-i, the main exponent of this theory of the special nature of the southeast, has argued that Chaozhou's merchant culture "led the way" in the region's history of overseas exploration and was at the same time "a product of a seaborne *yangwu* [foreign-learning] culture.[63]

In conclusion, *qiaopi* scholarship suggests a different pedigree for the *qiaopi* trade than one of lateral assimilation into modern capitalism as a result of technological developments. Instead, its roots and strength lay in centuries of Chinese enterprise in Fujian and Guangdong, Southeast Asia, and the Pacific, where migrant traders and, in some cases, their locally born descendants mobilized cultural capital and their cultural and familial affinities in the ancestral homeland to run their businesses. Despite its apparent "traditionalism," the *qiaopi* phenomenon enabled Chinese entrepreneurs to compete successfully for more than a century with modern state-run banks and postal services both in China and overseas. The mobilizations in support of *qiaopi* institutions in the face of government attacks on the trade in China, Singapore, Thailand, and elsewhere were part of a national and transnational (or diasporic) awakening of Chinese migrants. Although primarily economic, they also had great political potential, as well as the deeply emotional connotation of maintaining the tie to hearth and home. They not only reinforced the migrants' national identity but created a new sense of diasporic unity by fixing on an issue Chinese migrants everywhere jointly faced. They were matched in vigor and extent only by the anti-Japanese mobilizations of Chinese in Southeast Asia in the 1930s.[64] Chinese immigrants' linkages with China through *qiaopi* and the *qiaopi* trade reaffirm, methodologically, the importance of approaching the Chinese diaspora as "a series of moments in which reconnections with a putative homeland take place."[65]

4

Qiaopi Geography

This chapter explores differences in the *qiaopi* trade from place to place, and their causes and consequences. The trade arose separately on multiple sites to serve the same aim in settings that were broadly similar. Its transnational practitioners constantly copied one another's best ideas, for the trade was not hard to learn and enter. All it needed, at a minimum, was a table, a measure of good repute, the necessary contacts, and hard work. The system was reasonably simple and the set-up capital required was minimal. For these reasons, the trade was strikingly uniform across different regions, both in China and abroad, despite its geographic spread.[1]

This uniformity was most marked in the trade's great domestic centers in Shantou, Xiamen, and elsewhere, and in its principal overseas hubs in Singapore, Bangkok, Manila, and other cities. Here, the trade conformed to the archetype described in the previous chapter and in Chinese studies on the subject, so there is no need to deal with them separately in this chapter on its differential geography.

However, some of the smaller or more peripheral *qiaoxiang* and those in the hinterland exhibited special features. This is not surprising. The trade sprang up from below and spread along paths trodden by generations. Most *qiaoxiang* were relatively remote, and some more so than others; the poverty and economic backwardness concomitant with remoteness was, after all, a main push in the migration. Inevitably, the *qiaopi* trade was shaped by local circumstance and experience, but even though its broad contours did not alter, it was more likely to assume special forms in the furthest-flung *qiaoxiang* than in other migrant-sending areas, which diverged less from the economic and cultural mainstream. Geography affected it at both ends of the migration chain, in China and abroad. It took a somewhat different form in some parts of China and in some foreign settings. In the latter case, the

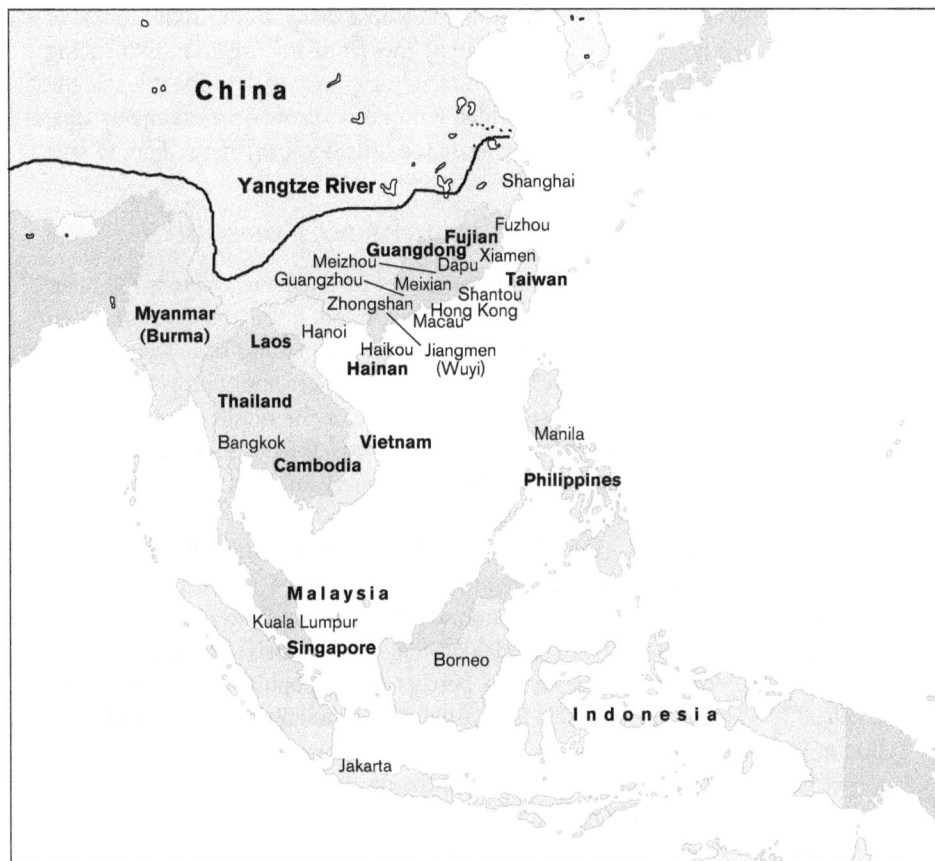

MAP 2. China and Southeast Asia. Map by authors.

Chinese emigrants communities' relative distance from China and the nature of the receiving society and economy shaped the *qiaopi* trade (see map 2). This chapter discusses regional distinctions that many studies have neglected.[2]

Places where the trade diverged most obviously from the norm included Guangdong's and Fujian's Hakka counties, the island of Hainan, and Guangdong's Guangfu and Wuyi (or Siyi) regions. Other early peripheral *qiaoxiang*, in Zhejiang (Qingtian), Hubei (Tianmen), central Fujian (Fuzhou), and Guangxi (Rongxian), also developed along different lines, but relatively little research has been done on the remittance system in these four places, so we cannot say much about them and we therefore leave them aside for the present.[3] Outside China, the trade developed special features in North America and Australasia, which had relatively advanced economies and administrative structures and whose *qiaopi* trade, in the course of time, consequently developed along different lines from other regions, influencing and interacting with special features of the sending *qiaoxiang*. It is possible that the same was true of other places from which remittances came—for example, Cuba, South Africa, India, and Europe—but again too little is known about them to say.[4]

THE HAKKA COUNTIES AND THE ROLE OF *SHUIKE*

Meizhou, along with the neighboring counties of Meixian and Dabu, is the main homeland of the Hakka people and a major *qiaoxiang*. It was much poorer than surrounding regions because of both its turbulent history and its rugged terrain and remote location.[5] Meizhou received fewer and smaller remittances than other *qiaoxiang*, mostly from Southeast Asia, and many of the remittances were first shipped through Shantou to the south.[6] (In the 1930s, foreign remittances worth fifteen to twenty million yuan were said to have flowed annually into Meixian, rising to thirty million in 1940.[7])

In the Hakka counties, the *piju* system developed later than elsewhere, and *shuike* played a much more prominent role in them. As a result, relatively few Hakka remittance letters, a phenomenon associated most closely with *piju*, have been found.[8] The *shuike* trade in the Hakka villages was massive: in some places, it is said to have employed as many as 5 percent of the population in one way or another.[9] It is tempting to link this fact with the exceptionally high levels of education in Hakka regions. *Shuike* needed to be both literate and educated, and thus respectable. In some Hakka communities, the number of degree-holders in the late Qing was 40 percent higher than among non-Hakkas.[10]

Hakka *piju* were not only fewer but smaller than in other places, with an average of 2.5 staff members.[11] Very few of the *piju* were actually started up by Hakkas; most were branches of Shantou *piju*.[12] The Hakka *piju* were divided into two systems, focused on Meixian and Dabu respectively, but there was little common feeling or geographical connection between them and very few links.[13] This was because of the region's poverty, difficult geography, and lack of direct access to the sea, and also because of Chaoshan's demographic and financial preponderance in many of Southeast Asia's Chinese communities.[14] *Piju* belonging to the Hakka *bang* often followed different procedures from those belonging to other *bang*. Some, after receiving remittances, issued money orders that the remitters themselves mailed back to the recipient. Others used *pijiao* or *shuike* at a time when bigger *piju* had switched to other methods.[15]

One reason for the big role played by *shuike* in Hakka counties was local people's vulnerability on the region's roads and rivers, where bandits often struck. It was therefore inadvisable to risk fetching remittances from the town-based *piju*, and *shuike* were the preferred medium. Hakka *shuike* were renowned for their martial skills, but they inevitably took precautions. When delivering remittances from Shantou, they liked to take back not cash but goods. This tactic killed two birds with one stone. It provided a less tempting target than money, which was more portable and therefore easier to steal, and it generated stock and thus revenue for the village stores with which the *shuike* were associated.[16]

In 1911, there were said to be 822 *shuike* in Meizhou.[17] Several hundred *shuike* continued to serve the region at the height of the Sino-Japanese War in 1941.[18] Modern banking also arrived late, and in 1937 fewer than 20 percent of the region's villages were linked up to the modern postal system.[19] But even after the banks arrived, *shuike* continued to import one-third of the region's remittances, and they also worked for the banks themselves.[20] Even as late as 1950, more than one thousand *shuike* were registered in Meizhou and Meixian, where they were organized into an association, and many continued to ply their trade well into the 1960s.[21]

HAINAN AND OVERSEAS CHINESE DOMINANCE IN THE *QIAOPI* TRADE

Hainan, a large island to the south of Guangdong and the east of Vietnam, also had a distinct *qiaopi* tradition. Historically, its *qiaopi* trade lagged behind that of mainland Guangdong (of which Hainan was part until 1988) and Fujian. Until 1882, the trade was carried out by *shuike* rather than by *piju*, and even *shuike* were far fewer in number in Hainan than elsewhere. This was because Hainanese migrants tended to earn a lot less than other migrants, and in any case they mostly returned home every few years, taking their earnings with them. They could afford to go to and fro because the distance between Haikou, Hainan's main port, and Haiphong, the nearest big port in Vietnam, where most Hainanese migrants went to work, was less than 250 miles, compared with the nearly 2,000 miles between Xiamen and Singapore. Even between 1900 and 1938, Haikou, the island's capital, never had more than twelve *piju*.

In the first half of the twentieth century, most remittances to Haikou went by way of Hong Kong. The *qiaopi* trade in Hainan was run almost exclusively by overseas Chinese. This was because people did not trust local entrepreneurs due to their generally low level of capitalization. A lack of statistical material makes quantification difficult, but it is thought that hundreds of millions of yuan were remitted to Hainan between 1927 and 1938.[22] Usually, payees received their remittances in Vietnamese currency—unlike in other *qiaoxiang*, where remittances were first changed into Chinese or Hong Kong money. This was because the Vietnamese piastre or dong circulated widely on the island, either sent or brought back by the large group of seasonal workers that spent the summer in Vietnam.[23]

WUYI AND NORTH AMERICA

Wuyi is the collective name of five counties centered on Jiangmen (the other four being Enping, Heshan, Kaiping, Taishan, and Xinhui) in Guangdong's Pearl River Delta. It is sometimes linked with the Guangfu region, which includes Zhongshan and other Cantonese-speaking *qiaoxiang* that share some characteristics with the Wuyi counties.[24] Its system of remittances also differed in certain respects from that in other *qiaoxiang*. Most of its early emigrants went not to Southeast Asia but to the United States, Canada, and Australia, drawn by the gold rushes of the mid-nineteenth century, and some went to Latin America and the Caribbean.[25] A smaller number turned up in Europe, where they opened laundries. The sources of the region's remittance letters (known as *yinxin* rather than *qiaopi*) are therefore different from and more varied than those of other regions. Most were from North America followed by Australia, with a smaller number from Southeast Asia, Cuba, and Peru.[26]

The presence of Chinese migrants in California and the start of the *yinxin* trade did not go unremarked by American administrators and scholars, who began studying and commenting on the Chinese remittance habit and its institutions well before their counterparts in most other places. Early commentators on remittances included anonymous officials as well as scholars such as H. B. Morse, S. R. Wagel, C. S. See, and A. G. Coons. Articles mentioning the practice started appearing in the *San Francisco Morning Call* as early as 1877.[27]

Right from the start, the *yinxin* trade in Wuyi was organized differently from the general *qiaopi* trade. In the 1860s, remittances from San Francisco and Hawaii were handled by a business specializing in import and export, or by a *tongxiang hui* ("native-place association"), a *zongqin hui* ("clanspeople's association"), or a *huiguan*, most of which had links to shipping companies and China ports.[28]

In later years, whereas in eastern Guangdong and southern Fujian many firms specialized mainly or exclusively in *qiaopi*, in Wuyi *yinxin* tended to be handled as a sideline by businesses dealing otherwise in commodities (rice, food, hardware) or services (a laundry, even a clinic) or by *yinhao* (traditional banks).[29] The trade never achieved the same degree of intensity and specialization as in other *qiaoxiang*. Only later did some firms begin to specialize in remittances, exchange, and savings. Such businesses were usually run as an investment, often by a returned *shuike* or migrant or by a migrant's dependent. By the early years of the Chinese Republic, there were several hundred of them in Wuyi. Like the *piju* in other places, they were mostly joint-stock companies with several or several dozen owners, linked to each other and to their clients by ties of kinship or locality.[30]

In the early years, remittances were taken to Wuyi by *shuike*, often in the form of cash or silver, but couriering from overseas had fallen into disuse by the late nineteenth century.[31] The distance between America or Australia and China was too great, and in any case both America and Australia had highly developed financial and postal institutions that were quicker, safer, and more convenient to use. Chinese migrants soon realized that the best way of remitting was to mail a cashier's check obtained from a bank, to be cashed in Guangzhou or Hong Kong or in one of the "exchange shops" that came to proliferate in the region, rather than to remit money in the same way as the Chaoshanese and Fujianese did.[32] Many migrants in North America from Wuyi and other places themselves returned every five to six years to distribute and invest their savings, which further limited the opportunity for a specialist trade of the sort that grew up elsewhere.[33]

Although the banking system in America and Australia was more developed than in Southeast Asia, even there the banks did not, initially, fully extend to all the places where Chinese had settled or were working, nor, in China, did they extend to most of the *qiaoxiang* and the interior. The resulting gap was filled at first by *shuike* and later by Gold Mountain shops and *yinhao*, which served both ends of the migration chain. These shops engaged mainly in export and import, currency exchange, and the sale of Chinese goods such as silk and Chinese medicine, while also helping migrants with paperwork connected with their arrival or departure or buying boat tickets for them. But they also remitted money on migrants' behalf.[34]

The role played in other regions by *shuike* was to some extent played in Wuyi by another important actor in the local remittance trade, nicknamed the *xunchengma* or "town-patrolling horse." The *xunchengma*, a relic of an older system of communication in the region, was similar in many respects to the *shuike* except that his role was narrower, for it was confined largely to domestic communication. Although *xunchengma* did on rare occasions escort migrants to and from China, like the *ketou* elsewhere, overseas travel was not their primary occupation. Their main job was to deliver *yinxin* and other goods and products, notably medicine, to the towns and villages, and to transmit secret commercial intelligence. *Xunchengma* worked on behalf of the Gold Mountain shops or *yinhao*. They were less numerous than the *shuike*: for example, in Zhongshan only around half a dozen were employed. They worked routes between the counties and the big cities—Hong Kong, Macau, Guangzhou, and Foshan—on tours that usually lasted three to four days. They acted on trust, without receipts, and received a regular payment and travel expenses after completing their missions. Like the *shuike*, they needed to be strong and brave and to be good at forming and maintaining strong personal ties and networks. Unlike *shuike*, the *xunchengma* seem never to have formed a trade association.[35]

At first, the checks from North America were mailed to an agent in one of the hundreds of Gold Mountain shops in Hong Kong, whence they were either collected by relatives or delivered by the *xunchengma*, who sailed north on the paddle steamers linking Hong Kong and Wuyi.[36] Later, once the post office and the Bank of China had extended their coverage throughout the region as well as to North America and its Chinatowns, remittances could be mailed directly to payees, who either cashed them or sold them to a local store.[37] The San Francisco post office set up a link to China very early on, at the start of the 1850s, and by the early 1880s it was offering a money-order service.[38] For decades, small remitters continued to prefer the stores. In the war years, however, the stores were no longer able to perform this function and telegraphic transfer through the Bank of China became the norm. After the war, official corruption and inflation drove remitters to revert to unofficial channels that bypassed the modern banking system.[39]

Yinxin in Wuyi were usually fewer in number but of greater value than in other *qiaoxiang*. For a while, their relative rarity convinced many philatelists and *qiaopi* collectors in China that the *yinxin* system in Wuyi was less developed than elsewhere. Where Chaoshan families could boast of runs of hundreds and in a few cases thousands of *qiaopi*, in Wuyi most had just a few or a few dozen *yinxin*. But the lower frequency of the correspondence can be explained not by the lesser vibrancy of the tie but by the greater—often much greater—size of individual remittances.

Remittances from North America overshadowed those from other areas, despite the far smaller size of the North American Chinese population.[40] According to statistics gathered by the American economist C. F. Remer, between 1930 and 1932 just over 50 percent of remittances sent to China through Hong Kong were from the United States and Canada.[41] This was a reflection of America's (and also of Australia's) greater prosperity.[42] US$4 million was remitted to Kaiping alone in 1946.

The greater volume of remittances can also be explained by the inability of the Chinese in North America to penetrate the economic mainstream, from which they were usually excluded, and to invest in it; the greater power of the dollar; and the greater absence of Chinese women from North America and Australia as a result of exclusion, and thus the greater need to send home remittances to sustain them.[43] (This compounded the racial antagonism: whites perceived Chinese migrants' resulting frugality as "unfair competition" in business and at work.[44]) In the postwar period, the effects of restrictions imposed by Southeast Asian governments on the size of individual remittances made the volume of remittances from America seem even greater by comparison.[45]

The role played by kinship was even more intense in the case of the Wuyi remittance trade than in other *qiaoxiang*, so *yinxin* could be administered even more informally than *qiaopi*. There was no serial number on the envelope, and not all businesses or *yinhao* working in the remittance field provided an envelope and paper for the *huipi*. In the *qiaopi* trade, the *piju* often supervised every step on the way, but in Wuyi *yinxin* delivery was delegated to the businesses or the *yinhao*.[46]

In the United States and Canada, many early laborers were seasonal workers with no fixed address, so relatives wrote to them care of stores run by relatives or fellow villagers, who passed the letters on or displayed them in the store window ready for collection. Others addressed their letters to clan associations. This practice was virtually universal in the early years, when few Chinese migrants in North America had permanent homes.[47] The letters were either mailed or they were smuggled: in 1889, customs officers in San Francisco reported finding nearly twenty thousand letters in Chinese passengers' luggage on just three ships, in violation of postal rules.[48] Letters to China also passed through stores, whence they were shipped home together with a consignment of goods. Such stores were run on the basis of ties of lineage or native place.[49]

This connection between remittances and overseas-Chinese trade was typical of both North America and Australia, especially in the early years. The link was cemented through Hong Kong, Guangzhou, Wuyi, and Zhongshan's Gold Mountain shops, of which there were hundreds, usually run by remitters' kin and organized, in Hong Kong, into a federation, the Hua'an Jinshanzhuang Gonghui. For these firms, remitting was secondary to the trade in goods, which was two-way, from China to the Chinatowns and vice versa. This was a poor person's method of remitting, usually in amounts of less than US$100, accompanied by the usual letter with the amount stated on the envelope. Richer remitters used the banks.[50] A processing charge was usually levied, set at around 0.2 percent of the remittance.[51]

In the postwar years, sending remittances through channels other than those formally established by the Chinese authorities, notably the Bank of China, became a feature of emigrant remittances to China from North America, just as it did in the case of Southeast Asian *qiaopi*. In Southeast Asia, the postwar battle to control remittances led to a sharp confrontation between the *piju* and the formal institutions of the Chinese state, but in North America nongovernmental channels played an increasingly diminishing role, and the confrontation that ensued was more directly between the Chinese state and the remitters and recipients. As a result, resistance in the Guangfu region of Guangdong and surrounding places was more widespread and deeply rooted, exacerbated by the direct experience of government bullying and corruption.

As elsewhere, the first cause for anger and frustration was the seeming inability of the Bank of China to deal promptly and efficiently with the backlog of *qiaopi* that had accumulated during the war. In the event, it was not until after the end of 1947 that the delivery of the backlog was finally completed. Reforms of the remittance system were promised and attempted, but they were only partly successful, and not for long. The money supply in local branches of the bank was too little, a common failing not just in Guangfu, and the dollar rate was too low. Remittances sent through official channels were delayed and eaten away by inflation. Corrupt officials extorted and blackmailed recipients. Service in the banks was poor, and there was a lot of bullying.

During the war and in its immediate aftermath, many emigrants remitted through official channels from a feeling of patriotic obligation, but the backlog, the losses incurred, and the arrogance of counter staff alienated this support, and there was a dramatic turn in the mood of affected sections of the population in China and abroad. In America, emigrants began to circumvent formal institutions, and in the *qiaoxiang* the anger that resulted from the bank's negligence and indifference led to threats and violent attacks on officials and bank staff. The press weighed in on the side of aggrieved recipients, who provided journalists with information about what was happening and did their best to mobilize public opinion against the authorities.

After 1947 *taobi*, or financial "evasion," became the norm everywhere in China and the diaspora, but it took a different form in America from in Southeast Asia. In the latter case, evasion was quite a complicated process with several stages. In the former, it was quite simple. Chinese in North America did not, by the late 1940s, use private remittance firms to send money home, but simply bought a money order in American or Hong Kong currency and sent it home by registered post. In China, it could either be cashed directly or endorsed and sold to a third party, after which it would begin its ascent up the hierarchy of money markets, whose higher stages were in the county capital and Guangzhou (which had ties to the Shanghai financial market) or Hong Kong.

The items were actually delivered by the post office. Most of Guangfu and Wuyi—71.1 percent of Jiangmen, for example—was not directly served by the post office, but its *qiaoxiang* were, geographically, far more concentrated and compact than those in Chaoshan, Meixian, southern Fujian, and Hainan, and these concentrations were relatively well-connected to the postal system. This difference was probably due to the fact that overseas emigration from Guangfu and Wuyi only began around 1849 and was curtailed just thirty years later by the US Exclusion Laws. Even by the late 1940s, the Guangfu and Wuyi *qiaoxiang* was only a century old, unlike other *qiaoxiang*, which in some cases had been sending people overseas for up to six hundred years and had become much more widely scattered over time. Where the mail did not reach in Guangfu and Wuyi, a dense network of businesses (*shanghao*), including *yinhao* and medical stores, delivered on the emigrants' behalf with the help of the *xunchengma*. Many emigrants posted their remittances to relatives in Hong Kong or Guangzhou, cities that were relatively close to the *qiaoxiang* where large numbers of emigrants' dependents or returned emigrants lived. The post office was happy to perform this service, which brought in a regular and substantial income, and in 1948 it took measures to speed up deliveries and make them safer.

The remittances fueled a massive growth in the currency black market in the region. In other *qiaoxiang*, the foreign currency in which the remittance was originally made stayed with the *piju*, but in Guangfu and Wuyi it was commonly delivered directly into the hands of the recipient. There was a huge demand for foreign currency from import businesses and from people engaged in assisting or promoting the flight of capital from China to abroad, and the interests of these people coincided with those of the recipients of remittances from North America and elsewhere. Dealers preferred to acquire money orders rather than actual cash, which was conspicuous and vulnerable to thieves and officials, and they had a practically insatiable appetite for such money orders. The businesses that operated this underground market did so under deliberately misleading signboards, so it is impossible to estimate their actual number. However, there were said to be 104 underground *qianzhuang* in Taishan county capital alone at one point in 1948.

The government worked hard to put an end to the evasion by banning the private possession or exchange of foreign currency after the monetary reform of August 1948 and by attacking the black market. However, taking such measures was fraught with difficulties, and it was experienced as official theft by those affected. A register of exchange shops and *qianzhuang* was made: the shops were investigated, and large numbers of them were purged and shut down. In reality, though, most simply slid underground, where they continued to operate, constantly changing their locations to avoid detection and dealing only with familiar and trusted clients. Where necessary, local officials could be bought off or even threatened or assaulted, as in one incident in Xinchang in November 1948, when investigators were surrounded and beaten by a mob of two hundred.[52]

Because of the Chinese Exclusion Laws, the letters that flowed either way between China and North America as part of the remittance trade were likely to focus on different issues from those between China and Southeast Asia. Many focused on immigration, how to deal with interrogation by officials (on arrival), and how to get work in North America.[53] One set of letters shows how a family used kinship ties to construct a migration network that spanned the Pacific, North America, and Southeast Asia and provided family members with the information and paper resources (birth certificates, application forms, depositions, witness statements) necessary to circumvent the ban.[54] One lineage, the Guan from Wuyi, used letters to create a Guan diaspora several thousand strong with branches and outposts across much of the United States, Canada, and Cuba.[55]

Trading companies being the principal link in the *qiaopi* trade, and given the usually far greater obstacles in the way of Chinese immigration to North America than to Southeast Asia, it is not surprising that the companies that managed or controlled the trade played a central role in advising on and facilitating immigration. Would-be immigrants asked company employees about immigration procedures, including depositions and information about the all-important immigration interview, for which it was essential to prepare a convincing case, and, where necessary, about how to get fake documents and identities.

The correspondence associated in the early years with Chinese migrants in North America was not necessarily linked directly to the *qiaopi* phenomenon and was much more likely than migrant letters in the Southeast Asian context to be among emigrants (friends, relatives, and people from the village or county) in different cities in the receiving countries or even between different receiving countries—for example, the United States and Canada. However, although not generally accompanied by money, this correspondence often shared the same channels as the *qiaopi* trade. The differences between it and *qiaopi* in the stricter sense throw interesting light on variations in the nature of migrant networks of the sort that underlay migrant correspondence.

This greater volume in North America of intra-diasporic correspondence can be explained by the greater mobility of Chinese migrants in the Americas, between the United States and Canada to the north and Cuba and Peru to the south, in search of work, trading opportunities, or escape from persecution. Some of these movements (for example, the flight from California to Cuba) were to escape the persecutions to which Chinese migrants were regularly subjected in the United States and Australia. The large-scale remigration of Chinese gold prospectors from California to Australia in the late 1850s was probably also to some extent organized through correspondence. Remigrations by Chinese in Southeast Asia, especially international remigrations, were less extensive than by Chinese in the so-called "white immigrant states" with their open inner frontiers, across which even non-white groups were generally more mobile.

Many Chinese migrants arrived in North America on student visas, either to attend schools identified by relatives or to take advantage of schemes funded or assisted by Chinese governments. This was another important difference between Chinese migration to North America and to Southeast Asia, where educational opportunities were fewer. Educational matters therefore figured more prominently in the correspondence between North America and the sending communities in China, and remittances were often earmarked for use in facilitating educational migration.[56]

GUANGFU AND AUSTRALIA

Early remittances were taken to China from Australia by returning friends or relatives of migrants, or by the migrants themselves. Initially, cash was handed to the courier and dispensed by the courier.[57] When the volume of remitting grew, it became the preserve for a while of *shuike*, as elsewhere. At the same time a system arose, particularly around the goldfields, whereby Chinese general stores, usually patronized by kith and kin of the store owner or manager and known as "clan stores" and "clan banks," provided customers with credit, set up deposit accounts for them, and remitted to China on their behalf, not unlike the setup in North America.[58] They also acted as informal headquarters for the hometown (or home village) associations. In the early years, these stores and banks shepherded the migrants through a society and economy that was in most ways foreign to them, not just with regard to language, and provided them with familiar goods and necessary services. Entrepreneurs sent people to the goldfields to write letters for illiterate workers, collect their gold, and arrange to remit their earnings through a central office in Guangzhou said to have delivered more than ten thousand *yinxin* in 1865.[59] As in North America, they displayed the replies (*huipi*) in wooden racks in store windows or on the counter, ready for collection.[60] This system became particularly popular after a disastrous episode in 1857 when sixty-five Chinese boarding ships to Hong Kong were relieved by officials of 2,600 ounces of gold and 56 gold sovereigns on which they had paid no duty. In the wake of that experience, remitters preferred using the services of local merchants, who were deemed to know the ropes.[61]

Initially, in Australia in the nineteenth century, remittances through clan stores were usually in the form of gold. That practice died out with the gold rush. By the 1930s, the stores had begun to provide customers with bank drafts. The stores bought boat tickets for migrants, in part because shipping agents preferred not to deal directly with ordinary Chinese customers.[62] Some of the bigger stores set up branches in different Australian cities and in Hong Kong, Guangzhou, Xiamen, and Shantou. Some of these businesses became huge, and all played a part in the remittance trade as well as arranged immigration, found accommodation for new arrivals, and lent them money. The opening of regular shipping lines, including (for a short while) some run by Chinese and Japanese, helped boost the trade. Remitting was usually disguised as some other form of business to circumvent the Australian Government's ban on exporting currency through channels other than a bank.[63]

Australia's Wing On company, founded as a fruit store by the Kwok brothers, Kwok Lok and Kwok Chuen, in 1897 and re-founded as a department store in Hong Kong in 1907, had a special tie to the Guangdong *qiaoxiang* and especially to Guangfu's Zhongshan, of which the brothers were natives. Wing On was closely connected almost from the start with non-Chinese modern banks and, in China, with the traditional *yinhao*, to which it remitted on its customers' behalf. It earned an excellent reputation among migrants, and the great bulk of its original capital emanated from overseas-Chinese sources. In 1907 Wing On stopped sending remittances to China through the banks and *yinhao* and instead used Gold Mountain shops directly connected to it in what became one continuous operation, so that it was better able to use the remittances as working capital. It attracted a large volume of migrants' savings, and in 1931 it set up the Wing On Bank on the back of its own earlier banking ventures. Eventually, it practically monopolized the remittance trade in Zhongshan, where it set up a *yinhao* in 1910. Although there were dozens of *qianzhuang* and *yinhao* in the county, Wing On controlled between 75 and 80 percent of Zhongshan remittances.[64]

To conclude, there were important differences between Chinese migration to America and Australia on the one hand and the largely colonial countries of Southeast Asia on the other. These differences helped shape the *qiaopi* trade in Guangfu and Wuyi, where it had special features that set it somewhat apart from the wider trade. They followed differences of geography, politics, economy, and society and were reflected not just in the *qiaopi* system in the region but also in the subject matter of the migrant correspondence. Migrants in Southeast Asia were geographically closer to China. *Shuike* came and went more easily than in the case of the Americas and Australasia, and the *qiaopi* system was correspondingly faster and easier to use. As a result, the *shuike* system soon fell into disuse in the Americas and Australasia, and the *shuike* role was performed, at the China end of the service, by the *xunchengma*, who were exclusively domestic, and on its foreign end by stores and trading companies. The difficulties in the way of migrating in and out of the "white" countries, where procedures were stricter and more complex, impeded movement, at least internationally, and weakened the role of individual entrepreneurs in the remittance trade. So did the fact that Chinese companies in the "white" countries tended to be bigger than in Southeast Asia and better able to deal with non-Chinese administrators and their rules and regulations, and to cope with anti-Chinese prejudice and discrimination.

Qiaopi and Modern Chinese Economy and Politics

This chapter considers the role played by the Chinese state and state-associated organizations in setting, or trying to set, policies and guidelines for the *qiaopi* trade, as one part of the postal service that it saw as its due monopoly. The Chinese state, like states elsewhere in the world, sought to destroy or assimilate premodern postal services like the *qiaopi* system and to assert the authority of the post office, a state postal system that seeks to unify and monopolize the previous mix of local or private services and state-controlled offices charged with the distribution of documents, civil and sometimes military. The state's striving for a monopoly of postal services and its commitment to universal-service obligations (now a general term but one originally applied to the state postal system, and meaning uniformity in price and service) brought it into conflict with existing postal services, among them the *qiaopi* trade.

QIAOPI AND THE BANKS AND POST OFFICE

In its early years, the *qiaopi* trade had strong ties to China's traditional banks, as we have seen. In Xiamen, the rise of the *qianzhuang* went hand in hand with that of the *qiaopi* trade; the number rose from six in 1880 to thirty-nine in 1910 to ninety in 1933, some with a capital of between one hundred and two hundred thousand yuan.[1] These ties survived the rise in China of a modern banking system and its eventual penetration of parts of the *qiaoxiang*. In some ways, the *qiaopi* trade in the *qiaoxiang* and their nearby ports and in Chinese settlements overseas also, as we shall see, paved the way for modern banks and was a mainstay of modern postal services.

Foreign banks practically monopolized modern banking in China and areas of Chinese settlement overseas until well into the twentieth century. HSBC founded its first branch in Xiamen in 1873, followed by others in later years. Foreign banks controlled much of China's foreign trade and issued their own banknotes.[2] They also strove to gain control of the remittance trade, particularly in Fuzhou and Xiamen, provoking Chinese resistance.[3]

On Gulangyu Island, just off Xiamen, the British opened a consulate, a post office, and banks. Japan, Germany, France, and nine other nations later followed suit. Boardinghouses opened to serve the *shuike* that flocked to the island to avail themselves of the consulates' immigration services, and wealthy overseas-Chinese returners settled there to take advantage of Gulangyu's connections and relative security. *Yinzhuang* and *piju* opened on the island, forming a small web of enterprises. In time, Gulangyu's foreign banks snatched large parts of the local *qiaopi* trade from Chinese operators.[4]

Elsewhere in China, however, there was for many years far less interface between *qiaopi* and modern banking. Both the Qing, in its dying years, and the Beiyang government that succeeded it aspired to incorporate the remittance system into their financial structures. The Qing authorities, for example, set up associations in the southern ports to strengthen ties with Chinese migrants and tried to develop an effective policy on remittances. However, its measures largely failed, and those of the Beiyang government scarcely progressed beyond theorizing, since neither regime had the strength to assert itself and realize its goals.[5]

Overseas, the *qiaopi* trade also failed, at first, to build ties to foreign banks. In Singapore, for example, migrants saw the banks' procedures as slow, intimidating, and unfathomable, and they steered largely clear of them. One overseas bank (the Overseas-Chinese Banking Corporation, or OCBC, formed in 1932 in Singapore) that tried to muscle its way into the remittance trade in the late 1930s took several months to effect delivery. Not surprisingly, its customers reverted to the *piju*, where they could speak in dialect, demand assistance, and expect speedy delivery and a swift guaranteed response from the recipient.[6]

The Bank of China was founded in 1912 as the government's central bank, and in 1928 it became a government-authorized international exchange bank specializing in foreign exchange among other things. Other banks followed, including the Guangdong Provincial Bank, which set up branches in the big ports in Guangdong and (to a lesser extent) abroad. The central bank, and the provincial and other banks it marshaled into its overall strategy, were set on a collision course with the *piju*, for in the final years of the Qing, the Chinese state was determined to take control of the *qiaopi* trade, as it was a unique and dependable source of foreign currency. This determination became ever more fixed under the Republic, which had an even greater thirst for foreign currency with which to pay for the strengthening and modernization of its institutions—the army, the police, the courts, the customs, etc.—and for the extension and unification of its system of communications. It was a bureaucratic institution set on a monopolistic trajectory.

The new banks captured much of the *qiaopi* trade, especially in the 1930s and the later war years. The *qiaopi* trade could not entirely escape the efforts of the central authorities to incorporate it into their domain through the system of licensing and by other means. However, the authorities succeeded only partly in doing so, due to crises and constantly changing circumstances (including inflation and the war), the enduring reputation and advantages of the *piju*, and the latter's head start. The Bank of China did not even have branches in Shantou and Quanzhou until 1914 and 1916 respectively; many of its overseas branches, in New York, London, Singapore, and Osaka, were set up shortly before the Second World War.[7]

As for the post office, its evolution was roughly contemporaneous with that of China's modern banking system, and it too was destined for conflict with the *qiaopi* trade. The British opened their first post office in Hong Kong in 1842, followed in 1844 by foreign-controlled postal agencies (the *keyou*) in other coastal cities. Other countries did the same in later years (the Japanese had 344 agencies and the Germans 140 in 1918). These agencies siphoned off some of the *qiaopi* trade, and some *shuike* and Chinese merchants used their services. The Qing Court set up its own imperial post office (it later dropped the imperial designation) in 1896–7 as part of a broader set of reforms after some regional experimentation in the 1860s and the 1870s.[8] In 1892 a branch of the earlier customs post office had been established in Xiamen, and in 1896 the Qing authorities put it in charge of *qiaopi* delivery. However, a lot of leeway was built into the arrangement, given the *pijus'* greater experience and far-flung resources. Even in 1900, when the Xiamen postal authority was established on a more formal basis, it had only twenty-three staff members and was relatively expensive, so the public tended to stick with the *piju*.[9] By 1904, the post office had more than 1,300 branches across the whole of China, but even so it was unable to seize control of the *qiaopi* trade.[10]

As in the case of the foreign banks, the procedures of the new Chinese banks and the post office were too complicated and arcane for many migrants and dependents. For a long time, the two institutions were unable to compete with the *piju* in terms of customer relations, and customers complained that they took too long to deliver. Their branches, mainly in the cities, were often hard for villagers to access because of their location and opening hours. In the smaller Chinese towns and in the villages, the banks and the post office had little or no presence until after the start of the Sino-Japanese War.[11] Even so, the spread of postal services to rural areas, including some *qiaoxiang*, was an important element in the gradual assimilation of parts of the *qiaopi* trade to the state.

In the 1930s the post office strove to reform and modernize its procedures, including those pertaining to the *qiaopi* trade, which continued to be a main target of officials seeking to fill state coffers. The foreign postal services that sprang up in

China in the late nineteenth and early twentieth centuries had little impact on remittances, mainly because of language problems (few Chinese spoke anything other than Chinese at the time) and their complex procedures. The Chinese post office was much more successful. After 1930, it increased the number of its routes, offices, agents, post boxes, deliveries, and opening hours, and it increased its workers' wages. To weaken the *piju*, it cracked down even more heavily on remittance smuggling and roped in the customs as part of its campaign. It issued leaflets using local forms of Chinese. For the time being, however, it made barely a dent in the *qiaopi* trade; in 1937, it still handled only 1.1 percent of Guangdong's *qiaohui*, coming a poor third to the *piju* and the Bank of China. It did poorly in Fujian as well.

In 1937 postal leaders took measures that soon led to an improvement in performance. They initiated a fresh study of the methods used by the *piju*, which were still very buoyant, and of the modern and old-style banks, and set out to learn from them. The post office incorporated parts of the remittance system by signing contracts with banks, letter companies, and *piju* in China and abroad, paying them a commission of 0.5 percent. In 1938 it signed agreements with modern and old-style banks in Hong Kong and several Southeast Asian countries, including the OCBC, which became its main business partner in the trade. Internally, supervision of the remittance system was tightened up and officials gathered relatively accurate and comprehensive statistics as modern methods of business and administration percolated downward.

However, corrupt practices, including embezzling or absconding with remittances, and rampant inefficiency remained a problem at all levels of the official postal system, despite attempts to introduce greater transparency and make a clearer demarcation of duties and responsibilities. Conflicts and muddle continued within the post office and associated institutions. *Huipi* were kept back for up to two months, compared with the *pijus'* average of three weeks. *Qiaopi* recipients were harassed for shopkeepers' guarantees and for commission, which was against the regulations and alienated potential customers. Although the post office made headway in these years, it was unable to break free of government bureaucracy, red tape, and overstaffing, or to achieve its purpose, which was to monopolize the *qiaopi* trade. It failed to win the complete confidence of potential users. Far from replacing the *piju* root and branch, it was forced to borrow *piju* methods to make headway.[12]

By comparison with the banks and the post office, especially in pre-reform days, the *piju* and the *shuike* were reliable, quick, familiar, and flexible. They were prepared to deliver even the tiniest sums, which made up a large proportion of remittances.[13] In 1941, for example, only 10 percent of a sample of "family-maintenance remittances" were in what then counted as the higher bracket of four hundred yuan or more, while more than 80 percent were below three hundred yuan and 27 percent were below one hundred yuan.[14] In most *qiaoxiang*, *piju* and *shuike* continued to handle between 80 and 90 percent of remittances right up until 1937.[15]

The *piju* were also well equipped to deal with the measures taken against them by the postal authorities, whose powers and reach remained heavily circumscribed throughout the Republican period, despite the reforms. *Qiaopi* traders did not respond passively to the new constraints and continued to outwit the post office through campaigns of noncompliance and active protest. Until the 1930s, large numbers of traders refused to apply for licensing, and even those that did were barely affected by it. In Shantou in 1927, not a single one of the seventy-five *piju* had a license; in the eyes of the post office, they were "smugglers." During that period, unlicensed traders carried far more *qiaopi* and *huipi* than their licensed counterparts.

Shuike and *xunchengma* too flouted government authority. According to the rules, they were supposed to register their names, whereabouts, and addresses, but few did. *Piju* applying for licenses in China were supposed to give the names of their foreign-based companies and to register the details of their employees overseas, but again few did.

In the 1930s the government presence began to make itself more felt, and *piju* that failed to register found it ever harder to operate. Some were closed down, including in Shantou, previously a bastion of resistance to the authorities on the part of the *qiaopi* trade. However, official licenses were largely viewed as "legal outer garments" rather than as obligations of real substance, and the *piju* continued to thrive under the new regime. In the Guangfu region, the post office was no match for the black market run by the dense network of *qianzhuang*, *yinhao*, and other old-style money-shops (of which there were more than sixty in Taishan alone) supported by *xunchengma*, backed up by shops and stores that accepted foreign currency, and linked by waterways to Hong Kong and other nearby cities that managed the higher levels of the remittance trade. The *piju* in eastern Guangdong and southern Fujian remained equally extensive and effective. The government's and the post office's problems were exacerbated by the boom in remittances in the 1930s, which hugely outstretched their resources. One way in which *qiaopi* traders fought back against the authorities was by banding together in *qiaopi* and *yinxin* trade associations. These associations negotiated with governments in China and overseas on matters such as *huipi* postage rates, the license system, and the abolition of clubbed packets.

Apart from collective actions of this sort, individual *piju* evaded fees and constraints by smuggling remittances and correspondence into and out of China. There were various ways in which this was done. In some cases, to evade the new charges on clubbed packets, *piju* workers secretly stuffed two or more letters into one envelope or understated the number of envelopes in a packet. In the late 1920s, the government recognized this as a serious problem, and in the 1930s it began slapping fines on offending *piju* or withdrawing their licenses. But this government campaign again drew protests from business organizations, and the punishments were watered down.

So on the whole, the government failed to take control of the *qiaopi* trade, let alone gain a monopoly of it. The trade was too widely scattered, and the government's resources were insufficient to realize its ambition. The post office had too few offices and agents, especially in rural areas, where most *qiaopi* were bound. Perhaps most importantly, the post office was unable to counter the alliance of local and transnational interests, including emigrant organizations, Chambers of Commerce, the press, and the dependents who opposed or undermined its measures.

The state greatly increased its share of the remittance trade during the war against Japan, when most *piju* were unable to cope with the changed conditions and closed down, at least for the time being. However, the trade shrank in volume, so although it became, proportionately, a major source of foreign currency for the Nationalists, absolutely it declined steeply. (Its wartime development is described later in this chapter.)

The Qing Court's and the Nationalist government's attitude toward the *qiaopi* trade underwent a lengthy evolution. For a long time, they lacked information about the institution and failed to grasp its special nature. In particular, they failed to make the necessary distinction between *piju*, which tied the *qiaoxiang* to places abroad, and the *minxinju* that served a domestic clientele. They even lacked a unitary term to describe the *piju*, which featured under a variety of names in the official debate about the *qiaopi* trade. The Nationalists tried to ban both *piju* and *minxinju* in 1928, when they announced their dissolution "before the end of 1930," but this plan, and associated measures, provoked a furor and widespread protests. After that, the government continued to aspire, as a long-term aim, to bring all branches of the postal trade under central control, but in the meantime it made a clear distinction between ordinary domestic mail and remittance letters. It took measures against the former, but merely set in motion an investigation of the latter. Even its campaign against the *minxinju* was not victorious until January 1935, when the *minxinju* trade finally came to an end.

The investigation into the *qiaopi* trade concluded that the *qiaopi* system had special features and many different functions—as a bank, credit system, postal system, massive source of remittances, vehicle of foreign trade, and labor agency. Its most effective feature was the dense and massive network of relationships it had established between China and Chinese communities overseas, chiefly in Southeast Asia. To ban it would therefore harm multiple interests and destroy a vital and, for the time being, irreplaceable channel linking the diaspora and China.[16]

So although the idea of an official postal monopoly was reasserted, the distinction between *minxinju* and *piju* was upheld. The battle was rejoined in 1930, but the government again "went for wool and came home shorn," after another wave of resistance.[17] So it had no choice, for the time being, but to recognize its limits in this matter, for its greater size was still no match for the *qiaopi* trade's greater flexibility and speed.

In the remoter *qiaoxiang*, the case for allowing *piju* to continue was even more glaring. In Chenghai, for example, then a small coastal town serving a large migrant hinterland, the post office branch (set up in 1902) employed only four staff. Because of its complex river system, the region was cut up by numerous tributaries of the Han Jiang, and the post office found it hard to reach the inland villages and the migrants' dependents, who made up half the county's population.[18]

However, the authorities had not given up their aim of "destroying the *piju* root and branch" and bringing this lucrative trade under their own monopoly control.[19] One of their tactics was to try to license the trade. In 1914 the Beiyang warlord government in Beijing proclaimed a licensing system for private letter and remittance services, but to little effect. In 1919 the Guangdong postal authorities tried to force the *piju* to register, with similar results. In 1928 a majority of the *piju* investigated by the post office were still unlicensed. It was not until 1935 that the postal authorities took effective steps to bring the *piju* under control by forcing them to apply for licenses and renew the licenses annually. This system did not break the *piju* owners' hold on the trade, but it increased the authority of the post office, which could now refuse to license companies that flouted the rules and regulations.

Joining the Universal Postal Union in 1914 also ultimately strengthened the post office's position in relation to the *piju*.[20] Initially, in the absence of a single Chinese authority, membership meant little, but China's reunification in 1927 necessitated and legitimized measures that weakened the *piju* and strengthened the central authority. An important issue concerning *piju* in this period was the so-called clubbed packet system, whereby many small letters were enclosed in a single packet to save money on postage. Colonial governments in Southeast Asia were the first to abolish the system, whereupon the postal authorities in China came under pressure to do the same in regard to clubbed packets of *huipi*. This happened slowly at first, with various concessions designed to placate the remitters and their dependents as well as the *qiaopi* traders, but gradually the postage charged on *huipi* was increased, so that by 1932 in Guangdong it brought the post office an income of nearly one hundred thousand yuan.

During and after the Sino-Japanese War, the authorities again did all they could to break the *pijus'* hold, by simplifying their own procedures, concerting the resources of different banks, and mobilizing the combined power of the post office, the foreign office, and the government-sponsored Overseas Chinese Affairs Council. To capture the trade and at the same time bring relief to the war-stricken *qiaoxiang*, the Bank of China and the Guangdong Provincial Bank adopted a more flexible approach than in past. In Quanzhou, the Bank of China's newly founded branch co-opted the Hechang *piju* and copied its methods to the last detail, poaching *pijiao* to deliver to the villages and, like the *piju*, accepting remittances however small. It eventually gained an excellent reputation among many villagers. During most of the war, apart from in 1941 and 1942, the two bleakest years, the amount remitted through the banks grew more or less uninterruptedly. For example, the overall overseas remittance received by the Guangdong Provincial Bank increased from US$1.25 million in 1937 to more than US$50 million in 1945.[21]

However, the *piju*, despite briefly stumbling during the Pacific war, bounced back after 1945 with even greater vigor by diversifying and collaborating where necessary with its capital-rich official rivals.[22] The Nationalist state was forced to make concession after concession to the *piju* until it finally lost power on the mainland in 1949, leaving the battle in the hands of a more skilful and effective agency, the Communists.[23]

Despite numerous tormented episodes, the relationship between the *piju* on the one side and the banks and post office on the other was only partly antagonistic. Although competitors, the three institutions cooperated where it was in their interests to do so. The banks and the post office used *qiaopi* networks, including traditional banks and *shuike*, to reach places they themselves had difficulty in penetrating. This reconciliation was speeded by improved banking procedures, the post office's transition in the first half of the twentieth century from failure to relative efficiency, and the creation in China of a "postal culture."[24] For their part, the *piju* separated out the functions of letter and remittance, using the banks for the latter and the post office for the former, thus speeding and protecting transfers.[25] A division of labor evolved: the *piju* collected the *pi* and took them to the door, the post office handled their transnational dispatch, and the banks handled the financial transfer and exchange.[26] A minority of *piju* continued to send foreign money back to China or Hong Kong, where it was exchanged for Chinese money, but their number was small and shrinking.

In quite a few cases, Chinese banks—especially those with branches abroad—preferred the *piju* to the post office. Most villages had no postal connection, and the post office charged too much for remitting and providing receipts. It also fell well short of the *piju* in terms of general service: it took too long to deliver the *qiaopi* and demanded that recipients provide guarantors, it held on too long to the *huipi*, and its delivery men often tried to extort "commission."[27]

The *piju* profited in several ways from their relationship with banks. The tie sped up transactions as well as secured them, but there was nearly always an interval between banking and cashing remittances, during which the remittances remained in the *piju*'s bank account and accrued interest. Sometimes, the *piju* waited for a favorable movement in exchange rates before releasing accumulated funds or (like the early *shuike*) used them as a working fund. So the banks and the *piju* were not necessarily or in all circumstances competitors, but had a relationship that was sometimes mutually beneficial.

This relationship obtained both in China and abroad. In Singapore, for example, the post office started using steamers to transport mail in 1905, acting as a hub for the wider region. The *piju* took note of the post office's rapid growth and concentrated their offices in Singapore. *Piju* throughout Malaya bundled their remittances and sent them through Singapore, after which they were able to reach Shantou within a week to ten days.[28] A similar relationship developed in Thailand, which set up a post office in 1883, earlier than in China, and a special *qiaopi* branch of it in 1907. In both Thailand and China, the *qiaopi* trade and the post office were generally on good terms, except when the latter tried too brazenly to assert itself at the former's expense.[29]

Despite its particularism and traditional flavor, the *qiaopi* trade was an essential part of the emergence of a system of international finance in China, a relationship illustrated by its close ties with China's modern banking system. It was a hybridization of traditional trust, rooted in relations of blood, place, and tongue, and the modern, legally supported notion of trust. The former prevailed in the *piju*'s relations with its customers and among *piju* and the traditional banks and money-shops they did business with. *Piju* were by no means averse to dealing with strangers, but only if they were vouched for by a trusted intermediary or belonged to a respected lineage. The latter forms of trust played an increasingly important role in *piju* operations as the twentieth century wore on.[30]

In Xiamen, where several dozen modern banks operated, the *qiaopi* trade was one of the banks' major assets. This was especially so in the late 1940s, when colonial and other overseas governments tried increasingly to ensure that all remittances were made through formal banking channels. Most remittances in those years went through unofficial channels because of galloping inflation and official corruption, but the banks did their best to get a grip on those parts of the *qiaopi* trade that remained accessible. They handled remittances' import and exchange, facilitated the import-export trade associated with remittances, invested on behalf of remitters and recipients of remittances, made loans and arranged insurance, supervised enterprises and joint ventures at home and abroad, and managed deposit accounts, both overseas and in China or Hong Kong.[31]

The *piju* finally folded in the 1970s, after the Chinese and foreign governments had stepped up their regulation of the trade and modern financial and postal institutions had asserted their superiority. Meanwhile, new migrants largely ignored the *piju*, and by then most of the *pijus*' former customers in the old migrant generation had died.[32]

So the *qiaopi* trade had an ambiguous relationship with China's official banks, sometimes troubled, sometimes mutually beneficial. However, for patriotic reasons, those running it tried to avoid relying too much on foreign banks like HSBC and the Nederlandsch-Indische Handelsbank, which Chinese businesses usually approached through compradors. Where they required trade finance, they often engaged in "book-keeping barter" within networks based on kinship or dialect, a form of credit based on personal trust rather than on assets.

In the early twentieth century, Chinese entrepreneurs began to establish their own banks, also based on particularistic ties. In the 1920s, leaders of the *qiaopi* trade intersected with and forged special links with these "native" banks, the development of which they saw as being in their own and China's best interests. Three main overseas-Chinese banks formed between 1912 and 1919, merging in 1932 to form the OCBC, a defensive measure in response to the 1929 crash. The merger also aimed at rooting out the potential for cronyism that plagued banks based on dialect.

At first these "native" banks established themselves on the basis of Chinese business in the big cities of Southeast Asia (Singapore, Kuala Lumpur, Bangkok, Saigon, Rangoon, and Manila). After that, they branched out to a second tier of cities like Penang and Malacca, and finally to even smaller towns across Asia and the Pacific. Eventually, they spread to the Americas.[33] Although they failed to reverse foreign dominance of the banking sector, they won an increased share of remittances.[34]

The "native" banks' role in the *qiaopi* trade was (a) to allocate and transfer funds and ensure a reliable money supply on behalf of *piju* and (b) to engage in the direct management of *qiaopi* operations. In the early years of the trade, *piju* had transferred silver dollars to China, where they distributed them across the villages. This took time and was highly insecure. Some traders therefore made their transfers through the foreign and domestic branches of the "native" banks, which hugely sped up and safeguarded transactions. Transferring funds between foreign and domestic *piju* was laborious and time-consuming, so in 1932 the OCBC set up a special section to administer *qiaopi* in cooperation with the Ministry of Communications and the *piju*.[35]

QIAOPI AND CHINA'S GENERAL ECONOMY

Qiaopi, which comprised both a letter and a remittance, helped construct and sustain two of the most important ties linking the diaspora with China: an emotional (or intangible) tie and a material (or tangible) one. They mattered in the creation of a modern and transnational China both in themselves, as letters plus remittances, and because of the material connections they both utilized and created. Numerous studies explain the massive role remittances from overseas played in China's social and economic modernization in the late nineteenth and twentieth centuries, as an indispensable foundation of modern Chinese economy.[36]

The *qiaopi* trade was geographically peripheral, in that it was concentrated in Guangdong and Fujian, far from the political center and initially less touched by modern industry and commerce than other regions. Although it took massive advantage of modern banking facilities, modern forms of transportation, and modern postal services, including telecommunications, its internal organization and external ties were essentially premodern. It was mainly part of the informal sector and often more or less successfully resisted government attempts, in China and overseas, to monitor and tax it. It depended for support on a wide array of organizations, including general *qiaopi* associations, overseas-Chinese associations, Chinese chambers of commerce in China and abroad, public opinion, and sections of the press. Although its activities were typically deemed by governments at home and abroad to be illegal, or to verge on illegality (it was abidingly associated with smuggling and black markets), its impact on China's national economy and on the economy of the southeastern coastal region was far-reaching and profound, more so for many years than almost any other sector of the economy.

Its best-known and most remarked-upon economic impact was on China's balance of payments. Overseas-Chinese remittances, an invisible import, were "the only major item that always benefits China's balance of payments," noted the Japanese economist Fukuda Shozo, writing in 1937. (Much foreign investment only temporarily benefited the international balance of payments, since China had to pay interest on it and remit a large proportion of the profits.) Fukuda went on to declare that overseas Chinese "may be credited with the merit of saving China from international bankruptcy."[37] Their remittances hugely compensated for China's trade deficit. According to estimates of China's international balance of payments, the ratio of total remittances to total trade deficits was 168 percent in 1903, 98 percent in 1909, 39 percent in 1912, 47 percent in 1913, 41 percent in 1920–3, and 108 percent in 1928.[38] (Compare this with, say, Japan, where they were generally below 5 percent, and Russia, where they were lower still. Even in the 1990s, remittances remained one of China's major sources of foreign currency.[39])

This compensation was, for obvious reasons, even more striking in the case of regional economies closely associated with the *qiaopi* trade. In Xiamen, for example, the trade deficit between 1932 and 1938 was more than 230 million yuan, whereas overseas-Chinese remittances amounted to more than 360 million yuan, a surplus of more than 120 million yuan.[40] The same went for Guangdong's Chaoshan region. From 1912 to 1937, visible imports exceeded exports in every year but one (1920), but remittances reversed the balance by 1.35 times in 1936, 2.6 in 1937, and a massive 4.85 in 1938.

The importance of the *qiaopi* trade and its remittance to China's national and local economy is demonstrated in tables 1 and 2.

Remittance contributed to the economic and social development of *qiaoxiang* to a far greater extent, as demonstrated by the case of Fujian in the late Qing and Republican periods.

Remittance continued to play a crucial role in the Chinese economy after 1949. As Glen Peterson has shown, "in both absolute and strategic terms, the role of remittances remained formidable after 1949." Remittances were of "even greater strategic importance to the PRC than to previous Chinese governments" because of the economic embargo imposed and led by the United States during the Cold War. It was estimated that between 1950 and 1957 the total value of remittances reached US$1.17 billion, which nearly cancelled out the country's trade deficit of the same

TABLE 1 Estimated Balance of Payments, 1902–30 (Million current U.S. dollars)

Category	1902–13	1914–30	1902–30
Total imports:			
Annual average	258.4	720.7	529.4
Total for period	3,100.6	12,252.1	15,352.7
Import surplus:			
Annual average	88.6	139.7	118.6
Total for period	1,063.3	2,375.5	3,438.8
% of total imports	34.3%	19.4%	22.4%
Private foreign investment:			
Annual average	47.0	75.1	63.5
Total for period	563.6	1,276.7	1,840.3
% of import surplus	53.0%	53.7%	53.5%
Remittances from overseas Chinese:			
Annual average	45.0	89.5	71.0
Total for period	539.6	1,502.7	2,060.3
% of import surplus	50.7%	63.3%	59.9%

SOURCE: Data from Robert F. Dernberger, "The Role of the Foreigner in China's Economic Development, 1840–1949," in Dwight H. Perkins, ed., *China's Modern Economy in Historical Perspective* (Stanford: Stanford University Press, 1975), 19–47.

TABLE 2 Comparison of Overseas Remittances and Trade Deficit, 1950–88 (Million dollars)

Category	1950–7	1958–62	1963–5	1966–75	1976–80	1981–8	1950–88
Trade deficit:							
Annual average	172.5	124.5	321	NA	778	NA	157
Total for period	1,380	498	963	NA	3,890	NA	6,124
Remittances from overseas Chinese:							
Annual average	146.3	112.5	151.3	252.3	597.6	253	246.4
Total for period	1,170	450	454	2,523	2,988	2,024	9,610
% of trade deficit	84.8%	90.4%	47.1%	NA	76.8%	NA	156.9%

SOURCE: Data from China Ministry of Commerce website, *History of Commerce-Remittance Policies and Overseas Chinese Remittances*. Available at http://history.mofcom.gov.cn.

TABLE 3 Comparison of Overseas Fujianese Remittances and Trade Deficit (Thousands of yuan)

Period	Deficit	Remittance	Surplus
1905–38	902,240	1,284,466	382,226
Yearly average	26,536	37,778	11,242
1929–38	428,336	602,744	174,408
Yearly average	42,834	60,274	17,440

SOURCE: Data from Cheng Lin-k'uan, "Remittance by Overseas Fukien Chinese," in George L. Hicks, ed., *Overseas Chinese Remittances from Southeast Asia, 1910–1940* (Singapore: Select Books Pte Ltd, 1993), 216–314. Originally published in 1942.

period (around US$1.38 billion).[41] At the level of individual families, remittances accounted for about 50 percent of the total income of households of *qiaojuan* (overseas Chinese family dependents). It is estimated that right up to the early 1980s (especially before 1949), 80 to 90 percent of remittances sent back to China by the Chinese diaspora were transmitted by *qiaopi* carriers. It was said that before the 1970s, some 75 to 80 percent of remittances to Xiamen from Southeast Asia passed through *piju*, though the proportion had declined to around 5 percent by 1990.[42]

The impact of the *qiaopi* trade on China's national and regional economies was not just restricted to its role in helping to balance general trade. The profits from it were used to build and rebuild Xiamen, Shantou, Chaozhou, and other cities in the southeast. It also contributed to the birth in southeastern China of a capitalism far more robust than the *guandu shangban* ("official supervised, merchant managed") and *guanshang heban* ("official and merchant managed") enterprises of the late nineteenth century or than bureaucratic capitalism under Chiang Kai-shek. In the early nineteenth century, the Daoguang Emperor praised the *qiaoxiang* as his "southern storehouse." One *qiaopi* scholar has argued that the trade not only opened a seaway to Southeast Asia during the period of the "sea ban" but helped China to cope with the problems it encountered after Spain's launching of the Mexican silver dollar in 1775. Mexican silver flooded into Guangdong in the early nineteenth century and then flooded out again after the acceleration of the opium trade. However, the development of the *qiaopi* trade helped to reverse this disastrous outflow by importing silver, and it promoted the birth of an original financial system capable of dealing with the profusion of foreign currencies, including for a while by the creation of a local currency in the *qiaoxiang*.[43]

Today, some Chinese historians compare the *qiaopi* trade favorably with the Qing's Yangwu Movement (1860–95), which aimed to enrich China by establishing a modern enterprise culture.[44] They argue that it both preceded and outlived the Yangwu Movement and ended in victory, "single-handedly" transforming the economies of China's southeastern ports—unlike the Yangwu Movement, which ended in defeat.[45] Others argue that the *piju* was China's first international financial institution. This distinction had previously been awarded by historians to Shanxi's *piaohao* banks, but the revisionists point out that it was not until 1907 that the first *piaohao* entered the international market (in Japan), decades after the first *piju*.[46]

Far less remarked but perhaps equally important was the impact of the *qiaopi* trade on Chinese cities not directly linked to the *qiaoxiang*. Here, we look at two such cities, Hong Kong and Shanghai.

Hong Kong dominated the *qiaopi* trade almost from the start of its second, more organized stage. *Shuike* and *piju* used Hong Kong's banking system, traditional and modern, to transfer and change money, and to cash checks and money orders. It was the trade's main hub, with spokes into all the southern *qiaoxiang*. In the 1920s, nearly four hundred *yinhao* operated in the colony (most of them run by Wuyinese and Guangfunese). In the early twentieth century, 50 percent of remittances to Xiamen from Southeast Asia passed through Hong Kong, compared with 39 percent remitted directly to Xiamen.[47] By 1936, 67 percent of remittances to China went through Hong Kong.[48] By the late 1940s, 80 percent of remittances passed through the colony, in part to evade the controls that postwar governments in Southeast Asia sought to impose. Why did Hong Kong play such a central role in the *qiaopi* trade? Its convenient geography, free-port status, and reliable and well-connected financial institutions (including more than twenty branches of overseas-Chinese banks) were the pull. So were Hong Kong's plentiful voluntary associations, representing different localities, surnames, and occupations; these too facilitated the *qiaopi* trade. The push favoring Hong Kong was China's corrupt and bureaucratic administration, its dangerously unstable economy, its restive politics and population, and the raging inflation of the late 1940s.[49] The channeling of *qiaopi* through Hong Kong, both before and after 1949, was a major—though rarely acknowledged—source of the colony's prosperity.[50] Michael Williams argues that Hong Kong played a major role as a key link between the *qiaoxiang* and migrants' destinations as well as serving as a hub of remittance networks. The number of business associations dealing with money-changing and banking in Hong Kong rose from 152 in 1871 to 241 ten years later. The Hong Kong governor reported in 1913 that various Gold Mountain firms remitted $HK56 million to China, and the manager of a Sydney bank said in 1927, speaking of his branch alone, that "the Hong Kong exchange sold by us yearly averages £600,000 ($HK27 million)."[51]

In Shanghai, the Fujian *bang*, based on the Quanzhou-Zhangzhou *huiguan*, was considered small in the nineteenth century, but it soared in importance after 1919 and became second only to the Ningbo *bang*, with which it formed an alliance. Its rise was due partly to political factors connected with the emergence of modern nationalism in Shanghai and Fujian, but it also had an economic explanation. Overseas Chinese from Fujian invested in Shanghai, and the *jinzhuang* ("gold shops") and import-export businesses they set up in Shanghai handled *qiaopi* and other remittances from Southeast Asia. As a result of their activities, Shanghai became for the first time a major center of the *qiaopi* trade, a development that greatly boosted the Fujian *bang*'s status in the city. In the early twentieth century, a Japanese researcher ascertained that 11 percent of remittances from Southeast Asia to Xiamen passed through Shanghai.[52] This Shanghai link to the *qiaopi* trade is not generally known, resulting in an underestimation of the volume of the Fujian *qiaopi* trade and, conversely, an overestimation of its Guangdong equivalent. A large slice of Chinese remittances from Southeast Asia, particularly the Philippines, were transmitted by way of the United States, and on to Shanghai and then Fujian. Nearly all these remittance were Fujianese, but because 95 percent of Chinese in North America were Cantonese, these remittances have been wrongly reckoned as Cantonese (in fact, nearly all Cantonese remitted through Hong

Kong). As a result, the volume of Cantonese remittances was thought in the late 1930s to be more than twice that of Fujianese remittances, even though such a large disparity was merely apparent.[53]

The *qiaopi* trade was dynamic and protean, constantly adapting to changes in the economic, financial, and technological environment, though without ever shedding its special character. Before 1840 the trade was usually conducted in goods or gold conveyed by *shuike*. In this respect, it mirrored the first stage of international trade generally, also based on bullion. The second stage of the *qiaopi* trade saw a transition to a more sophisticated but less risky and laborious form of exchange based on fiduciary money rather than coins and material goods, which again mirrored the global transition to bills of exchange.[54] The close ties between the *qiaopi* trade and the emergence of a Chinese-owned modern banking sector in Southeast Asia and China made it easier for *piju* owners to extend their networks into European and North American markets, and to facilitate intra-diasporic migrations by overseas-Chinese people and capital.[55]

QIAOPI IN THE SINO-JAPANESE WAR (1937–45)

In 1937 the Japanese invasion of northern and central China, consolidated between May and October 1938 by the invasion of Fujian and Guangdong, threw the *qiaopi* trade into turmoil. In the first few months of the war in 1937, remittances increased.[56] However, after this initial phase of feverish, panicky remitting, in anticipation of the collapse of China's economy and the trade's expected demise, routes into China were for a while cut.[57] To meet the crisis, the *qiaopi* trade changed in different ways in different places, going essentially in two opposite directions. In some wartime transactions, the element of personal trust, which had been partly eroded in previous years by the trade's growing size and professionalization, made a comeback, while in others modern banks and the post office came to play a greater role than they had previously.

During the war, the *qiaopi* trade in China had to contend with rival political authorities in what had previously been a more or less united country. However, contrary to what some historians have assumed or asserted, the barriers created by the war did not put an end to the import of remittances, although they greatly complicated and hampered it in many places. The war instead brought into even more vigorous play the rootstalks on which the *qiaopi* trade had originally formed and which, for more than one hundred years, had been the secret of its strength.

In the early years of the Sino-Japanese War, before the Pacific war engulfed Southeast Asia, the *qiaopi* trade supported the resistance to Japan in whatever ways it could, chiefly by donating huge amounts of its own money and goods, encouraging and remitting others' donations, and backing the call to boycott Japan, a campaign *piju* advertised on their envelopes.[58] This was part of a massive political mobilization that has been called the "second overseas-Chinese patriotic high tide," after the first one at the time of the birth of the Republic.[59] Most donations went to the Guomindang government in Wuhan and later Chongqing, but some went to the Communists, discreetly, in the form of *koupi* ('oral *pi*') sent via friends in China to the Eighth Route Army Office in the Nationalist capital.[60] (The pro-Communist remitters received a reply from Zhou Enlai and other leaders proudly described by *qiaopi* historians as a *huipi*.[61])

In the *qiaoxiang*, maintaining the flow of remittances to dependents was difficult but essential, for more than 80 percent of dependents' income was estimated to derive from *qiaopi*.[62] During the war, the lack of labor power and dependence on remittances in the *qiaoxiang*, concomitants of a migrant society, plunged the villages deep into crisis. In the famine of 1943, two hundred thousand people died in Chaoyang; villages emptied; dependents' families sold their clothes and houses; parents sold their daughters into marriage, concubinage, or prostitution; and some families became extinct.[63] Inflation compounded the misery: a big rise in the amount remitted in 1940 was due mainly to the fall in value of the fabi.[64]

In the war, the Chinese authorities changed their attitude toward *qiaopi* from hostility and suspicion to support. They came to recognize more than ever the importance of remittances not just for the survival of emigrants' dependents but as a pillar of the national economy, at a time when industrial and other production was plummeting and military expenditure was soaring.[65] In the first four years of the war, from 1937 to 1940, *qiaopi* continued to play a vital economic role in China. Together, the *qiaopi* received in that four-year period amounted to a total import of just over four billion fabi, the equivalent of 126.8 percent of the annual average state revenue over the same period, and enabled the Nationalist authorities to supplement the military aid they were receiving from the West and the Soviet Union by buying military materials on the international market.[66] The wartime inflow peaked in 1940, when remittances equaled 329 percent of China's national trade deficit.[67] The wartime crisis wonderfully concentrated the minds of the Nationalist authorities, who took measures previously neglected or opposed and put the promotion of remittances and the removal of obstacles to them at the top of their financial agenda in southeastern China, while at the same time stepping up their efforts to seize control of the *qiaopi* trade. The Chinese Foreign Ministry and the Overseas Chinese Council worked together with the post office and the Bank of China to simplify remittance procedures in Southeast Asia, lower the cost to remitters of remitting, reduce harmful competition, and strengthen remittance networks. When the British raised postal charges in Hong Kong, the Nationalist authorities switched to using French planes and steamers to reach China from Hanoi.[68] For a while, until it was closed by Japanese bombers, a new route from Shantou to Hong Kong was opened through the port of Shayuyong (which happened to be the wartime headquarters of the Communists' Dong Jiang guerrillas in southern Guangdong).[69]

The authorities set up new overseas branches of the Bank of China to absorb remittances and ensure their rapid transfer.[70] In the period leading up to the outbreak of the Pacific war in December 1941, eighteen branches of the bank were founded in maritime Southeast Asia, Indochina, Burma, and India.[71] The biggest new branch was in Quanzhou, a city that was never occupied but suffered greatly under a Japanese naval blockade that led to a partial collapse of the remittance trade.[72] This Quanzhou branch set up a network of nearly two hundred agent offices in Southeast Asia as well as numerous lesser agencies, usually in Chinese-owned stores, until the Japanese invasion of the region starting in late 1941 put a temporary stop to the venture. In Quanzhou, an area that had never before known modern banking, the Bank of China, as we have already seen, purchased the license of a local *piju*, the Hechang, in an effort to break the *pijus*' stranglehold on the local trade, and employed their *pijiao* and couriers.[73] By 1938 this bank-controlled *piju* handled 70 percent of all remittances in southern Fujian.[74] Many families in the *qiaoxiang* opened accounts with the bank after the fall of Xiamen in May 1938.[75]

The authorities created a register of migrants' dependents and bodies to support them, and organized protection and relief (although these measures were often only minimally effective).[76] Under pressure from the local Overseas Chinese Committee, the Bank of China and the Guangdong Provincial Bank set up special units to serve dependents as well as a remittance section to manage the trade.[77] The two banks and the authorities worked together with *piju* that had fled inland to smuggle remittances to dependents in occupied areas.[78] The banks also used the *shuike*, who were particularly active in the Hakka counties of eastern Guangdong and southern Fujian in 1940 and 1941.[79] In the past, banks had found it difficult to attract remitters, but now, amid the wartime turmoil, the banks' official status ensured them support at China's and the provinces' highest levels, including in the ministries, and became a positive advantage.[80] In Guangdong's Wuyi region, too, the Bank of China became the main wartime channel for remittances, chiefly by telegraphic transfer by way of Chongqing.[81] Where the Bank of China lacked branches, the Guangdong Provincial Bank acted on its behalf.[82] At the same time, some *piju* made things worse for themselves, and better for the banks, by taking advantage of the war to retain remittances rather than deliver them promptly, and using them to speculate.[83]

The Hakka region around Meizhou also experienced a sudden inflow of coastal institutions, including banks. Its first modern bank, the Guangdong Provincial, was set up shortly before the war in April 1937 and was joined by around fifty branches of different banks in the war years.[84]

After the Japanese invasion, most *piju* stopped operating, at least for a while. Those that continued to operate in China moved inland, where most did their best to stay in touch with their customers at home and overseas. Most of those abroad closed down (although some persisted, as we shall see later in this chapter). All but a handful of Xiamen's *piju* fled in or around May 1938, first to the island of Gulangyu (an International Settlement until 1942) opposite Xiamen and then to Quanzhou, where more than twenty *piju* turned up.[85] The few remaining ones in Xiamen cut back their operations for a while to the barest minimum.[86] The amount remitted through Quanzhou leapt from 53 million guobi in 1938 to 120 million in 1939 and 365 million in 1941.[87]

In Meizhou, where *shuike* had always been particularly active, not only the *qiaopi* trade but the gold market was sustained during the war by their smuggling. Even the state bank got much of its foreign currency from *shuike*.[88] In the late 1930s, state authorities tried hard to introduce new regulations to bring the *shuike* under closer supervision, but the war and the government's lack of control at the village level thwarted them.

In this situation, Chinese state institutions became temporarily hegemonic in much of the *qiaopi* trade, more and more so as the war continued. After the outbreak of the European war, Britain, the Netherlands, and France tightened their grip on finances in their Southeast Asian colonies, but the Nationalist government negotiated a relaxation of the controls on remittances, a first step in the Chinese state's wartime assertion of its powers in this regard. Gradually, its role in the remittance trade stabilized, at the same time as that of the *piju* shrank or disappeared in many places. Even in areas, and periods, in which the *piju* survived or now and then revived, they usually depended on state banks and postal institutions to do the main part of their business; they themselves carried out no more than the first and final stages, the initial collection and the ultimate act of delivery. Between them, the *piju* and the state monopolized this style of remittance; in most places, the *shuike* no longer had much part in it.

In Japanese-occupied regions of southeastern China, the post office and its savings bank negotiated an agreement with the Japanese to keep remittance routes from Southeast Asia open, and for a while the volume of the trade increased. The Japanese and puppet authorities kept on nearly all of the old postal workers and preserved their work regime. For much of the war, the postal service kept up the flow of *huipi* at a more or less constant volume. In 1942, for example, the Japanese not only allowed the dispatch from Shantou of an accumulated backlog of more than ten thousand *huipi* but sent them free of charge, in the realization that without *huipi* further remittances would be unlikely. (However, they did insist on stamping the *huipi* with pro-Japanese political slogans.)

These contacts with the Japanese and the deliveries and collections of correspondence happened with the Guomindang's connivance or encouragement. *Pijiao* were allowed to deliver to villages on the condition that they reported their deliveries. Letters were delivered across enemy lines into occupied towns and villages "with seals unbroken"; in some senses, business carried on more or less as usual, at least for a while. In 1942 the Japanese and the puppets even negotiated direct deals on currency transfer with the Nationalist postal authorities in Qujiang, Guangdong, where the latter had reestablished their wartime headquarters. These authorities stayed in close touch with their branch in occupied Shantou. They not only supervised postal operations in occupied areas, especially regarding remittances, but issued policy directives.[89]

The Japanese and puppet authorities were keen to keep the remittances flowing directly into areas under their control (rather than by way of Qujiang), both in order to deny them to the Guomindang and to help buoy up the economy and the occupation with foreign currency. Both sides therefore competed to control the trade.[90] However, the Japanese needed time to stabilize their administration of the occupied areas, with the help of local puppets. In most of Southeast Asia, not yet under Japanese control, postal services continued to operate and ties to Hong Kong and Free China survived. In many cases, *piju* overseas continued to play their traditional role until late 1941, often using existing channels.[91] In China the Japanese sought to control the *piju*, *yinhao*, and *qianzhuang* by means of threats and inducements. After the start of the Pacific war and the Japanese invasion of Southeast Asia, the private remittance trade came under severe attack and largely closed down. Even so, *qiaopi* continued to arrive in occupied regions, where they greatly surpassed both the quantity and the value of those reaching the *qiaoxiang* of Free China.[92]

The pro-Japanese puppets reopened the post office in Shantou in July 1939, and a remittance service was restored within days. In the first six weeks after its reopening, the post office handled nearly three thousand *qiaopi* worth 319,219 yuan.[93] However, the goal was an even greater and more permanent inflow of resources. In September 1939, Japanese investigators asked what could be done to persuade more overseas Chinese to remit through Japanese banks, and they concluded that the main problem was the migrants' dislike of the currency used by the Japanese in China.[94]

The puppet authorities instituted a system of licenses for *pijiao* delivering *qiaopi* to the villages, in an effort to control them and stop them operating outside the Japanese "peace zone."[95] To shake up the trade, in February 1940 they organized Shantou's thirty-six surviving *piju* (there had been more than seventy in 1934–5) into a guild (*gonghui*) and ordered them to cooperate with Japanese-controlled banks in Taiwan to facilitate remittances.[96] The guild handled remittances worth 111 million yuan between March 1940 and February 1941, and it constituted a major part of the Japanese strategy to restore and control the *qiaopi* trade by co-opting its institutions.[97] By 1943 more than sixty *piju* were operating in occupied Shantou, with 658 sub-branches—only three fewer *piju* and seventy-five fewer sub-branches than in 1946.[98] However, not all *piju* stuck to the Japanese rules, and some secretly delivered to villages beyond Japanese control, at great personal risk.[99]

The Japanese also authorized branches of Taiwanese banks to open in Guangzhou and Shantou. They even arranged for remittances from Southeast Asia to be flown in military aircraft to Japanese consulates and embassies in Thailand and Vietnam, and from there to occupied cities in China, or directly from Thailand to Shantou.[100]

After the outbreak of the Pacific war in December 1941, only Thailand and Vietnam escaped formal occupation by Japan. Thailand's pact with the Japanese led to their de facto occupation of its cities and main lines of communication, but much of the local economy continued to operate along the old lines. The French Vichy regime allowed the Japanese to station troops in Indochina, but the Japanese never took over completely from the French. As a result, Thailand and Vietnam played a special role in keeping lines to China open.

Elsewhere in Southeast Asia, the Japanese occupation necessitated radical readjustments. In the immediate aftermath of the outbreak of the Pacific war, the *qiaopi* trade came to a standstill in the invaded countries when Japanese warships closed the sea lanes to Xiamen, Shantou, Guangdong, and Hainan. By 1943 the trade had started to revive, but it operated largely through Hong Kong. Some *piju* used the Taiwanese banks, as instructed by the occupying authorities, but these banks had branches only in Guangzhou and Shantou, which were beyond easy reach for most dependents. Eventually, nearly all the *qiaopi* from occupied Southeast Asia entered China by way of Hong Kong.[101]

In Thailand in 1942, the newly formed state bank took official control of the *qiaopi* trade (though the trade survived underground in independent but greatly shrunken form) and the Thai government allowed only *qiaopi* destined for Japanese-controlled parts of China to be officially remitted.[102] Before the Pacific war, the Japanese had found it hard to compete with the trade through Gulangyu or the Hong Kong banks. After 1941, they encouraged remittances from Singapore and elsewhere, but most overseas Chinese were fiercely anti-Japanese, and their families in China had little confidence in the chubeiquan currency imposed by the puppet authority in 1942, for it had an extremely adverse exchange rate.[103] So only a minority collaborated with the campaign, which was less effective than the Japanese had hoped. Remittances worth twenty million yuan were received in 1940. However, in December 1942, normally the busiest month of the year, only 802 remittances reached Shantou, totaling 123,000 fabi, and a much smaller amount reached the surrounding area.[104] Throughout the whole of 1943, only fourteen thousand *qiaopi* reached Shantou, compared with eighteen thousand each month in 1938.[105]

In the *qiaoxiang* and the nearby ports they occupied, the Japanese ordered *piju* to submit remittances for inspection and stamping on receiving them, and only then allowed the remittances' further passage into the Japanese-controlled "peace zone." *Qiaopi* addressed to destinations beyond the "peace zone" were subject to confiscation.[106]

THE DONGXING ROUTE INTO THE *QIAOXIANG*

How did remittances not under Japanese control reach the occupied and block-aded *qiaoxiang* in the war years? At one time, it was widely assumed that the *qiaopi* trade largely came to a halt as a result of the invasion, but recent *qiaopi* studies have identified various paths along which substantial remittances continued to flow into the region.

We have already seen that some *qiaopi* arrived in the occupied areas with the knowledge and collusion of the Chinese post office, especially at the beginning of the war. Later, other routes formed that did not depend on collusion. Before the outbreak of the Pacific war, Southeast Asian banks sent remittances through Hong Kong, after which they were smuggled by fishing boats to Lufeng on the Guang-dong coast and then taken inland. Others were sent by air to Shaoguan in northern Guangdong and then taken south. Searching out routes was a dangerous and dif-ficult business. One representative of the Guangdong Provincial Bank walked forty miles through wartorn villages to establish a viable (but short-lived) link between Hong Kong and Raoping. Some *piju* hired *shuike* to slip across enemy lines, and the *shuike* phenomenon underwent a marked revival in some regions (although four out of five *shuike* were said to have been killed in the war years).[107]

After the start of the Pacific war in 1941, however, these routes were no longer open, and new ones were urgently sought. At one point, Nationalist planners and Chaoshanese *piju* operators aimed to funnel remittances through Guangzhouwan (Kwangchowan), a small French enclave on Guangdong's Leizhou Peninsula ruled (anomalously) by Free France until 1943, in the belief that the route would be rela-tively secure. Merchants from Chaoshan controlled much of the enclave's economy and ran a guild hall, or *huiguan*, there. However, the plan failed, mainly because the route required a sea passage to Chaoshan, which was too hazardous at the time, and because the enclave lacked the facilities to deal with Southeast Asian currencies.[108]

Eventually, a way into China was opened not by Nationalist administrators but by *qiaopi* entrepreneurs acting on their own initiative. The breakthrough came in 1942. The *qiaopi* trade was in its deepest trough at the time, with most *piju* closed and their workforce scattered. During this crisis, some *shuike* routes revived, as we have seen, but they covered only a fraction of the trade's geography. The banks also played a role. But the boldest and most striking innovation was the blazing for this traditionally seaborne enterprise of new land routes through Guangxi and Yun-nan, provinces bordering on Indochina. These routes did not benefit all regions equally. Most migrants from southern Fujian, for example, lived in maritime Southeast Asia, so the new land route was irrelevant in their case, except for the minority of Fujianese in Thailand and Indochina.[109]

Finding the land routes required a perilous and protracted search. The search started in December 1941 when Chen Zhifang, a refugee in Haiphong from

Shantou, where he had worked as a fishnet maker, offered to take some *qiaopi* to fisherman acquaintances of his on the coast who were familiar with the sea routes to China. It occurred to him that a land route out of Vietnam might also be possible, so he set about reconnoitering the Chinese border. He worked alone, often sleeping rough in the mountains. He investigated three routes before finally settling on Dongxing (then in Guangdong, but now in Guangxi), the only established crossing into China still more or less open to traffic. By that time, much of the Chinese coast was under Japanese control, so Dongxing was a rare lifeline. Traditionally, it was a crossroads for trade from Sichuan, Yunnan, Guizhou, and Guangxi as well as Vietnam. Chinese and Vietnamese currencies intermingled in the local economy. The mountain roads into Dongxing were relatively safe from Japanese attack.[110] After sending a couple of test remittances from Dongxing to Chaoshan and checking that they had arrived safely, he returned to Haiphong and organized a visit to the border by local *piju* owners to show them his discovery.[111]

Initially the *qiaopi* traders in Vietnam doubted Chen's proposal, but eventually the owners of more than a dozen *piju* and bank branches (traditional and modern) were sufficiently convinced to send staff to Dongxing, which for a couple of years assumed the pivotal role in the *qiaopi* business previously played (on a far greater scale) by Hong Kong.[112] Chen became an iconic figure in the trade and showed courage and daring. When the Japanese arrested and tortured *piju* owners in Vietnam and forced them to reveal his name, he became a hunted man, but he continued to tour the region under assumed identities.[113]

The flow of remittances through Dongxing mitigated the Chaoshan famine of 1943 by injecting around $10 million per month, mainly in Vietnamese currency, into the *qiaoxiang* economy.[114] (The precise amount is impossible to quantify, given that the trade was secret.) *Piju* from Chaoshan, along with a smaller number from southern Fujian, set up liaison stations in Dongxing. At first, the town served only Vietnamese routes, but it soon incorporated Bangkok as well, and through Bangkok news of the Dongxing route spread to Cambodia and Laos. In Thailand and Indochina, the Japanese controlled only the cities: smaller towns were under puppet rule, which was easier to circumvent. The *piju* in these places revived old methods: representatives fanned out across the towns and villages, collecting remittances from the mines and factories either directly or through agents (mainly shopkeepers). In Bangkok itself, four new *piju* started up between 1942 and 1944.[115] China's post office and state banks also played a crucial role in the Dongxing operation.[116]

The currency scene in occupied Southeast Asia was chaotic, so the wartime *qiaopi* trade tended to be conducted in the form of small gold bars, slotted into a sort of ammunition belt hidden by the courier inside an army-style greatcoat. There were four principal routes from Southeast Asia to Dongxing by way of Hanoi and Haiphong. Bangkok couriers went by train to Udon Thani in northern Thailand and then took a motor vehicle to the river (a day's drive) and crossed into

Laos, then eastwards into Vietnam. The crossing point was at Nghe An, one of the poorest parts of the north, known as Vietnam's Yan'an because many of Ho Chi Minh's generals came from there. From Nghe An, they took the train to Hanoi, where they changed the gold into Chinese guobi at a courier station. They then went on to Haiphong, where they took a steamer to Mong Cai, hugging the coast and traveling by night to evade Japanese warplanes. Across the river, which was crossable in winter, were Guangxi and the relatively unfortified town of Dongxing. However, the border between China and Vietnam was not entirely uncontrolled and had to be crossed in secret by fording the river.[117]

Dongxing boomed as a result of the trade. Teahouses and restaurants sprang up to serve the scores of employees of the banks and *piju*. New hostels opened for the growing number of migrants that passed into and out of China through the town, helped by a special station set up by the government's Office for Overseas Chinese Affairs.[118] The office also assisted several thousand Chinese refugees from Vietnam, who reached Dongxing in some twenty batches.[119]

In Dongxing, the remittances (70 percent of which were in Vietnamese currency) were changed into Nationalist or puppet currency, depending on their end destination. From Dongxing, they were either taken directly to the *qiaoxiang* or were routed through Chongqing, Guilin, and other Chinese-controlled cities.[120] The routes out of Dongxing into China were arduous and risky, along bandit-infested mountain paths.[121] Some couriers lost their lives in attacks.[122] To protect the trade, Shantou entrepreneurs set up a well-armed bodyguard several dozen strong.[123] From Dongxing, representatives of the Shantou *piju* took the remittances back to the *qiaoxiang* villages, where the *huipi* was reduced, for security reasons, to a mere signature on a slip of paper. Inevitably, the war slowed the trade enormously. Remittances that normally would have taken a fortnight now took one to three months, with the couriers travelling by car, lorry, and boat and sometimes on foot. Because of the delays and the insubstantial receipts, remitters were understandably anxious, and there were frequent quarrels between them and the *piju* staff.[124]

The Dongxing route remained open for three years, from July 1942 until the summer of 1944, when Japan's Operation Ichi-Go led to the fall of Nanning and endangered the entire region, forcing the banks and *piju* to retreat from the border town. The final act was in September 1945, when Chen Zhifang returned briefly to sell off gold bars left behind during the retreat and sent the proceeds on to Chaoshan.[125] Thus the curtain fell on a heroic interlude in the *qiaopi* trade.

During the war, China was broken into pieces under two rival regimes, or three counting the Communists. The framework of the nation-state disintegrated, and even provinces and regions ceased to function as coherent units. In those years, the *qiaopi* trade survived by reviving or focusing even more intently on the traditional networks that had given birth to it, knitted together in the wider context of rival political forces, social classes under intense pressure, new and old associations, and competing states.[126]

Where the *qiaopi* trade was concerned, the main effect of the war was to drive most *piju* to the wall, at least until after the Japanese surrender in 1945. Only a few *piju* survived, and the dense web of *qiaopi* routes thinned out into a few separate or barely connected stems. The main Chinese beneficiary of the war was the state, together with its banks and postal services, whose relative weight in the remittance trade shot up. This happened because the war pitted the Chinese and Japanese states against one another and required the fullest possible mobilization of each side in every field. After the war, however, the Chinese state lost much of the ground it had gained during it because of its general failings, including corruption and its inability to maintain a stable government and a modicum of prosperity and security. An augur of its incompetence and unreliability was the fate of the great backlog of *qiaopi* that had amassed during the war, when old routes were blocked. By the time the *qiaopi* reached the villages, months or years after their initial remitting, they had been whittled down to a small fraction of their original value by inflation and devaluation; the state, whose role in the trade had grown so massively in the war years, proved incapable of protecting the interests of *qiaopi* recipients against the effects of its policies.[127]

QIAOPI IN THE POSTWAR YEARS, 1945–49

After the war, the prospects looked anything but good for the *piju*, given the banks' wartime weakening of the *pijus'* hold on the *qiaopi* trade. The Nanjing government was keener than ever to tighten its grip on remittances in preparation for the civil war with the Communists, the resumption of which was clearly imminent in the wake of the Japanese surrender. In what everyone knew would be a fight to the death, control over the lucrative *qiaopi* trade was deemed essential.

Starting shortly after the Japanese surrender in 1945, Chinese authorities presided over the full and rapid restoration of the remittance system, in which the Bank of China and various provincial banks and the post office exercised an unprecedented level of authority. In 1945 and early 1946, the Bank of China established, strengthened, or reestablished branches at home and abroad, and also set up agreements with various agencies (including the OCBC) that agreed to act on its behalf. Its main priority in 1945 was to deal with the wartime backlog of *qiaopi*. In the Guangdong *qiaoxiang*, the post office was better entrenched than other government bodies, and it played a major role in the remittance trade in the immediate postwar years. The authorities aimed not just to restore the trade but to reform it by simplifying its procedures and making them more efficient. In the long run, however, their plans collapsed, and the remittances they had dreamed of bringing under their secure and permanent control were instead smuggled into the country by illegal means.

The smuggling grew in volume throughout the second half of the 1940s, reaching a crescendo in 1948–9, during the Guomindang's brief remaining half-life. The official institutions designated to run the *qiaopi* trade were largely sidelined by recrudescent *piju* and other similar organizations. In Hainan in 1947, for example, only 15 percent of remittances passed through official hands; the remaining 85 percent navigated private channels. In Chaoshan in 1947, 14.9 percent were handled by state banks or the post office, while *piju* controlled the rest. Siyi presented a similar picture. In Guangdong in 1946, 61.5 percent of remittances happened through nonofficial channels, and by 1948 this figure had reached nearly 99 percent. The significance of this loss cannot be overstated; in 1947 alone, the overall amount remitted was just under US$60 million.

Why did the *piju* win out over the state in the postwar battle of remittances? The main reason was the inability of the latter to find a way to deal with the onrush of inflation that destroyed much of the value of remittances in the interval between dispatch and receipt. The background to this inflation was the ever-worsening state of the Nationalist government's finances in the postwar years, mainly as a result of military expenditure to fund the civil war against the Communists. Between 1946 and 1948, this rose from 60 to 64 percent of state expenditure. The resulting gap in finances was filled by the massive printing of new money: the amount of fabi in circulation in 1948 was 578 times that in 1946 and 506,637 times that in 1937, on the eve of the Japanese invasion, and prices in Shanghai in July 1948 were nearly three million times higher than in prewar times.

The government's strategy for dealing with inflation was to "stabilize" prices, including the price of foreign currency, which was kept below the market price. Inevitably, a black market sprang up, offering a more realistic rate of exchange far higher than the official one. The government tried various remedies, but none worked for more than a short while. The official exchange rate in 1947 oscillated between 24.1 and 69 percent of the black-market rate and averaged 31 percent. State organizations urged a change of strategy, but the central bank failed to act, in the belief that its nominal monopoly of remittances was sufficient to keep a grip on the situation.

Other reasons for the *piju* ascendancy included shortcomings, most of them long-standing, in the handling of *qiaopi* by state institutions like banks and the postal service. The Bank of China dominated the remittance economy in the late 1940s, and although regional banks like the Guangdong Provincial Bank were well represented locally, they were refused permission to expand overseas, where they had far fewer branches than the central bank. As a result, the Guangdong Provincial Bank was forced to rely extensively on agents to act for it abroad. Its relations with these agents were not always stable and predictable. Some agents represented multiple clients in the same field. The post office savings bank, which was even better represented within China than regional banks, had even less representation than those banks outside the Chinese mainland—just one office, in Hong Kong. The networks run by these state bodies had practically no presence in the rural *qiaoxiang*. In the Chaoshan region, 91.6 percent of villages and small towns had no postal service; in the Xingning-Meixian region, 83.6 percent had none.

Non-state organizations—principally *piju*, but also *yinhao*, *qianzhuang*, *piao-hao*, and various sorts of trading companies—had many strengths and advantages, and a better reputation than their official rivals. They had far more branches in all the *qiaoxiang* and in all the Chinese communities overseas. Unlike the banks and their agents, they did not sit back and wait for customers to come knocking, but actively sought them out. The banks, in contrast, opened their overseas branches in the financial districts alongside Western banks, rather than in Chinatown, and in China they largely ignored the rural areas inhabited by emigrants' dependents.

The speed with which the *qiaopi* arrived in China and the *huipi* bounced back mattered a lot to remitters and recipients alike. Here, the *piju* owners left the official traders standing. In most cases, the receipt and further transmission of remittances was organized with military precision by the *piju* in the offices, docks, and villages. The race to be quickest was not between *piju* and the state but among the *piju*, each of which bent every effort to reducing to an absolute minimum the time spent on each separate phase of the operation. The official trade, by contrast, was reliant on agencies (usually privately owned) that tended to let the *qiaopi* grow into a backlog in order to save costs. The longer the delay, the fewer the remittances they received—leading to a vicious cycle in which *qiaopi* were left unattended for ever-lengthening periods. Delivery was further delayed by the agencies' habit of employing delivery men with little knowledge of or contacts in the villages they served. Even trading companies that delivered remittances as a sideline had better ties to their clientele than the official traders did, for they too had extensive networks and long-standing relationships to one another and, where necessary, to the *piju*.

Moreover, official traders were hampered by regulations, many of them seemingly irrational: for example, they were required to register remittances in fabi, regardless of the currency in which they were received, which cost the remitter money; and they tended to summon the recipient to receive the remittance, which again cost him or her time and effort (unlike the *piju*, which took them straight to the door). They were also denied an adequate money supply, which further delayed dispensing the remittances and made it hard for them to respond flexibly to changing circumstances. At one point, they were instructed to demand that shopkeepers act as guarantors when dependents turned up to collect their remittances, which was highly inconvenient for the recipients, especially in remote areas without shops, or that recipients verify their identity by using specimen impressions of seals filed for checking purposes in local banks. The *piju*, by contrast, employed only local people and were therefore able to operate a system of "payment on sight" (*jianmian jifu*). This was a difference between two historic forms of individual identification—on the one hand, the method of the aspirant modern state with its anonymous but tabulated citizenry, which is required to confirm its identity bureaucratically, and on the other the traditional method of identification, with reference to personal relations based on blood and place.

Huipi were an essential moment in the remittance process; without their prompt receipt, most remitters would hesitate to remit a second time. The *qiaopi* phenomenon was complex and meant different things to different people. For some, the financial remittance was the main thing, even to the extent that some remitters did not even send an accompanying note. At the other extreme, the act and content of the written communication (*qiaopi* or *huipi*) was more important than the money, a negligible appendage to the letter, with the same symbolic meaning as a *hongbao*, the pennies given to children in a red envelope as a New Year gift. However, state organizations paid *huipi* relatively little attention and took their time in delivering them.

To satisfy their customers and increase their own income from the trade at a time of runaway inflation, the *piju* adopted various strategies and tactics. Because the official rate of exchange in China was far below that on the black market, *piju* transferred remittances by way of money orders through Hong Kong, secretly rather than through official Chinese channels. Being close to all the major *qiaoxiang*, Hong Kong was ideal for smuggling into them. It was a main gateway into south China. It had a strong currency, and it permitted the free exchange of foreign currencies. Another way of evading official currency controls and the high fees levied on exchange in China was to export money in the form of goods, a tactic first developed to circumvent Southeast Asian controls on currency export. Finally, the *piju* smuggled gold and silver or cash into Hong Kong, where they sold it to buy fabi. By methods of this sort, they made an ever-greater killing as the discrepancy between the official and the black-market price of the fabi widened.

Licensing was supposed to put an end to evasion, but it largely failed to do so. A minority of *piju* and other firms failed to register with the authorities, and even the great majority of those that did so continued their evading. Needless to say, *shuike* and *xunchengma* were even less likely to conform to the requirements of officialdom.

State financial organizations like the central or provincial banks and the post office begged the government to work more energetically to control or outlaw evasion by the *piju* and other private firms, but this proved impossible. The *piju* had a special relationship with the post office from which both sides benefited. The volume of *qiaopi* that passed through the post office was many times greater than that through the Bank of China. In Shantou, for example, the post office derived 70 percent of its income from the *qiaopi* and *huipi* trade.

Moreover, the *piju* were like knotweed, linked by a ubiquitous and ineradicable rhizome system with hundreds of outlets in China and abroad. Even though the authorities could take some measures against domestic firms, they were usually helpless in the case of those operating from overseas. Even foreign governments were often at a loss: during the prohibition on *piju* in Vietnam in 1948, for example, most *shuike* and *piju* managed to evade controls. The *piju* utilized several different channels to transfer remittances into China, including foreign banks and other institutions. Government laxness and corruption usually rendered counter-measures ineffective.

Because they were unable to suppress the *qiaopi* trade, the authorities tried a dual strategy in the late 1940s of simultaneously restricting and exploiting it for the authorities' own purposes. *Piju* sometimes even used local overseas branches of the Bank of China as their agents, although some of their operations were technically illegal. In some instances the Guangdong Provincial Bank strove to form ties to the overseas *piju* and to transfer funds on their behalf at preferential rates of exchange, and even used some domestic *piju* as its agents.

Why did the state fail to achieve its aim of monopolizing the remittance trade? There were, in sum, three main reasons. First, its currency policy was perceived by emigrants and their dependents to be unreasonable and unfair. By artificially inflating the price of the fabi on the exchange market, it sought to reduce the value of remittances in the state's interests. However, this price was in reality set by international market relations, which could not be arbitrarily manipulated from Nanjing. The paper money belched out by its minters lost it the confidence of Chinese everywhere, including in the *qiaoxiang*. Second, state administration of the *qiaopi* system was wholly inadequate and incapable of competing with the private version of the trade. It was too poorly spread (the post office reached just 10 percent of the Chaoshan region), and it failed to win people's trust and confidence. Its method of identification (seals, cards, guarantors) was inappropriate in backward rural areas. Even in Guangfu, which was much more open to modern influences and where the Gold Mountain shops had already started to decline as a result of those influences, evasion was impossible to eradicate and took modern forms. Third, the Nationalist authorities were generally corrupt and incompetent at all levels, from top to bottom. Far from arresting the evaders, in many cases they secretly shielded them, and where they took firm action against the *piju*, they risked sparking mass disaffection.

These official shortcomings and abuses were no secret even at the time. Studies published in China between 1946 and 1949 openly concluded that the widespread evasion of controls by remitters was due to unfair exchange rates and poor management of remittances by corrupt and incompetent officials. These studies also noted that the principal method of evasion was to use checks in the case of North American remittances and to use the services of the *piju* in Southeast Asia.

The state never won its war against the *qiaopi* traders, and its efforts to stem the trade grew ever weaker and less convincing as its own final and general collapse in

1949 approached. It tried out various reforms in its dying years, but they were largely designed to suit its own interests rather than those of the remitters and recipients. The central state also alienated the official and semiofficial provincial and local organizations working in the remittance field by relentlessly squeezing the trade, so that very soon those organizations spent more time and effort trying to defend their own sectional interests than dealing with the problem of evasion. Some local state bodies came almost to a standstill as the crisis of remittances, and of China, deepened. In mid-1948, the Shantou post office sacked all its delivery men to save money. Instructions issued by the central authorities were increasingly ignored, and evasion became increasingly commonplace, if not universal. In 1949 the authorities loosened controls on both remittances and its local representatives working in the remittance trade, but although these measures were undoubtedly fairer than those that preceded them, they had little effect on evasion and have gone down in histories of the Chinese post office as "a final radiance of the setting sun."[128]

So the *piju* as an institution not only survived the Sino-Japanese War but bounced back with renewed vigor after it, and on an even greater scale, by diversifying its operations and cooperating where necessary with the banks. As soon as the Japanese surrendered, Chinese migrants and their descendants in Southeast Asia rushed to renew contact with China. The *piju* stayed open day and night, and a huge pile of remittances built up. New *piju* sprang up on all sides, many of them unlicensed. During these catch-up years, the private *qiaopi* trade entered its most hectic period ever.[129]

Manila, for example, had more than 180 *piju* in 1948, despite hostile measures by the Chinese post office, whose employees deliberately delayed remittances, committed fraud, and stole money.[130] There were other *piju* in other towns and cities of the Philippines.[131] (The post office's actions led to a wave of protests, including by members of the famous Philippine Overseas Chinese Anti-Japanese Army.[132]) In Singapore and Thailand, historians describe the years 1946–8 as the *qiaopi* trade's "golden age." There were seventy-nine *piju* in Bangkok's Sampeng Lane and hundreds more that did not officially advertise themselves as *piju*.[133] The Shantou region had 130 domestic *piju* in 1946 and a further 451 overseas. These received more than five million *qiaopi* between 1947 and 1949, peaking at just under two million in 1948, a total remittance of more than HK$100 million annually.[134] In southern Fujian, sub-branches of urban *piju* spread like wildfire across the villages to cope with the upsurge in demand. In 1949 there were 1,282 such branches in the Fujian interior.[135]

Starting in 1945, the *qiaopi* trade was hit simultaneously by (a) bans and restrictions imposed by colonial and newly independent governments in Southeast Asia, which did their best to force remitters to act through the banks and tried to prevent relief funds reaching China; and (b) by chaos and anti-*qiaopi* measures in China.[136] The trade also suffered from internally induced decline. Couriers were hard to recruit, for the *qiaopi* routes were fraught with danger as China descended into economic and political turmoil, and the *piju* had lost touch with many of their prewar agents. To add to the general sense of crisis, generational change and the Southeast Asian block on new migration from China led to a loss of custom.[137]

Couriers were widely deemed to have become less trustworthy and were observed to abscond more frequently than in the past, despite attempts to tighten up tracking and regulation. This was in part because of the postwar rise of a black market in the *qiaopi* trade. The *qiaopi* trade's underbelly had always verged on the mildly criminal, and the increasing resort to secrecy put its traditional mechanisms under severe pressure.[138]

For these and other reasons, the *shuike* phenomenon shrank after the peace, when the *piju*, sidelined for much of the war, came to play an ever greater role. However, the reputation of the *piju* also began to suffer. Because of China's galloping inflation and confusion of currencies, as well as the new restrictions in China and overseas, the entire trade tended to slip underground, leading to even greater chaos. If remittance smugglers were caught, they were fined heavily and the remittances they had in their possession were likely to be confiscated. Some *piju* owners deliberately held on to remittances for as long as possible to make an easy killing from the inflation. As a result of this procrastination, some dependents received a remittance several times smaller than its original value; when it finally did arrive, they rushed immediately to buy things in the local store, where prices were shooting up by the minute. (In 1949, most *piju* switched to using the Hong Kong dollar to deal with this problem.) The increasing corruption of the *piju* in the late 1940s caused many remitters to lose confidence in them as an institution.[139]

However, the newly revived *piju* continued to hold their own against the banks, which were unable to match the black-market rates observed by the *piju*.[140] For example, in March 1946 the US dollar was officially worth 20 yuan, but on the black market it fetched between 1,459 and 2,022 yuan. In 1947, 87,800 million yuan entered Shantou through *piju*, compared with just 9,453 million through the local branch of the Bank of China.[141] The *piju* were also a safeguard against official corruption, which soared to ever greater heights in the Guomindang's last years on the mainland (though not, of course, against the *pijus'* own proclivity, which also grew with the chaos, to act corruptly). After 1948, however, China's collapse into chaos dealt a severe blow to the *qiaopi* trade, and many *piju* stopped trading, in most cases for good.[142]

QIAOPI UNDER THE COMMUNISTS

It is a wry fact that the *qiaopi* trade, born of the masses, was finally wound up after 1949 by a government that proclaimed itself guardian, product, and representative of the masses. But the trade's demise did not happen all at once. The Communists, like the Nationalists before them, were deeply aware of its benefits and uses, not just for migrants' dependents but for the national economy. Moreover, they ran a far stronger and, at least in the early years, more honest and effective state that was better able to realize its goals than the one it overthrew.

The Communists' acquaintance with *qiaopi* preceded their ascent to power. Communist guerrillas controlled many of the villages in or around the Fujian and Guangdong *qiaoxiang* in the 1930s and the 1940s (though in many cases spasmodically), and during the civil war of 1946–9, they issued their own temporary local currency, the *yuminjuan*, in an effort to stabilize prices. The Communists required transfer into this currency of *qiaopi* brought into guerrilla areas by couriers.[143]

We know little about Communist involvement in the internal workings of the *qiaopi* trade. Given the radical inclinations of many young overseas Chinese, especially just before, during, and after the Sino-Japanese War, and given the nature of the trade, which was both financially attractive to the party and offered it a secret path and line of communications into parts of China where it had been strongly rooted ever since the 1920s, it would not be surprising to learn that Communists did infiltrate the *piju*, but we have only one record of such infiltration. That is the case of Zhang Bogong, who was born in Thailand in 1921, "returned" to China in 1925, and joined the Communist party in 1939 in Puning in southeastern Guangdong, where he ran its liaison station. Zhang Bogong gave the party three thousand yuan of remittance money to fund its Chaozhou-Meixian Committee and a bookshop, and in 1942 the party located him back to Thailand. There he ran a remittance office that was highly lucrative and employed up-to-date electronic equipment; he used some of the profit to fund the party and used the radio to send political, military, and economic intelligence back to China.[144] Zhang's activity is the only evidence we have so far of a Communist association with the *qiaopi* trade in the revolutionary years.

The *piju* as a corporate body embracing both workers and employers did not survive the revolution of 1949. During the transition to state socialism in the 1950s and the early 1960s, the *qiaopi* trade was politicized and reengineered by the authorities along lines of social class by separating the *piju* workers from the *piju* owners. (This campaign was probably less successful than first envisaged, in a trade still dominated by ties of kinship.) The *pijiao* and other toilers acquired a new designation, *qiaopi* officers, and were organized into trade unions. Thus a new labor politics was injected into the *qiaopi* system. *Qiaopi* workers now attended union meetings and conferences. However, the *qiaopi* union was a typical Communist-style trade union, designed to act as a "school of socialism" and a tool with which the authorities sought to mobilize labor activism rather than as an authentic voice of the workers.

The Communist authorities in China staged several rounds of major conferences in Fujian and Guangdong in the 1950s to sing the praises of the *qiaopi* trade and "consult" its practitioners.[145] At the time, remittances were still one of China's two main sources of foreign currency (the other being the sale of domestic products overseas, usually conducted on highly disadvantageous terms). For several years, the young state formulated its policy regarding "overseas Chinese," their dependents in China, and the *qiaopi* carefully and sensitively. Policy conducted under He Xiangning (1878–1972), a Guomindang leftist loyal to the new regime and director-general of the PRC State Council's Overseas Chinese Affairs Committee when it was established in October 1949, was not unfavorable to dependents and their overseas relatives, who continued to remit on a relatively large scale.[146]

At first, the Communists left in place much of the legislation and many of the practices regarding *qiaopi* that they had inherited from the Nationalist era. The trade continued in good health for a while, and the volume of remittances rose in places. More than 150,000 *qiaopi* reached Shantou between November 1949 and mid-January 1950, with a value of 7.97 million yuan. In 1951 even more money was remitted, as prices in China stabilized, Southeast Asian economies grew, *qiaopi* systems in China settled back into place, and remitters started to understand and gain confidence in the new setup. The impact of land reform on wealthy families also played a role, for the loss of rent and interest forced some previously landowning dependents to request additional remittances from migrants.[147] In Quanzhou, 2,165.3 million renminbi were remitted after 1951 (the figures cover the period up to 1990). Jinjiang received US$105 million between 1954 and 1975.[148] Meixian received US$4.85 million in 1952 and US$5.63 million in 1957. In 1953 more than 60 percent of remittances continued to be made through *piju*, and in 1955 the percentage had barely dropped.[149] Even between 1958 and 1964, generally a low point for the trade, 14 million Singapore dollars were remitted annually from Singapore and Malaysia. Political donations were also remitted to official causes.[150]

Piju played a major role in the early years of the new regime. For a few months, everything continued in the same old way. There was no longer any great disparity between the bank's and the black-market rate for the Hong Kong dollar, so the *piju* were happy to cooperate with the People's Bank of China, especially after the renminbi began to stabilize. Remittances were paid out promptly, and the currency black market quickly disappeared. In March 1950, *piju* were registered under the new authorities.[151] Of the 57 *piju* in Meizhou in 1949, 39 were allowed to register, including 23 with direct ties to *piju* overseas.[152] In southern Fujian, 185 registered.[153] In August 1950, a national conference called on *piju* to defend migrants' interests and pledged to leave profits from the trade in private hands.[154] In 1953 and 1954, at the urging of a conference in Guangzhou on the welfare of *qiaojuan* ("migrants' dependents"), the postal authorities in Shantou and Xiamen abolished the domestic surcharge on *qiaopi* on the grounds that postage had already been paid overseas and that to levy a second charge would be inappropriate.[155] In 1955 the State Council confirmed in a declaration that remittances were legal income, and it encouraged the *piju* to cooperate with the state and expand their networks. Even during the "socialist high tide" of 1956, the distinction between private and public interest was maintained in the case of *qiaopi*.[156]

Shuike were also encouraged to register with the authorities; several hundred did in Meizhou in 1950. The *shuike* also acquired a new official title, *qiaopiyuan* ("*qiaopi* officer"), in recognition of their incorporation into the state. However, by 1960 the trade had practically died out.[157]

The *pijus'* days were also numbered because of changes both at home and abroad. In Thailand, the biggest single source of remittances, the government took measures to control foreign currency in the early 1950s that radically affected their functioning. Seventy closed down, and although the measure was revoked after protests and campaigning, not all reopened.[158] In 1951, the US Foreign Assets Control Board forbade remittances to China, and most of its Southeast Asian allies did the same.[159]

Qiaopi officials in China reverted to underground methods invented in earlier years to deal with foreign governments' attempts to ban or restrict remittances. To outwit foreign inspectors, they stopped writing words in their communications with remitters that might be potentially incriminating or switched to oral communication though trusted intermediaries.[160] Secret codes were revived. For example, receipt of "100 pounds of rice" acknowledged in a *huipi* might stand for "HK$100." To defeat the blockade, *piju* serving overseas remitters also revived "tricks" (usually derived from popular handbooks like *Sanshiliu ji*, "Thirty-six stratagems") from earlier years. These included "representing many by few" (understating the amount remitted), "breaking up the whole into parts" (to get round restrictive quotas), and "crossing the sea by trickery" (concealing the amount remitted, by recording it underneath the postage stamp, for example).[161] In Guangdong, a special "*huipi* team" was set up to supervise the writing of *huipi* and to ensure that they observed guidelines aimed at ensuring secrecy. Remittances were overwhelmingly routed through Hong Kong's Chinese banks, also to evade controls.[162]

In the late 1950s, the *qiaopi* trade was put under the direction and control of the People's Bank of China. Each county in the *qiaoxiang* set up a remittance section under the bank and campaigned energetically, through small teams of workers, to increase the amount remitted, as a contribution to China's national reconstruction. *Qiaopi* officers, the *shuike* and *pijiao* of the old days, encouraged dependents to badger their relatives for money to build houses, and rival teams competed with one another to see who could raise the most foreign currency from targets. Often, team members wrote letters on the recipients' behalf: one team in Zhangzhou wrote more than 3,500 letters and traced 267 migrated relatives between 1956 and 1960 in the endless search for new sources of remittance.[163] They also encouraged the illiterate wives of migrants to learn to read and write so they could request remittances themselves.[164]

This campaign to boost remittances sometimes backfired. In Canada, for example, reports or rumors in Chinatown of Communists writing "blackmail" letters to Chinese migrants urging them to send more money (together with reports of anti-Chinese "investigations" in Canada) led to a drop in the volume of remittances.[165]

Remittances were a crucial lifeline during the famine of 1959–61, when *shuike* were said to have turned up in the villages bearing money and food, which was declared tax-free in the final year of the crisis. In 1961, 13 million kilos of grain and 5.7 million kilos of other food were sent through Chaoshan.[166] In the 1970s, *piju* assisted dependents by importing cement, steel, and chemical fertilizer on their behalf.[167]

Despite these developments, the trade started to decline in the late 1950s. There were several reasons for this development. In some Southeast Asian countries, the authorities clamped down ever more forcibly on remittances and arrested traders and couriers. In Vietnam, an anti-Chinese campaign in 1956 led to a bout of persecution of the Chinese minority. In China itself, the authorities took action against currency smuggling, which revived toward the end of the decade, and placed the trade under "mass surveillance." The socialization of agriculture in the mid-1950s frightened many migrants, who feared being denounced as "class enemies" if they sent money back to China. Whatever government spokespersons might say to reassure remitters, envious or radical local leaders often acted on their own authority, harassing recipients of big remittances and even confiscating the remittances.[168] In 1956 the *qiaopi* trade was reorganized and federated, although *piju* were still allowed to operate under their old names and signboards.[169] In 1958 the ownership of the remaining *piju* changed from "collective" to "of the whole people," a further move in the direction of their complete subjection to state control.[170] In the course of the 1950s, the number of *piju* fell, by nearly half in southern Fujian, to around one hundred.[171] As a result of all these factors, the volume of remittances started to shrink in 1957 and fell to a new low in 1959, when Spring Festival remittances fell by more than half over the previous year.[172] In 1962 the amount remitted through Chaoshan stood at one-fifth of the 1952 level. This was followed by a brief revival, to which the Cultural Revolution then put an end.[173]

During the Cultural Revolution, prosperous migrants and their dependents or descendants who had bought property in the *qiaoxiang* became "objects of dictatorship" and, for the most part, stopped remitting. As for their dependents, they risked persecution and criminalization.[174] Some wrote letters breaking off relations with their relatives overseas. Authorities stamped the envelopes bearing their *huipi* with strident and intimidating political slogans and directives.[175] In 1969 the *piju* were incorporated under the People's Bank of China as so-called "*qiaopi* stations." It was not until the early 1970s that the hostility toward the trade abated.[176]

In 1979 the *qiaopi* trade was fully subsumed into the state financial system (though it seems to have lasted a little longer in some places than in others).[177] It became an integral part of the People's Bank of China, which now guaranteed delivery of remittances within five days. Thus, the *piju* finally disappeared from the stage.[178] At the same time, the accent in government pronouncements (following the party's Third Plenum in 1978) switched from remitting to investing, as well as to donating to good causes in China.[179] The *shuike* were also decreed out of existence in 1977.[180]

This chapter traces the evolution and roles of the *qiaopi* trade in modern China's economic and political transformations. It leads to three conclusions. First, the *qiaopi* trade was one of a number of key financial institutions that proved to be indispensable for China's economic modernization and for its political survival as an independent nation-state. Second, in the course of interacting with and participating in China's domestic economy and body politic, the agents and institutions that underlay the *qiaopi* trade (principally, *piju* and *shuike*) underwent tremendous changes, although their mode of operation remained, at bottom, largely identical from the mid-nineteenth to the mid-twentieth centuries: they built on trust and sustained their operations by depending on primordial ties of place, kinship, and dialect and a complex set of associated transnational mechanisms. Third, in the course of the century in which *qiaopi* culture arose and flourished, the nation-state, in China and the world, grew rapidly in power and influence. This was particularly the case after the founding of the PRC and the emergence of newly independent nation-states in Southeast Asia, where most diasporic Chinese lived. The *qiaopi* trade and its agents and mechanisms evolved against precisely this backdrop. The Chinese state (and, to a lesser extent, other states) sought to bring this channel of financial and social connections between China and the outside world under its formal jurisdiction. This was especially true after 1949, when the changed political environment in China and Southeast Asia and the fuller emergence of a modern banking system backed by state resources finally led to the demise of the *qiaopi* trade and the closing of an important, though largely forgotten, chapter in the making of modern China.

6

Qiaopi, Qiaoxiang, and Charity

This chapter examines a dimension of the *qiaopi* trade often overlooked in the existing literature (and, more broadly, in diasporic Chinese studies): its role in charity, and the operational mechanisms, impact, and theoretical implications of *qiaopi* charity. In this chapter, we argue that *qiaopi* and the associated remittance networks served as important arenas of diasporic Chinese philanthropy, which in turn further cemented the relationship between Chinese overseas and China.

QIAOPI AND CHARITABLE GIVING

Charity and *qiaopi* are closely linked in two main ways. First, family remittances of the sort that make up the great bulk of *qiaopi* were and are (as we shall argue) by nature a form of charity, one that seems at first sight minor in kind but that nevertheless, in terms of its aggregate global volume across all migrant-sending countries, in fact puts all other forms, including the philanthropy practiced by major foundations, deep in shade. Family remittances throughout the world not only act to mitigate the inequalities caused or tolerated by markets and governments but have done so on an ever-increasing scale in modern times.[1] Second, at higher levels, China's remittance trade was part of a massive voluntary and charitable transfer of resources in the form of social expenditure on major projects and collective donations by trusts and associations. So the *qiaopi* trade was associated with two main types of giving, personal or private and public or collective, that transformed the *qiaoxiang*, ancestral hometowns of the Chinese diaspora.

Glen Peterson has noted that "philanthropy is an understudied subject in Chinese history. . . . A similar lack of scholarly attention applies to the study of overseas Chinese philanthropy."[2] Christopher Baker too has pointed out that "while the traditions and institutions of charitable giving are as ancient and honoured in Chinese society as they are in the West, westerners have historically failed to properly identify and acknowledge Chinese charitable traditions because of our own narrowly defined and simplistic notions about philanthropy and the mono-cultural lens employed."[3] It has been argued that "philanthropy, as defined and practiced by the Chinese, is mainly giving on an individual basis, which includes charity, mutual aid, and giving to one's family and community." The Western concept of philanthropy, in contrast, "is exhibited mainly through giving towards institutions to solve root problems of society."[4]

Research into charity as practiced by migrants is a relatively new field of study. Some studies refer to such charity as "diasporic philanthropy"; others prefer the term "social investment" to emphasize the transformative potential and intent of diasporic giving.[5] Charity is usually defined as voluntary giving, so it is sometimes argued that remittances sent to support family members, being semi-obligatory and prescribed, cannot be classed as charity. In the Chinese case, for example, remittances are usually intended as an exercise in *xiao* ("filial piety") directed toward parents or as fulfilment of related obligations toward siblings, wives, children, and other kin. Charity, in contrast, is not seen as intrinsically socially binding and is directed toward nonkin, who figure much more rarely than kin at the lower level of China's remittance culture.

Other studies, however, maintain that diasporic giving can and should be defined as charity in societies organized by clan (like China) or by tribe. In such societies, the distinction between family and the larger community—and therefore between philanthropy and self-help or mutual aid—is far less relevant than in Western societies. In non-Western contexts, family as a main focus of charitable giving shades gradually into "institutions that support family spirit" at the level of community and society, including schools and temples.[6] This is also true of *qiaopi*, whose charitable dimension extended beyond kinship even if a firm dividing line between kin and nonkin is accepted, for this line was repeatedly crossed by remitters.

Friendship and neighborliness were regularly cited alongside consanguinity and affinity in remitters' instructions in *qiaopi* regarding the distribution of remittance money, and recipients often contributed part of the remittance to broader clan or community projects, either from a sense of compassion or obligation, or to enhance their own status (and that of the remitter). For example, in a *qiaopi* to his wife in Chenghai, Liu Chenghai in Thailand specified friends and neighbors as beneficiaries alongside his mother, sister, cousin, son, daughter, and various uncles.[7] So there is no way of quantifying the proportion of the resources migrants transferred to their country of origin or ancestry that constituted social investment for the public good as opposed to narrower investment in the interests of the family.[8]

New institutions evolved to tie migrants to the community as a whole, not just to their immediate families. As Madeline Hsu explains, these included new community media, the *qiaokan*, which were designed to strengthen transnational community and migrant loyalties: "In the physically dispersed community of Taishan, the people who commanded the highest levels of loyalty from overseas Taishanese were relatives: wives, parents, children, siblings and, to a lesser degree, uncles, aunts, nephews, and nieces. Beyond the relationships secured by ties of blood, connections to clan and native place also compelled the loyalty and support of overseas Taishanese. The responsibilities associated with these bonds were, however, less clearly defined and in need of reinforcement and organization in order to be of systematic benefit for native place and clan. Within the far-flung borders of their transnational community, Taishanese developed a means of conveying expressions of belonging, duty, and need to those overseas in the form of magazines known as *qiaokan*."[9] In many parts of rural China, including most *qiaoxiang*, society in premodern times was (and to some extent remains) clan based and clan governed. Clans were the locus of cooperation and morality, and their obligations applied mainly to kin. Scholars call this limited as opposed to generalized morality, allowing a further distinction between personal and impersonal charity, with the former applying to clan-based rural China. Greif and Tabellini, in their study on the Chinese clan, argue that "charity is personal when the giver donates to specific individuals he knows and it is impersonal otherwise. If limited morality prevailed in China, personal charity among kin was more likely to predominate. In contrast, if generalised morality prevailed in Europe, impersonal charity to non-kin was more likely to predominate." Under this definition, the charitable trusts that provided religious, educational, and other services were personal charity.[10] Moreover, even generalized morality and the associated impersonal charity is not necessarily or always universal, for they are commonly circumscribed by citizenship, class, residence, or religion.[11] So generalized morality has more in common with limited morality than it seems at first sight.

Who were the donors and recipients of *qiaopi* charity; what was the donors' motivation; what were the types and antecedents of charitable giving; what were its objects, occasions, and purposes; through what means and institutions was it channeled; and what were its impediments? What special features characterize diasporic charity, what distinguishes it from other forms of charity, and what distinguishes Chinese diasporic charity from that of comparable diasporas—for example, the Indian diaspora? These are some of the questions this chapter asks. Finally, in what ways did and does Chinese diasporic charity depart from other previously existing and new forms of charity in China, associated with China's old and new social institutions and religions and with Western influence?

Discussions of gifting distinguish between charity and philanthropy, with the former defined as "a short-term, emotional, immediate response, focused primarily on rescue and relief," and the latter "more long-term, more strategic, focused on rebuilding."[12] By that definition, leaders of the *qiaopi* system like Guo Youpin and others can better be described as philanthropists than as charity-givers, for they invested considerable sums in charitable enterprises at both ends of the migration chain, in China and overseas, in a systematic, long-term, and organized way. They did so at the same time as giving on an individual and family basis; one could even say that simultaneously engaging with both institutions and the family is a defining characteristic of diasporic Chinese philanthropy, in line with the Confucian maxim that "when one's personal life is cultivated and one's family is well regulated, the state will be well governed, and there will be peace and harmony throughout the world." They helped build and fund schools in China and abroad while participating in their supervision, and they invested in the construction of new roads and amenities in the *qiaoxiang*. During famines and crises induced by war or natural disasters, they mobilized support for and themselves contributed to charitable campaigns. They did the same to support Chinese political movements at home and abroad, using *qiaopi* channels and connections.

The distinction between *qiaopi* entrepreneurs and ordinary remitters does not hold in all regards. It is true that low-level remittances were often used to deal with short-term problems, especially during the migrant's early years abroad, but in many if not most cases they were highly regular and systematic, stretching over decades and amounting over the years to a big and long-term homeward-bound investment, realized in part in buildings or businesses. The remitters sometimes left decisions about the remittance to the recipient, especially if he (or sometimes she) was genealogically senior, but at other times they laid out in great detail how the remittance should be used. So although remitting had some features usually associated with charity, it was also strategic and long-term, features usually associated with philanthropy.

A common instruction was to buy land or build a house. For example, Li Huan in China wrote in a *huipi* to his father in Canada about purchasing land in the village. He pointed out that a fellow villager had put land on the market that was centrally located, enjoyed good *fengshui*, and cost no more than three to four hundred dollars.[13]

Although charity is usually defined as voluntary and selfless, *qiaopi* were in part a material as well as an emotional investment on the part of the remitter, with his return home as an expected (though often, in the event, unconsummated) part of the arrangement. To that extent, they were self-interested. However, most forms of charity have a self-interested dimension, if not core. For example, Christian and Buddhist charity is sustained by the notion of the accumulation of goodness—good deeds are rewarded in the afterlife—and much large-scale giving is designed to render society harmonious and stable, which is in everybody's interest, especially that of the richer giver. So it is usual in discussions of philanthropy to decline normative judgments about it and to define it instead as "the voluntary transfer of resources . . . for the benefit of others, irrespective of either the motives of the donor or any benefits that may accrue to the donor."[14]

Most donors acted in the capacity of sons, fathers, brothers, or husbands of the recipients. This sort of donor is a familiar figure throughout the world. The motivation thus asserted is deep-seated and universal: there is nothing new about male migrants supporting their families from abroad. However, many of these lowly donors played new roles in the new setting. Emigration and the sudden access to relative wealth cast them in a new light. Their status and role in the village was magnified by migration and by remitting, thus disordering the village's tradition-bound hierarchies. Men (and sometimes women) normally low and junior in the village hierarchy were catapulted into its upper levels after infusing wealth into their ancestral community, thus acquiring a new political role and status in the sending place. These included both people still resident overseas, who could be consulted about village matters by letter, and returnees. John Kuo Wei Tschen described the Chinese laundryman in America as "not only a mediator in personal and private affairs but also an elderman in village politics," even more authoritative than elders in the village.[15] They were expected to help steer village life from afar and to donate to its institutions. Madeline Hsu, talking of Taishan, described how "homebound Taishanese restructured social and economic hierarchies in order to elevate the absentee Taishanese who, in light of their greater opportunities and good fortunes in living and working abroad, bore an even greater share of the burden, not just for maintaining, but also for improving standards of living in Taishan."[16] Back-and-forth correspondence between Ye Tang, an emigrant in the United States, and his relatives in China, in this case concerning the building of watchtowers and a school, illustrates the process of consultation.[17]

Most donors were private and individual, but others were collective, organized in hometown associations, guilds, professional associations, and temples, over which Chinatown bigwigs and social luminaries held sway. At this higher end of the charity ladder, an even more striking departure from established ways took place. Local and regional projects that were by tradition the domain of China's gentry class devolved as a result of remittances to other normally disesteemed social groups and classes. In China before the 1905 reforms and the 1911 revolution, the merchant was generally a despised class. However, after the collapse of the Qing, when titles and degrees became redundant, merchants—including, in southern China, merchant leaders of the *qiaopi* trade—began to assume new functions and perform new tasks in local and regional society. As benefactors, they could expect to get official positions and government jobs on retiring to their native places.[18]

As we have seen, in the southeastern littoral region, class structure and class relations differed in some ways from those in other regions, and local historians talk of an oceanic culture in which trade and enterprise were valued even before the changes wrought by Sun Yat-sen's "bourgeois" revolution. The *qiaopi* trade required cultural capital that rougher trades usually lacked. *Qiaopi* practitioners had to be literate and to appear morally impeccable, in the Confucian sense, for their clients were entrusting them with hard-earned savings. So the *qiaopi* trade's strong association with promoting education in the *qiaoxiang* was in one sense a new departure, with entrepreneurs acquiring a sort of gentry status, yet in other senses a continuation of local ways.[19]

The channels along which *qiaopi*-type charity flowed home included traditional associations, traditional and modern banks, and the Chinese embassy or its consulates. However, even in such cases the *qiaopi* trade sometimes played the central role, as a tried, tested, and trusted institution of Chinese migrant life. *Qiaopi* managers not only donated from their own pockets to educational funds and had their names prominently displayed at the top of lists of contributors to disaster funds and political campaigns, but used their connections and prestige to mobilize broad circles to support them.[20]

Clan records suggest that most *qiaopi* addressed one or more of six main issues: supporting one's immediate family, building or repairing the family house, helping brothers marry, helping relatives or clan members buy land, lending relatives or clan members money to go into business, and assisting kin to emigrate. Over the years, investing in businesses climbed steadily up the agenda in correspondence. So did assisting during natural disasters, building temples, and supporting revolutionary movements. However, family support remained the overriding focus into the twentieth century.[21] Most *qiaopi* insisted that the money sent should be "used within the home." In a letter from Thailand, for example, Zeng Jin told his son in Chenghai that "these twelve hundred dollars must only be used to repair the house."[22]

Remittances were also used for weddings and funerals, and for building new houses or extending old ones.[23] In a *qiaopi* sent from Thailand, Huang Rensheng said the remittance should be put toward his cousin's forthcoming marriage.[24] An example of a funerary contribution is a *qiaopi* sent from Thailand by Huang Rensheng after his mother's death so that his brother in Chenghai could organize prayers for her.[25] In his essay on the new Gold Mountain (Australia), Michael Williams lists "health clinics, schools, street lights, reading rooms, tea pavilions, communal buildings, village watch-towers and bridges." He also mentions roads. Letters often talked about health matters, and medicines and restoratives were regularly sent through the *qiaopi* system while the community elite funded clinics, hospitals, and health schemes.

EDUCATION AND OTHER *QIAOPI*-RELATED CHARITABLE ACTIVITIES

While *qiaopi* correspondence covered a wide range of issues, it was strongest on education (traditional and modern), which, after everyday finance and family

survival, was a main focus of *qiaopi* giving. The *qiaopi* impact on educational culture and school politics was twofold. Early leaders of the *qiaopi* trade like Guo
Youpin promoted Confucian values in the schools they set up, whereas their sons
and heirs reformed education along modern lines. They set up hundreds of schools
in the *qiaoxiang* and funded evening classes, libraries, and other schemes. Even so,
they remained part of the establishment, which vaunted their efforts. Lower down
the social scale, remitters enabled their children, including many girls, and their
younger relatives and in-laws to go to school. Some even went to universities,
including prestigious foreign universities.

A good school system arose in the *qiaoxiang* earlier than in other regions
because of the migrant tie. Workers' and petty entrepreneurs' *qiaopi* specified
sums for the education of their younger relatives while high-ups built schools and
libraries for the lineage or the whole community. An analysis of 114 *qiaopi* from
one lineage shows that 86 percent discussed education.[26] Some talked of the need
to send girls as well as boys to school. One letter writer made arrangements for his
daughter to study overseas; Cai Quan in Malaya asked his mother to complete the
formalities necessary for his daughter to go to school in Singapore.[27] Some writers
even proposed educating their daughters-in-law, a new departure that would previously have been inconceivable.[28] Remittances also promoted adult education at
night schools. Education has always been a major focus of traditional Chinese
social thinking, even before the confrontation with Western technology in China
and overseas created a new realization that "knowledge is strength." In the *qiaopi*
age, this focus became practically an obsession.

Qiaopi letters stressed the need for constant study and frugal living. Politically
aware migrants wrote in them about political issues and affairs of state to educate
their families, and they demanded information about the political situation at home.
Many migrants sent children born overseas to China to acquire a Chinese education,
not to prepare them for a life in China but to equip them to promote Chinese culture
and customs overseas and to thrive as teachers and entrepreneurs in Chinatown.[29]

Remittances were strikingly effective in transforming patterns of education in
the *qiaoxiang*. By the 1930s, migrants' children and younger relatives were enrolled
at schools and universities not just in Guangzhou, Hong Kong, and Shanghai but
also in the United States and Japan. In the 1920s and 1930s, 20 to 30 percent of
students at Hong Kong University were migrants' dependents.[30] For example, in a
huipi to his father in the United States, one man revealed that he and his two sisters
were studying in Hong Kong, while another from a younger sister to her older
sister in New York mentioned an application to Fordham University in the United
States or, failing that, the possibility of gaining free admission to a music school.[31]
Schools in the *qiaoxiang* focused not just on Chinese learning but on the transmission of skills necessary for children whose future probably lay abroad, including
English language and commercial training.[32]

Migrants' introduction into the *qiaoxiang* of a modern education system nurtured a great pool of talent that was employed at both ends and all levels of the migration chain in education, enterprise, politics, and community leadership. Alumni associations became a main channel of international communication and a strong sinew of diasporic and domestic community.[33]

This promotion of schooling advanced the politicization of *qiaoxiang* society. The focus on schooling in the *qiaoxiang* was synchronic with political developments in wider society. The schools movement in the nineteenth century, at around the time of the Wuxu Reforms of 1898, had as their goal the founding of a modern math- and science-based system of education. The schools movement in the *qiaoxiang* entered its heyday after the Revolution of 1911, when local schools opened their doors to the general population.[34]

The earliest education-related remittance so far identified in studies was by a *guiqiao* father and son from Huian, who, after returning to China, donated two thousand taels to restore the local examination sheds in 1827.[35] In Chaoshan, the first migrant-sponsored *sishu* (old-style private school) was founded in 1880. Others followed later in the nineteenth century.

Between 1915 and 1949, overseas Chinese founded 48 secondary schools and 967 primary schools in Fujian. The total sum donated for this purpose has been put at RMB 54.9 million.[36] In Jinjiang alone, more than 200 middle and primary schools were founded before 1937, most of them privately funded—90 percent through remittances by overseas Chinese or with their help.[37]

Overseas-Chinese donations to and investment in schooling was the main reason for the extraordinary boom in education in southern Fujian and eastern and southern Guangdong in the late Qing and the early Republic and in the Chinatowns of Southeast Asia. Institutions thus funded included universities in Fujian and Nanyang University in Singapore. The most prominent donor was Singapore's Tan Kah Kee (Chen Jiageng, 1874–1962), founder of Amoy University in Fujian in 1921 and famous for saying that "education is the key to saving the nation." Tan continued his donations after 1949, when he is said to have given more than RMB 20 million.[38]

Guangfu also acquired new schools, partly as a result of migrants' *qiaopi*. The number of schools in Taishan rose from five to forty-seven between 1850 and 1911. Despite this investment, before 1911 the Wuyi counties were considered backward, with a literacy rate of just 50 percent in the towns and far lower in the villages. In the years 1912 to 1921, however, education in the region shot ahead because of migrant encouragement and pressure. By 1935, 75 percent of Taishan's children were attending school.[39] The schools followed a modern and westernized syllabus in which math and English replaced the Confucian classics. As a result, Jiangmen, the capital of Wuyi, took top place in Guangdong's table of educational achievement.

Overseas Chinese funded the establishment of around one thousand schools in Wuyi, and returned migrants came to the fore in directing and administering them. Some schools became famous throughout the province. Headmasters and headmistresses canvassed energetically among migrants and returnees for donations. One campaign in support of Taishan Middle School set up a foundation in Canada with branches in more than fifty places. The foundation collected 247,596 Canadian dollars and sent back three people to Taishan to supervise the school. On another occasion, the head of another school spent several months in the United States, where he collected US$240,000. In a third campaign, the headmistress of Taishan's County Girls' Normal School (which developed out of a primary school set up in the late Qing) went abroad twice and collected enough money for a new building. Some graduates of these schools studied abroad, including at leading American universities, where five former village children gained master's degrees and four gained doctorates. In 1932 in Xicun, a village of four thousand people, 1 percent (a large proportion, relative to other similar areas) had studied at university, including at PhD level in America.[40]

In 1940 *Kaiping Huaqiao yuekan* (*Kaiping Overseas Chinese Monthly*) carried numerous stories about emigrants contributing to educational projects in the *qiaoxiang*: "Overseas Chinese enthusiastically support education and contribute to lineage school funds," "Migrants returned from the Philippines donate educational funding," "Emigrants in America have raised US$4,000 for their lineage school," "Lineage members in America have contributed a huge amount of money to lineage schools."[41]

Another migrant who focused on education, in his case at both ends of the migration chain, was Singapore's Lim Soo Gan (1913–1993), a prominent leader of the *qiaopi* trade. Lim founded and funded a middle school in his native Anxi, to which he donated ten million yuan. He also directed or served on the boards of four middle schools in Singapore, two of them for girls.[42] A *qiaopi*-related charitable activity also linked to Chinese schooling overseas was the decision by *piju* owners to levy a small additional charge on *qiaopi* to help the board of directors of two Hakka schools tide the schools through a temporary financial crisis.[43]

Hakkas are usually said to have put a greater emphasis on schooling as an avenue for upward social mobility than other Chinese because of the poor quality of their mountain farmland and their resulting concentration in the army and public administration, professions that required greater literacy.[44] Hakka *qiaoxiang* are famous for the schools funded by Hakka migrants. In the Hakka county of Fengshun, migrants are said to have established several schools in the late Ming and early Qing.[45] When in 1903 the Qing started a campaign to promote education in the region, middle and primary schools sprang up on all sides, supported by Hakkas overseas.[46] Like other groups, Hakka philanthropists connected to the *qiaopi* trade set up schools for girls as well as boys; Meixian Girls' School was founded as early as 1898 and lasted until 1949. Although Meixian was, at the time, economically underdeveloped and remote from modern life, it joined the vanguard of modern change in the run-up to the New Culture Movement of the late 1910s, which led to the transformation of China's education system.[47]

The donations continued after 1949. Eight new middle schools were founded under the Communists with overseas-Chinese money, and the authorities tactfully encouraged migrants to set up schools named after themselves. In Jinjiang between 1949 and 1976, the amount overseas Chinese donated through remittances to educational causes was three times that donated during the Republican period.[48] However, during the Cultural Revolution, when the emphasis in China fell on self-reliance and overseas connections were discouraged, donations dried up for several years. Only after the Third Plenum of 1978 did they resume.[49]

Qiaopi leaders and ordinary remitters also played a major role in the provision of Chinese education in overseas migrant destinations. In chapter two, we described the entrepreneurial career of the *qiaopi* trader Guo Youpin, who founded the famous Tianyi *piju*. Guo Youpin and his family were also well-known philanthropists, and Guo was the *qiaopi* trade's most prominent educational philanthropist. His sons took over both of his roles, as company leader and donor. He and his family present a perfect case study of the link between *qiaopi* and charity.

In 1898 Guo Youpin set up a community-run school (*yishu*) in his native place with free teaching, food, and board, and he hired and paid a teacher to run it. The school was called Huanxing Tang ("Awakening School"), a name that showed that Guo Youpin's ambition extended beyond promoting traditional beliefs to turning China into a strong and modern nation. However, Confucian moral principles were his central concern, not just for pupils but for the wider community, and on the fifteenth day of each month, the teacher was required to deliver a public lecture on Confucian themes urging loyalty, filial piety, and "self-restraint and a return to rites." His charity initiatives were commended by both the Qing Court and the Republic, and local dignitaries wrote inscriptions praising them.

After Guo Youpin's death in 1905, his son Yongzhong, in a traditional gesture of benefaction, donated ten *mu* (0.67 acres) of paddy to support the school. He also transformed it into a modern-style school with more pupils, more teachers, better buildings, and a curriculum that combined Confucianism with modern education, including math, history, geography, and physical education. Yongzhong appointed himself headmaster and continued to fund the school until the early 1950s. He too was honored by the Qing Court for his efforts and was praised by local bigwigs.

Guo Youpin paid close attention to children who had "gone astray," which happened quite often in regions affected by the sudden influx of wealth and the consumerism and life of leisure associated with dependence on emigration. He bought such children tickets to Southeast Asia so that they would be able to earn their living abroad and turn over a new leaf.

Guo Youpin's investment in Confucian culture in his village and lineage extended beyond a concern for schooling. He also founded a hall for the poor, providing free medicine and coffins. Guo Youpin's successors continued to support education, and they set up and funded a modern primary school with a nine-year curriculum and, in 1921, a Girls' National School.

Another famous overseas *qiaopi* philanthropist, Zeng Yangmei, founder of the Zhengshengxing remittance firm, set up a boys' and girls' school. Zeng is lauded in folklore and publications for his legendary philanthropy and altruism. Whenever he returned from Thailand to his native place in eastern Guangdong, he took with him great quantities of medicine for fellow villagers. In Thailand, he erected a tea pavilion on a river bank not far from his company office to refresh passersby, and he also put up sun-rain shelters. According to one account, on one occasion he personally plunged into the floods in Chaoshan to help prevent a dyke from bursting its banks.[50]

Migrants and returned migrants were famous for building libraries, for both their lineages and the general public, as part of the effort to bring education and enlightenment to the *qiaoxiang*.[51] Overseas Chinese leaders were painfully aware that many younger dependents had become used to a life of relative idleness and that some spent their time in "immoral" pursuits, ranging from playing mahjong to visiting prostitutes. The leaders' remedy was to try to promote a healthy lifestyle in both body and mind. They had volleyball and basketball courts laid out and made provision for music and other "healthy" pastimes, but their most enduring legacy was a system of libraries, often magnificent in contents and construction. The Guan lineage library, built in 1929, occupies five stories and continues in operation to this day, open to all. Another in Xinhui, also open to the general public, has a stock of sixty thousand volumes and occupies one thousand square meters.[52]

Qiaopi letters discussed schooling both at home, in China, and in diaspora, where *qiaopi* entrepreneurs helped set up, manage, and fund modern-style Chinese-language schools. We have already noted the case of Lim Soo Gan in Singapore and the Hakka traders in Thailand. Similar campaigns were waged in most migrant destinations and were supported in part by wealthy *qiaopi* traders and reported on in *qiaopi* correspondence.[53]

Publishing thrived in the *qiaoxiang* as a result of migration. As we have already mentioned, migrant and community leaders produced *qiaokan* ("overseas Chinese magazines") in the villages and counties and mailed them to expatriates to inform them of events at home and to encourage them to donate to local causes.[54] They also set up publishing enterprises to the same end. In the decades leading up to 1949, scores of *qiaokan* were published in Wuyi, including 127 in Taishan, 25 in Kaiping, and 26 in Xinhui.[55]

Remittances were also used to fund roads and bridges, build hospitals, provide medical care, and build parks.[56] Some of these activities were in part entrepreneurial, but it is difficult to distinguish in such cases between enterprise pursued for profit and that pursued with the intention of raising native places out of poverty by improving transport and communications. In 1922 a Chinese philanthropist in Thailand donated two hundred thousand baht to build a rural hospital in Chaoshan after the outbreak of an epidemic. Others too funded hospitals and clinics.[57] In Fengshun, fifty-nine bridges and scores of hospitals had been built by the late 1980s, at a cost of more than RMB 60 million.[58]

QIAOPI CHARITY, THE NATIONAL CAUSE, AND THE STATE

In normal times, most ordinary Chinese remitted only or principally to their families and at most to their native villages or counties, but during wars and crises, donations to the wider cause surged, both to boost China's military defenses and to relieve distress. One Singapore man, Lin Shouzhi, sold his own and his wife's possessions to support Sun Yat-sen's Revolutionary Alliance in 1911. The *qiaokan* founded to bind migrants to their native places played a big role in this mobilization before and during the war against Japan by advertising appeals. Between 1937 and 1939, Chinese in Singapore raised 3.6 million yuan to support the anti-Japanese resistance, and they set up a system of monthly contributions.[59] For example, in 1937 a Chaozhou *huiguan* in Singapore raised S$470,000. In 1939, after the fall of Chaozhou, it contributed more than S$100,000 to aid Chaozhou refugees.[60] In the years 1937 to 1941, overseas Chinese on a world scale are said to have donated the equivalent of around SG$1.1 billion to patriotic causes.[61]

Radical Chinese sent financial help and messages of political support to left-wing Nationalists and to the Communists in Yan'an. In 1931 Chinese in Vietnam donated 2,600 silver dollars to the Nineteenth Route Army in Shanghai, where it fought the Japanese at a time when Chiang Kai-shek was deemed to favor appeasement. In 1937, after the Marco Polo Bridge Incident, Chinese in Singapore immediately set about raising funds to support the Chinese resistance to Japan.[62] In 1938 young Chinese in Thailand sent 2 million guobi to the Communists' Eighth Route Army office in Wuhan.[63] Political donations continued after 1949. During the Korean War, *shuike* in Meixian raised more than 235 million yuan to help "resist America and aid Korea."[64]

Overseas Chinese also responded when necessary to natural disasters. In 1918, when an earthquake in Chaozhou caused the Han Jiang to burst its banks, individuals and associations donated money and goods to relieve the devastation caused by the flooding.[65] In Thailand, Zheng Zhiyong donated 380,000 silver dollars and sent materials by steamer to Shantou to repair the dykes. He also sent his son and nephew to supervise this work. Chinese in Malaya and Indonesia donated hundreds of thousands of yuan.[66] The Chaoshanese in Singapore donated S$400,000, followed in 1922 by another S$30–40,000 after another disaster. In 1936, when the dykes again came under threat, they again donated S$37,000.[67] Overseas

Chinese from Tianmen in Hubei were less closely tied to their ancestral homes than those from other places, probably because they tended to practice whole-family rather than male migration, but Tianmenese in India, Indonesia, Malaysia, and Singapore sent donations whenever disasters happened, either personally through the Chinese Embassy, or through their associations.[68] Usually people donated to their native regions, but in some cases they donated to relieve disasters in other regions, such as north China.[69] In the late 1950s and early 1960s, during the hardships exacerbated by the failure of the Great Leap Forward, emigrants and their descendants used the *qiaopi* system to send grain, flour, pig fat, chemical fertilizer, and building supplies to villages in China.[70] For example, in 1962 Thailand's Zeng Ruifan sent home "a bag of rice, two packets of flour, and thirty pounds of lard" to his family in Chenghai.[71]

Since the start of the 1980s, overseas Chinese have resumed donating to promote local welfare in their native towns and villages. The great majority of these donors are first-generation migrants. Ethnic Chinese born and bred in countries outside China rarely evince the same degree of attachment.[72] As the generations multiply, attitudes and orientations change: some forget their ancestral roots and identify with their places of birth, others have little notion of their exact ancestral provenance and identify at most with China, broadly conceived, instead of with their ancestral counties. With the gradual demise of the *qiaopi* trade and the consolidation of a modern banking system, donations to the hometowns and China were channeled less and less frequently through *qiaopi*, and eventually not at all.

The *qiaopi* trade played an important part in mobilizing overseas Chinese on a pan-Chinese basis, and this was reflected in the postwar years in their charitable giving. For example, in 1945 Thailand's six sub-ethnic Chinese *huiguan* set up the Famine Relief Committee with 148 branches across the country. When famine struck nineteen provinces of China in 1946, the committee raised more than 1 million baht in fifty days, followed by another 1.1 million baht raised by ethnic Chinese in the Thai interior.[73]

Diasporic giving cannot be fully understood without paying some attention to the role of official institutions. Governments in China and overseas played a role over many decades in the development of charitable giving, either by hindering it in some periods (in the latter case) or generally promoting it (in the case of the Chinese authorities). The Chinese authorities promoted it chiefly because they recognized that remittances hugely compensated for China's trade deficit.[74] In recent years, other poor countries with big overseas diasporas have begun actively wooing them on a scale in most cases unprecedented, but in China this has been happening for more than a century.

In some periods, the Chinese government tried to commandeer the *qiaopi* trade. As we have seen, however, it was forced in the 1920s and 1930s to back down and compromise, since the remittance companies had a greater reach in the *qiaoxiang* and in Chinatown and overseas-Chinese communities than the modern banks and postal services. During the war against Japan, when remittances threatened to dry up, the authorities acted energetically to support the *qiaopi* trade under the new conditions and in synergy with it. After 1949 the new Communist authorities supported and encouraged the trade for the first fifteen years of their regime.

Diasporic philanthropy was to some extent synchronous with government initiatives in China and sometimes inextricable from them. This is most obvious in the case of wars, when overseas Chinese united behind the homeland effort. However, charity also chimed with government initiatives in other ways. For example, the 1898 Wuxu Reforms, although in themselves unsuccessful at the time, coincided with and inspired investment in education in the *qiaoxiang*.

Governments sometimes impeded remittances and *qiaopi* charity for economic or political and ideological reasons. In the postwar years, colonial and other governments in Southeast Asia tried to restrict remittances to safeguard their own currencies and economies, and after 1947 some banned sending relief funds to China.[75] During the Cultural Revolution, the Chinese government and local authorities discouraged remittances and stigmatized their recipients.

The overseas-Chinese banks, set up in part with *qiaopi* capital and an essential element in the *qiaopi* system, played a crucial role in charitable giving. In 1931 their remittances accounted for 17 percent of China's national relief mission, and in 1939 and 1940 they donated relief funds of more than one hundred million yuan.[76] As we have already seen, the post office sometimes promoted and sometimes sought to hamper the *qiaopi* trade, depending on whether it was out to capture or co-opt it.[77]

QIAOPI, RELIGIOUS CHARITIES, AND MODERN PHILANTHROPY

China is often depicted as a society without a strong inclination to practice charity toward nonkin. In fact, China has a long history of charitable institutions, known as *shanshe* or *shanhui* and described by the scholar Tan Chee Beng as permanent and professional charity associations, in both China and Southeast Asia. Although *shanshe* were sometimes secular, they did have a religious dimension, chiefly Buddhist and Taoist but with some Confucian input. There were many *shanshe* in Chaoshan, the unofficial capital of one of China's two main *qiaoxiang*, which helps explain their spread across Southeast Asia.[78]

Qiaopi-related charity was linked to the *shanshe* tradition through the Chaoshan connection, but there were important differences between the two forms. In premodern China, charitable associations were more commonly found in Beijing and the cities of eastern China. They were an urban phenomenon, whereas *qiaopi* charity was overwhelmingly focused on migrants' native places in rural areas.[79]

Unlike official relief associations in the Ming and Qing, *shanshe* in China attended to the needs not just of the local poor but of migrant workers from other places. *Shanshe* in Southeast Asia also did this, but there is less evidence of *qiaopi*-related charities in the *qiaoxiang* doing so. Finally, charitable institutions like those run by Guo Youpin and his sons in Liuchuan had a different moral inspiration from the *shanshe*, which largely drew on Buddhist and Taoist religions, unlike the Guos' more secularly framed Confucian motivation.

Some migrants, through their remittances, funded the establishment and maintenance of Buddhist and Taoist temples.[80] Even small contributions are recorded. For example, one donor gave HK$100 to pay for a new temple drum.[81] This tradition dated back to the Kangxi reign (1662–1722), when two migrants in Batavia (modern-day Jakarta) donated money for the repair of a temple in Fujian's Longhai.[82] Once abroad, migrants often developed a more modern outlook than their relatives and friends left behind in the villages, and many saw traditional village customs as a waste of money. Even so, they sponsored religious celebrations in China, particularly in the Hakka villages, where people were even more likely to worship gods and spirits than on the coast.[83] (This practice continues in the United States among new migrants from Fujian, who have funded the reconstruction of ancestral halls and graves destroyed in the Cultural Revolution and collected donations, in some cases huge, to build Buddhist temples and Christian churches, as well as for secular development and relief.[84])

Studies on diasporic philanthropy assume that it focuses, like philanthropy in general, on elites and that remittances and charity have a "stratifying effect" on receiving communities. Indian diasporic philanthropy in particular is criticized for its "counterequity thrust."[85] Charitable funding that "directly reaches the poor" is said to be rare, for philanthropy is, supposedly by nature, "conducted by elites and the beneficiary institutions are often elitist."[86] Yet the thrust of the *qiaopi* system was in many ways upwardly leveling rather than stratifying. It brought prosperity to parts of China that had long been mired in desperate poverty, and it transformed the lives and chances of generations of dependents in society's lowest strata. However, it is true that the *qiaopi* phenomenon created a wealth gap in the *qiaoxiang* between those with relatives overseas and those without.

The infusion of wealth into the *qiaoxiang* did not bring modernization and sustainable development to the villages. Some money other than that needed for direct sustenance was invested in land and small businesses, but much was spent on luxury items like jewelry or on entertainment and conspicuous consumption.

Another assumption of studies on diasporic philanthropy is that it is, essentially, a newborn thing of the late twentieth and twenty-first centuries. It is, so it is supposed, a recent phenomenon that has become important in the years since the 1980s, much in the same way that transnationalism is often seen as a child of the late twentieth century, the age of unprecedented compression of time and space.[87] This assumption too, so it transpires, has little relevance in the Chinese case. *Qiaopi* donations and diasporic philanthropy are practically as old as modern Chinese migration, with a history of 150 years before their eventual demise after 1949, and although their form and objects changed over time, in part as a result of donors' exposure to Western ways, the donations preceded such exposure and were indigenous in execution and inspiration.

The role of "diaspora associations," mainly hometown associations (*tongxiang hui* and *huiguan*), professional associations, and faith-based organizations, also has a far longer history in China and among Chinese overseas than one might conclude from the general literature on diasporic philanthropy. Paula Johnson asserts that associations' role in the past was limited, mainly to emergency provision, and implies that only now are they emerging as "powerful philanthropic players."[88] This may be true of the hometown associations Johnson studies, but it is not true of the Chinese case. Nor was membership of such associations low in Chinatown. In the United States, only around 5 percent of contemporary migrants from Latin America and the Caribbean are thought to belong to these associations, but in many Chinese communities in the past, membership was, for a long time, practically obligatory and universal.[89]

Professional associations have long played a major role in organizing Chinese communities overseas. Of particular relevance in this regard is the role of *qiaopi*-related trade associations. They helped to unify the trade economically, and the institutions they set up provided a model and example for subsequent political campaigns, especially during and after the run-up to the Japanese invasion. They created a new communal ethos and not only facilitated personal charity in the form of family remittances but acted as channels for collective and impersonal forms of charitable giving.

One argument for why diasporic givers today supposedly differ greatly from those in the past is the "increasing mobility of talent," so that contemporary "venture philanthropists" are more likely to become personally involved in the management and monitoring of their social investments. Another is that an "organizational revolution" has taken place, whereby new technologies enabling instantaneous communication make community organizing far easier now than in the past, particularly for poorer migrants.[90] But while it is true that "venture philanthropy" has become more prominent in some settings in recent years and that new technologies facilitate it, this should not blind us to the fact that Chinese charitable donors even in the early years of overseas settlement closely supervised or played an active part in the projects they funded (particularly but not only in the field of education). It also underestimates the speed and reliability of communications under the *qiaopi* system, which eventually became as quick as modern airmail.[91] However, unlike the professional associations Johnson discusses, which often focus on national rather than local issues, overseas-Chinese trade associations were regionally or locally directed.[92] They did unite and cohere at a supra-regional level at times of political crisis or when their common professional interests came under threat, but this was the exception rather than the norm.

QIAOPI AND THE *QIAOXIANG*

Emigration transforms not just migrants but the communities they leave behind. This is particularly true in the case of a group, like the Chinese, that tends to send only young males abroad, and to keep women, children, and old men in the sending places, where they depend on remittances. *Qiaopi*, together with all the other importations associated with emigration, wrought deep transformations on both the physical and the mental landscape of the *qiaoxiang*.

The mental changes in the *qiaoxiang* were an initially unintended consequence of the *qiaopi* trade, which was run by people steeped in traditional morality and cultural values on behalf of clients whose expectations were informed by a similarly conservative set of values. Although the trade was based on notions of commerce and exchange that had strong modern and nontraditional associations, traditional moral values lay at its heart.[93] This is obvious from the names adopted by the *piju*, formed by characters drawn from Confucian maxims.[94] Confucian values—of benevolence, filial piety, love, and respect for one's elder brother; valuing righteousness above material gain; and prizing modesty, yielding, sincerity, and trust—were reflected not only in the organization of the *qiaopi* trade but in the contents of the letters it delivered.[95] These values, rather than laws and regulations, defined the essential nature of the trade, even after its maturation. In today's China, where Confucian values are once again praised after a century of vituperation, many of the essays written about the *qiaopi* trade by local historians focus on its traditional morality. In 2014 one group of *qiaopi* enthusiasts even went so far as to propose declaring a Day of Filial Piety and Fraternal Duty (*xiaoqin ri*) in honor of it.[96]

The remitters continued to support traditional customs in the villages, and religious life in the *qiaoxiang* was largely financed by overseas Chinese, even though traditional religious influences were far less evident among migrants than among their dependents.[97] However, letters home often expressed opinions on village matters that reflected modern influences on the writers. For example, some enjoined villagers to respect the interests of every household rather than just of one's own family or lineage, and to ensure that the burden of taxation was fairly distributed.[98]

Many letters were deeply conservative, especially regarding the wives, mothers, and daughters their writers had left behind, and enjoined wives and daughters to be passive, submissive, virtuous, and filial. The culture reflected in them remained largely closed and conservative, up to and even after 1949.[99] However, migrants' exposure to a society and polity further than China along the road to modernity and to new customs, viewpoints, and institutions changed the thinking of some on basic social issues such as girls' schooling, and on political issues such as democracy, freedom of assembly and expression, fair taxation, etc. There is plenty of evidence to show that, in many cases, *qiaopi* transformed the politics of gender and generation in the *qiaoxiang*, overthrowing established principles of power and status. The changed thinking of some remitters was reflected in their letters home and in their instructions regarding girls' and women's rights, particularly (as we have seen) in the field of education. The new approach was not always well received. One *qiaopi* addressed not to the mother, as custom dictated, but to the wife drew a strong reproach from the mother, who decried it as a violation of traditional propriety.[100]

The transformations in mentality were not necessarily progressive; living off *qiaopi* did not always change outlooks for the better. Life in the *qiaoxiang* became more leisure oriented than in the past. Some youngsters developed an aversion to farming or working in the shop and preferred to spend recklessly and to idle away their time in tea-houses, gambling dens, and brothels, despite the efforts of migrant leaders to revive a work-ethic among dependents.[101]

The gifts remitted, and the products that flowed into the *qiaoxiang* as a result of the prosperity remittances brought in their wake, deeply transformed local habits and material life in migrant communities. Remitters' dependents dressed differently from other people and were immediately recognizable as dependents. They wore clothes made of nontraditional materials, which they sometimes worked up themselves on newly acquired sewing machines, and they flaunted expensive jewelry. Female Hakka dependents (who had natural feet) wore high heels. Old men wore slippers or leather shoes. They regularly ate meat and consumed tinned food, MSG, and nutritious supplements. The more prosperous dependents built modern houses and summer houses, and repaired or extended their clans' ancestral halls. Bikes, motor vehicles, and—in some regions—trains financed by overseas Chinese investment carried them from place to place. Gramophones, flashlights, and knives and forks made their appearance, as did cameras and photo studios, so the migrant could see photos of his family.[102]

As a direct result of the activities of *shuike* and other traders, a huge range of precious metals and metal and paper currencies flooded the southern *qiaoxiang*. Silver dollars were mentioned in Zhangzhou as early as 1516, and in the Ming's Wanli reign (1573–1619), as many as half a million pesos were flowing annually into the port.[103] The Qing-dynasty currency was the silver tael (*yinliang*), but its irregular shape and weight made it unpopular with traders, who increasingly switched to the foreign silver dollar. Other Chinese currencies in the late nineteenth and early twentieth centuries included the dragon dollar, issued by provincial banks. In 1830 ships from Thailand took sixty thousand Spanish silver dollars to migrants' dependents in the Chaoshan region. The early *shuike* and returning migrants brought back silver coins (*fanyin*, "foreign silver") issued by all the colonial powers represented in the region, as well as Mexican, Spanish, and Philippine silver dollars and British, Dutch, French, and American money.[104] Local Chinese called the coins "Buddha-face silver" or "ghost-face money," to describe the unfamiliar Western faces inscribed on them, and used them for dowries, lucky charms, and headdress jewelry as well as for paying taxes and buying goods and services.[105] They were followed in later years by currencies issued by the Nationalists, the puppets and Japanese, and Communist guerrillas.[106] These mingled in the streets and markets with Hong Kong, Singaporean, Thai, and Vietnamese currencies and various paper currencies issued by local traditional banks.[107] In the 1930s, the Nationalists forbade the import of foreign currencies, but this had scant effect. In the *qiaoxiang*, foreign currencies continued to circulate, and some merchants would accept nothing but.[108] (Needless to say, this profusion of currencies makes studying and cataloging *qiaopi* even more difficult.[109])

The invasion of the *qiaoxiang* by gold and precious metals reached startling levels in some places. Jewelry became an everyday thing for the more prosperous class of migrant women in the early twentieth century. Large numbers of gold and silver shops opened in Quanzhou, where making jewelry became quite an industry, in defiance of a Nationalist ban on dealing in precious metals. Quanzhou is said to have become the center of China's gold trade. Some women, Gold Mountain women in particular, wore eight rings on two hands, together with bracelets and other adornments. When the war started and remittances became scarcer, the gold and silver was sold back to the shops at knock-down prices, but the trade revived after the war, supported by the *piju*. The rush into gold after 1945 was fueled by the postwar inflation, which killed off the Chinese currency.

The flow of wealth into the villagers attracted the unwelcome attention of bandits and corrupt local leaders, which led in turn to even more conspicuous material changes in the local scene. To guard against kidnappings, migrants built defensive towers for their families, consolidating the trend toward new architectural styles throughout the *qiaoxiang*, and they hired armed men to protect the towers.[110]

On occasion, changes in the mental landscape culminated in a new political mind-set in some *qiaoxiang* villages. During the Sino-Japanese War, the collapse of the general economy was reflected even more acutely in villages that were no longer able to receive remittances. Government promises of protection and relief usually came to nothing, and taxes continued to rise. This sparked resistance, both passive and active, and demonstrations, including by the *fankeshen*, or migrants' wives, and by local mobs.[111] Political protest against attempts by the authorities to restrict the *qiaopi* trade broke out at all levels of society, in the villages, the towns, the cities, and even the national capital (both in Beijing and Nanjing), as well as in Chinese communities abroad.

Protests in the villages and the smaller towns were probably in most cases organized by local powerholders intent on protecting local interests and their own interests, in which sense they differed little from traditional protest and cannot count as manifestations of modern political change. But although nearly all these protest movements, particularly those closest to the villages, were deeply rooted in organizations and networks based on long-standing particularistic ties, over time they ripened in some places into a broadly based political culture that later paved the way, both in China and overseas, for an extensive mobilization of patriotic forces. That women sometimes came to the fore in these movements is not surprising, given that they made up the great majority of youthful dependents, but it was nevertheless uncommon and a sign of the times and of rural women's elevation into the political domain.

CHINESE DIASPORIC CHARITY IN HISTORICAL AND INSTITUTIONAL PERSPECTIVE

Most studies concede that diasporic philanthropy merits a longer history, but they raise scant evidence of one. Why is diasporic giving associated principally with the third wave of globalization that started in the late 1980s rather than projected further backward? Partly because, outside China, the Chinese case has been all along glaringly absent from the debate. This is because the Chinese scholarly focus on the *qiaopi* trade is relatively recent. Although much work has been done on it, nearly all of the publications are in Chinese and thus inaccessible to most Western scholars.[112]

Another way in which Chinese philanthropy differs from philanthropy associated with other emerging economies in more recent times is its greater transparency and measurability. Studies note that there has been little attempt to measure charitable giving to India. There are no general surveys and few studies.[113] China, on the other hand, has a huge amount of statistical information about *qiaopi* and associated forms of giving, including charity, stretching back to the nineteenth century and even earlier. This is not only because the *qiaopi* trade was highly organized. It was not necessarily in the traders' or remitters' interest to reveal the extent of remittances, and in some circumstances they did their best to hide or understate it. However, the remittance houses necessarily registered and recorded traffic, and China's modern banks and post office also kept a beady eye on their transactions so that they could levy postal charges and get a slice of the profits of what was an exceptionally lucrative trade. So although it was rarely possible to say for certain how much money was entering China, officials and investigators could, on the basis of spot checks in the remittance-receiving ports, estimate the total more or less accurately by multiplying the number of letters by the likely average remittance. Local authorities and clan associations also recorded charitable donations, including *qiaopi*-based donations.

However, in some respects the *qiaopi* trade and early Chinese diasporic philanthropy strikingly foreshadowed some of its contemporary non-Chinese manifestations. Studies suggest a correlation between high levels of charitable giving and migrants' expectation of a return to the homeland, and that a concentrated pattern of migrant settlement overseas boosts giving.[114] Both premises hold in the early Chinese case, where the idea (though not necessarily the reality) of return was normative and where white and other forms of racism led to both exclusion and residential concentration, thus reinforcing the sojourner mentality.

Qiaopi activity took many forms, both private and collective, delegatory and micromanaging. It covered most of the same areas as contemporary social investment by members of other diasporic groups, and it particularly emphasised schools, hospitals, roads, temples, ancestral halls, and politics. This chapter shows that *qiaopi* exemplified a key characteristic of diasporic Chinese philanthropy: its systemic combination of individual and family giving and donations to institutions. It was a *sui generis* form of charity that exemplified the intense interaction, created by the Chinese system of family and lineage control and sealed by the racist exclusion Chinese experienced almost everywhere, between the Chinese migrant's sending place and his or her migratory destination. *Qiaopi* enabled a massive transfer of resources that combined remittances and philanthropy in a seamless, inextricable tangle. This transfer staved off China's financial ruin for nearly a century and lifted large numbers of dependents out of penury, for a while or for good. The *qiaopi* system prefigured rather than paralleled or mimicked modern forms of diasporic philanthropy. Although it borrowed technology and some attitudes from the West, as a form of social investment it preceded Western influence. In other words, in China, charity truly "began at home," and in two senses: family and friends came first, and the charitable idea was in large part indigenous in shape and conception.

Qiaopi and European Migrants' Letters Compared

Migration is a universal condition of human life, as much a fact of it as feet. It is rarely complete and final. Mass exoduses in the sense of a complete divorce or emptying are exceptional in modern times. Most migrants stay in touch with their sending places, at least for a generation. Communication is by physical return, word of mouth, or—after the eighteenth century—correspondence in the form, until recently, of letters. Staying in touch by letter became almost as universal as migration.

China is just one of the developing nations migrants have left. In the nineteenth and twentieth centuries, the "great migrations" were by Europeans to white-settled and white-ruled places. Their story dominates writing about migrants' letters, and their letters fill the anthologies. Chinese also migrated to white-ruled places, but as "perpetual foreigners." They are the only non-European migrants whose letters and letter institutions have been widely studied. However, the studies are nearly all in Chinese, and thus inaccessible to most non-Chinese scholars. This chapter asks what was special about Chinese migrants' letters, and why.

The chapter compares *qiaopi* letters and institutions with their European equivalent. Some will see a European conflation as occidentalizing and a denial of national specificity. The study assumes that white migrant epistolaries have much in common, including a reliance on the post office, shared attitudes and values, and a strong sense of nationhood. Their writers had whiteness, however graduated, which ensured their inclusion, partial or complete, in the hegemonic culture and polity. They also had alphabetization and forms of modern schooling that often predated emigration and that Chinese migrants generally lacked.

Eric Richards, regretting the consignment of migrants' letters to "isolated ethnic clusters" that play up differences, calls for their juxtaposition to transcend "the limits of specific selections" and find "their exceptional and common characteristics."[1] This chapter takes up Richards' challenge to discover Chinese and European letters' differences and commonalities. It first examines the different institutional settings in which migrant letters were written and the emergence of postal culture. It then goes on to discuss features of Chinese and European migrant letters connected to the letters' materiality, including the cost of postage and letter-writing techniques. It ends by analyzing Chinese and European migrant letters' contents and literary excursions, and matters such as privacy and the role of letters as a substitute for guidebooks.

MIGRANT SETTINGS AND THE EMERGENCE OF POSTAL CULTURE

European and Chinese migrants shared many characteristics, but their sending places and the communities they formed abroad differed greatly. These differences were reflected in their letters.

Most European migrants came from rural communities threatened by dissolution. The collapse of the old order occasioned much of the migration. Among entities under threat were old forms of kinship and community that had once integrated local life. Many European families sponsored and depended on migrants who sent back huge amounts of money, often to fund sequential migration. However, the home tie was weakened by whole-family migration, which became ever more common. Even elderly parents left to join their children. Few Europeans saw emigration as temporary. Most aimed to start a new life overseas.[2]

European migrants were often individualistic and independent minded. As Richards points out, domestic disharmony and dislike of family authority, bitterly expressed in letters, was a powerful force in British emigration.[3] Migrants left home for a variety of reasons, described by David Gerber as "individualized discontents" rather than a structural economic push.[4]

The Chinese orientation was, at bottom, collective, with family and lineage as its bedrock. Chinese migrated on behalf of their families and the clans that governed rural life in the migrant-sending south. They were overwhelmingly male—even as late as the 1940s, Chinese men outnumbered women in New York by six to one.[5] In theory (though less so in practice), they were sojourners. Their task was to send back money and accumulate enough for a return in triumph.

If the question is whether migrants were "violently uprooted" or "strategically transplanted," Chinese tended to be both.[6] They had no less agency than European migrants, but material circumstances put them under pressure.

The communities that Chinese and European migrants formed overseas reflected their different backgrounds. Although European migrants started out in ethnic enclaves, most quickly dispersed.[7] European enclaves grew as immigration grew, but they were bridges rather than fortresses. Chinatown arose in response to exclusion, but also because it let Chinese remain culturally distinct.[8] It was governed by ties of kinship and dialect derived from migrants' places of origin. The ties changed in the transition but survived essentially intact.

Gerber argues that "emigration puts a singular strain on personal identity, because it is a radical challenge to continuity,"[9] and writing letters helped migrants establish new identities. The Chinese too experienced rupture and upheaval as a result of emigration, but the element of continuity was greater.

A study on Dutch migrants to America found that they were more likely to write home and less ready to strike new notes if they stayed enclaved.[10] Chinese migrants, for their part, had their own institutions, born of home society and culture and adapted for overseas use. They were the most enclaved because of racist exclusion and their own collectivism, a confirmation of the link between enclaving and ancestral loyalty.

Most European migrants joined the mainstream economy, often in their old jobs. This smoothed the transition and facilitated a comparison with the old country, usually favorable to the new.[11] Far fewer Chinese worked in the mainstream. They joined the ethnic economy, adding a rice-bowl dimension to their enclavement.

The Piju *versus the Post Office*

The *piju* overlapped in character, and even in functions and operations, with the modern post office, but the two institutions differed in many respects. The post office was a globally regulated service open to all, whereas the *piju* was indigenous to the diaspora. It grew organically from the migrant setting to which it was consummately suited. A transnational product of the translation of old postal practices to Chinatown, it served clients organized by kinship, provenance, or dialect, affiliations that framed their migration, in a mix with no European equivalent. Like the clan associations that established it, the *qiaopi* system was practically inescapable, a homeland institution in an unfamiliar environment, into which customers were recruited straight off the boat. The *piju* was the migrant's bank, and his link to home. It was his post office, though neither universal nor even national in scope, but a blend of modern and premodern.

Many studies have explored the role played by communication and print culture in creating national identities. Karen Lemiski mentions the propaganda effect of depicting national themes on postage stamps. However, *qiaopi* envelopes were not necessarily stamped and were adorned with administrative marks and symbols added by the *piju*. (In the anti-Japanese war and after 1949, political slogans were added.[12]) They cemented the migrant's identification with his place of ancestry rather than with national culture.

Qiaopi-style institutions were not exclusively Chinese, as we have seen. The *hawala* system in the Middle East and South Asia strongly resembles the old *qiaopi* model, as do and did other migrant services. In New York in the 1830s, merchants ran ethnic businesses that handled migrants' remittances, letters, jobs, and travel. They also worked (like *piju*) in insurance and currency exchange and as shipping agents, translators, and legal advisors. The clerks were the bosses' conationals and kin, as in the *piju*.[13]

Migrants in many places developed unofficial courier services, far sketchier than the Chinese system but similar. For example, Welsh in America and Scots in New Zealand paid returners to act as couriers.[14] But customers complained (like Chinese who used informal services) that the couriers were unreliable and slow: they took up to half a year to deliver, if they delivered at all.[15]

During the great migrations, even modern post offices retained older practices that resembled the *qiaopi* system. Vincenzo Pietropaolo's description of the Italian postal service in a 1950s village is richly evocative of the arrival of the *qiaopi* man:

> As the houses did not have street addresses with numbers, . . . the postman had to rely on his detailed knowledge of almost every family in the population of 3,000. There were no mailboxes or letter slots . . ., so upon reaching the intended house, the mail-man called out the name of the recipient. . . . The addressee, usually a woman, would open the door, or perhaps hurry down a flight of stairs, and, as she clutched the letter in her hands, the look of great anticipation on her face became etched in my mind. . . . The arrival of a letter became nothing less than a public event. Neighbors would gather quickly, or would lean from their windows or stoops, to hear once more the name of that magical place that was the letter's most likely point of origin: New York.[16]

But the *qiaopi* trade was not, like the New York firms, a modern extemporization but a reversion, in new settings, to old ways. America's modern postal services were the best in the world in the late 1820s.[17] Singapore had a weaker service, and China had no post office at all for decades. In Singapore and China, the *qiaopi* trade preceded and survived the founding of the post office. The post office in America quickly eclipsed unofficial services, but there was scope elsewhere for their Chinese equivalent to flourish. Even in America the *qiaopi* trade survived, though in a commensal relationship with the post office.

Postal Culture

The mass migrations of the nineteenth and twentieth centuries overlapped with the emergence of a postal culture. Narrowly defined, as an institution for the universal conveying of mail, postal culture made mass migrant epistolarity possible. However, the Chinese case shows that the post office was not a sine qua non of migrant correspondence, though *qiaopi* traders often used it for part of the delivery.

Mass-based postal culture arose after the start of the great migrations and peaked after the proliferation of new rail and shipping routes. The best studies are on Italy, where writing letters and postcards, publishing letters in the press, and producing letter-writing manuals took off in the 1870s and contributed to creating an Italian national identity. Gabriella Romani sees Italy's postal transformation as a key moment in Italy's modernization and democratization and in engendering a "shared language of sociability." Letters created an "incorporeal" interlocutor that became the nation.[18] In other countries, the spread of letter-writing to the poor also intersected with the rise of a postal culture and national identity.[19]

As part of postal culture, letter-writing manuals became popular throughout the world at the end of the nineteenth century. Hundreds appeared in English and other languages.[20] However, the craze followed the start of large-scale emigration, whose migrant writers borrowed their style from other sources (notably, the Bible).

In America and elsewhere, letters became a main form of life-writing in the nineteenth century, the "foundational genre of American journalism" and the "most prevalent literary form."[21] Epistolary fiction, a genre rooted in European literature and linked with the publication of letter books, also became popular.[22]

Fitzpatrick and others argue that the conventions migrants' letters followed were not copied from manuals or textbooks. Most writers were unfamiliar with epistolary conventions and drew their "untutored eloquence" from other sources. Fitzpatrick cannot say how the forms of the migrants' letter came into being, but he rejects the idea that it was modeled on "formal rhetoric, popular manuals, or elementary education." Instead, it evolved through "practice and imitation," like a dialect.[23] Miguel Angel Vargas agrees that migrants' letters evolved independently of manuals and followed their own "particular practices of writing and reading."[24] Some later migrants consulted the manuals and drew inspiration from them, but most were probably put off by the cost and their own poor reading ability.[25]

The same goes for Chinese migrants. China too had a long tradition of letter books, and the tradition revived in the twentieth century among urban women.[26] The epistolary novel had indigenous roots in China and was instantiated in the diaspora.[27] Chapbooks were available in Chinatown as a way of learning pidgin. However, there is no evidence that letter books played a role in Chinese migrants' writing.

FEATURES AND MATERIALITY OF THE LETTER

Of the many definitions of the letter, that followed here, chosen for its clarity, is from Antje Richter's book on Chinese letters. For Richter, a letter "is a communication written on a tangible medium by one historical person and addressed to another (or, as the case may be, by one narrowly circumscribed group to another), which, in order to reach its spatially removed addressee, undergoes some form of physical transmission involving a third party and is, more often than not, part of an exchange."

Letters are, by nature, self-referential, illocutionary, and subject to occasionality—i.e., written by an author whose stance is overtly positioned to effect an intention, and in specific circumstances. They are also, says Liz Stanley, a writer on letters as "documents of life," both dialogic (part of an exchange) and perspectival (they change with the recipient and "take on the perspective of the 'moment'"). Richter calls their form, content, and function indeterminate, for the epistolary situation, like all social interaction, knows endless permutations.[28]

Richter classifies letters as informal, literary, or open. Given the indeterminacy, these categories are not mutually exclusive. Most migrants' letters are personal, sent by one individual to another, a friend or relative, concerning personal rather than other matters. Personal correspondence includes letters of thanks, recommendation, and admonition.[29] It also includes ritual correspondence expressing condolences or reporting on births, deaths, marriages, etc.

Like other letters, some migrants' letters were written or addressed collectively. This is especially true of *qiaopi*. They were more likely than other migrants' letters to straddle the boundary between personal and business matters. In some cases, they were mere chits or memoranda recording financial transactions. As we have seen, in times of war, when secrecy was essential, couriers memorized amounts and addresses and delivered an "oral letter," the *kouxin*—i.e., no letter at all.

Do similar conventions apply to all letters, regardless of nationality? Stanley thinks yes, but they "provide a loose shape rather than being determining." They have remained stable over time. Letters have "specific recognizable rhetorical features, including a salutation to an addressee, greetings and excuses, other usually descriptive content, closing material, a closure, and a signature." Letters written centuries and continents apart are recognizably "the same kind." However, they can mutate into other genres, like the British banknote, which began as a letter "promising to 'pay the bearer on demand' its weight in gold coinage," in an evolution not unlike that of some forms of *qiaopi*.[30] So there is a sameness of epistolary traditions.

In classical theory formulated along Ciceronian lines, letters had a *salutatio*, *exordium*, *narratio*, *petitio*, *conclusio*, *subscriptio*, and *inscriptio* or *superscriptio*. In the seventeenth century, this model gave way to a more spontaneous, colloquial style.[31] However, a shadow of the seven *topoi* still stalks the genre.

According to Richter, "letters all over the world" take the form of a "tripartite composition" comprising salutation, letter body, and closing words. This structure can be stretched into five parts, corresponding roughly to the divisions of classical rhetoric, if the salutation is divided into a prescript and a proem (the *exordium*, usually aimed at establishing goodwill) and the closure into an epilogue and postscript. This scheme applies to non-Western letters, too.[32]

Writing about Irish migrants' correspondence, David Fitzpatrick described its functions as supplying public and private information, sustaining material and emotional ties, and helping to shape future migration. It varied in type, depending on the writer's provenance, gender, social class, schooling, etc., but evinced a "distinctive blend of ceremonial and conversational elements" and a complex routine of formulaic phrases that kept elements of the classical structure. It was framed around references to the correspondents and to health matters, religious evocations, and personal messages.[33] Across the world, it had a similar structure. Daiva Markelis, writing about Lithuanian letters, notes a sameness of tone and of established forms and rituals.[34] Portuguese migrants wrote according to a formula comprising "date, opening, [religious] invocation, greeting, discussions, greetings, best wishes, blessings, and farewells."[35]

The passage in letter-writing from the formal, the pedagogical, and the literary to the informal and the conversational was steepest during the mass migrations of the nineteenth century, when lower classes, including semiliterates, started writing home. Migration from village to town had spread the letter-writing habit past the educated elite, but overseas emigration, together with the birth of a postal culture, led millions more to write, giving rise a new style based on the stunted skills of migrant "scribes" who, as Bill Jones said, would otherwise never have dreamed of putting pen to paper.[36] The letters' informal tone magnified the dialogity and occasionality, making them doubly opaque.[37] On the whole, however, they conformed to Richter's schema.

Are migrants' letters a subset of personal letters? They have features in common that are not exclusive to them but are probably more likely to be found in them than in other letters. The time lag between writing and delivery, and the overall turnaround time, was far greater than the normal interval, heightening the sense of expectation. The sudden and complete change in the writers' circumstances and the disparity between their new and old lives dramatized the exchange.

But despite commonalities, scholars find more diversity and formlessness in European migrants' letters than linkages, "core common purpose," and "grand emplotment schemes."[38] They have a less sophisticated style than elite letters but treat a broader range of themes than the mere practicalities of migration.

Qiaopi letters do many of the same things as general migrant correspondence. They maintain the tie of family solidarity and convey personal and domestic news and migratory intelligence. Like all letters, they generally conform to the imperatives of epistography as set out in classical texts. However, they have fewer styles and types than other migrants' letters, mainly because of their narrower focus on remittance.

Chinese migrants' letters fall into three classes, although these do not exhaust the types and some letters have an individual character. The classes are (1) letters to the head of the senior generation, usually the migrant's parent, nominally the decision-maker and the most likely addressee; (2) letters to the wife; and (3) letters to younger siblings, cousins, sons, daughters, and other relatives. Letters to the head were deferential. Letters to wives could be intimate. Letters to younger relatives were often to instruct them or tell them off. The types were not absolute: elements of one can be found in another.

Qiaopi letters were even less likely than European migrants' letters to be influenced by letter-writing of the elite, the literati, and the gentry class. China had a rooted indigenous epistolary tradition, but it served a world apart from that of the villagers who were the majority of migrants. However, Chinese migrants' educational level and social class were not entirely uniform. Some belonged to the lower gentry or professional classes and were familiar with letter-writing.

Since few Chinese migrants were educated, most got professional scribes to write their *qiaopi*. As a result, many *qiaopi* shared the same format and similar, stereotyped sentences. Few of the *qiaopi* letters were written in standard Chinese, and many were unpunctuated. Most were written partly in dialect.

The Letter's Materiality

The handwritten and individually addressed letter is a unique artefact with a seductive materiality few literary genres can match. Richter calls it more tangible than other writing, being physical, singular, and specific. Concealed in an envelope, it can be accompanied by or in response to gifts, and it is specially transmitted.[39]

The magic materiality of the traditional Chinese letter was magnified by the decoration of its paper. The scholar's fourth treasure (after brush, inkstick, and inkslab), paper had been visually enhanced ever since its invention in the Eastern Han. Papermakers started coloring and decorating writing paper in the fourth century at the latest. The decoration later incorporated designs printed by woodblock, ranging from columns to guide the handwriting to border designs featuring bamboo, animals (especially geese and fish, symbolizing distance), landscapes, etc., including modern-day images of the fight against imperialism.[40]

Europeans started illustrating letter paper in the late eighteenth century, after the birth of postcards. When envelopes were introduced in Britain around 1840, they too sometimes featured pictures.[41] However, pre-decorated stationery never became as popular as in China.

Qiaopi entrepreneurs embraced the Chinese tradition of epistolary decoration and extended it to the envelope. They decorated *qiaopi* and *huipi* envelopes with adverts for their services, cultural motifs, patriotic slogans, and a red seal stripe featuring orchids, jade, or other symbols of virtue, family harmony, fertility, longevity, etc., as well as examples of painting and calligraphy.[42] However, the letter paper provided as part of the service was kept small to minimize the weight of the clubbed packages. This curtailed the extent of the decoration.

The *qiaopi* letter was the most tangible of letters, not just because of its design but also because of the remittance. This came either in prized gold or silver coinage (in the early days) or recorded on imposing official slips.

Whatever their nationality, most migrants wrote poorly in a jumble of styles, daunted by the technology of writing. Writers were not unaware of style conventions and tried to apply them, but rarely to much effect.[43] The Chinese letter has been associated with calligraphy ever since the later Han Dynasty.[44] The link added to its lustre, and the calligraphy was displayed, blurring the epistolary distinction between public and private.[45] Most Chinese migrants' letters were in a rough hand, except for those done professionally, for a fee, or by a *piju* employee. However, some writers prided themselves on their penmanship, learned at school in China or overseas, and displayed it on the envelope and in the letter.

The Cost of Postage

The cost of postage, paper, envelopes, and pens bore on the form of postal culture in migrant communities. During the nineteenth century, the price of stamps and stationery fell in real terms, but a letter was never cheap. In the early nineteenth century, writing home and getting return mail could take a week's wages.

A letter to Europe cost "enough to deter most plebeian correspondents from dashing off trivial notes." As a precious investment, it was usually composed with great care, straying as little as possible from the point and making full use of the available space.[46] The cost of stamps encouraged writers to share letters.[47]

Qiaopi, in contrast, cost little or nothing and were part of a regular routine tied to the schedule of the ships that carried them. The *qiaopi* trade was very competitive and made most of its profit by manipulating the exchange rate and using remittances as capital to finance trading schemes. Some firms charged no fee at all and provided free paper and envelopes. All provided a free answer service for the recipient. A *qiaopi* envelope needed, in principle, include no more than the bare notice of dispatch. Most remitters used the opportunity to write a letter, but with scant sense of occasion. European migrants, who did not enjoy a free or cheap letter service, weighed the cost of postage against their general budget. Over time, it could become an obstacle to preserving ties.[48]

Letter Contents

Qiaopi letters were delivered in the same envelope as a remittance. Not all Chinese migrants' letters were sent as *qiaopi*, but little work has appeared on non-*qiaopi* letters, so one cannot say to what extent they resemble *qiaopi* letters.[49] Even *qiaopi* letters come in many forms and treat a wide range of subjects, so they resist simple categorizing and are not necessarily distinguishable from other letters. They form a subgenre, but like all epistolary genres, its boundary is porous.

European migrants sometimes sent money with a letter. However, remittances were not part of the letter by definition, and the sums remitted were usually small and had an emotional rather than an economic impact; bigger amounts went through the formal sector.[50] In the *qiaopi* trade, amounts big and small followed the same route.

Migrants in the nineteenth and twentieth centuries were agents and objects of massive global change, but their letters rarely reflected on big issues of the day and stuck mainly to practicalities, domestic business, consolation, and reassurance.[51] This is true of both European migrants' letters and *qiaopi* letters. Few *qiaopi* letters ever talked about political topics, except when political change directly affected their lives—for example, during the Second World War and during anti-Chinese campaigns. However, Western migrants were more likely than *qiaopi* writers to reflect on novel encounters overseas and engage in self-revelation.

How to explain the greater fullness of European migrants' letters? The cost of stamps drove writers to make the most of the paper. Levels of literacy and the extent to which letter-writing was habitual were part of the explanation. Even among European migrants, literacy levels differed widely. Lithuanians in America were among the least literate, whereas Jews and Swedes were natural letter writers. Most Welsh migrants could read and write because of church schools, while in Italy literacy programs had taught many migrants to do so by the time migration took off.[52]

The literacy rate among early Chinese emigrants was low, and in America it declined in the course of the nineteenth century because of the "coolie" trade.[53] Like Western migrants, Chinese wrote home with the help of relatives and friends, but roadside scribes and *piju* employees, whose services were sometimes free, often helped. Migrants of many nationalities used preprinted letters: the Lithuanian version offered advice and notices ranging from the practical to the religious and the sentimental, and Swedes used both preprinted forms and "ghost" writers.[54] However, preprinted and "ghosted" or dictated letters were probably commonest among Chinese because of illiteracy, *qiaopi* services (which were usually free), and the *qiaopi* letters' frequency and routineness.

Migrants' social background differed strikingly from person to person and group to group. However, an overall distinction can be drawn between Chinese and European migrants. Europeans of all nationalities came from a wider range of places and, in general, higher social classes than the Chinese, nearly all of whom were poor rural dwellers from a handful of counties. European migrants were usually more literate and had wider intellectual and political horizons than both their nonmigrant conationals and the Chinese.

However, this generalization did not apply everywhere. Although the great majority of Chinese in Southeast Asia were "coolies" driven abroad by poverty, most early Chinese in America were middle and lower-middle class.[55] Other migrant Chinese communities were also more socially diverse than is often thought.

The main reason for the difference in European migrants' letters and *qiaopi* letters is that they served different ends. The European letters strove toward relative fullness because they sought to maintain or repair a family tie. They were liberally punctuated with expressions of warmth.[56] Chinese migrants were less isolated, having sailed abroad with kith and kin and landed in a home from home of sorts. Their letters were more likely to focus on money and promoting family migration.

Some themes in European and Chinese migrant letters are the same, but beyond a core of matters such as transoceanic separation and the maintenance of the migration chain, they tend to address different issues in different ways. These differences can be explained in part by each group's relationship to its sending and receiving places, and its purpose in going abroad and staying in touch with home.

Relative distance between sending and receiving place shapes migrants' perception of their situation and their relationship to home. Most Europeans in the New World and the even further antipodes had gone to settle permanently, or quickly accepted that they would.[57] At the height of European migration to America, some returned—ranging from a third of English (mostly only briefly) to 5 percent of Dutch and Germans—but the great majority stayed.[58] From Australia, fewer still returned.[59]

Chinese went home from America in relatively large numbers—probably around half—between 1850 and 1889.[60] A similar proportion is thought to have returned from Australia.[61] The proportion returning from Southeast Asia was higher than the general European return. The sense of rupture was less in the Nanyang than for Europeans in America and Australasia, and that of uninterrupted belonging to the homeland greater. Returning was well organized and cheaper than for Europeans, many of whom could not afford to go. Southeast Asia's urban culture and physical geography was influenced by the Chinese presence and resembled that of Guangdong and Fujian, while Chinatown heightened the sense of familiarity. The fields were worked differently, but the underlying landscape was similar. Chinese tended, initially, to concentrate in just a few places, members of dialect and kinship groups even more so. Southeast Asia, especially its continental portion, was nearer to China than white settlements were to Europe, and getting home was easier. For Europeans the distance was vast, as was the degree of scattering. As many as one in four migrants' letters failed to arrive from the remotest settlements. Even members of a single family were scattered across the world with little chance of staying in touch.[62]

For Europeans, the physical discontinuity and the feeling of "no going back" was matched by a sense of existential rupture.[63] White migrants craved a fresh start, free from constraints and inhibitions. Gerber notes the role played by proletarianization at home and the allure of "rural self-sufficiency" abroad.[64] Some turned their back on home; others reimagined it in line with their new self-image.[65] According to Richards, most British migrants survived transplantation by "sloughing off their British past."[66] Chinese, in contrast, were emissaries of their families; few risked ostracism and isolation by striking out alone.

"Race" and religion were the main underpinnings of European migrants' confidence. The sense of moral superiority was greatest among those with cultural and "racial" attributes of the WASP ascendancy, which reached its apogee in the early twentieth century, displayed in abundance in Scandinavian migrants' letters.[67]

Qiaopi letters show that migrants and their families lived their lives, for the most part, in the traditional way and were guided by traditional thinking. For example, some spoke about praying and religion, and uttered religious invocations. However, there is less explicit discussion of religious issues in Chinese migrants' letters than in European migrants' letters. The latter not only opened, typically, with a religious intercession but articulated religious viewpoints that led them to describe social practices and reveal their own inner feelings. Welsh commented on the lack of chapels in America, the Catholics taking over, the dangers of drink and profligacy, the duplicity of the Mormons, and so on.[68] Dutch expressed faith in God's providence and church fellowship.[69] Norwegians praised the lay or trained preacher.[70] Much of the rhetoric in British letters copied preaching styles and the Bible.[71]

Letters from migrants fleeing persecution and members of discriminated religious minorities identified closely with the new freedom. Germans after 1848 rejoiced in their liberation and did not write about returning.[72] In America, they created a new language of citizenship and "became the most passionate and powerful pluralists."[73]

Letters renegotiated the writers' relationship with home, but they also initiated would-be migrants into the ways of the new society, what Nicholas Tavuchis (borrowing from Robert K. Merton) called "anticipatory socialization."[74] Letters from migrants en route to New Zealand demonstrated an uplifted spirit, free of class oppression, well before arrival.[75] Italian letters spoke of abundance, richness, and freedom.[76] Irish letter writers in the eighteenth century created a "paradisiacal" image of America and reshaped their view of Ireland and their own Irishness in line with their new perceptions.[77] Norwegian letters praised American laws and institutions.[78]

In the late nineteenth century, a new tone of disillusion entered the letters. Migration was equated with liberation up to 1848, in the era of democratic revolution, but later letters saw it more critically.[79] Many German letters from America switched from celebrating the republic and universal values to criticizing materialism. However, the overseas identification survived the fading of the ideal. America had become not repulsive but normal.[80]

Gerber explains that most European migrants' letters focused on family concerns, practicalities, and maintaining the writers' sense of personal identity and continuity in an unfamiliar and unpredictable context. The letters enabled "a collaborative process of interpersonal communication," the "narrative construction of self," and the repair of intimate relationships "rendered vulnerable by . . . separation." They lay at the conceptual conjunct "of the self-in-relationship, personal identity, the narrative construction of the self, discourse, and acts of literacy."[81] A study on Swedish migrants' letters agrees that they allowed migrants to come to terms with "the tensions inherent in the displacement" and to engage in self-reflection and reimagine their own identities.[82] Richards says that migrants were more likely than nonmigrants "to reflect on their condition," and to experience collective mind-sets bordering on madness.[83] Dutch migrants' letters were far more open than the culture of the time.[84]

European migrants' letters did not always tell the truth, to spare addressees concern and avoid personal embarrassment. Gerber uses the term "masquerades" to denote their tendency to "exaggerate the gains" of emigration and downplay the hardship. Serra identifies a tendency among Italian migrants to omit negative comments from their letters; in this regard, the sub-genre of migrants' letters differed from the wider genre of personal letters, with its premium on "clarity and truth."[85]

However, most European migrants avoided painting an excessively euphoric picture for which they might be held to account by new arrivals. Many candidly admitted their failures and dashed hopes. Inevitably, those who adapted best to their destinations were less likely to write home than the failures. Richards even says that migrants' letters can best be seen as a record of failure.[86]

Gerber establishes a three-fold division of European migrants' letters. *Regulative* letters aimed at "organizing and maintaining" relationships and networks, including the "schedule of epistolary exchange." *Expressive* letters sought "to represent lived experience [and] emotional states" and to realize the relationship through endearments and professions of feeling. *Descriptive* letters told of "daily concerns, events, and routines."[87]

European migrants mostly wrote regulative letters. Most *qiaopi* letters were also regulative, by Gerber's definition. They were also descriptive, particularly in regard to the advisability of further emigration. But they were far less given to self-expression, imagination, and creativity. They were, on the whole, less demonstrative, more reserved, and less likely to betray innermost feelings. Some touched on family scandals, but personal and family affairs could rarely be kept secret for long in lineage settlements, so the scandals were public anyway.

Can the expressive deficit be explained by the writers' maleness and the rigidity of Chinese gender roles? Gerber doubts whether there is a simple correlation between "gender and the expression of emotion in [European] immigrant epistolarity" and points out that male migrants also engaged in it.[88] However, its absence from most *qiaopi* letters can probably be explained by the lesser intensity of emotional display and expression of intimacy in Chinese culture, particularly in males.

Chinese letters were more uniform and less given to self-reflection and self-display. Writers, overwhelmingly male, avoided distressing accounts of hardship and struck a stoic tone. Roles mattered more in Chinese society than individual experience, and mutual dependence more than self-reliance. Admissions of failure were avoided. Self-doubt was concealed beneath a cult of face—and fear of the loss of face as a result of others' perception of the wearer's incompetence.

Personal feelings mattered less in China, where the self was interdependent, than in societies that prized independence. Personality in China was expressed more in interpersonal relations, social roles, and moral deeds than in emotions and self-assertion. In societies constituted more by individuals than by collectives, self-expression is expected. This difference explains the self-restraint of Chinese letters, which focused on practical matters and formal relations.

Collective obligations disinclined Chinese migrants to gloss over the difficulties for the sake of those intending to follow them abroad. Their roles were to provide for the family by remitting at predictable intervals and to pave the way for further migration. The remittances told their own tale: Were they punctual, substantial, and increasing? Was the overseas economy buoyant? Critical decisions depended on the accuracy of the information sent along *qiaopi* channels. Prevarication, equivocation, and the withholding of bad news could backfire. So whereas European migrants practiced "strategic silence," Chinese were under pressure to provide reliable and regular intelligence.[89] The *qiaopi* system created a transnational community of migrants and their dependents whose business at either end of the chain was hard to hide.

One function of letters for non-Anglophone migrants was to keep ancestral languages alive.[90] Chinese writers, however, lived in Chinatown, a Chinese world, and used a Chinese-language postal service that even let them write their envelopes in Chinese. People did not use Chinese to make a statement. Their situation resembled that of English speakers in the big migrant countries, save that they identified with the homeland, not the Anglophone receiving place.

A subset of letters concerned with preserving relationships was the "romance epistolary," keeping love alive despite separation. Love letters, though rare, are a part of European migrant correspondence, and there is even a book on them.[91] They are rarer still in Chinese migrant epistography. China has a long indigenous tradition of love letters, but *qiaopi* letters avoided not just expressions of spousal love but even endearments of the sort that were commonplace in European migrants' letters.[92]

The renegotiation of relationships with fellow migrants or people at home also features less in *qiaopi* correspondence. Chinese migrants' relationships did change. Their earnings increased their power in the family and their social standing. They became financially independent and, in many cases, important. However, this change rarely resulted in overt self-questioning or relational readjustment. Instead, people adapted their behavior to accord with changed norms and expectations.

The sure knowledge that letters would be passed from hand to hand or read aloud inhibited some Chinese from writing at all. Instead, they used the pre-printed forms provided by the *piju* and inscribed with platitudes, including a standard message or a choice of several such. This was less because the remitter was afraid of writing about things better kept private between himself and the addressee than because he feared being held up to ridicule if he spoke clumsily or offended conventions.

Respect and Deference

Studies on European migrants' letters mention the ways in which they convey deference and obligation. One of the first studies in the field, Thomas and Znaniecki's book on Polish migrants, coined the term "bowing letters" to capture it.[93] Chinese migrants' letters were even more likely to express deference, using a rich repertoire of linguistic markers denoting honorification and self-deprecation. They frequently contained terms such as "kneeling" and "bowing" before the "honored" and "respected" recipient, and writers often signed off (in letters to older relatives) as "stupid" or "kowtowing."

In historical Chinese, these practices were even more pronounced than their equivalent in medieval Europe.[94] One way to express deference and politeness was to avoid first- and second-person pronouns because they do not indicate status and instead to address people using kinship terms or "quasi-familial forms," even in family contexts. European migrants often called people by their personal names, whereas Chinese were more likely to address people in ways that indicated their seniority in age or generation.[95] It was also common for writers to make exaggerated apologies or self-inculpations. Not all *qiaopi* letters followed these conventions. Some used ordinary pronouns and non-deferential language. But most applied strategies of respect and deference that conveyed a strong sense of hierarchy.

OTHER ISSUES IN MIGRANT EPISTOGRAPHY

The previous section examined the materiality of Chinese and European migrant letters as well as their differences and commonalities. The following section focuses on epistolary scholarship, the blurring of the boundary between public and private, letters' literary excursions, and their role as guidebooks.

Epistolary Scholarship and Curation

Letters appear in all literate societies, but studies on letter-writing as a social and literary practice are quite rare. This is especially true of China, surprisingly, given that Chinese have been writing letters for more than two millennia. Richter attributes the lack in part to letters' absence from the Confucian canon. Classic texts have none of the epistles of the New Testament, which brought epistolary scholarship into being.[96]

Qiaopi studies are, as we have seen, a notable exception to this neglect. The interest is greatest in the provinces that engendered the *qiaopi* trade, whose registering in 2013 under UNESCO's Memory of the World Register brought it to wider attention.

Scholars of European migrants' letters regret the failure of museums, archives, and descendants to preserve them, and the fact that most preservers are middle class so the letters they collect usually have a narrow social range.[97] One study says that "only a tiny, infinitesimal fraction [of migrant letters] has been preserved and is available to researchers," and that the research population is defined not by researchers but by donors.[98] It is difficult, in most cases, to know what proportion preserved letters are of the total sent. The same goes for all European migrants' letters.[99] Inbound letters from Europe, which matched the outgoing in volume, are rarer still, given migrants' mobility and assimilation into the mainstream, where they shed their past.[100] Only 2 percent of letters in one German archive are "westbound."[101] But if even the epistolaria of well-known individuals are incomplete because of the "quintessentially fragmentary and dispersed nature of letter writing and receiving," group collections are inevitably more so.[102] This incompleteness reduces the value of preserved letters, which are often obscure out of context and sequence and unless they reflect the emigrant enterprise's "full unwinding."[103]

Collections of *qiaopi* letters are more complete than those of European migrants' letters, and in fuller runs, as we have seen. They were retained because of their remittance function and for cultural, demographic, and institutional reasons. Historically, Chinese revered written characters. There was particular cause to preserve *qiaopi*, which documented financial transactions that might need consulting and so were kept as a matter of course. Many were letters of admonition, their prescriptions permanently valid.

Scholars of European migrants' letters regret that collections are not just incomplete but atypical because of the underrepresentation of poor people and women. Gerber's writers were a "distinctly middling group" with "significant personal resources."[104] Richards' were richer and more literate than the general population in both the sending and the receiving places.[105]

Qiaopi collections, in contrast, are socially more inclusive. All classes remitted, and lowly recipients had no less need to document transactions by retaining stubs and correspondence than the high-placed.

However, the *qiaopi* collections are no less lacking in letters from home, for Chinese migrants and their descendants often abandoned their papers, which most could not read anyway. Families in China were far more likely to stay in the same place and to venerate the letters.[106] Chinese local government has played a part in rescuing letters by identifying descendants and getting them to help reconstruct the history of "the people without history." However, there has been less corresponding effort by overseas Chinese libraries and associations.

The attitude toward Western migrants' letters has changed greatly since Thomas and Znaniecki brought out their book on the Polish peasant in 1958, using migrants' letters to research the impact of modernization. Others have published letters in anthologies, as migrants' "authentic" voice, or used them to illustrate wider theses. Today, however, experts in the field have begun to focus on the letter as "the object to be studied rather than a source that advances the study of other phenomena," and as a means of inscribing "human relations and personal and social identities through the mobilization of language."[107] These approaches have little equivalent in *qiaopi* studies.

Migrants' letters in both China and the West have attracted the notice of linguists. Stephan Elspass has argued that they can be used to discover how ordinary people spoke in the past, since they largely ignored the prescriptions of grammarians and schoolteachers.[108] In China similar conclusions have been drawn. But other methods—for example, Emma Moreton's subjection of large corpus of migrant letters to linguistic analysis and "inferring outwards" from them—have no Chinese parallel.[109]

Western scholarship on migrant letters drew inspiration in the 1990s from the rise of transnationalism, contemporary and historical. The transnational turn led to a new view of migrants as straddling two or more places, the homeland, the new land, and perhaps the wider diaspora, between which letters were, for decades, the main link. Transnationalism is an emergent theme in Chinese migration studies, where it jibes with provincial and central authorities' interest in global networks. In both China and the West, the transnational turn has created an even stronger interest in finding the rarer *huipi*, which document a vital dimension of the exchange.[110]

Scores of articles have appeared on *qiaopi* and the *qiaopi* trade, but more effort has gone into producing sets of photostated material than into analyzing its contents. Chinese *qiaopi* scholars focus mainly on the historical, economic, and institutional setting, from the letter's collection in Chinatown and conveyance to China along networks to its delivery in the village. Why do they favor context over content? Few are familiar with discourse analysis, cultural studies, and the linguistic turn. Their Marxist approach foregrounds the objective setting and the bigger issues, rather than the minutiae of daily life. As local historians, they value the special features of *qiaopi* institutions. Finally, the practical nature of *qiaopi* letters makes them less responsive to literary, textual, and content analysis. They are more likely to be uniform and insubstantial.

Literary Excursions

Some European migrants wrote at length about their travel and encounters.[111] First letters often described the ocean journey, which took up to fourteen weeks to America in the early nineteenth century and longer to Australia.[112] The passage was difficult and dangerous, and its length signaled the depth of the rupture. Detailed accounts were sent home as shipboard journals and copied or bound as diaries for circulation. Letters about the crossing were the first in a series culminating in the migrants settling into their new homes.[113] "Arrival narratives" made detailed comparisons of the places left and reached.[114] Accounts of the hardships of pioneer life and of the "novelty of the entire process of migration from one country to another" followed. Elliott describes how even the travel narratives of uneducated migrants "conformed to literary conventions to some degree." Some narrated a voyage "from civilization to 'howling wilderness' and back," drawing on "popular culture, the press, Biblical language and metaphors, sermon literature and Shakespeare," turning new landscapes into familiar ones.[115] Even laborers' letters helped "make sense of and make their mark on their new landscapes" by engaging with "the tropes of civilization and savagery."[116]

The *qiaopi* letters rarely matched the creativity and poetry of these travel chronicles. Few recounted their writers' experiences at sea and in foreign ports with the same sense of wonderment and adventure. One reason is that the journey from China was often hellish, unlike the European crossings. New Chinese arrivals usually sent at most a note to say they had arrived "safe and sound," enclosing a couple of dollars (provided by the *piju*) as a token of future remittances.

However, some *qiaopi* and *huipi* talked about aspects of Western culture and lifestyle. Many showed a keen interest in photography. The benefits of drinking milk were among topics discussed in the correspondence. Family members in China wrote asking the migrants to send home modern products including clothes and medicine.

But the great majority of *qiaopi* letters were directed toward China-related concerns and business. Education was a common topic of *qiaopi* letters, far more so than in European migrants' correspondence. Writers instructed the younger generation left behind in the villages to study hard and to avoid gambling and other vices. Some *qiaopi* and *huipi*, especially those passing between Guangdong and the United States, discussed or arranged for dependent relatives or children to study abroad. However, this topic was unlikely to feature in *qiaopi* and *huipi* letters sent from and to Southeast Asia. *Qiaopi* letters inevitably reflected traditional thinking about the migrant's family responsibilities. "There are three unfilial acts, of which going without progeny is the least forgivable" was the best-known precept in premodern China and was frequently intoned. Some letters talked about adopting or buying a son or daughter for the migrant, who was in some cases childless after years of marital separation. There is no equivalent of this practice in European migrants' letters. *Qiaopi* letters often evoked the trope of "falling leaves settle on the roots," a sentiment used to reinforce the ideology of sojourning. Many letters ended with stock phrases about returning and the obstacles to it. Letters from the senior generation and from wives and children begged the migrants to return. This happened far more frequently than in European migrants' correspondence.

Abiding features of the Chinese letters are anxiety, pessimism, and the craving for mutual reassurance. European migrants also voiced concerns in letters, but less intensely, unremittingly, and inevitably. *Ping'an*, "safe and sound," was such a stand-ard cliché of attempted reassurance in both *qiaopi* and *huipi* that the first letter home after the migrant's arrival was known, colloquially, as the "safe-and-sound letter." The injunction on recipients at either end "not to worry" was similarly ubiq-uitous. Many letters from home started with a string of invocations wishing the recipient good things, principally good health and lots of money. The focus of *qiaopi* letters was, by definition, on remittance, so money matters and money quar-rels predominated, especially in the *huipi*, whose writers vied to control the remit-tance, shut others out from it, or get a bigger slice of it. Because Guangdong and Fujian were ravaged for a century by banditry and by civil wars, war with Japan, and a return to civil war, in that order, the correspondence is far more steeped than its European equivalent in a strong sense of personal and national tragedy—but only when directly experienced, and rarely as general political reflection.

Chinese and European letter writers responded differently to the experience of geographic dislocation because of physical and cultural distance and differences in social psychology. Even more important, however, was the exclusion of Chinese migrants from the social and political mainstream and their confinement to an ethnic enclave. If they developed a political awareness, it centered, of necessity, on Chinatown and China, just as their economic schemes were, for a long time, mostly an extension of their Chinese lives.

Privacy

A personal letter is, in principle, meant only for the recipient, who might or might not circulate it. This is one reason why it is sealed in an envelope—the other being to keep it from physical harm. This practice has applied to letters everywhere and at all times, including in China.

The epistolary boundary between public and private is not impermeable. Let-ters are passed around among intimates. Letters everywhere enter the public arena because of their intellectual or literary content, which can endure through genera-tions, as models of beautiful writing, eloquent expression, or fine reasoning. In China, letters' close connection with calligraphy has led to their circulation as cal-ligraphies.[117]

Scholars argue that migrants' letters were more public than most.[118] They were shown around informally and read aloud at the kitchen table, in the fields, at com-munal gatherings, or from the pulpit. In Italy, readings were held in "religious silence."[119] In European migrant communities where literacy levels were low, letter-writing was communal or collaborative, or a job for children who learned to write at school.[120]

To name this feature of the migrant letter, Gerber borrowed the term "vernacu-lar publication" (coined by Stephen Fender in *Sea Changes* for archived migrants' letters) to describe "acts of sharing personal letters through oral communications, which not only served to make public a private letter, but also elevated it within its own lifetime from a private writing to a social document."[121]

European migrants' letters were sometimes circulated in the press, by business interests or by charities and political groups that promoted emigration as a solution to social problems, or to serve a local network or propagate political ideas about democracy and reform (in an age of political change).[122] European migration agents even invented letters to drum up trade.[123] A charity scheme organized to send emigrants to Canada from England published "good letters" in pamphlet form.[124] Other schemes published letters from successful migrants urging people to migrate.[125] However, potential migrants rarely made their decision without receiving assurances from a friend or relative.[126]

Such practices further blur the distinction between private and public letters. Some scholars dismiss published migrants' letters as not necessarily representative, hard to verify, and probably edited, but others point to the close relationship between the press at home and the ethnic press overseas on the one hand and the migrants and their families on the other, as a sign of the emergence of a modern public sphere in the years before the fuller professionalization of the press and diasporic ethnicization and assimilation.[127]

Letters to the press were a feature of Chinese newspapers in the nineteenth century, just as they were throughout the world. Like published migrant letters, they have been neglected by social scientists. Natascha Gentz links these letters to Anderson's idea of an "imagined community" of readers, but she concedes that they were designed to promote consensus rather than debate and that their writers were literati, merchants, and professionals.[128]

Chinese migrants' letters offer a different perspective on Gentz's idea. As we explained in a previous chapter, the *qiaopi* trade was closely linked with the *qiaokan*, or migrant newspapers, that proliferated in China's migrant counties and were sometimes called "collective family letters." *Piju* owners supported the *qiaokan* financially, advertised in them, and helped in their distribution. However, the community "imagined" was not of nation but of dialect and place. In crises, the *qiaokan* backed the national effort, but its face was usually turned toward the migrant heartland.

Qiaopi letters were not published in the *qiaokan* in the same way as European migrants' letters—to promote migration. They were rarely circulated outside the family. However, if a migrant, a migrant's family, or a *qiaopi* trader wrote to the *qiaokan* offering a donation, the letter would usually be published. In Hong Kong after the Cultural Revolution, migrants' letters were published by the colonial government as propaganda to strengthen the migrants' Hong Kong attachment.

Qiaopi letters were less likely to express private sentiments than their European counterparts, but senders and recipients insisted on privacy in at least one respect. The sender's prime purpose was to remit money and get a receipt. Small remittances did not need to be concealed, since they were predictable, but big remittances could attract the attention of indigent relatives, local leaders demanding "donations," and bandits. So while the arrival of *qiaopi* letters was public knowledge, big remittances were hidden. The deliverer was also expected to keep quiet about them so they could be concealed until the time came to spend or bank them. But the secrecy had to do with the size of the remittance, not with a concern for personal privacy.

Migrants' Letters as Guidebooks

Migrants' letters were used not just to maintain family bonds but to encourage others to migrate, along the chain. They helped by providing information about the sea crossing, the reception, bureaucratic procedures at the port of entry, the availability of jobs, and prices and wages, and were seen everywhere as the most realistic guide.

In Europe, letters greatly stimulated migration and were widely transcribed and distributed. In Scandinavia, Ireland, and elsewhere, they were known as "America letters." They praised America and, where possible, enclosed prepaid tickets for relatives.[129] In the Jewish shtetl, letters played a bigger role in deciding to emigrate than the press.[130] In Italy, they built up the American myth by accentuating positive factors and playing down problems, either to avoid worrying recipients or through a reluctance to advertise their own anxieties. Together with remittances, they were "the conjunctive rings" of Italian migration.[131] Walter D. Kamphoefner, however, says that German migrants' letters offered "a nuanced portrait of conditions in America rather than euphoric immigration propaganda" because of the constraint that chain migration exercised. They were, he says, "the Real Guidebooks."[132]

Chinese migrants' letters played the same role, but with added dimensions. Chinese migrant chains were exceptionally long and well organized by clan. The correspondence of the American Chinese family studied by Haiming Liu was not one-way but "a network of communication among more than a dozen people" who exchanged "information, ideas, and feelings" to sustain social networks and expand chain migration. Some clans used letter networks to establish routes used by hundreds and even thousands of their members across the world. European migrants could, on the whole, migrate relatively freely for most of the nineteenth and twentieth centuries, but authorities nearly everywhere did their best to stop Chinese immigration. How to circumvent these obstacles by following the right routes and methods and how to provide satisfactory answers to immigration officials, in interrogations that could go on for days or weeks, was a main subject of the letters.

The problem of interrogations is usually associated with the "paper son" strategy, where Chinese who would otherwise have been refused admission to America used false papers to claim to be the sons of settled migrants, their "paper fathers."

Migrants bought "coaching letters" from professional coaches. But even some real sons were subject to interrogation and received coaching, in letters, on how to deal with it.[133]

Letters of Admonition

Historically, nearly all migrants were men. Their power was great, especially when their families lived off their remittances, and they exercised it by writing letters in which they made or interfered in decisions or adjudicated in disputes.

Didacticism is a feature, to a degree, of most male migrants' letters. Irish migrants, for example, wrote home for the edification of posterity, "to admonish their descendants to emulate the memoirists' alleged virtues and successes."[134] Dialogicity is said to be a key feature of the letter, but most didactic letters were monologues.[135] Monologic admonition was common in Chinese migrants' letters. This is reflected in the replies, which acknowledge receipt of letters of "instruction" and "guidance."

The letter of admonition has been part of Chinese epistolarity for centuries. Studies on Chinese letters in medieval times note the absence from them of "private matters" and their similarity and even "genetic filiation" to memorials. They were mostly between people of unequal status and were formulated according to strict rules and codes. The exercise of state power was personal and patriarchal, making the distinction between public and private redundant. Even family letters had the same style as official missives. In a society in which the literate worked in administration, most writing, even epistolary, was colored by bureaucratic procedures.[136] Richter, writing about the sub-genre of "letters of familial admonition," which have featured prominently in the Chinese epistolary tradition ever since the Han Dynasty, finds they have characteristics of the testament. They were pedagogic and might address future as well as present generations, and they were not always delivered over distance.[137]

Haiming Liu, in his study on the correspondence of a transnational Chinese family, showed how letter-writing remained a vehicle for transmitting moral values and ethical advice across generations and, in the case of migrants, oceans. China-bound letters (not in this case *qiaopi*-related) emphasized the importance of education, hard work, thrift, filial piety, and moral character, based on examples from history and family history. The letters spawned further letters in their turn, by lesser figures further down the family chain, who copied their style and precepts.[138]

There was no direct line of descent between the traditional letter of admonition and the *qiaopi*, for the literatus and the laborer or petty entrepreneur inhabited different spheres. However, they did have common features. Both sorts were designed to transmit moral values and instructions to relatives and to censure bad behavior. Unlike other correspondence, they tended to dispense with the proem, given that their authors were addressing inferiors and had no need to beat about the bush.[139] According to Richter, official letters were "content-oriented, formal, and literary," unlike personal letters, which were "relationship-oriented, informal, and quotidian."[140] By that definition, qiaopi letters of instruction had more in common with official than with personal letters. Like the traditional letter of admonition, they shared features with two other genres, the family instruction and the testament, documents to be passed down the generations. Both were either interventional ("occasioned by an occurrence in the life of the addressee") or testamentary ("precipitated by an existential experience of the writer"). However, only the qiaopi is, because of geography, transmitted of necessity by a third party, whereas the traditional letter of admonition did not always travel across space.[141]

The peremptory tone of some qiaopi correspondence sounded like a rough echo of bureaucratic language. This is not surprising, in a society in which writing was generally the preserve of authorities. It is reflected in the writers' habit of presenting their letters as "reports" (bing) to the senior generation. It has a match in the letters of poor people in other cultures, including migrants. Italian migrants, for example, signed letters home with both their first and their last names—because, says Serra, they "still smell bureaucracy in papers and pens."[142]

The generic likeness reflected similarities in the cultural setting of the two sorts of correspondence. The imperial state and the rural communities of the qiaopi writers coexisted symbiotically in a chain of authority that stretched from the court to the village. In this chain, few relationships were between equals. The villages were integrated by lineages and bound together by ancestor worship. The agrarian state used lineages to spread Confucian values to the villages and get villagers to bow to its authority. Family and clan interacted remotely with the state, ensured its stability and cohesion, and engaged in symbolic dialogue with it. The patriarchal family mirrored the state hierarchy, whose local representative was the "father-mother official," with the emperor as the people's father.

This helps explain the likeness between letters of admonition written by literati and qiaopi. Socially, their writers were poles apart, but they belonged to the same cultural tradition. Their task was to issue moral instruction and moral censure. They had no need to embellish their letters with prefaces and circumlocutions, for they were engaged not in negotiation but in blunt assertion. So their messages belonged to the same genetic type, as a result of parallel development rather than diffusion.

Not only Chinese migrants wrote letters of admonition. Most migrants worried about their wives, children, and siblings, and sent instructions along with the remittances. However, the Chinese tie was stronger, and many more Chinese letters contained instructions and advice. This was especially so in the case of families that depended on remittances, when male emigration became the norm and farming fell into decay. In such circumstances, the remitter's responsibility was all the greater. At the same time, young people in the villages felt they no longer needed to work or study, got used to a life of ease, and developed bad habits that led the providers to write rebuking them. This happened less in European countries, where the ratio of male to female migrants was more equal and whole families migrated.

In conclusion, *Qiaopi* letters shared some features with European migrants' letters because of the convergence of cultures, the spread of markets, the commonalities of the migrant condition, and the universality of epistolary conventions. However, the role played by *qiaopi* letters gave a special shape to their style and content.

The *qiaopi* trade was designed to remit money, to which the letter and the reply were necessary but incidental accompaniments to mark payment and receipt. The letter did not need to be substantial, and it was often a mere note. European migrants' letters were not, by definition, adjuncts to a remittance, and they tended to be fuller and more individual.

Qiaopi letters and European migrants' letters were mainly personal, but they were written with less regard to privacy and confidentiality than most personal letters. They were typically passed around or read aloud. In the case of *qiaopi* letters, where senders and recipients were illiterate, the courier might both read the letter and write the reply. On the whole, however, *qiaopi* letters were sent to named individuals and circulated only within the family rather than in public.

Migrants' correspondence differed according to demography, economics, and cultural traditions. The *qiaopi* trade served a society of sojourners that reproduced, overseas, basic structures of the kinship system of the sending place. That system, and the Confucian ideology underpinning it, was the frame of the migration and its institutions, including the *qiaopi* trade. *Qiaopi* correspondents observed conventions and proprieties appropriate to writer and addressee. Relationships within the Chinese family were less equal than those in the European family. Social, generational, and gender roles were, at the time, more fixed than European ones, a rigidity reflected in *qiaopi* letters' writing style. Most *qiaopi* were addressed to senior figures in the family, such as parents and grandparents, and to men rather than to women. Nearly all the migrants were men, who continued to play the role of master of the family by issuing instructions through letters.

Chinese emigration was a response to China's multiple crisis of sovereignty. This, together with kinship obligations, focused migrants' attention on the homeland. The cultural and geographic closeness to China of most Chinese migrant communities and their marginal status in white-ruled or majority-white countries inclined them (but not their descendants) to retain their ancestral identifications and uphold them by sending *qiaopi*. Many European migrants went abroad as individuals rather than as communities, and through choice rather than in response to a communal imperative. They migrated as part of the Western ascendancy to places that took them in and made them settlers, with a corresponding mindset. Few Chinese experienced migrating as liberation and rebirth. Most lived life in a Chinese key, in Chinatown. Migrating turned the affairs of migrants of all nationalities upside down, and some Chinese migrants became modern entrepreneurs and revolutionary activists. However, the Chinese migrant community's guiding beliefs, values, and habits remained relatively stable, which was reflected in the quieter, less radical, more practical and humdrum tone of their letters home.

Conclusions

The *qiaopi* trade was the basis for one of China's earliest excursions into the modern world economy. It quickly progressed from the one-man operations of the early years to the *piju* that formed to take advantage of the opportunities offered by the swift growth of Chinese emigration and remittance. It eventually matured into a stable industry with its own perfected mechanisms patched onto China's other modern institutions, like the banks and the post office, and linked to modern forms of communication and transport. It also gave an impetus to other forms of transnational and domestic industry and to urban growth in coastal cities adjacent to the *qiaoxiang*. Initially based on networks of blood, place, and tongue, it later joined or created national, transnational, and international networks based on trade, finance, and general migration, mainly in territories around the South China Sea but also in the goldrush Pacific—the Americas, Australia, and the South Pacific. These networks, maritime and terrestrial, were not just economic but also had deep cultural and social dimensions. Along them ran not just cash, capital, and goods but people, ideas, and information.

The *qiaopi* trade was, for the most part, except in the case of the big firms, diffuse rather than specialized. The average *piju*, especially the smaller ones, engaged in all sorts of business alongside *qiaopi*—far from interfering with the development of its *qiaopi* trade, this diversity increased clients' confidence and cut administrative costs.[1]

The trade was deeply embedded in tradition and its associated forms of trust, which defined relations between the *piju* and the remitter and recipient, between the *piju* and the hostel or *shanghao* with which the *piju* were associated, and among *piju*. However, the character of the trade was protean, not static, and over the years it underwent many transformations. These changes were not unidirectional or irreversible. The *qiaopi* system was characterized above all by its flexibility and adaptability. When a modern banking system and modern postal services took hold in China and in Chinese migrants' overseas destinations, *qiaopi* traders took advantage of the strong points of these institutions and, where it was profitable to do, entered into or initiated legally defined trust relations with them while taking care to adapt their new-style practices to local social conditions in the *qiaoxiang* and the diaspora. From these interactions there emerged a new synthetic system that hybridized ancient and modern forms of trust, the one *in personam*, the other *in rem*—the one rooted in social relations and community, the other in the market and society. Yet the former remained primary throughout.

The *qiaopi* trade was further defined by its strictly and exclusively regional nature, its "richness in human feeling," and its professional diffuseness and multiformity. Its regionalism was broadly drawn in the case of the bigger *piju* but sometimes exercised, in the case of smaller firms, on the tiniest scale: transgressing its regional limits reduced the intensity of trust. "Richness in human feeling" at first infused the entire *qiaopi* and *huipi* process. Even after the resort to banks and the post office in the middle stage of transmission, from abroad to China and vice versa, receipt and delivery retained that element of intimacy and fellow-feeling. Its multiformity—its engagement in many interlinked forms of business and social action—underlay its extensive ties to Chinese and ethnic-Chinese society and its intersecting, interlocking, and overlapping social and business networks, both regional and transnational.[2]

The *qiaopi* trade was a local and regional phenomenon that embraced only a small proportion of the Chinese population. It served those parts of China— mainly in Guangdong (including Hainan, which was part of Guangdong before 1988) and Fujian, but also in Hubei (Tianmen), Zhejiang (Qingtian), and Guangxi (Rongxian)—from which large numbers of migrants had left to work overseas as laborers or traders. Even within Guangdong and Fujian, only a small proportion of the forty or so counties in each province were major sources of emigration. Although the *qiaoxiang* in different parts of southern China shared similar interests and problems, Guangdong and Fujian had different provincial identities, and within each province the *qiaoxiang* were further subdivided by sub-ethnic and other loyalties and by dialect.[3]

Despite the trade's Chinese-ethnic diversity and the lack of direct geographic contiguity or of necessary political and cultural affinity between the counties and parts of counties it served, there were practical grounds for joint action and solidarity. Competition was not necessarily a barrier to cooperation. Although *piju* and *shuike* serving the same sub-ethnic segment of population were, actually or potentially, in rivalry with one another, those serving different places with which they almost invariably had an ascriptive relationship were unlikely to clash with one another. This was particularly true of *qiaopi* traders overseas, although traders from different places were more likely to be in close physical proximity with one another overseas than their counterparts in China. The only obvious case of intra-trade conflict in China was between Hakka traders and the Teochew-speaking Chaoshanese, who controlled the ports that received *qiaopi* destined for the Hakka hinterland and used their advantage, where possible, to extend their control into the Hakka counties.

Because of the deep segmentation of the *qiaopi* trade along sub-ethnic lines, a commonality of political and economic interest took decades to emerge and was never fully or lastingly consummated. The eventual trigger to its formation was state interference in the trade, both in China and overseas, by governments seeking to extend to it the concept of postal monopoly. On the whole, these state efforts to encroach on the trade failed because of the trade's vigorous resistance and its own intractability and impermeability—its transnational nature and amorphousness (to which neither the colonial and other non-Chinese states nor the Chinese state had much of an answer). Within China, they also failed because of the state's precarious hold on society and the economy, and the failure of the banks and the post office to establish a reliable service across the *qiaoxiang*; outside China, they failed because for decades Chinese tended to live separately in all-male ghettos, isolated from the non-Chinese around them and largely impervious to the efforts of the colonial (and Thai) states to control them. However, this onslaught by predatory authorities was not repulsed (to the extent that it was repulsed) without a political struggle, in the course of which the grounds for a new ethnic-Chinese political identity were greatly extended.

Was the new identity created by *qiaopi* and other outcomes of migration in the *qiaoxiang* an equivalent, in the *qiaopi* sphere, of the postal culture that in Italy, North America, and elsewhere brought into being a communicative network that helped generate and was coterminous with the nation? Not really, for it formed in large part in opposition to national authority, with which it was in competition. It was a newborn thing, but not one that fed directly, solely, and irreversibly into nationalist politics. In China, it expressed a corporate regional identity; overseas, it expressed a corporate Chinese-diasporic identity. Even so, there was a strong lateral link between *qiaopi* politics and Chinese national identity overseas.

A nationalist consciousness of the foreign threat to China arose most strongly among Chinese who experienced foreign power firsthand, along the Chinese coast and in Chinese settlements overseas. At first, the identity of Chinese overseas was chiefly cultural, and it remained deeply segmented. Not until the start of the twentieth century did it begin to take a political form, culminating in an attachment to the idea of Chinese nationhood. At first, Chinese politics overseas were confined to a minority of the educated elite, but in the 1920s these politics spread, in China and abroad, to large numbers of educated young people. In the 1930s, it became a mass movement representing all classes.

In Chinatown, *shuike* and *piju* owners were well equipped to play a part in ethnic-Chinese and diasporan politics because of their innate force of character, entrepreneurial ability, resources, and extensive ties in China and Chinatown and throughout the diaspora. In time, *qiaopi* networks stretched across regions and continents, and they packed political as well as economic clout. *Qiaopi* traders often played leading roles in chambers of commerce, the main site of political and economic activity at home and abroad, in the sending and receiving ports. They did so because of their position in the *qiaopi* trade and also because most big *qiaopi* traders had wide-ranging interests in all areas of society and the economy. This involvement of *qiaopi* traders in Chinatown politics was evident practically from the start. In eighteenth-century Batavia, for example, as we have seen, *shuike* were active in local Chinese institutions and regularly appeared before a tribunal of the local Chinese association to defend their practices.

Political mobilizations in support of the *qiaopi* trade preceded mobilizations in support of modern nationalism in China and the diaspora and, after nationalism's first full flowering, kept time with them. These political mobilizations could not have happened but for the prior consolidation of the trade in China and abroad, which came about after *qiaopi* agents were impelled on economic grounds to act together. Abroad, the organizations that formed initially on sub-ethnic lines later started to develop along pan-Chinese lines. These trade associations were tipped into politics by the hostile actions of the Chinese and other state authorities, which were seen to require a unified response.

Benedict Anderson's genealogy of nationhood in the Third World has been criticized for asserting that Third-World nationalists copied their idea of the nation from American and European models and for neglecting the nationalists' creativity.[4] The emergence in the *qiaoxiang* of Guangdong and Fujian of an indigenous political and social culture of print and post—based on the *qiaopi* trade and intent (at least initially) not on stoking nationalism or overthrowing the ancien régime but on maintaining emotional and economic ties between migrants and their sending places—supports the critics' view.

So the *qiaoxiang* case shows, yet again, that Third-World nation-building was not just an iteration of North American and European models but a phenomenon with sturdy indigenous roots. There is not just "one modernity" or "vision of modernization": the path to modernity outside Europe is not a repetition of "modular" forms first generated by whites or a convergence with them.[5] Although the *qiaopi* trade intersected and interacted with Western forms of economic organization and profit-making, and although *qiaopi* traders often copied new Western technologies to develop their businesses transnationally, they appropriated these technologies creatively, on the basis of structural, cultural, and institutional premises and in settings shaped by Chinese regional and national histories and traditions. This process of adaptation and selective appropriation generated a new national and transnational dynamic that has features in common with other modern societies but also draws strongly on China's internal cultural and institutional resources.

For many years, however, the unique role of the *qiaopi* trade in promoting the modernization of southeastern China and contributing to the economic health of the whole of China was obscured. This was partly because of the centralist fixation of Chinese governments of all stripes, starting with the imperial court. Beijing, later joined by Shanghai, was the main focus of China's central institutions, just as the eastern seaboard and the northern administrative region have been the main focus of its historians and thinkers. Although China's modern revolutions either began in the south (in the Nationalist case) or retreated there in the late 1920s (in the case of the Communists, whose geography starting in the early 1930s extended, more or less uninterruptedly through until 1949, to many of the *qiaoxiang*), this was forgotten or neglected under the consolidated regimes, whose history was rewritten with a bias to reflect the hegemony first of Chiang Kai-shek and then of Mao Zedong, leaders whose tie to the south frayed. The neglect was also due, in part, to a relative lack of source materials for historians to write from. The documentary record was far more copious in the case of the Shanxi traders and bankers of the north, who founded China's modern banking system, and the banks and industries of Shanghai and Tianjin.[6]

Since the 1990s, however, the founding of *qiaopi* archives in Guangdong and Fujian has turned the *qiaoxiang* and their nearby cities into a new focus of historical and sociological research. Departments of local and regional government have also begun to promote *qiaopi* studies as a topic in "patriotic education" and an early example of transnationalism and economic expansion, a "silk road on water," to match the northern land-based New Silk Road through Central Asia. The *qiaopi* trade now has its dedicated museums and exhibition halls, and some of the surviving sites of former *piju* have come under the protection of the authorities. In September 2014, the State Council even agreed to designate Shantou's Special Economic Zone as "an important passageway to 'the Maritime Silk Road,'" China's first such.[7]

Chinese economic culture is often reduced to a single stereotype rooted in Confucian ideas about Chinese society, which supposedly could be jolted into the modern world only by exogenous shocks, but studies on the *qiaopi* trade have started to rewrite the history and geography of Chinese modernism. This rewriting, which resurrects old ideas about the special nature of China's southeastern littoral, is closely connected with new trends in regional politics, now tolerated by a system formerly keener on homogeny than distinctions.

Qiaopi describe and embody the lives of ordinary Chinese migrants and their descendants and dependents, their hopes and fears, and their daily routines of business, labor, leisure, kinship, and fellowship in Chinatown and China. They present a rich mixture of intimacy and practicality. Unlike the official documents and elite observations from which accounts of migration and its impact at either end of the chain are usually written, they mostly depict individuals and communities on the margins of society or in its depths. They are not fine literature, and they lack the precision and aspiration to objectivity of scholarship. They are, for the most part, honest and unadorned by rhetoric. At times, they touch on politics in China and abroad and world affairs and crises, but through the rare prism of the eyes of ordinary Chinese, whose angles seldom figure in mainstream commentary. They are, as China's *qiaopi* historians like to say, a unique and "non-renewable" cultural resource.

Over the years, *qiaopi* generated a rich culture with many regional and national variants in China and the world. This culture includes folk songs, poems, stories and anecdotes about stock characters of the *qiaopi* world, and legends about its heroes. *Qiaopi* closely reflect the communities within which they circulated and preserve ethnographic information that would otherwise be impossible to retrieve, as well as linguistic evidence of how ordinary Chinese expressed themselves in the nineteenth and twentieth centuries, including in many remote dialects that are now dead or dying. In recent years, as part of the campaign to get *qiaopi* recognized as part of the world's documentary heritage, *qiaopi* historians in Fujian, Guangdong, and Chinese communities in many countries have worked hard to rescue this tradition from the oblivion into which it seemed destined to sink, and they told the story of the trade and the letters as a special branch of China's national and transnational story with its own strong local colors. In the course of its rediscovery and reimagining, it has become entwined with regional and diasporic identity, which has not just a cultural dimension but a solid material and financial one. As economic, administrative, and political decision-making in China becomes increasingly devolved and as old regional political traditions start to regain traction and new political identities begin to emerge, the history of the *qiaopi* trade is woven into China's budding polycentric politics.

The *qiaopi* trade, from its small geographic base, had a profound impact on China's national economy. The focus of research on China's modern economy in the early years has been overwhelmingly on Shanghai and the eastern seaboard, but research into the *qiaopi* trade shows that Shanghai and Hong Kong were, to a much larger extent than previously thought, indebted to it: without its input, their economies would have been substantially weaker.

The trade also transformed coastal parts of southern Fujian and eastern Guangdong. True, it did not lead to the creation of a sustainable modern economy in the *qiaoxiang* because of the ubiquitous political and military chaos and other factors, including a lack of transport and modern communications, but it did fuel the development of modern cities in the southeast and led to the introduction into economically backward regions of some modern forms of administration, notably banks and a postal culture. One of its greatest achievements was to catapult schools in the previously impoverished and marginal *qiaoxiang* to the top of regional and even national school leagues in China.

In Italy and the United States, the emergence of a postal culture led to greater literacy among the lower classes and thus created the potential for their participation in community and state affairs—i.e., politics. In the Chinese case, much of the correspondence from migrants to dependents, and even more so vice versa, was written on their behalf by others, including friends and relatives, *piju* staff, and professional roadside letter writers. However, the correspondence acted as a catalyst for the promotion of literacy. There is no statistical proof of this proposition, but in their letters home, many migrants urged their female relatives and their children to learn to read and write, and they funded schooling for their children, including girls, and even, in some cases, for wives and daughters-in-law.

Perhaps the most important legacy of the *qiaopi* trade to China and Southeast Asia was its creation of numerous bridges and transnational ties between China's *qiaoxiang* and their nearby cities on the one hand and migrant communities overseas on the other. These ties extended far beyond their original scope, as conduits for remittances, and swelled over time into a broader channel for the exchange of goods and people. The flow of capital, ideas, and population between Chinese in diaspora and their families and communities in China was a key driver in the remaking of China along modern and transnational lines. The *qiaopi* trade provided a foundation in institutions for transnational linkages, through *piju* and other associated mechanisms, and at the same time sustained an emotional connection between migrants and their friends and families through the letters they sent, with their rich messages and sentiments, and fulfilled the obsession of many of their writers with providing modern education in the towns and villages of the *qiaoxiang*.

The ties upon which the *qiaopi* trade rested were mainly prescribed, of blood, place, affinity, and sometimes friendship, but in some cases they were elective, in that they came to encompass ties of business or of politics. However, even in those cases they were reinforced and consolidated by social connections, so even the elective ties can be best described as particularistic.[8] Such ties were not an optional embellishment of the trade but lay at its very heart: they were its strength, but also (for example, in 1928 when the Tianyi remittance company collapsed) its weakness. This persistence of particularism in a trade that at its top end had numerous modern trappings and was closely linked with modern institutions like banks and the post office shows that in a community of migrants, culture and tradition can trump technology and economic determinism.

The *qiaopi* trade differed greatly from place to place, in relation both to the migrants' sending areas and to their destinations. The most obvious differences were those between Hakkas and non-Hakkas and between the trade in Southeast Asia and the "white" countries. A comparison brings to light the *qiaopi* system's enormous flexibility and adaptability, so that Chinese migrants throughout the world were able to apply network principles, maintain them smoothly and largely uninterruptedly over long periods of time, and link Chinese throughout the world both with their hometowns and villages and, where it was profitable or necessary to do so, with other diasporic outposts.

Appendix

Selected Qiaopi *and* Huipi *Letters*

1. REMITTANCE AND IMMIGRATION PROCEDURES
(NORTH AMERICA), 1905

*From Li Rurong in Vancouver to [his younger
brother] Li Rurong in Tangshan*

Third day of the fourth month, 1905.

Respected [Brother]

I have already received your two letters. I have also received the two seals sent by Uncle Li Wuchang. You say you want to come to Gold Mountain, but it's very difficult to get in.[1] In July and August, the Westerners didn't allow anyone into [North] America, new migrants and [returning] old migrants alike. If you want to come, you can go to Chicao.[2] Brother Huangde knows it is very difficult for people to get in. Once you reach Saltwater Port, the Westerners will cut your eyes.[3] If you really want to come, there's someone in Hong Kong who stands guarantor for people. You can wait and see if there is someone that can help to settle the migration procedure and be your guarantor in a few years' time. If there is someone who can do this, write and let me know. If there is no guarantor to carry out the procedure, you might need 1,300 silver dollars. Geji and I are in Yunlibi [in Canada]. We're both safe and sound, there's no need to worry. Here in the exterior, so far I don't have money to send back. I reckon I'll be able to send some in July or August at the latest. You told me in detail about the troubles you've been having in China, but my situation overseas is also difficult.

All best wishes,

Please pass on this letter to Huangde

Li Rurong

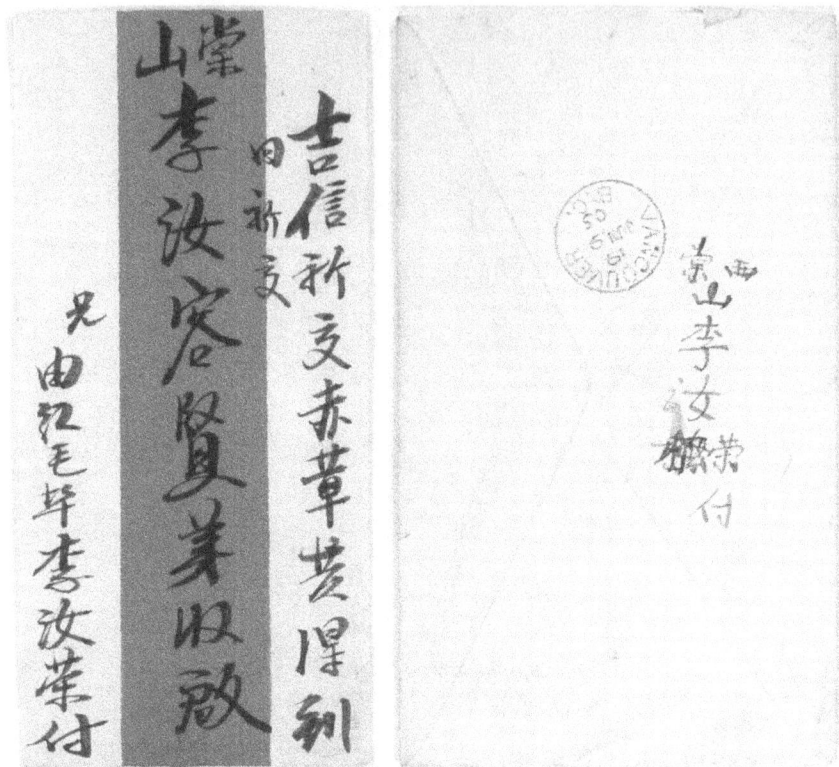

Remittance and Immigration Procedures (North America), 1905. Envelope. Source: City of Vancouver Archives, no. 1108334.

2. BUSINESS IN SINGAPORE
AND ARRANGED MARRIAGE, 1932

Song Jiarui in Singapore to his family in Chenghai

Reporting to Grandmother and Parents,

I honor my predecessors, to whom I respectfully report.

On the twenty-fourth of this month, I received your reply, all is clear to me. In your letter, you ask whether I have yet met my Uncle. I have been in Singapore for several months now, but during the day I am busy in the shop and unable to go out, so I have not met him, that's the fact of it. At night I also went to look for him in the Nansheng Shop, but he was not there either. I asked people in the shop to tell him. I went three or four times on consecutive nights, but failed to find him. Since arriving here, I've been more than a dozen times, always in vain. There's nothing that can be done.

Remittance and Immigration Procedures (North America), 1905. Source: City of Vancouver Archives, no. 1108334.

It's not that I don't want to find him. You wrote to give me an introduction. I've told you everything that happened. However, the Nansheng Shop has now closed down, and I have no idea where Uncle lives. It's very hard to track him down, as I told you. Also, I don't have a permanent job in the Qiansheng Shop—at present it's not easy to find work in Singapore. Businesses are closing down on every street. It seems to me there's nothing can

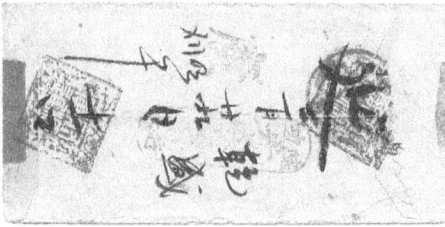

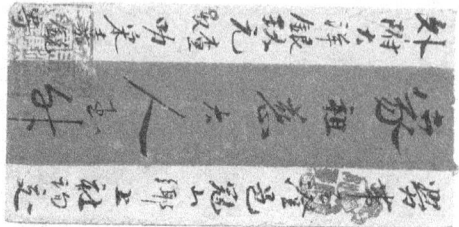

Business in Singapore and Arranged Marriage, 1932. Source: Chaoshan lishi wenhua yanjiu zhongxin ("Chaoshan Historical and Cultural Research Center"). 2007. Vol. 1, no. 4, of *Chaoshan qiaopi jicheng* ("Collection of Chaoshan *Qiaopi*"). Nanning: Guangxi shifan daxue chuban she, 2.

be done. They're not even boiling sugar in the [sweet] shop. When they start boiling again, I'll see if Elder Brother will pay my wages.[4] I will let you know at the time. Every month Elder Brother posts the family letter on my behalf, and gives me a dollar or two to live on. Everything costs a lot in Singapore, and I can never save much, I save just a little. About getting married: if you, my parents, want me to, then choose a wife for me. But Uncle is nearly fifty.[5] He must not leave the the home to live outside. Under no circumstances! He must continue to live at home, where you are safe and sound. If he really does decide to go somewhere else to live, then it would be better not to find me a wife. Be sure to do as I say in this regard. According to the letter, Uncle's legs no longer work properly. That worries me no end. Uncle is old. He must pay attention to his health, so that I can cease to worry. Today a ship is about to sail, so I'm sending a letter with nine dollars for you to spend. Let's talk about the other business later.

Humbly,

Your Son Jiarui
Twenty-ninth day of the third month, 1932

3. RAMPANT INFLATION, 1938

*Letter from Chen Yingchuan in Malaya to his younger
sister and brother-in-law in Chenghai*

1938

Dear Brother-in-Law Bingfa and Younger Sister Xuanqing,

I hope the harvest is good. I hope you are all as you should be.

I received the letter, what Brother-in-Law said filled me with emotions. Younger Sister Xuanqing wants me to send more money for housekeeping. I take this very much to heart. It's not that I don't know the pain suffered by my family, that is really Heaven's will. The sooner the Government acts correctly, the sooner we can expect happiness. The money I send each time I write is all for the family budget. But what can I do, every time I take money to the remittance shop, it gets smaller day by day, and only half the amount reaches home. Prices are rising day by day, and the money buys less and less. Both sides lose out, it's really hard to swallow. Like the forty dollars I sent, it takes a month to reach home, but in the meantime one hundred dollars has fallen in value by sixteen Singapore dollars. One hundred dollars is equal to seventy seven dollars at the time sent. On the ninth of this month I sent $100, and on the twentieth I sent $100, so in forty days I sent a total of $240, and up to now you haven't written back. I heard recently that I got a baby boy, and Younger Sister did too, that can really be called double happiness. I was really relieved to hear it. I'm in good health. You ask me to send photographs, I will enclose them in the next letter. I'm interested in photography, and I've done some research on it. Recently I took some registration photos for various people. In future, if I get the chance, I would like to recruit friends to open a photography shop. I don't know if I can achieve my aim. I'll let you know if I do. If you have some money left over, get Mother and Father's concubine to pose for a family photo. You can change the Singapore dollars I'm sending and use the money for clothes. Next month I'll send more money, don't worry.

Best wishes.

Peace.

November 27, twenty-seventh year of the Republic
Stupid Chen Yingchuan

4. DISTRIBUTION OF REMITTANCES, 1939

*Letter from Song Jiarui in Singapore
to his mother in Chenghai*

1939
Reporting

Dear Mother,

Kneeling before you I report:

I received a reply from the remittance shop. I've read it and know its contents. On the eighth of this month, I sent a letter and sixty dollars, you should have received it and your reply is probably underway. I also gave a remittance of $50 to the remittance shop, check

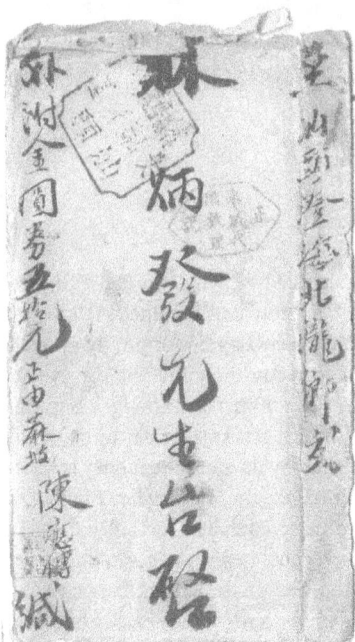

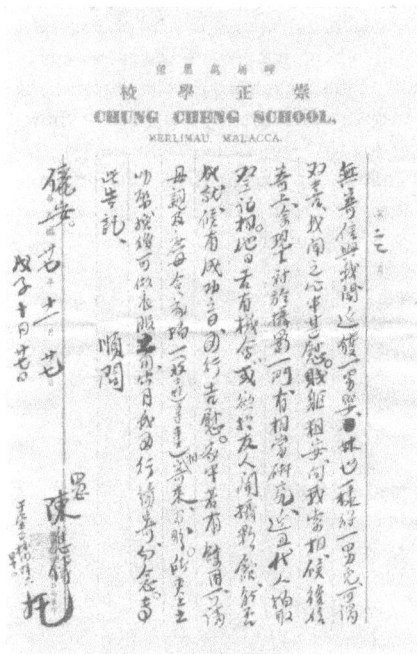

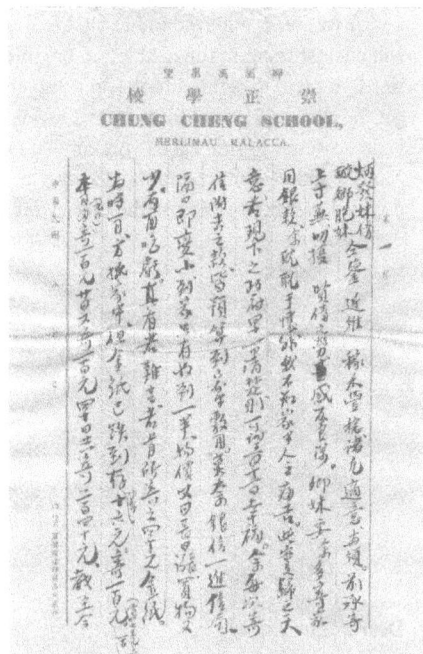

Rampant Inflation, 1938. Source: Chaoshan lishi wenhua yanjiu zhongxin ("Chaoshan Historical and Cultural Research Center"). 2007. Vol. 1, no. 5, of *Chaoshan qiaopi jicheng* ("Collection of Chaoshan *Qiaopi*"). Nanning: Guangxi shifan daxue chuban she, 498.

when it arrives. Six dollars are for [wife] Lin and two dollars for Mushen's mother to keep. The rest is for home use. I'm glad everyone at home, young and old, is safe and sound. But the letter says the Yang family have a child they want to give to me as a son. I don't know who this is and what the father's name is, write back and tell me. I think at present I have the resources to raise him, but I don't really want a child from our own village, it would be better if he was from another village. Also, it would be more appropriate if the child's age were one year less than that of [my daughter] Jinmei. Also, Lin herself should agree and personally see to it, to avoid future trouble, this is essential. Yingwei is in Jiting state [perhaps Kedah in Malaya]. When you receive a remittance from him, let me know. I will write again later.

> Thirtieth day of the eighth month of the twenty-eighth year of the Republic
> *Your Son Jiarui reporting*

I send money in monthly installments, but sometimes I forget to include Mushen, so make sure he gets a few dollars too.

5. FAMILY VALUES, 1940

Letter from Zeng Baofa in Thailand to his son
Zeng Congliang in Tuhao Village in Chenghai

1940

Congliang my Son,

I have received the *huipi* sent on the second of the month. I read the many things you said. Although everything is now very expensive in China, our household should remain exceptionally frugal in its expenditure. You should put more effort into things for the sake of the family, and not remain idle. Whatever it is, if it is of benefit to the family, every effort should be bent towards it, only then you can be treated as a man of talent and will be worthy of heaven and earth, of your parents and of yourself. You must know that your father, here overseas, has suffered people's bullying, that it is difficult to make a profit, people are always requesting me to do things, only thus can I get a little money. Do not think that money is thrown from Heaven for us to use. You are growing up year by year, you need to learn to endure hardship, don't copy that spoiled-boy behavior such as depending on your father or brother, for it is irresponsible. You can believe my words, if you follow what I say, there will finally be good results for you. Otherwise, you depend on me for everything, but the powers of myself alone are limited, it is very hard to help you all your life. If something unexpected or unfortunate were to happen, such as illness, unemployment, etc., ask yourself who you could turn to. How great the pain would be! Remember these words, don't see them as pointless or trivial.

I send eighty dollars in the national currency, please check. Four yuan is for Fourth Uncle's wife, two yuan is for Biqin, the rest is for household expenses. If there are debts, use what I send each time to gradually reduce them. Please note this.

> Twentieth day of the third month of the twenty-ninth year of the Republic

澄海對山衛上社逓交

家慈親大人金展

外寄去□民伍拾元□收如宗□□

金宝

廿六年□月

The Oversea Photographic Store.
Outdoor and Indoor Photographers
148, SELEC[T]IE. ROAD.

字宝

慈親大人尊前敬稟者

Distribution of Remittances, 1939. Source: Chaoshan lishi wenhua
yanjiu zhongxin ("Chaoshan Historical and Cultural Research Center")
2007. Vol. 1, no. 4, of *Chaoshan qiaopi jicheng* ("Collection of Chaoshan
Qiaopi"). Nanning: Guangxi shifan daxue chuban she, 76.

Family Values, 1940. Source: Chaoshan lishi wenhua yanjiu zhongxin ("Chaoshan Historical and Cultural Research Center"). 2007. Vol. 1, no. 6, of *Chaoshan qiaopi jicheng* ("Collection of Chaoshan *Qiaopi*"). Nanning: Guangxi shifan daxue chuban she, 555.

6. LOCAL POLITICS AND SOCIETY AFTER THE WAR, 1946

Letter from Huang Wenbin in Thailand to
his younger brother in Chenghai

My dear Younger Brother Songhao,

After a decade of war, the enemy has put down his arms and the Allies are victorious. Our country has gone from being a semi-colony to being one of the Four Great Powers. Our compatriots at home and abroad are feverishly rejoicing. They hope that from now we can live and work in peace and without fear. But who would have thought that as soon as the man-made disaster is over, natural disaster strikes. The land is arid and we cannot sow the fields, so that people dying of starvation block the roads and wailing can be heard everywhere. Hearing this terrible news, overseas Chinese bend their efforts to provide relief, but it is a mere drop in the ocean. Bandits swarm everywhere, and the people are anxious day and night. I heard the bandits are everywhere to be found. I don't know if it's true or not. Write to let me know how things are in the village. I enclose $10,000 in national currency. Uncle sends two thousand dollars.

Best wishes,
In spirit and in health.

Thirty-fifth year of the Republic, May 4
Signed Elder Brother Wenbin

7. LAND REFORM IN THE PEOPLE'S REPUBLIC, 1951

Letter from Xiao Junbo in Thailand to his mother in Chenghai

Kneeling before Mother and respectfully reporting:

Spring is about to arrive. It is a time of renewal. The earth echoes with new slogans. The Motherland's economy is striding towards a glorious new foundation. In the countryside, everything is conformng to the new practices. I hear there will be land reform when spring comes. Our family is a family of dependents of overseas Chinese, and they will definitely receive preferential treatment from the government. "Previously the government issued the contents of the principles of land reform, including the protection of the property of overseas Chinese and their preferential treatment." Mother, when our family registers, ask the government official so that you understand everything. I now send a letter with HK $130, please check on arrival, it's for household expenses, there's nothing more to say.

Blessings.

Son Junbo sends this letter
Seventeenth day of the first month

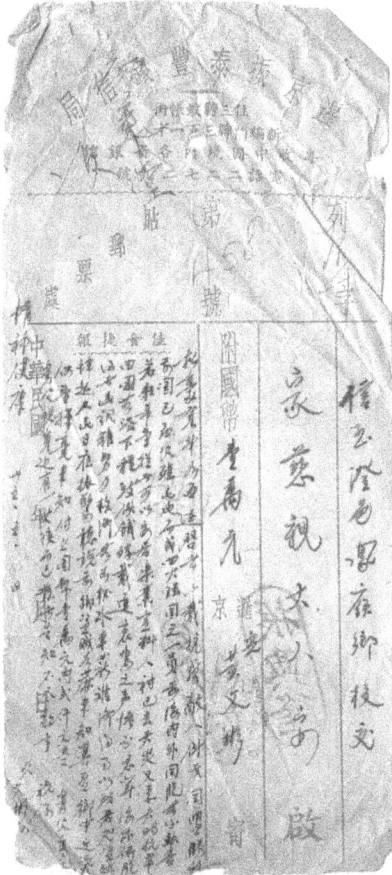

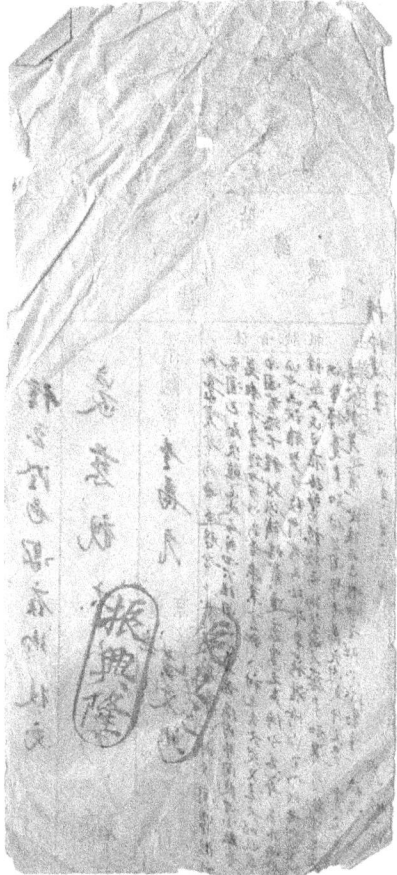

Local Politics and Society after the War, 1946. Source: Chaoshan lishi wenhua yanjiu zhongxin ("Chaoshan Historical and Cultural Research Center"). 2007. Vol. 1, no. 3, of *Chaoshan qiaopi jicheng* ("Collection of Chaoshan *Qiaopi*"), Nanning: Guangxi shifan daxue chuban she, 67.

8. FAMILY REUNION, 1957

Letter from Zeng Jiafeng in Thailand to wife, Xiubi, and mother in Chenghai[6]

My Wife Xiubi,

I have received and read your words. Today I sent Elder Brother Qinhui HK $50, fifteen dollars each for Younger Brothers Qinran and Yiran and twenty for Elder Brother Qinhui. You say you intend to come to Siam with Mother. I'm so happy to hear that, because I am constantly thinking of Mother and you. I fully understand that I left as a last resort, and the hardships you have suffered. That is why, until today, although it is many years since I left

Land Reform in the People's Republic, 1951. Source: Chaoshan lishi wenhua yanjiu zhongxin ("Chaoshan Historical and Cultural Research Center"). 2007. Vol. 1, no. 3, of *Chaoshan qiaopi jicheng* ("Collection of Chaoshan *Qiaopi*"). Nanning: Guangxi shifan daxue chuban she, 198.

you, I have not yet taken another wife in Siam. Siam does not yet have diplomatic relations with our Motherland, so if Mother and you enter Siam officially, you have to pay HK $20,000, otherwise you will not be allowed in. I want you to apply for entrance via Penang and pretend to be the wife of one of our friends (this is the local law, an applicant can apply for his wife to come in). The friend is working in Penang at the Tongcheng Trading Company. He and I are working under the same boss, the headquarters are based in Penang, and it has branches in Siam too. I work in this shop. If you dare to come, then try to apply. If you get permission, you can come. When the boat arrives in Penang, the boss in Penang and friends will come to the docks to take you to the Penang store, where you can

Family Reunion, 1957. Source: Chaoshan lishi wenhua yanjiu zhongxin ("Chaoshan Historical and Cultural Research Center"). 2007. Vol. 1, no. 6, of *Chaoshan qiaopi jicheng* ("Collection of Chaoshan *Qiaopi*"). Nanning: Guangxi shifan daxue chuban she, 164.

stay for a while. After that, we'll see how things stand, and look for a chance to arrange for you to enter Siam and come and live with me, because from Penang to my place in Siam is only one day's drive. As for Mother, I don't think she can come with you, it's a real headache. But if we wait a bit longer, world peace will come, and then she can come. These are my views for your consideration. I don't know what you think, and whether Mother has agreed for you to come. Don't worry, leave the headache to me.

Best wishes.

Blessings.

Jiafeng
January 18, 1957

9. USING REMITTANCES, 1974

Huang Zuoshu in Singapore to his mother in Chenghai in Guangdong

I kneel before my venerable mother.

I received the *huipi* and took careful note of everything you said. It comforts your son to know that the older generation is in good health. The house's leaking roof must be repaired, wait for your son to send some small amount. Because today Mother's birthday is imminent, your son and daughter-in-law send money to bring you joy. When the time comes for family members to congratulate you, Mother must have good meat and fish dishes ready, or familial affection will not be properly displayed. Today I will take advantage of the steamer to remit HK$100. This includes ten dollars for Weiqin, ten dollars for my sister's daughter, ten dollars for Auntie Sairou, and the remaining seventy dollars for Mother's birthday.

Happiness and peace,

Zuoshu
Third day of the fourth month

10. REMITTANCE AND IMMIGRATION PROCEDURES (SOUTHEAST ASIA), YEAR UNKNOWN

Letter from Gao Xiongcai in Hong Kong to his parents in Chenghai, year unknown

Kneeling before my respected parents I report:

I have received and read your letters of instruction of the nineteenth and the twenty-first and know their contents. However, on the nineteenth I had already sent a report on how this man [whom you mention] got to Hong Kong. I also sent five Shanghai dollars. I think you should have received the letter and will know the details. Regarding the man coming to Hong Kong, although he said his father had already discussed this with you, I haven't received your letter of instruction, I have some questions. However, it seems to me that he is in a hurry, I can't not attend to this, and I have not sent him away. He is a new arrival, so if I don't help he's bound to be cheated. He is kith and kin, so I would not feel good if I didn't help him. I know that regulations must be followed, but personal feelings must also be respected, or I will be despised. If I don't help him, how

Using Remittances, 1974. Source: Chaoshan lishi wenhua yanjiu zhongxin ("Chaoshan Historical and Cultural Research Center"). 2007. Vol. 1, no. 2, of *Chaoshan qiaopi jicheng* ("Collection of Chaoshan *Qiaopi*"). Nanning: Guangxi shifan daxue chuban she, 195.

can I then ask others to help me in future? So I decided to take responsibility for helping him. I immediately told Brother Zizhao everything. The man brought some money. I asked Brother Zizhao to let him live in the hostel, and he kindly agreed. Brother Zizhao asked about the man's father and his grandfather's name, and I told him everything. He sighed and said it's not easy to get a job in Siam. I said after reaching Siam the man can go and live in Liang Chengfa's place for a while. Zizhao said the people in the shop there are very nice, and he has some communication with the owner and has exchanged letters with him. Brother Zizhao is very kind-hearted. Recently Brother Zixu returned to Hong Kong. I also told him about all this. He also expressed sympathy. I have already discussed with those in the relevant business about booking a ticket [to Siam] from the shipping company. I hope sooner or later he can get a seat. Another way would be to join the crew and then jump ship [in Siam]. To jump ship you needed $50–60 in the past, now it's gone up to $70–80. It's half the cost of a normal ticket. In Siam the agent of the shipping company will send him to the shop. In the trade, this is the procedure for getting to Siam. I've recently heard that the Siam government is discussing raising the cost of resident permits from one hundred to two hundred baht from January 1. So if this decision goes through, in future going to Siam will cost more than three hundred Shanghai dollars. When you receive this letter, tell his father all this. Tell him not to worry that I won't do these things. The day before yesterday I received and read Uncle Rangchu's letter, and learned that Elder Brother Gongpu will fly from Siam to Hong Kong today or tomorrow. I'm telling you this by the way. I enclose twenty Shanghai dollars. I'll report again later.

Reporting herewith.

Respectfully,

Best wishes,

Hoping the whole family is safe,

Xiongcai
November 22

11. "AN AGE WITHOUT MORALS" AND CHAOS IN THE HOMELAND, 1903

Huipi *from Liu Hongyao in Taishan in Guangdong to his father Liu Mingming in Vancouver*

Kneeling before my stern father and reporting:

The money-letters you sent last year were one of thirty dollars, one of twenty dollars, and one of one hundred dollars. All were received. So why does someone say I didn't give any money to Uncle Biqin, it's not true. At present I've seen with my own eyes how bandits run rampant, disturbing the villages. It's worst in Nazhang and in our village, now all the women in Nazhang are escaping to hide with their kin, so our village elders are forcing all the families with relatives in Gold Mountain [North America] to buy guns to fight the bandits, and to pay money for ammunition, and every family must contribute to improve security and build defensive walls round the village. As for the bandits causing explosions night after night, robbing people, causing panic, and terrifying everyone, there's no apparent antidote,

Remittance and Immigration Procedures (Southeast Asia), Year Unknown. Source: Chaoshan lishi wenhua yanjiu zhongxin ("Chaoshan Historical and Cultural Research Center"). 2007. Vol. 1, no. 3, of *Chaoshan qiaopi jicheng* ("Collection of Chaoshan *Qiaopi*"). Nanning: Guangxi shifan daxue chuban she, 165.

"An Age without Morals" and Chaos in the Homeland, 1903. Envelope. Source: City of Vancouver Archives, no. 1108002.

no one knows what the next day will bring. This is an age without morals, grain is as expensive as gemstones, one *dan* costs five taels, it's difficult to keep the household going, and the burden of the household is great, I am in more and more of a panic. You may recall that a long time ago you borrowed money from Banqin in Canada, he's now come back to China to do farming, and the harvest is poor. It's very difficult. Our own family is short of money, we can't return the money. I wish Father would send him back a little money now and again. At present your son's annual school fees are more than twenty dollars. In my previous letter I mentioned several times about how Great Grandfather's memorial tablet cost ten dollars, but you didn't reply. When you receive this letter, whatever month and day it is, be sure to let me know and give me your instructions. My marrage has already happened,

"An Age without Morals" and Chaos in the Homeland, 1903. Source: City of Vancouver Archives, no. 1108002.

the daughter-in-law is called Zhu, from Namei Village. You left word that there should be a wedding gift. The situation in the family is critical, we have borrowed money from others and given a wedding gift. I hope you read the letter and understand this point. If Heaven helps you in everything and your ancestors support you, you can get money with their help in six months or a year. You can return home early to reunite with your family and you will no longer need to stay overseas in a barbarian land. The whole family, old and young, are happy, you do not need to worry. I simply write this. I send my respects.

Blessings on my Father Liu Mingming.

Twenty-seventh day of the second month
Signed, unfilial Son Liu Hongyao

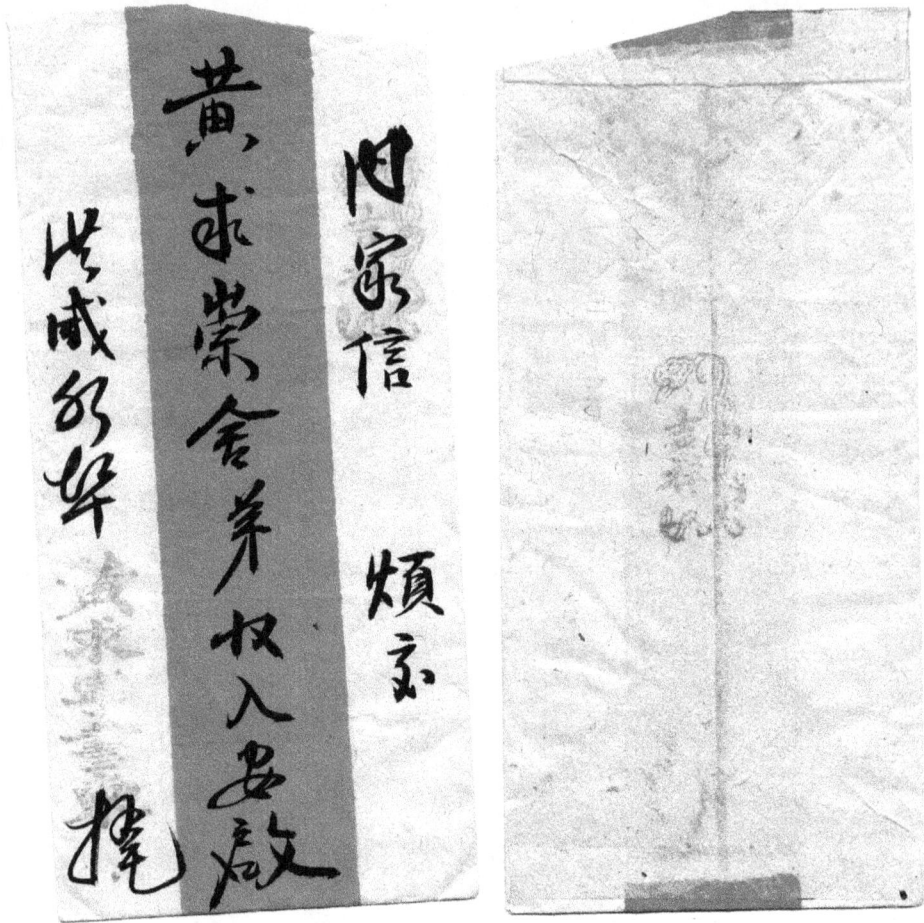

Family Values, 1903. Envelope. Source: City of Vancouver Archives, no. 1108117.

12. FAMILY VALUES, 1903

Letter from Ms. Chen to her son Huang Qiuchong in Vancouver

Qiuchong my son, read and know this,

Now all of us at home, old and young, are safe and sound, there is no need to worry. But because of a poor harvest, the price of rice is currently rising. Goods are expensive, and it's hard for the poor to make ends meet, but what can you do? It's important that you avoid drinking, visiting prostitutes, and gambling. And you must not be idle at work, or engage in luxury. Don't drink, or engage in bribery or gambling. Make sure you send

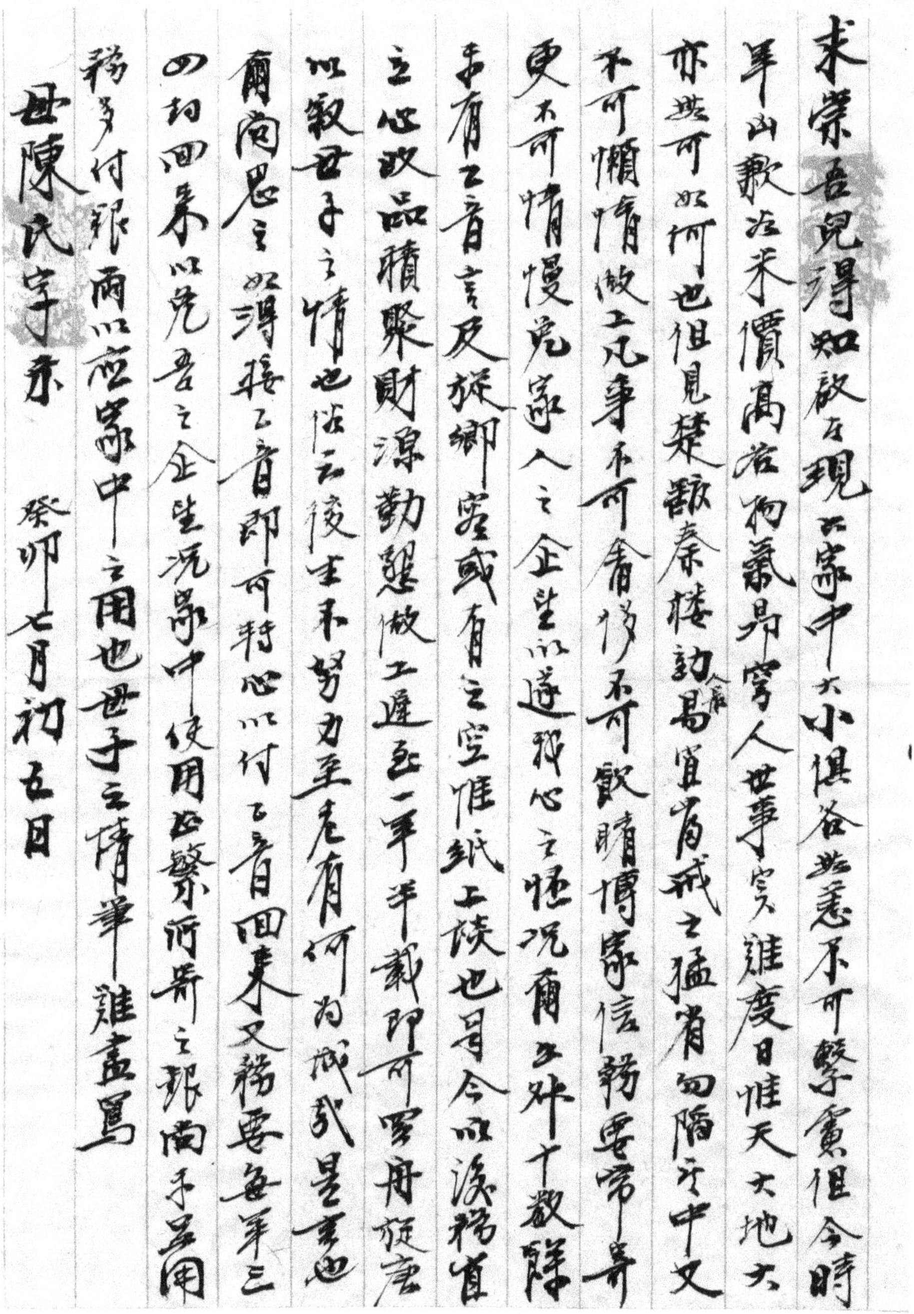

求崇吾兒得知啟者現下家中大小俱各無恙不可掛慮但今時
年山歉治米價高若物氣昂窮人無事窮難度日惟天大地大
亦無可如何也但見楚館秦樓勾易宜首戒之猛省勿陷於中又
不可懶惰做工凡事不可奢侈不可飲賭博寄信務要常寄
更不可惰慢免家人之企望以慰我心之懷況爾出外十數餘
年有工音言及旋鄉空或有之空惟紙上談也自今以後務宜
之心改品積聚財源勤懇做工遲至一年半載即可買舟旋唐
以叙母子之情也倘云後生不努力至老有何為哉是要也
爾宜思之如得接工音即可持心以付工音回來又務要每年三
四封回來以免吾之企望況家中使用甚緊所寄之銀尚予無用
務多付銀兩以應家中之用也母子之情筆難盡寫
母陳氏字示
癸卯七月初五日

Family Values, 1903. Source: City of Vancouver Archives, no. 1108117.

民國廿八年七月

幸林氏上

Wish to Join Husband in Singapore, 1939. Source: Chaoshan lishi wenhua yanjiu zhongxin ("Chaoshan Historical and Cultural Research Center"). 2007. Vol. 1, no. 4, of *Chaoshan qiaopi jicheng* ("Collection of Chaoshan *Qiaopi*"). Nanning: Guangxi shifan daxue chuban she, 211.

frequent letters home, and that you are not idle, you must do everything properly, to meet my expectations. You have been overseas for more than ten years and never say anything about coming home. If you have, it has remained on paper. From now on you must make sure that you maintain a good character, and accumulate financial resources, by means of hard work. In a year or so's time at the latest, you can buy a boat ticket to return to China and tell Mother what has been happening. There's a general saying, if you don't work hard when you're young, what can you do when you're old? This is true, you must think about it. Once you receive this letter, tell me your thinking. Be sure to send three or four letters a year to stop me worrying. For household expenses, things are tight, the money is not enough, be sure to send more money for use at home. It's not possible for me to tell you everything.

Sent by Mother Chen
Fifth day of the seventh month

13. WISH TO JOIN HUSBAND IN SINGAPORE, 1939

Wife Lin, in Chenghai, to Song Jiarui in Singapore

Reporting to my respected husband Jiarui

We received your letter and money. Now I have asked a villager to post this letter to you. Now here in China the head of the village security system is pressurizing households to hand over money. Every month there are three or four collections. Anyone who doesn't pay, for whatever reason, is abused with harsh words, cursed, and insulted. How can your wife listen to these cruel tirades? It is truly impossible to bear. Sometimes if you don't pay, you're likely to get dragged before the headman and humiliated. When sons and daughters see their elders dragged off in this way, they are naturally scared and start weeping. Now, with China in a state of turmoil and chaos, the misery is indescribable. But you have a task to fulfill, you cannot come back to China to witness this, it is something you cannot know. Since the Japanese occupation, we have suffered terrible starvation. I am unable to tell you about this hard situation face to face. Here, people are quarrelling and gossiping. I beg you to find a way to get me and our children to Singapore, so I no longer have to suffer fights about trifles. Now those in the village with money are all leaving, to avoid being blackmailed by the headman. So now he blackmails me even more. I want to go to Singapore to get away from him. At home, I'm taking charge of worshipping the ancestors, some relatives can help me if I leave, you don't need to worry. Daughter Jinmei has already grown up, she's fourteen now. If she was with you, it would be good if she could learn how to do business, so she can help you in future. When you read this, I hope you agree to us coming to Singapore, so we can meet and talk together about our bitter sufferings. There's lots more to say but too little paper to say it on, so some things must wait until another day.

Wishing you prosperity and peace,

The seventh month of the twentieth-eighth year of the Republic
Concubine Lin[7]

GLOSSARY

Pinyin	Chinese character	English
anpi	暗批	"secret *pi*," remittances sent in code to evade overseas government bans, especially between 1945 and 1949
baixin	白信	a letter without money
banghao	帮号	shipment number of *qiaopi*
baojia	保甲	local system of collective responsibility in pre-modern and modern China
bianhao	编号	a serial number on the counterfoil provided on receipt of a *qiaopi* letter
chaitou	差头	"messenger boss," who fetched the *qiaopi* from the *piju*
chidanshui	吃淡水	"freshwater eater," a *qiaopi* courier at the domestic end of the chain
chuanbang	船帮	"shipment"
citang	祠堂	"ancestral hall"
daipiren	带批人	"*pi* deliverer," deliverer of *qiaopi*
dapi	大批	"big *pi*," a substantial remittance
datou	搭头	"[guest] sender," coolie broker
dianhui	电汇	telegraphic transfer
difang zhi	地方志	local gazetteer
duangong	短工	casual laborer

ersanju	二三局	"second and third *piju*"
fanke	番客	overseas migrant
fankeshen	番客婶	migrants' wife
fanpi	番批	"foreign *pi* or barbarian *pi*," a variant name for *qiaopi*
fanyin	番银	"foreign silver," i.e., remittance
feiqian	飞钱	"flying money," postal system in the Tang dynasty
fenpi	分批	"distributing *pi*," the distribution of remittance letters around the houses
ganzhi	干支	the old Sexagenary Cycle based on the Ten Heavenly Stems and Twelve Earthly Branches, traditionally used to record a fixed cycle of sixty years
gonghui	公会	guild, association
guandu shangban	官督商办	"official supervised, merchant managed"
guanshang heban	官商合办	"official and merchant jointly managed"
guanzai	馆仔	a variant name for *piju*
guiqiao	归侨	returned or returning Chinese migrant
haijin	海禁	"sea bans"
hangguan	行馆	"trade house," the premises couriers lived in overseas
hongbao	红包	"red packet," the money given to children in a red envelope as a New Year gift
huama	花码	an indigenous "positional' numeral used at the start of a *bianhao*
Huaqiao	华侨	Chinese sojourner
Huaqiao qiaoxinju lianhehui	华侨侨信局联合会	Overseas Chinese Federation of Remittance Offices
Huaren xiao youzhengju	华人小邮政局	Chinese Sub-Post Office
Huayi	华裔	descendant of a Chinese migrant
huiduiju	汇兑局	remittance office, a variant name for *piju*
huidui zhuang	汇兑庄	remittance shop, a variant name for *piju*
huiguan	会馆	guild
huipi	回批	"return *pi*," a recipient's reply to a *qiaopi*
jianmian jifu	见面即付	"payment on sight"
jiapu	家谱	family records

jiaofu	脚夫	"foot man," last-stage bearer in the chain of remittance delivery
jingshang shuike	经商水客	commercial *shuike*
jinshan	金山	Gold Mountain, i.e., western regions of North America
jinshanbo	金山伯	Gold Mountain guest/uncle, Chinese laborer in North America
jinshanke	金山客	Chinese laborer in North America
jinshanpo	金山婆	Gold Mountain woman, wife of a *jinshanke*
jinshanshao	金山少	Gold Mountain youngster, child of a *jinshanke*
jinshan xin	金山信	Gold Mountain letter, a variant name for *qiaopi*
jinzhuang	金庄	gold shop
jiu jinshan	旧金山	Old Gold Mountain, renamed from *jinshan*, after gold was discovered in Australia. Today Chinese use it for San Francisco.
jiyi	辑佚	"gathering rare and scattered [classical] writings"
kaishu	楷书	regular script, a style of writing often used in *qiaopi* letters
kaopi	靠批	"relying on *pi*," an expression of the sense of *pi* as a lifeline
kejian	客间	"guest space," the hostel or barracoon migrants lodged in
ketou	客头	"guest chief," often written as *kheh-tau* and translated as crimp or coolie broker
keyou	客邮	foreign-controlled postal agency
kezhan	客栈	"guest hostel," the hostel or barracoon migrants lodged in
koupi	口批	"oral *pi*," a message transmitted by word of mouth when a remittance was delivered
kouxin	口信	a variant name for an oral *pi*
lianhao	联号	chain of independent agents
liezi	列字	a list character used for *bianhao*
liucushui	溜粗水	"saltwater skater," a *qiaopi* courier connecting China and the outside world
menshi	门市	"door-market trade"
minjian shufa	民间书法	people's calligraphy, a popular art form for *qiaopi* letter writing in the twentieth century

minxinju	民信局	"people's letter office," a variant name for the offices run by the *qiaopi* trade
Nanyang	南洋	"Southern Ocean," or Southeast Asia
Nanyangke	南洋客	"South Ocean guest," *qiaopi* courier
Nanyang shuike lianhehui	南洋水客联合会	Federation of Southeast Asian *Shuike*
Nanyang Zhonghua huiye zonghui	南洋中华汇业总会	Nanyang Chinese Remittance Association
neifu	内付	"handed over internally," money order placed inside the envelope
nianhao	年号	year specified by reign name
panpi	盼批	"hoping for *pi*," an indication of the sense of *pi* as a lifeline
pi	批	"letter" in southern Fujian dialect
piaohao	票号	traditional bank
piaohui	票汇	draft remittance
piban	批伴	"*pi* companion," a deliverer of *qiaopi*
pibao	批包	*qiaopi* deliverer's sack
pidai	批带	*qiaopi* deliverer's sack
piduan	批断	"the breaking off of *pi*," a term used in the Sino-Japanese War when the *qiaopi* trade was disastrously interrupted
piguan	批馆	"*pi* building," the premises couriers lived in overseas
pijiao	批脚	"*pi* foot," deliverer of *qiaopi*
piju	批局	remittance shop
piguan	批馆	"*pi* shop," a variant name for the companies that ran the *qiaopi* trade
pigong	批工	"*pi* worker," employee in the *qiaopi* trade
pikuan	批款	a *pi* remittance
ping'anpi	平安批	"safe-and sound *pi*," the initial *qiaopi* sent back home by immigrants
pixin	批信	letter
pixinju	批信局	"remittance-letter office," a variant name for the offices run by the *qiaopi* trade
pizai	批仔	"*pi* child," the tiny sheet of paper glued to the back of the *qiaopi* envelope by the *piju* for the recipient's *huipi*
qianzhuang	钱庄	traditional bank

qiaohui	侨汇	emigrant remittance
qiaohuiye	侨汇业	remittance trade
qiaohui zhuan	侨汇庄	remittance shop
qiaojuan	侨眷	migrants' dependent
qiaokan	侨刊	overseas-Chinese magazine
qiaopi	侨批	letter sent together with a remittance
qiaopiju	侨批局	*qiaopi* office, a variant name for *piju*
qiaopiyuan	侨批员	"*qiaopi* officer," the official title *shuike* acquired in the 1950s
qiaoxiang	侨乡	sending region of Chinese emigrants
sanpan	三盘	"three coils," an operational model of the *qiaopi* trade
sanshiliu ji	三十六计	Thirty-Six Stratagems, a traditional book of tricks
shandan	山单	"mountain unit," coupon or credit
shanghao	商号	a dense network of businesses
shanhui	善会	charitable institution
shanpiao	山票	"mountain note," coupon or credits note
shanshe	善社	charitable institution
Shantou qiaopi tongye gonghui	汕头侨批同业公会	Shantou *Qiaopi* Trade Association
shilipai	实力派	local powerholder
shili youting	十里邮亭	courier station
shoupi	收批	"gathering the *pi*," when *huipi* were gathered together in the village
shuike	水客	"water guest," *qiaopi* courier
shuxin yinliang	书信银两	a variant name for *qiaopi*
sishu	私塾	old-style private school
taifu	台伏	coupon or credit note used by *piju*
Tangren	唐人	"Tang person," a Chinese emigrant
taobi	逃避	financial evasion
touju	透局	"all-round *piju*"
tongxianghui	同乡会	native-place association
tuhao	土豪	local bullies
waifu	外付	"handed over externally," with the amount of remittance recorded on the left-hand side of the *qiaopi* envelope

wenshi ziliao	文史资料	officially approved writings on local history and culture under the Communists
xiangkan	乡刊	village publication
xiangxian	乡贤	village scholar
xiangxun	乡讯	village bulletin
xiaohao	消号	"cancelling the number" for the shipping documents of *qiaopi* and *huipi*
xiaopiao	小票	"small note," coupon or credit note
xiaoqin ri	孝亲日	Day of Filial Piety and Fraternal Duty
xinchai	信差	letter courier
xingshu	行书	running script, a style of writing sometimes used in *qiaopi* letters
xinhui	信汇	mail transfer
xin jinshan	新金山	New Gold Mountain, name used for Australia after gold was discovered there
xinju	信局	letter office, a variant name for *piju*
xinke	新客	"new guest," a China-born immigrant
xinke	信客	letter courier
xin Tang	新唐	"new Tang person," a China-born immigrant
xin yimin	新移民	"new migrant," originating from China starting in the late 1970s
xinyin	信银	a variant name for *qiaopi*, short for *shuxin yinliang*
xunchengma	巡城马	domestic courier
yangshuike	洋水客	"foreign water guest," a *qiaopi* courier
yangyin	洋银	foreign silver dollar
yi	驿	the postal system founded in the Han dynasty
yinliang	银两	silver tael
yinpi	银批	"silver *pi*"
yinxin	银信	"silver plus letter," one of the names used for *qiaopi*
yinxinju	银信局	"*yinxin* office," a variant name for *piju*
yinxinju gongsuo	银信局公所	Overseas-Chinese Remittance Office Association
yishu	义塾	community-run school

yi tiao bian	一条鞭	"single whip," the vertical hierarchy in the remittance process from receipt to delivery
youyi	邮驿	postal station
yuminquan	裕民券	temporary local currency issued by the Communist guerrillas in the Fujian and Guangdong *qiaoxiang* during the Civil War of 1946-9
zai	仔	a youngster who worked under the *chaitou*
zhan	栈	hostel
zhengpi	正批	"main *pi*," a variant name for *qiaopi*
zongpu	宗谱	clan records
zongxianghui	宗乡会	clanspeople's association
zoudabang	走大帮	"big batch," *qiaopi* deliveries tied to big festivals during the first, fifth, and ninth lunar months
zoudanbang	走单帮	"lone traveller," a courier who specialized in carrying goods
zouxiaobang	走小帮	"small batch," *qiaopi* deliveries tied to small festivals during second, seventh, and tenth lunar months
zoushui	走水	"water goer," a *qiaopi* courier
zuoke	做客	"being the guest," a process in which the *ketou* helped track down his charges' migrant kin and find work
zukan	族刊	lineage publication
zupu	族谱	lineage records

NOTES

INTRODUCTION

1. Out of a total population of 11,456,000 Chinese overseas in 1955, 11,074,000, or 96.7 percent, resided in Asia (predominantly Southeast Asia). Peter Li and Eva Li 2013, 20–21.

2. McKeown 1999; Wang 2000; Hong Liu 2006; Kuhn 2008.

3. Thunø 2007; Hong Liu 2011.

4. On voluntary associations: Li Minghuan 2010; Benton and Gomez 2015. On investment, trade, and business networks: Godley 2002; McKeown 2002; Hicks 1993; Hong Liu 2012; Peterson 2012. On participation in Chinese politics: Hong Liu 2006; Yow 2013. On remittances: Fukuda 1995; Hamashita 2001, 2013; Cheong Kee Cheok, Lee Kam Hing, and Poh Ping Lee 2013; Harris 2015.

5. Haiming Liu 2005, 1.

6. Fei 1992, 41.

7. Wong 1985, 58.

8. See, e.g., Chan 1997; Waters 2005; Faure 2006.

9. Chen Ta (1940) focuses on the emigrant sending regions; Haiming Liu (2005) focuses on America; Douw, Huang, and Godley 1999.

10. Deng Dahong 2013c, 94. Jin Wenjian (2014, 245) says that according to a conservative estimate there are around 200,000 items in Chaoshan alone.

11. Accessed at http://www.unesco.org/new/en/communication-and-information/flagship-project-activities/memory-of-the-world/homepage/.

12. On the project, see Batto 2006.

13. Su Wenjing and Huang Qinghai 2013b, 35.

14. Ong and Nonini 1997; McKeown 2010; Chan 2015.

15. For examples of trade, see Fairbank 1953; A. G. Frank 1998; Hamashita 2008. For examples of diplomacy, see Kirby 1984. For examples of commercial culture, see

Cochran 2000; Cochran 2006. For examples of diaspora, see Duara 1997; Benton and Gomez 2015.

16. Mei-hui Mayfair Yang 1999, 7.

17. See, e.g., Guobin Yang 2003; Marchetti 2006.

18. Dean Yang 2011.

19. Accessed at https://siteresources.worldbank.org/INTPROSPECTS/Resources/334934-1199807908806/4549025-1450455807487/Factbookpart1.pdf.

20. See, e.g., Vertovec 2004; McKeown 1999.

21. Tsai 2010; Min Zhou and Li 2016.

22. Deng Dahong 2009, 45; Chen Xinyuan 2009, 113–4; Chen Hua 2010, 193.

23. Hong Lin 2004, 22.

24. Wu Hongli 2008, 359.

25. Zhang Guoxiong 2010, 70.

26. Li Lianxi 1994; Chen Hua 2010, 194; Huang Qinghai 2016a, 53. Note, however, that the *qiaopi* trade on the island of Jinmen, controlled from Taipei, continued until 2001. The Jinmen *piju* were part of the Xiamen network until 1949, after which they received their *qiaopi* through Taipei (Jiang Bowei and Cai Mingsong 2008, 266–8; Tang Cunfang 2008).

27. Zhang Guoxiong 2010, 73–4.

28. Zeng Xubo 2010, 421.

29. Jiao Jianhua 2005, 66.

30. *Xiamen wenshi ziliao* 2004, 428; Lin Sha 2008, 355; Li Wenhai, ed., 2009, 801.

31. Sinn 2013, 176.

32. Sinn 2013, 301.

33. Chen Chunsheng 2000, 61–2.

34. A Confucian text written in triplets for easy memorization and used to teach children.

35. Zou Jinsheng 2010, 404; Zeng Xubo 2010, 420; Jia Junying 2012, 91–3.

36. Jia Junying 2012, 13; Jiao Jianhua 2005, 65–6.

37. Yang Qunxi, ed., 2004, 53.

38. Fujian sheng dang'an guan, eds., 2013, 103.

39. Chen Youyi and Xue Can 2010, 362.

40. Chen Xiaojie et al. 2008, 442–3. Please refer to the appendix of this book for selected letters.

41. Wan Dongqing 2010, 296.

42. Zou Jinsheng 2010, 404.

43. Huang Zijian 2013, 138.

44. Du Shimin 2004, 286.

45. Wu Baoguo 2014, 201.

46. Li Wenhai, ed., 2009, 801.

47. "The Earliest Remittance Centres," 2. Wang Gungwu's preface to this book similarly reflects on letter-writing in Southeast Asia before World War II.

48. Zhang Mingshan 2006, 101.

49. Wan Dongqing 2010, 295; Chen Chuangyi 2004, 303.

50. Pan Meizhu n.d., 3.

51. Zhang Guoxiong 2010, 79.

52. Xie Jiaolan 2014, 274.

53. Kraus 1991.
54. Chen Jiashun 2014.
55. Wan Dongqing 2009, 88.
56. Kuhn 2008, 96.
57. Fujian sheng dang'an guan, eds., 2013, 187.
58. Chen Xiaojie et al. 2008, 442–3; Huang Jiaxiang 2008, 342.
59. Chen Xiaojie et al. 2008, 448; Chen Xunxian 2006, 95; Xu Hanjun 2006, 99.
60. Liu Jin 2013a, 147–9; Wang Hanwu 2010, 244.
61. Pan Meizhu n.d.
62. Shi Jianping 2013, 308.
63. Liu Jin 2013b. On the evolution of the Guan lineage in post-1949 China, see Woon 1989.
64. Chen Xiaojie et al. 2008, 446–7.
65. Zhang Guoxiong 2010, 74–8.
66. Wang Hanwu 2010, 127.
67. Chen Hua 2010, 196; Liao Yun and Wu Erchi 2010, 263.
68. Wang Hanwu 2010.
69. Chen Haizhong 2013.
70. Wang Weizhong 2007, 55.
71. Luo Zeyang 2008; Xu Guanghua and Cai Jinhe 2010.
72. Li Wenhai, ed., 2009, 801; Wu Baoguo 2014, 201.
73. Dai Yifeng 2003, 75.
74. Jiao Jianhua 2005, 67.
75. Chen Hanchu 2010, 88.
76. Williams 1999b, 22; Liu Jin 2009, 51.
77. City of Vancouver Archives n.d.
78. Zou Qiudong and Su Tonghai 2009, 71–4.
79. Huifen Shen 2012, 90.
80. Ke Mulin 2013. Even in 1939, just 15 percent of Fujianese migrants were female (Huifen Shen 2012, 5–6).
81. Wang Gungwu 2000; Yuan Ding, Chen Liyuan, and Zhong Yunrong 2014, 23–4.
82. Lin Nanzhong 2010, 492.
83. Liu Jin 2009, 12.
84. Wu Hongli 2008, 361.
85. Jia Junying 2012, 53; Wang Weizhong 2007, 15–6.
86. Yang Qunxi, ed., 2004, 57–62, 481.
87. Yen Ching-hwang 2013, 75.
88. Wang Weizhong 2007, 16–7.
89. Yang Qunxi, ed., 2004, 57, 62; 481–3.
90. On genealogy of the Chinese diaspora, see Wang Gungwu 2000; Hong Liu 2006; Kuhn 2008; Benton and Gomez 2015.
91. Zeng Xubo 2014, 175.
92. Lin Qingxi 2010; Guo Mafeng 2004.
93. Zeng Xubo 2014.
94. Chen Hanchu 2010, 83.

95. Zeng Xubo 2014, 172.

96. Lin Qingxi 2010; Guo Mafeng 2004.

97. Liu Jin (2009) says he has never encountered the term *qiaopi* in the Wuyi counties.

98. Zeng Xubo 2014, 168–9.

99. Jiang Bowei and Cai Mingsong 2008, 267.

100. Chen Xunxian 2010, 184–5.

101. Yang Qunxi, ed., 2004, 60.

102. Xiamen wenshi ziliao 2004, 428; Yang Qunxi, ed., 2004, 360.

103. Lu Yongguang 2006, 156; Lin Qingxi 2010, 216; Chen Shengsheng 2013, 227; Huang Shaoxiong 2010, 489.

CHAPTER 1. THE GENEALOGY OF *QIAOPI* STUDIES

1. Examples include Fitzpatrick 1994; Jones 2005; Kamphoefner 2007; Kamphoefner and Helbich, eds., 2006; Lyons, ed., 2007; Reynolds 2009; Richards 2005; Schrier 1958. The main exception is Haiming Liu 2005, but it too concerns the letters of a better-off and better-educated American Chinese family.

2. Rogler 1994; McKeown 2004.

3. Rao Min 2010, 482.

4. Oyen 2007, 320; around 1900, 3.7 million Australians (who wrote and received twice as many letters per capita as Canadians and more than people in the United States) sent only one million letters abroad per annum (Richards 2006), compared with six million exchanged in South China in 1955 with the then eleven million overseas Chinese (i.e., twice the Australian rate). In 1854 British emigrants in the United States sent home more than two million letters, a figure that had exceeded six million by 1874 (Schrier 1958, 22, cited in Jones 2005, 25). The 1955 figure for China may partly reflect improvements in the meantime in the international postal service, but this would be offset by the greater rate of literacy in Australia and the United States as well the Western blockade of China in the mid-1950s.

5. The literacy rate among Chinese emigrants to the United States, never high, consistently declined in the mid- to late nineteenth century as a result of the "coolie" trade (Zhongping Chen 2011).

6. Hsu 2000a, 310.

7. Richards 2005, 103n56; Lyons 2012, 197.

8. Jin Wenjian 2014, 247.

9. Peterson 2012.

10. Kollewe 2010.

11. Chang Zengshu 2010, 67; Chen Hanchu 2010, 84.

12. Wang Weizhong 2010a, 44, 48.

13. Freedman 1967, 87.

14. Zhang Meisheng 2014, 294.

15. For English-language works on the *qiaoxiang*, see Chen Ta 1940; Leo Dow, Huang Ceng, Godley 1999; Peterson 2012; Candela 2013; Yow 2013.

16. The rise of "social history" in China since the 1970s is sometimes depicted as a Western import, involving a switch from "elite history" to "mass history" (Shuo Wang 2006, 315), but "mass history" has been practiced in China far longer than this argument supposes.

17. Williams 2003, 86.

18. Portes, Guarnizo, and Landolt 1999. On the growing body of literature on transnationalism, its critics, and its relevance to the Chinese diaspora, see Vertovec 1999; Ong and Nonini 2003; Liu and Van Dongen 2013; Tan 2013.

19. For example, Madeline Hsu's excellent book (2000b) on transnational Chinese migrants pays scant attention to *qiaopi* and their uses.

20. Jao Tsung-i (1917.8–2018.2) was a Sinologist who taught in Hong Kong, India, Singapore, the United States, and Japan. In 1962 the Académie des Inscriptions et Belles-Lettres awarded him the Prix Stanislas Julien. Jao's main publications and contributions to Sinology can be found in a collection dedicated to his scholarship housed at Hong Kong University; http://www.jaotipe.hku.hk/jaoti/ao_intro. For a detailed study of Jao's contribution to *qiaopi* studies, see Liu Jin 2015.

21. Held on two main sites.

22. Wang Weizhong 2007, 1; Jin Wenjian 2014, 245. Chaoshan (Teoswa in the local dialect) is a contraction of Chaozhou (Teochew) and Shantou (Swatow), two adjacent cities now agglomerated into one.

23. Ma Chujian 2010, 21, 26; Shantou University.

24. Yuan Ding, Chen Liyuan, and Zhong Yunrong 2014, 2, 22.

25. See, e.g., Morse 1904; Muhse 1916; Moore 1918.

26. Fukuda Shozo 1939; Hicks 1993.

27. The English version was published in 1940 as *Emigrant Communities in South China: A Study of Overseas Migration and its Influence on Standards of Living and Social Change* (New York: IPR); Chen Ta 1940.

28. On the early Chinese-language literature, see Yuan Ding, Chen Liyuan, and Zhong Yunrong 2014, 3–4.

29. Chen Shengsheng 2014. In the 1980s, scholars at Xiamen University undertook fieldwork and collected data about overseas Chinese investment in Fujian and Guangdong. Some of the data are also related to *qiaopi*, though not directly. See Lin Jinzhi 1983; Lin Jinzhi and Zhuang Weiji 1985; Lin Jinzhi and Zhuang Weiji 1989.

30. Chen Shuisheng 2014.

31. Wang Weizhong 2010a, 45–7; Wang Weizhong 2010b, 1–2.

32. Ma Chujian 2010, 21–6; http://www.wxy.stu.edu.cn/Eng/Intro/index.aspx?fkID=6.

33. Chen Shuisheng 2014, 9.

34. Yuan Ding, Chen Liyuan, and Zhong Yunrong 2014.

35. Huang Haiqing 2016b.

36. Volume 1 published in 2007 and volume 2 in 2011, by Guangxi shifan daxue chuban she in Nanning.

37. Edited by Huang Haiqing, Lin Nanzhong, and Su Tonghai, and published by Fujian renmin chuban she in Fuzhou in 2016.

38. Edited by Chaoshan lishi wenhua yanjiu zhongxin, qiaopi dang'an guan, and published by Ji'nan daxue chuban she in Guangzhou in 2017; edited by Luo Daquan, Zhang Xiuming, and Liu Jin, and published by Guangdong renmin chuban she in Guangzhou in 2016; Huang Qinghai 2015; Huang Qinghai 2016b.

39. In December 2013, an international workshop titled "Comparison, Exchange and New Perspectives: International Symposium on Transnational Migration Letters" was

organized by the Editorial Board of *History of Overseas Chinese of Guangdong*, Guangdong *Qiaoxiang* Cultural Research Center, Wuyi University, China Institute of Overseas Chinese History, and Immigration History Research Center, University of Minnesota. It was held at Wuyi University. After the conference, a volume titled *Bijiao, jiejian yu qianzhan: Guoji yimin shuxin yanjiu* (*Comparison, Exchange and New Perspectives: Studies on Transnational Migration Letters*) was edited by Liu Jin and published in 2014 by Guangdong remin chuban she. The Second Symposium on International Migration Correspondence was held in June 2016, and the conference proceeding has not been published.

40. Edited by the Guangdong *Qiangoxiang* wenhua yanjiu zhongxin (Guangdong *Qiaoxiang* Culture Studies Center) and published by Zhongguo Huaqiao Chubanshe. For a review of recent *qiaoxiang* (including *qiaopi*) studies originated from Guangdong, see Lai and Yuan 2013.

41. Zhang Guoxiong 2014.

42. Hu and Chen 2013; Hu and Chen 2015; Harris 2015. Chapter 3 of this book has a more detailed discussion on Harris' work on *qiaopi*.

43. Young 1966; Yang 1983; Hamashita 2013.

44. Yamagishi Takeshi 2013.

45. Hamashita 2013; Hamashita 2008.

46. Wang Weizhong 2010a, 47.

47. Yang Qunxi, ed., 2004, 206.

48. On the problems of dating *qiaopi*, see Yang Jian 2014 and Kang Yefeng 2014, 264.

49. On this theory, see Zeng Xubo 2014.

50. Jin Wenjian 2014.

51. Jin Wenjian 2014, 245–6.

52. Xu Jianping 2010, 64; Huang Shaoxiong 2004, 108. In 2013, only a few hours of interviews with *qiaopi* workers and entrepreneurs had been videoed or recorded (Ye Fangrong and Yang Huichang 2013, 8).

53. Zheng Songhui 2008.

54. Wu Rongqing, Li Lipeng, and Wang Lisha's work (2014) is a plea for and exercise in the supplementing of *qiaopi* studies with oral-history interviews.

55. On Dunhuang studies, see Xinjiang Rong 2013.

56. On the Huizhou collection, see McDermott 2013.

57. Huang Qinghai 2009a, 64; Wang Weizhong 2008, 198–201; Zhang Guoxiong 2010, 75–9.

58. Wang Weizhong 2010a, 45.

59. On the gazetteers, see Zurndorfer 1995, 187–95.

60. Zhang Linyou 2014, 223–4.

61. On Hainan: Zhang Shuoren 2013; Yang Qunxi, ed., 2004, 490; Lin Jiajing et al. 1999, 17; Li Wenhai, ed., 2009, 855. On Tianmen: Tianmen ren lüju haiwai shi bianzuan weiyuan hui, eds., 2001. On Rongxian: Zheng Yisheng 2013.

62. Chang Zengshu 2010, 67.

63. Li Daogang 2006b, 58–9; Santasombat 2015.

64. Liu Jin 2013a, 150.

65. Chen Shuisheng 2014, 9.

66. See, e.g., Iriye and Saunier 2009; Lake and Curthoys 2013.

CHAPTER 2. THE STRUCTURE OF THE *QIAOPI* TRADE AND
TRANSNATIONAL NETWORKS

1. Zou Jinsheng 2010, 403.
2. Li Zhixian 2014, 6.
3. Ma Mingda and Huang Zechun 2004, 124.
4. Huang Zijian 2013, 134.
5. Liao Yun and Wu Erchi 2010, 266.
6. Harris 2012, 148–53.
7. Zhang Guoxiong 2010, 72.
8. The Earliest Remittance Centres, 1.
9. Wang Weizhong 2008, 210; Liu Bozi 2010, 282; Benton and Gomez 2008, 208. Some remitted with the shipping company's help. The practice of migrants paying other migrants to take things back to China from abroad on their own behalf survives throughout the world. In Spain, migrants advertise on Chinese e-commerce websites if they have free space in their luggage, and even operate a pick-up service at Madrid airport (Masdeu Torruella 2014, 123).
10. Yang Qunxi, ed., 2004, 58.
11. Zhang Shuoren 2013, 205; Xiao Wenping 2004, 255; Yang Qunxi, ed., 2004, 57–9; Wu Hongli 2008, 362, 366.
12. Chan 2007, 158, 163.
13. Benton and Gomez 2008, 208.
14. Huang Qinghai 2009a, 60; Dai Yifeng 2003, 71.
15. Hong Lin 2004, 22; Wang Zhuchun 2004, 153; Yang Qunxi, ed., 2004, 61.
16. Huang Ting 2008, 209.
17. Yang Qunxi, ed., 2004, 55–6, 66.
18. Zhang Guoxiong 2010, 71.
19. Wang Weizhong 2007, 18; Yang Qunxi, ed., 2004, 61, 443.
20. Ma Chujian 2008, 25; Li Wenhai, ed., 2009, 854.
21. Yang Qunxi, ed., 2004, 56–7.
22. Li Zhixian 2014, 6.
23. Huang Zijian 2013, 133.
24. Fujian sheng dang'an guan, eds., 2013, 41.
25. The Earliest Remittance Centres, 1.
26. Wang Weizhong 2007, 16.
27. Huang Ting 2008, 213–4.
28. Li Wenhai, ed., 2009, 794.
29. Xia Yuanming 2008, 374.
30. Jiao Jianhua and Xu Cuihong 2004, 167–8; Yang Qunxi, ed., 2004, 58–9.
31. Xiamen wenshi ziliao 2004, 426.
32. Yuan Ding, Chen Liyuan, and Zhong Yunrong 2014, 16.
33. Ma Zhenhui 2008, 91; Zhang Mingshan 2006, 103.
34. Ma Chujian 2008, 24–5; Yuan Ding, Chen Liyuan, and Zhong Yunrong 2014, 15.
35. Yang Qunxi, ed., 2004, 58; Jiao Jianhua 2005, 64.
36. Li Wenhai, ed., 2009, 855.

37. Wang Weizhong 2007, 17.

38. Huang Shaoxiong 2010, 489; Chen Haizhong 2013.

39. Zou Qiudong and Su Tonghai 2009, 70–1.

40. Yang Qunxi, ed., 2004, 58.

41. Xiao Wenping 2004, 256.

42. Yang Qunxi, ed., 2004, 63, 443; Li Xiaoyan 2004, 52.

43. Jiao Jianhua and Xu Cuihong 2004, 166.

44. Yang Qunxi, ed., 2004, 62; Xia Yuanming 2008, 388.

45. Lin Sha 2008, 355; Yang Qunxi, ed., 2004, 62.

46. Wang Weizhong 2007, 16–7; Wu Hongli 2008, 366.

47. Huang Qinghai 2009a, 60.

48. Chen Lie 2008, 228.

49. Hong Lin 2004, 28; Huang Jiaxiang 2010, 503–4; Xiamen wenshi ziliao 2004, 433.

50. Xiao Wenping 2004, 256.

51. Wu Kuixin 2004, 200–1.

52. Wang Weizhong 2007, 17–8; Huang Shaoxiong 2004, 108. The father of the Communist General Ye Jianying, a Hakka, was a well-known *shuike* and martial-arts teacher (Li Xiaoyan 2004, 51).

53. Zhang Shuoren 2013, 205–6; Li Wenhai, ed., 2009, 855.

54. Li Xiaoyan 2004, 51–2.

55. Su Wenjing, ed. 2013, 254; Su Wenjing and Huang Qinghai 2013a, 20; Su Wenjing and Huang Qinghai 2013b, 41.

56. Ma Chujian 2008, 26; Zou Jinsheng 2010, 403.

57. Yang Qunxi, ed., 2004, 443.

58. Liao Yun and Wu Erchi 2010, 267.

59. Yuan Ding, Chen Liyuan, and Zhong Yunrong 2014, 18.

60. Li Xiaoyan 2004, 52; Huang Ting 2008, 215.

61. Liu Bozi 2010, 282.

62. Yuan Ding, Chen Liyuan, and Zhong Yunrong 2014, 16.

63. Chen Xinyuan 2009, 113.

64. See, respectively, Wang Zhuchun 2004, 154; Yang Qunxi, ed., 2004, 80 (Huang Shaoxiong 2004, 107, says 1835); Zhang Guoxiong 2010, 71; Huang Shaoxiong 2004, 109; Yang Qunxi, ed., 2004, 200.

65. Yang Qunxi, ed., 2004, 68; Wu Kuixin 2004, 201; Li Zhixian 2014, 6–7.

66. Jia Junying 2012, 25.

67. Zeng Xubo 2010, 423.

68. Li Zhixian 2014, 6.

69. Jiao Jianhua and Xu Cuihong 2004, 167.

70. Yang Qunxi, ed., 2004, 337; Yang Qunxi 2004, 198.

71. Shantou shi renmin zhengfu, eds., 2004, 462; Li Zhixian 2014, 13.

72. Zeng Xubo 2010, 423; Yang Qunxi, ed., 2004, 60; Yang Qunxi 2004, 198.

73. Yang Qunxi, ed., 2004, 50; Jia Junying 2012, 26.

74. Jiao Jianhua and Xu Cuihong 2004, 167; Jiao Jianhua 2005, 65.

75. Yuan Ding, Chen Liyuan, and Zhong Yunrong 2014, 22.

76. Li Zhixian 2014, 13.

77. Lin Qingxi 2010, 213.
78. Jiao Jianhua and Xu Cuihong 2004, 167; Dai Yifeng 2003, 71.
79. Yang Qunxi, ed., 2004, 483; Jia Junying 2012, 26; Xiamen wenshi ziliao 2004, 431.
80. Chen Lie 2008, 228; Su Wenjing and Huang Qinghai 2013a, 21.
81. Yang Qunxi, ed., 2004, 68; Chen Lie 2008, 228.
82. Su Wenjing, ed. 2013, 255; Yang Qunxi, ed., 2004, 59.
83. Li Zhixian 2014, 7.
84. Yang Qunxi 2004, 197–8.
85. Chen Chunsheng 2000, 60.
86. Chen Haizhong 2013, 299; Huifen Shen 2012, 3.
87. Li Wenhai, ed., 2009, 802.
88. Jiao Jianhua and Xu Cuihong 2004, 165–6.
89. Yang Qunxi, ed., 2004, 56.
90. Wang Weizhong 2007, 18–25.
91. Huang Jiaxiang 2010, 503–4.
92. Yang Qunxi, ed., 2004, 57.
93. Wang Weizhong 2007, 25; Fujian sheng dang'an guan, eds., 2013, 47.
94. Zeng Xubo 2010, 419.
95. Yuan Ding, Chen Liyuan, and Zhong Yunrong 2014, 33–4.
96. Yang Qunxi, ed., 2004, 442; Jiao Jianhua 2007, 142.
97. Chen Xunxian 2010, 183.
98. Ma Chujian 2003, 58–61.
99. Harris 2012, 129–36; Zeng Xubo 2010, 419.
100. Jiang Bowei and Cai Mingsong 2008, 266–7; Harris 2012, 135–8.
101. Fujian sheng dang'an guan, eds., 1990, 311–2.
102. Chen Xunxian 2010, 183–5; Yang Qunxi, ed., 2004, 69.
103. Harris 2012, 132–6; Zeng Xubo 2010, 419.
104. Zeng Xubo 2010, 419–20; Yang Qunxi, ed., 2004, 54–6.
105. Jia Junying 2012, 37; Wang Dongxu 2009, 105.
106. Wu Baoguo 2008, 62–5.
107. Yang Qunxi, ed., 2004, 53; Deng Rui 2010, 114.
108. Lin Jiajing et al. 1999, 13.
109. Liu Jin 2009, 22–31.
110. Wang Weizhong 2007, 88.
111. Hou Weixiong 2009, 140.
112. Huang Jiaxiang 2008, 343; Jiao Jianhua 2005, 65.
113. Lin Sha 2008, 356.
114. Jiao Jianhua 2005, 68.
115. Wu Baoguo 2014, 201–2.
116. Chen Yingxun 2010, 135; Jiao Jianhua 2005, 66.
117. Li Wenhai, ed., 2009, 846.
118. Gu Zi 2006, 128–9.
119. Zeng Xubo 2010, 422–3; Li Wenhai, ed., 2009, 846–7.
120. Yang Qunxi, ed., 2004, 481.

121. Su Wenjing, ed. 2013, 260.

122. Huang Jiaxiang 2008, 341; Chen Hanchu 2010, 87–8; Ma Chujian 2008, 28–9.

123. Wang Weizhong 2007, 62.

124. Chen Haizhong 2013.

125. Jiao Jianhua 2005, 68.

126. Porter 1993, 160.

127. In Hainan, one or two thousand yuan was enough (Yang Qunxi, ed., 2004, 493).

128. Yang Qunxi, ed., 2004, 419.

129. Huang Jiaxiang 2010, 507.

130. Li Wenhai, ed., 2009, 796, 848. For *minxinju* wages, see Harris 2012, 133.

131. Xiamen wenshi ziliao 2004, 432.

132. Yang Qunxi, ed., 2004, 462, 493; Jiao Jianhua and Xu Cuihong 2004, 165; Dai Yifeng 2003, 72.

133. Liu Jin 2010, 301–2.

134. Yang Qunxi, ed., 2004, 332; Liu Jin 2010, 300–2.

135. Liu Jin 2010, 303, 308.

136. Jia Junying 2012, 60–1, 89–91; Jiao Jianhua 2005, 65–6.

137. Huang Zijian 2013, 134; Chen Chunsheng 2000, 59.

138. Hong Lin 2010, 118–9; Yang Qunxi, ed., 2004, 269.

139. Jia Junying 2012, 60; Jia Junying 2014, 149.

140. Jia Junying 2012, 91; Jiao Jianhua and Xu Cuihong 2004, 166.

141. Chen Liyuan 2008, 188.

142. Yang Qunxi, ed., 2004, 335–6.

143. Chen Hua 2010, 195.

144. Li Wenhai, ed., 2009, 849.

145. Dai Yifeng 2003, 73.

146. Ma Mingda and Huang Zechun 2004, 125–7.

147. Jiao Jianhua 2005, 67.

148. Li Zhixian 2014, 14.

149. Zeng Xubo 2010, 418; Wang Weizhong 2007, 9.

150. Liu Youyuan 2008, 54; Chen Hua 2010, 194–5.

151. Yang Qunxi 2004, 10, 96, 100–1.

152. Chen Xunxian 2010, 187.

153. Chen Hua 2010, 197.

154. Chen Liyuan 2008.

155. Yang Qunxi, ed., 2004, 58, 64; Mo Zhen, ed., 2013, 32.

156. Chen Chunsheng 2000, 58.

157. Jia Junying n.d., 9–14; Chen Liyuan 2008, 186–1.

158. Yang Qunxi, ed., 2004, 332, 463–4; Jiao Jianhua and Xu Cuihong 2004, 166.

159. Jia Junying n.d., 24.

160. Huang Jiaxiang 2008, 339; Jiao Jianhua and Xu Cuihong 2004, 168–9.

161. Yang Qunxi, ed., 2004, 487; Jiao Jianhua 2005, 67–8.

162. Jiao Jianhua and Xu Cuihong 2004, 168–9.

163. Xiamen wenshi ziliao 2004, 431–2.

164. Jia Junying n.d., 24–5; Jia Junying 2012, 84.

165. El Qorchi, Maimbo, and Wilson 2003; Jost and Singh Sandhu n.d. On the historical coincidence of the *hawala* and the *hundi*, see Martin 2009.

166. Gulshan and Kapoor 2003, 271.

167. Zhang Linyou 2014, 225–6.

168. For case studies on Chaoshan *piju*, see Chen Chunsheng 2000.

169. This section is based, except where otherwise stated, on Jia Junying n.d., 2012, and 2014; Guo Boling 2009 and 2014; and Chen Xunxian 2010.

170. On Guo Youpin's ancestry and biography, see Jia Junying 2012, 34–6.

171. Su Wenjing, ed., 2013, 261. According to Wu Hongli 2008, 366, Tianyi at one time had branches in more than a score of countries.

172. Jia Junying 2014, 140.

173. Harris 2012, 133; Zeng Xubo 2010, 419–20. *Pijiao* were nearly always male, though some studies note the occasional female *pijiao* (e.g., Wang Weizhong 2007, 51).

174. On *pijiao*, see Wang Weizhong 2008, 204–5; Huang Jiaxiang 2010, 508; Yang Qunxi, ed., 2004, 360; Jia Junying n.d., 5–6.

175. Wang Weizhong 2007, 51.

176. Wang Weizhong 2007, 51; Wang Weizhong 2008, 205.

177. Huang Jiaxiang 2010, 508; Jia Junying n.d., 6.

178. Wang Weizhong 2008, 204–5; Yang Qunxi, ed., 2004, 360; Jia Junying n.d., 24.

179. Mo Zhen, ed., 2013, 51.

180. Jia Junying n.d., 18.

181. Wang Weizhong 2010a, 47–8.

182. Yuan Ding, Chen Liyuan, and Zhong Yunrong 2014, 121.

183. The job tended to be inherited (three generations of *pijiao* in one family was not uncommon), and it was usually for life. Wang Weizhong 2008, 204; Li Xiaoyan 2004, 53.

184. Yang Qunxi, ed., 2004, 467.

185. Jiao Jianhua 2010, 314.

186. Guo Boling 2009, 124; Li Wenhai, ed., 2009, 848.

187. Huang Jiaxiang 2010, 508.

188. Chen Haizhong 2013.

189. Jia Junying n.d., 6; Chen Haizhong 2013.

190. Jiao Jianhua 2005, 66.

191. Wan Dongqing 2009, 89; Wan Dongqing 2010, 294.

192. Wang Weizhong 2007, 55.

193. Wan Dongqing 2010, 294.

194. On *pijiao* security, see Huang Jiaxiang 2010, 508; Yang Qunxi, ed., 2004, 360; Xiamen wenshi ziliao 2004, 432; Jia Junying n.d., 24; Chen Haizhong 2013.

195. Huifen Shen 2012, 51–66.

196. Li Zhixian 2014, 10–11.

197. Jia Junying 2012, 93.

198. Chen Lie 2008, 227; Shen Jianhua 2014.

199. Huang Qinghai and Liu Bozi 2010, 396–7; Jiang Ning 2010, 328–9.

200. Zheng Yisheng 2013, 313–6.

201. Cai Shaoming 2008.

202. Xiamen wenshi ziliao 2004, 430.

203. Ma Mingda and Huang Zechun 2004, 127.

204. Chen Chunsheng 2000, 60–1.

205. Jia Junying n.d., 8–9.

206. It changed its name in 1926 to Shantou qiaopi tongye gonghui (Shantou *Qiaopi* Trade Association).

207. Wang Weizhong 2007, 30–3.

208. Li Zhixian 2013, 252–3; Harris 2013.

209. Yang Qunxi, ed., 2004, 212.

210. Li Daogang 2008; Hong Lin 2006b, 30; Hong Lin 2006c, 221; Yang Qunxi, ed., 2004, 214.

211. Yang Qunxi, ed., 2004, 467–8.

212. Liu Bozi 2009, 77; Liu Bozi 2010, 282–3.

213. On efforts to unify the *qiaopi* trade, see Chen Liyuan 2003, 98–9; Yang Qunxi, ed., 2004, 91–6; Jia Junying 2012, 66; Wu Kuixin 2004, 206–7; Jiao Jianhua 2007, 143.

214. Chen Hanchu 2014, 120.

215. On Singapore's position as the nexus of ethnic Chinese social and business networks in Asia, see Hong Liu 1999 and Hong Liu and S. K. Wong 2004.

216. Chen Liyuan 2010, 166–79.

217. Huang Qinghai and Liu Bozi 2010, 396; Ke Mulin 2008, 470–4; Huang Qinghai 2016b, 162–174.

218. Li Zhixian 2014, 11–2.

219. Wu Kuixin 2004, 202–3.

220. Ke Mulin 2008.

221. Chen Liyuan 2010.

CHAPTER 3. THE *QIAOPI* TRADE AS A DISTINCTIVE FORM OF CHINESE CAPITALISM

1. Harris 2012, 2013, and 2015. Part of the materials and interpretations in this chapter has appeared in Liu and Benton 2016.

2. Here, we leave aside the wider question of the role ethnicity and identity might play in matured diasporic business culture, consolidated by generational depth.

3. The role of sub-ethnicity in ethnic Chinese identity is discussed in Gomez and Benton, 2004, 1–19. The term "sub-ethnic" is, from an anthropological point of view, questionable (see Honig 1992, 10), and is here used as an expedient. Honig prefers to call local attachments "ethnic."

4. Harris 2012, 32–3.

5. Malay "deliverer," in this context "guarantor," rendered in Chinese as *anda*.

6. Huang Ting 2008, 211–6; Chen Lie 2008, 229.

7. Liao Yun and Wu Erchi 2010, 268; Yang Qunxi, ed., 2004, 102–3.

8. Huang Jiaxiang 2010, 503–4.

9. Harris 2015.

10. Cooke Johnson 1993, 164–5. Zhongping Chen 2011, 20, and Di Wang 2008, 59, point to the intermeshing and interchangeability of the two types of organization. Hong Liu argues that "ethnic Chinese have had to resort to various types of formal and informal net-

works in order to overcome this institutional barrier. It is in this context that Chinese values and practices—which are constantly evolving themselves—continue to be relevant in the globalising world." He points out that "instead of seeing networks just as relationships based upon cultural and ethnic commonalities, it is imperative to configure networks between the state and society and to conceptualise them as a nexus, both spatially within the country and horizontally across the region, not just in the evolution of diasporic Chinese business, but more broadly, in the East Asian political economy" (Hong Liu 2012, 27, 30–1).

11. Zhang Mingshan 2006, 100.
12. Romani 2013, 4.
13. Henkin 2006, 6, 93.
14. Harris 2012, 181.
15. Anderson 1991.
16. Romani 2013, 4; Quoted in John 1995, 3; Maclachen 2011.
17. John 1995, 4–13.
18. Chatterjee 1993, 5.
19. Desai 2009.
20. Williams 2003, 104.
21. Liu Jin 2007, 33.
22. Liu Jin 2009, 75, 85; Mei Weiqiang and Mei Xue, 2007, 6.
23. Liu Jin 2007, 33.
24. Huang and Godley 1999, 313–9; Yao Ting and Mei Weiqiang 2009.
25. Huang and Godley 1999, 317; Liu Jin 2009, 75, 85.
26. Huang Annian Science Blog 2014.
27. Hsu 2000b, 139.
28. Liu Jin 2007, 33–4; Yao Ting 2011, 24.
29. Zurndorfer 1995, 187–95. On genealogical records, see Meskill 1970, 139–61.
30. Meskill 1970, 141–3.
31. Yao Ting and Mei Weiqiang 2009, 1–5.
32. Mei Weiqiang and Guan Zefeng 2010, 289.
33. Chen Chunsheng 2004, 8–9.
34. Chen Chunsheng 2005, 334–48.
35. Wu Yixiang 1949; Xinjiapo Shunde Tongxiang Hui 1948.
36. Jao Tsung-i 1965, 870–1.
37. Ke Mulin 1991, 70–6.
38. Yuan and Wu 2012, 65–100; Yuan 2011, chapter 5.
39. Yao Ting and Mei Weiqiang, 2009, 6.
40. Benton and Gomez 2008, 192–3.
41. Cai Jinhe and Xu Guanghua 2014.
42. Hsu 2000a, 313–4.
43. Hsu 2000a, 312n11, 326.
44. Hsu 2000a, 315–6, 324–8.
45. Harris 2015.
46. This is a theme of Benton 1992.
47. Hegel 1991 [1820], 268–9.
48. Zheng Youguo 2013.

49. Su Wenjing and Huang Qinghai 2013b, 40.

50. Wu Hongli 2008, 367.

51. Huang Qinghai 2009b, 55. This name is also applied to the Wenzhounese, another sub-ethnic group in southeastern China with a global trading reputation.

52. Su Wenjing and Huang Qinghai 2013b, 40.

53. Rana and Chia, 2014.

54. Su Wenjing and Huang Qinghai 2013b, 40–1.

55. Wang Weizhong 2007, 4.

56. Chen Xunxian 2010, 183–6.

57. Luo Zeyang 2004, 208–10.

58. Zhang Linyou 2014, 226–7.

59. Wang Weizhong 2007, 9. Ma Chujian 2008, 23, says six million.

60. Huang Qinghai 2009b, 55.

61. Ye Fangrong and Yang Huichang 2013, 7.

62. Wu Hongli 2008, 362.

63. Chen Xunxian 2008, 168. The Yangwu ("foreign affairs") Movement paralleled the Self-Strengthening Movement at the time of the late-Qing reforms.

64. Chen Liyuan 2010.

65. Chan 2015.

CHAPTER 4. *QIAOPI* GEOGRAPHY

1. Overseas Chinese enterprise is often based on a single idea exported by the pioneers' kinsmen or sub-ethnic associates through a process of cellular expansion (Benton and Gomez 2008, 101).

2. Xiao Wenping 2004, 253.

3. On Fuzhou's *qiaopi* trade (which, unusually, served migrants in Japan and the United States), see Wang Dongxu 2009, 104–5; on Rongxian's, Zheng Yisheng 2013. Also barely studied is the *qiaopi* trade in western Fujian, another Hakka region (Wang Dongxu 2009, 106). The *qiaopi* trade in Fujian was subdivided into four separate systems, each of which had its special features (Wang Dongxu 2009, 103).

4. For Cuba, see Li Boda 2013. Fujian sheng dang'an guan, eds., 2013, 34–5, reports *qiaopi* from South Africa.

5. Xia Yuanming 2008, 370–2.

6. Zhang Guoxiong 2010, 72.

7. Deng Rui 2010, 107.

8. Li Daogang 2006b, 59.

9. Li Xiaoyan 2004, 52–3.

10. Xiao Wenping 2004, 254–6.

11. Xia Yuanming 2008, 380; Deng Rui 2004, 61–2.

12. Xiao Wenping 2004, 257.

13. Chen Hanchu 2014, 115.

14. On the relationship between the *qiaopi* trade in Chaoshan and Meizhou, see Xia Yuanming 2008, 384–5; Lin Tengyun 2008; Lin Qingxi 2010, 215. Of the 110 *piju* in Bangkok, only a handful were Hakka-owned (Xia Shuiping and Fang Xuejia 2004, 183; Lin Jiajing et al. 1999, 14).

15. Li Zhixian 2014, 10–1.
16. Xiao Wenping 2004, 257–8.
17. Deng Rui 2008, 85.
18. On Hakka *shuike* in the early war years, see Xia Yuanming 2008, 375; Deng Rui 2010, 114; Xia Shuiping and Fang Xuejia 2004, 180.
19. Deng Rui 2008, 88; Xia Yuanming 2008, 386.
20. Xia Shuiping and Fang Xuejia 2004, 182.
21. Xia Yuanming 2008, 374–6, 383–4; Li Xiaoyan 2004, 52.
22. Zhang Shuoren 2013.
23. Li Wenhai, ed., 2009, 855.
24. Olson 1998, 86.
25. Zhang Guoxiong and Zhao Hongying 2013.
26. Zhang Guoxiong 2010, 71–2.
27. *San Francisco Morning Call*, various issues, 1877–8; Morse 1904, 11–5; Blakeslee, ed., 1910, 107; Wagel 1914, 473–4; See 1919, 334–6; Remer 1926; Coons 1930, 183; Remer 1933. See Ban Guorui, Liu Hong, and Zhang Huimei 2014, 23, citing Jiao Jianhua 2006.
28. Liu Jin 2009, 48.
29. Mai Guopei 2004, 242.
30. Liu Jin 2009, 3–4 and 21–32.
31. Liu Jin 2009, 42; Yang Qunxi, ed., 2004, 66.
32. Mai Guopei 2004, 242; Zhang Guoxiong 2010, 73–4.
33. Li Wenhai, ed., 2009, 845; Xinyang Wang 2001, 44.
34. Pei Yan 2013, 47.
35. Liu Jin 2008; Liu Jin 2009, 60–2; Pei Yan 2013, 47–8.
36. Zhang Guoxiong 2010, 73; Pei Yan 2013, 47.
37. Liu Jin 2009, 34–47.
38. Yong Chen 2000, 100–1.
39. Liu Jin 2009, 54–8; Li Zhixian 2014, 11.
40. Sung 1967, 282–3.
41. Cited in Hsu 2000a, 311.
42. Mai Guopei 2004, 242.
43. The interruption of remittances in postwar Vancouver coincided with an upsurge in corporate property ownership among Chinese there (Ng 1999, 69).
44. Peter Li 1988, 70.
45. Lin Jiajing et al. 1999, 146.
46. Liu Jin 2009, 49–52.
47. Hsu 2000b, 224n61.
48. Yong Chen 2000, 100.
49. Pan Meizhu n.d.; Yee 2005, 27–8.
50. Li Wenhai, ed., 2009, 840–1; Char, ed., 1975, 127–8.
51. Pei Yan 2013, 47.
52. Yuan Ding, Chen Liyuan, and Zhong Yunrong 2014, 255–78.
53. Pan Meizhu n.d.
54. Shi Jianping 2013, 308.
55. Liu Jin 2013b.

56. Ban Guorui, Liu Hong, and Zhang Huimei 2014, 25–8.

57. Zhang Guoxiong and Zhao Hongying 2013, 7.

58. Walden 1995, 183; Fitzgerald 1996, 46.

59. Guo Cunxiao 2013, 298–301.

60. Pei Yan 2013, 47.

61. Fitzgerald 1996, 47.

62. Williams 1999b, 22–3.

63. On the Australian connection, see Chang Zengshu 2008; Zhang Guoxiong and Zhao Hongying 2013; Williams 1999a, 16.

64. Pei Yan 2013, 48–9.

CHAPTER 5. *QIAOPI* AND MODERN CHINESE ECONOMY AND POLITICS

1. Wang Fubing 2013, 59.

2. Jia Junying 2012, 26–9.

3. Wang Zhuchun 2008, 117–8.

4. Jia Junying 2012, 30–1; Hou Weixiong 2009, 137–9.

5. Yuan Ding, Chen Liyuan, and Zhong Yunrong 2014, 24–5.

6. Huang Qinghai and Liu Bozi 2010, 393; Xiamen wenshi ziliao 2004, 436.

7. Liu Bozi 2009, 77–8; Liu Bozi 2010, 283–4; Liu Jin 2009, 35–6.

8. Yuan Ding, Chen Liyuan, and Zhong Yunrong 2014, 34.

9. Jia Junying 2012, 31–2; Guo Boling 2009, 124–6; Zou Jinsheng 2010, 404–5.

10. Yuan Ding, Chen Liyuan, and Zhong Yunrong 2014, 36.

11. Xiamen wenshi ziliao 2004, 429–30.

12. Yuan Ding, Chen Liyuan, and Zhong Yunrong 2014, 64–108.

13. An excellent English-language analysis of their relationship with the post office is Harris 2012.

14. Yuan Ding, Chen Liyuan, and Zhong Yunrong 2014, 26.

15. Li Wenhai, ed., 2009, 797.

16. Yuan Ding, Chen Liyuan, and Zhong Yunrong 2014, 43–51.

17. Jiao Jianhua 2010, 315–6; Jiao Jianhua 2013.

18. Zou Jinsheng 2010, 406.

19. Jiao Jianhua 2010, 315.

20. Cotreau 1975.

21. Yuan Ding, Chen Liyuan, and Zhong Yunrong 2014, 11, table 1-1, 53–63.

22. Liu Bozi 2010, 284; Liu Bozi 2009, 77–8; Xia Yuanming 2008, 375.

23. Jiao Jianhua 2010, 319–24.

24. Harris 2012, 179–81.

25. Lin Jiajing et al. 1999, 16; Jia Junying 2012, 48.

26. Huang Qinghai 2009a, 60.

27. Chen Chunsheng 2000, 62–3.

28. Li Zhixian 2014, 7–8.

29. Zeng Xubo 2010, 421–2; Yang Qunxi, ed., 2004, 212.

30. Jiao Jianhua 2005, 68.

31. Jia Junying 2012, 51–2; Cheong, Lee, and Lee 2013, 85–93.

32. Gu Zi 2006, 129.

33. Zeng Xubo 2008, 152; Wang Zhuchun 2008, 117–8.

34. Cheong, Lee, and Lee 2013, 84–5.

35. Liu Bozi 2014.

36. E.g., Godley 2002; Hicks 1993; Yamagaki 2005; Hamashita 2008; Shiroyama 2008.

37. Fukuda 1995, 192–202.

38. Shiroyama 2008, 32–3.

39. Mo Zhen, ed., 2013, 240.

40. Zhang Xing 2013, 329.

41. Peterson 2012, 67.

42. Huang Qinghai 2016b, 45, 196; Yamagishi 2013, 178.

43. Hou Weixiong 2009, 139; Chen Xunxian 2004; Wang Weizhong 2007.

44. The Yangwu Movement was long held to have failed, and to have been feudalistic and comprador-led. However, recent Chinese and other scholarship has evaluated it more positively.

45. Chen Xunxian 2010, 182; Xia Shuiping and Fang Xuejia 2004, 192.

46. Wang Weizhong 2013, 294–5.

47. Dai Yifeng 2003, 74.

48. Ma Mingda and Huang Zechun 2004, 125.

49. Yi Jian 2010; Li Wenhai, ed., 2009, 854.

50. Yang Qunxi, ed., 2004, 269–70.

51. Cited in Williams 2004, 266–7. For a detailed study on Hong Kong's pivotal role in Chinese emigration, see Sinn 2013.

52. Dai Yifeng 2003, 74.

53. Chen Chucai and Chen Xinyuan 2009; Jia Junying 2012, 74. According to official statistics, Guangdong (including Hainan) received more than 80 percent of remittances in the modern period (Yuan Ding, Chen Liyuan, and Zhong Yunrong 2014, 8), but Shanghai's role in the trade may necessitate a revision of this estimate.

54. Wang Weizhong 2013, 292–3.

55. Su Wenjing and Huang Qinghai 2013b, 45–6.

56. Zhang Xing 2013, 327.

57. Li Daogang 2008, 180.

58. Fujian sheng dang'an guan, eds., 2013, 157; Jiang Ning 2008, 97.

59. Ren Guixiang 1989.

60. Wang Weizhong 2009, 52.

61. Chen Shengsheng 2013, 227.

62. These are Chen Da's figures, cited in Wang Fubing 2013, 58.

63. On the wartime crisis, see Chen Shengsheng 2013, 227; Huang Shaoxiong 2010, 490–1; Wang Fubing 2013, 59.

64. Zhang Xing 2013, 331.

65. Chen Shengsheng 2013, 227.

66. Shen Dunwu 2014, 238.

67. Yuan Ding, Chen Liyuan, and Zhong Yunrong 2014, 135–6.

68. Zhang Xing 2013, 329–30; Hong Lin 2006a, 76.

69. Li Daogang 2006a, 122.
70. Liu Bozi 2009, 78; Jiang Ning 2008, 102–3.
71. Zhang Huimei 2004, 171–2.
72. Lary 2010, 133.
73. Su Wenjing, ed. 2013, 257.
74. Jia Junying 2012, 85; Zhang Xing 2013, 332.
75. Chen Xinyuan 2009, 114.
76. Huifen Shen 2012, 146–7.
77. Su Wenjing, ed., 2013, 257; Li Daogang 2006a, 107–10.
78. Jiang Ning 2008, 102–3.
79. Xia Yuanming 2008, 275–6.
80. Zhang Xing 2013, 333.
81. Liu Jin 2009, 36, 53–5.
82. Yuan Ding, Chen Liyuan, and Zhong Yunrong 2014, 10.
83. Wu Kuixin 2004, 202.
84. Deng Rui 2008, 88.
85. Jia Junying 2012, 85; Shen Dunwu 2014, 238.
86. Yang Qunxi, ed., 2004, 101.
87. Zhang Xing 2013, 327.
88. Xia Shuiping and Fang Xuejia 2004, 181–2.
89. Yuan Ding, Chen Liyuan, and Zhong Yunrong 2014, 134–80.
90. Chen Haizhong 2013, 300.
91. Zhang Huimei 2004, 160–1.
92. Yuan Ding, Chen Liyuan, and Zhong Yunrong 2014, 159–61.
93. Zhang Huimei 2004, 158.
94. Cui Pi and Yao Yumin 2011, 102.
95. Yang Qunxi, ed., 2004, 105; Zhang Huimei 2004, 182.
96. Jiang Ning 2008, 102.
97. Zhang Xing 2013, 331. For a full discussion of Japanese measures to control the trade, see Zhang Huimei 2004, 172–81.
98. Chen Chunsheng 2000, 57.
99. Zhang Huimei 2004, 179–83.
100. Zhang Xing 2013, 331; Yang Qunxi, ed., 2004, 102.
101. Zhang Huimei 2004, 162–87.
102. Hong Lin 2006b, 31; Yang Qunxi, ed., 2004, 107.
103. Chen Shengsheng 2013, 226; Zhang Xing 2013, 331–2.
104. Jiang Ning 2008, 107; Chen Xuanzhu 2008, 488–91.
105. Yang Qunxi, ed., 2004, 106.
106. Shen Dunwu 2014, 238.
107. Liao Yun and Wu Erchi 2010, 268; Yang Qunxi, ed., 2004, 102–3.
108. Jiang Ning 2008, 95–6, 103–4; Wang Weizhong 2008, 205–7; Wang Weizhong 2007, 34–40.
109. Zhang Xing 2013, 335–6.
110. Wang Weizhong 2008, 205–6; Chen Shengsheng 2013, 222–4.
111. Wang Weizhong 2007, 35.

112. Wang Weizhong 2009, 54.

113. Chen Shengsheng 2013, 224.

114. Jiang Ning 2008, 106.

115. Yang Qunxi, ed., 2004, 102–17; Hong Lin 2006b, 32.

116. Yuan Ding, Chen Liyuan, and Zhong Yunrong 2014, 167.

117. Xu Hanjun 2006; Zhang Huimei 2004, 167.

118. Yang Qunxi, ed., 2004, 117.

119. Chen Shengsheng 2013, 223.

120. Yuan Ding, Chen Liyuan, and Zhong Yunrong 2014, 10.

121. Yang Qunxi, ed., 2004, 114–8.

122. Jiang Ning 2008, 106.

123. Chen Shengsheng 2013, 222.

124. Wang Weizhong 2009, 54; Wang Weizhong 2007, 36; Xu Hanjun 2006, 99.

125. Wang Weizhong 2007, 37–8; Wu Kuixin 2004, 205.

126. This is the thesis of Zhang Huimei 2004.

127. Yuan Ding, Chen Liyuan, and Zhong Yunrong 2014, 173.

128. Yan Xing, ed., 1994, 270. The preceding paragraphs on the postwar situation are based on Yuan Ding, Chen Liyuan, and Zhong Yunrong 2014, 4, 174–254, 279–90.

129. Yang Qunxi, ed., 2004, 122; Hong Lin 2004, 24.

130. Liu Bozi 2009, 78; Wan Dongqing 2010, 298.

131. Liu Bozi 2010, 284.

132. Zhang Xing 2013, 336–7.

133. Hong Lin 2010, 118–9; Yang Qunxi, ed., 2004, 269.

134. Rao Min 2010, 482; Yang Qunxi, ed., 2004, 118–22.

135. Yang Qunxi, ed., 2004, 447.

136. Xiamen wenshi ziliao 2004, 433; Wu Kuixin 2004, 202–3.

137. Cheong Kee Cheok, Lee Kam Hing, and Poh Ping Lee 2013, 85–94.

138. Shiroyama forthcoming.

139. Yang Qunxi, ed., 2004, 54, 122–9, 332, 463–4; Wu Kuixin 2004, 203–4.

140. Jia Junying 2012, 85–6.

141. Zeng Xubo 2004, 219.

142. Li Zhixian 2014, 15.

143. Zhang Mingshan 2006, 103; Chen Haizhong 2013.

144. Luo Zeyang 2010.

145. Fujian sheng dang'an guan, eds., 2013, 96.

146. Jiang Guohua 2009, 56–7.

147. Yang Qunxi, ed., 2004, 131–2.

148. Jiang Guohua 2009, 56–7.

149. Yuan Ding, Chen Liyuan, and Zhong Yunrong 2014, 293.

150. Deng Rui 2010, 107–8; Fujian sheng dang'an guan, eds., 1990, 58.

151. Huang Jiaxiang 2010, 506.

152. Deng Rui 2010, 107.

153. Jiao Jianhua and Xu Cuihong 2004, 165.

154. Jiang Ning 2010, 332–3.

155. Cai Huanqin 2014, 176–7.

156. Shantou shi renmin zhengfu, eds., 2004, 134–5.
157. Deng Rui 2004, 59–61; Xia Shuiping and Fang Xuejia 2004, 180.
158. Li Daogang 2010, 128–32.
159. Peterson 2012, 68; Sung 1967, 19–20.
160. Zhang Mingshan 2006, 104.
161. Wang Fubing 2013, 62.
162. Lu Yongguang 2006, 157; Xiamen wenshi ziliao 2004, 437; Zeng Xubo 2004, 220–9.
163. Zou Qiudong and Su Tonghai 2009, 72–3; Ma Zhenhui 2008.
164. Huifen Shen 2012, 90.
165. Ng 1999, 83.
166. Wang Linqian 2008, 465.
167. Jiang Ning 2010, 333.
168. Chen Haizhong 2013.
169. Yang Qunxi 2004, 195; Wang Weizhong 2007, 49.
170. Jia Junying 2012, 87–8.
171. Jiao Jianhua and Xu Cuihong 2004, 165.
172. Shantou shi renmin zhengfu, eds., 2004, 131–7.
173. Yang Qunxi, ed., 2004, 182–5.
174. Yang Qunxi, ed., 2004, 375.
175. Chen Chuangyi 2004, 305.
176. Wang Linqian 2008, 465; Huang Jiaxiang 2010, 506–9.
177. E.g., Huang Jiaxiang 2010, 506.
178. Jiang Ning 2010, 334; Zou Jinsheng 2010, 406.
179. Deng Rui 2004, 64.
180. Xia Shuiping and Fang Xuejia 2004, 181.

CHAPTER 6. *QIAOPI, QIAOXIANG,* AND CHARITY

1. Dunn 2004.
2. Peterson 2005, 88.
3. Baker n.d.
4. Menkhoff and Hoon 2010.
5. Newland, Terrazas, and Munster 2010, 4.
6. Young and Shih 2004, 129, 145–6; Kapur, Mehta, and Dutt 2004, 193; Newland, Terrazas, and Munster 2010, 3.
7. *Qiaopi* sent by Liu Zhongshi in Thailand to Liu Zhuwei in Chenghai in Guangdong in 1967, in Chaoshan lishi wenhua yanjiu zhongxin, eds., 2007, no. 1, 135.
8. Johnson 2007, 3.
9. Hsu 2000a, 312.
10. Greif and Tabellini 2012, 18. The assertion that generalized morality prevailed in the West is perhaps open to question, for migrants everywhere, including those from European countries, remit on an often massive scale. That kinship is a social rather than a natural construction, independent of biology, and has long been a central tenet of critical anthropology. "A kinship system does not exist in the objective ties of descent or consanguinity between individuals: It exists only in human consciousness" (Lévi-Strauss 1963, 50, cited in

Frishkopf 2003). That the construction of clans in biological terms is theoretically no less immune to criticism than that of race renders the distinction between kin and nonkin doubly questionable. The practice of adopting and fostering children not genetically related to the adopter or fosterer falsifies the biological definition of family and kinship, defined at best as "partly putative" (Lee 2013).

11. Greif and Tabellini 2012, 16.

12. Gunderson 2006.

13. *Huipi* sent by Li Huanyou in Zhixing village (county unknown) to his father Li Huanchong in Vancouver in 1903 (City of Vancouver Archives, no. 1108060).

14. Young and Shih 2004, 129.

15. Siu 1987, 169.

16. Hsu 2000a, 309.

17. *Qiaopi* sent by Ye Tang in the United States to his younger brother in China in 1925 (Courtesy of the Museum of the Chinese in America).

18. Williams 2003, 97–8; 104–5.

19. *Qiaopi* managers and the owners of remittance shops were not always willing donors. Handling *qiaopi* was a lucrative enterprise that stuck out prominently in places where prosperity was new, and it was hard to hide from powerful local factions. Authorities and local strongmen constantly demanded "donations" to "social" funds that might or might not have lived up to their name. *Qiaopi* managers had to factor in this pestering for "donations" as a necessary expense (Huang Jiaxiang 2010, 503–4; Yang Qunxi, ed., 2004, 467).

20. Wang Weizhong 2007, 93.

21. Williams 2003, 95.

22. *Qiaopi* sent by Zeng Jinming in Thailand to Zeng Zhijian in Chenghai in 1973 (Courtesy of the Museum of Chaoshan Qiaopi Archives).

23. Deng Rui 2010, 107.

24. *Qiaopi* sent by Huang Renshen in Thailand to Huang Binshen in Chenghai in 1955 (Chaoshan lishi wenhua yanjiu zhongxin 2007, no. 2, 443).

25. *Qiaopi* sent by Huang Lixing in Thailand to Huang Libao in Chenghai in 1974 (Chaoshan lishi wenhua yanjiu zhongxin 2007, no. 2, 110).

26. Deng Dahong 2013a, 339–40.

27. *Qiaopi* sent by Cai Gaiquan in Malaya to his mother in Chenghai in 1955 (Chaoshan lishi wenhua yanjiu zhongxin 2007, no. 7, 206).

28. Luo Dunjin 2008, 426–7.

29. Deng Dahong 2013b.

30. Williams 2003, 96–102.

31. *Qiaopi* sent by Jing in Hong Kong to his father in America (date unknown); *qiaopi* sent by Ji in Hong Kong to Lin in New York (Courtesy of the Museum of the Chinese in America).

32. Deng Dahong 2013b, 294.

33. Deng Dahong 2014, 108.

34. Wang Weizhong 2007, 90–2.

35. Deng Dahong 2013a, 339–47.

36. Fujian sheng dang'an guan, eds., 2013, 118.

37. Wang Fubing 2013, 59.

38. Cai Huanqin 2009, 142. The most authoritative study on Tan Kah Kee is Yong 2013.

39. Williams 2003, 100. The percentages for other Guangfu counties were Zhongshan (36), Enping (68), Kaiping (36), and Shunde (56).

40. Liu Jin 2009, 75–84.

41. Kaiping Huaqiao yuekan she 1940.

42. Ke Mulin 2008, 475; Su Wenjing, ed., 2013, 262.

43. Lu Xiaoxia 2014, 271.

44. Lutz and Lutz 1998, 235.

45. Luo Peiheng and Zhan Guoshuang 2008, 352–3.

46. Deng Rui 2010, 261–2.

47. Xiao Wenping, Tian Lu, and Xu Ying 2014.

48. Wang Fubing 2013, 59.

49. Luo Peiheng and Zhan Guoshuang 2008, 352–3; Deng Rui 2004, 63–4.

50. Wang Weizhong 2007, 56.

51. Wang Weizhong 2006, 63.

52. Liu Jin 2009, 85–8.

53. For *qiaopi* materials relating to Hakka schools in Indonesia, see Xiao Wenping, Tian Lu, and Xu Ying 2014.

54. Williams 2003, 104.

55. Liu Jin 2009, 75, 85.

56. Fujian sheng dang'an guan, eds., 2013, 118; Wang Weizhong 2006, 63.

57. Wang Weizhong 2007, 97.

58. Luo Peiheng and Zhan Guoshuang 2008, 353; Xia Yuanming 2008, 372.

59. Wang Weizhong 2007, 99–1; Liu Jin 2009, 86.

60. Singapore Chaozhou Bayi Association 1937, 1939.

61. Jiang Ning 2008, 97. For country totals, see Liu Weisen 1999, 201, and Benton and Gomez 2008, 242, who give a total figure for 1937–40 of 294.3 million Chinese dollars.

62. *Sin Chew Jit Poh*, July 17, 1937.

63. Wang Weizhong 2007, 101–2.

64. Deng Rui 2010, 107.

65. Wang Weizhong 2006, 63.

66. Wang Weizhong 2007, 96–7.

67. Singapore Chaozhou Bayi Association 1922, 1936; Ma Chujian 2003, 80; Wang Weizhong 2007, 93–4.

68. Benton and Gomez 2008, 205; Tianmen ren lüju haiwai shi bianzuan weiyuan hui, eds., 2001, 139–59.

69. Deng Rui 2010, 108.

70. Chen Xiaojie et al. 2008, 442–3; Huang Jiaxiang 2008, 342.

71. *Qiaopi* sent by Zeng Ruipan in Thailand to Zeng Ruicheng and Zeng Ruixu in Chenghai in 1962 (Courtesy of the Museum of Chaoshan *Qiaopi* Archives).

72. Yang Ximing 2008, 279–86.

73. Wang Weizhong 2007, 93–5.

74. Jiao Jianhua 2013, 324.

75. Cheong Kee Cheok, Lee Kam Hing, and Poh Ping Lee 2013, 92–4.

76. Huang Zijian 2013, 135–8.

77. The best study, and the only one in English, is Harris 2012.
78. Tan Chee Beng 2012.
79. Tan Chee Beng 2012, 79.
80. Wang Weizhong 2006, 63.
81. Fujian sheng dang'an guan, eds., 2013, 118.
82. Wang Fubing 2013, 59.
83. Deng Rui 2010, 260–1.
84. Guest 2003, 72–87, 133–8.
85. Sidel 2004, 239.
86. Geithner, Johnson, and Chen, eds., 2004, xix.
87. Gaberman 2004, vii-viii; Johnson 2007, 3.
88. Johnson 2007, 16; Newland, Terrazas, and Munster 2010, 12–5.
89. See, for example, Lee 2014, 98.
90. Newland, Terrazas, and Munster 2010, 8–9.
91. Ma Chujian 2008, 28–9.
92. Johnson 2007, 24.
93. Liao Yun and Wu Erchi 2010, 267–8.
94. Wan Dongqing 2010, 294.
95. Chen Xiaojie et al. 2008, 442–3.
96. *Fujian qiaobao*, July 4, 2014.
97. Xiao Wenping 2004, 260–1.
98. Zhang Guoxiong 2010, 78.
99. Du Shimin 2004, 286–7.
100. Zhang Guoxiong 2010, 78; Chen Hanchu 2010, 90.
101. Li Xiaoyan 2008, 294; Iris Chang 2004, 67–8.
102. Li Xiaoyan 2008.
103. Lin Nanzhong 2014, 216.
104. Yang Qunxi, ed., 2004, 68, 209.
105. Lin Nanzhong 2010, 493–8.
106. Chen Xuanzhu 2008.
107. Chen Jiaxun and Hu Dingbo 2010, 349.
108. Liu Jin 2009, 42–3.
109. Wang Weizhong 2010a, 47–8.
110. Wu Baoguo 2008, 65–8; Williams 2003, 92, 105–8.
111. Huifen Shen 2012, 146–59.
112. The main exceptions are Harris 2012, 2013, and 2015.
113. Sidel 2004, 236–7.
114. Johnson 2007, 40–1.

CHAPTER 7. *QIAOPI* AND EUROPEAN MIGRANTS' LETTERS COMPARED

1. Richards 2006a, 69–70.
2. Stott 1990, 80–5.
3. Richards 2006a, 61–2.

4. Gerber 2006b, 15.

5. Min Zhou 2009, 172.

6. Gerber 2006b, 14.

7. Stott 1990, 85.

8. Min Zhou 1992.

9. Gerber 2006b, 67.

10. Brinks 1995, 3, 421.

11. Nadel 1953, 257–8.

12. Lemiski 2006, 248.

13. Ernst 1994, 96–7.

14. Conway, ed., 1961, 234; Bueltmann 2011, 58.

15. Cameron, Haines, and Maude 2000, xxxv.

16. Pietropaolo 2002, 2.

17. John 1995, 5.

18. Romani 2013, 4, 35.

19. Jones 2005.

20. Trasciatti 2009, 73–94; Markelis 2006, 117.

21. Harris and Gaul, eds. 2009, 10–2.

22. Richter, ed., 2015, 246.

23. Fitzpatrick 2006, 101–6.

24. Vargas 2006, 136.

25. Markelis 2006, 117–8.

26. Oi Man Cheng 2012, 106.

27. Richter, ed., 2015, 246.

28. Richter 2013, 37–8, 51; Stanley 2004, 202–3.

29. Richter 2015b, 1–14.

30. Stanley 2004, 217–8.

31. Grafton, Most, and Settis 2010, 521–3.

32. Richter 2013, 75.

33. Fitzpatrick 2006, 97–100.

34. Markelis 2006, 113.

35. Truzzi and Matos 2015.

36. Jones 2005, 25.

37. Richter 2015b, 8.

38. Gerber 2006b, 7.

39. Richter 2015b, 3–4.

40. Wright 2015, 97–134.

41. Milne 2012.

42. Fujian sheng dang'an guan, eds., 2013, 24, 157, 190.

43. Markelis 2006, 108, 115; Fitzpatrick 2006, 105; Vargas 2006, 126–31.

44. McNair 2015, 53.

45. Richter 2013, 42.

46. Fitzpatrick 2006, 97.

47. Cameron, Haines, and Maude 2000, xxx.

48. Barton 2007, 130.

49. Haiming Liu 2005.

50. These are assumptions based on a study of Mexican migrant families in the 1980s (Vargas 2006, 124–38).

51. Richards 2006a, 60.

52. Markelis 2006, 107–11; Jones 2006, 182; Cancian 2010, 11.

53. Chen 2011.

54. Markelis 2006, 115–6; DeHaan 2001, 68n4.

55. Haiming Liu 2002, 24.

56. Fitzpatrick 2006, 99.

57. Gerber 2006b, 13.

58. Stott 1975.

59. Harper 2005, 81.

60. Hooper and Batalova 2015.

61. Fitzgerald 2007.

62. Bueltmann 2011, 51.

63. Blegen, ed., 1955.

64. Gerber 2006b, 16.

65. See Miller, Schrier, Boling, and Doyle, eds. and authors, 2003 for the Irish.

66. Richards 2006a, 69.

67. Ureland and Clarkson, eds. 1993, 241–7; Barton 2007, 13.

68. Conway, ed. 1961, 231–4.

69. Stellingwerff 1975.

70. Blegen, ed., 1955, 9.

71. Cameron, Haines, and Maude, eds., 2000, 49.

72. Nadel 1953, 257–8.

73. Efford 2013, 12, 45.

74. Tavuchis 1963, 21.

75. Arnold 1981, 238; Bueltmann 2011, 47.

76. Serra 2009, 139.

77. Miller, Schrier, Boling, and Doyle, eds., 2003, 9.

78. Flom 1909, 80.

79. Debouzy 1992, 13.

80. Helbich 1997, 128–9.

81. Gerber 2006a, 143–4; Gerber 2006b, 57.

82. DeHaan 2001, 67–8.

83. Richards 1991, 20; Richards 2006b, 5.

84. Ganzevoort, trans. and ed., 1999, 19–21.

85. Gerber 2006a, 147–57; Serra 2009, 137–8.

86. Richards 2006a, 61–2.

87. Gerber 2006b, 101–36.

88. Gerber 2006b, 116–29.

89. Gerber 2006a, 151.

90. Ureland and Clarkson, eds., 1993, 240; Jones 2006.

91. Cancian 2010.

92. McDougall 2015, 546–81.

93. Thomas and Znaniecki 1958.

94. Pan and Kádár 2011, 60.

95. Pan and Kádár 2011, 54, 61.

96. Richter 2013, 5–6; Richter 2015b, 1.

97. Donna Gabaccia, cited in Baran 2010.

98. Helbich and Kamphoefner 2006, 29–30, 50.

99. See Bielenberg, ed., 2000, 137n41 for Irish letters.

100. Elliott, Gerber, and Sinke 2006, 3.

101. Helbich 1997, 126.

102. Stanley 2004, 204.

103. Richards 2006a, 68.

104. Gerber 2006b, 14–5.

105. Richards 2006a, 58, 62–5.

106. In Germany, farm families are also more likely to preserve letters than urbanites (Helbich and Kamphoefner 2006, 45).

107. Elliott, Gerber, and Sinke 2006, 5–9.

108. Kamphoefner 2007, 139.

109. Moreton 2013, chapter 4.

110. On Western scholarship, see Elliott, Gerber, and Sinke 2006, 11–2.

111. Barton 2007, 131.

112. Stellingwerff 2014. The letter typically starts at sea.

113. DeHaan 2001, 53.

114. See, e.g., Bueltmann 2011, 60.

115. Elliott 2017.

116. Middleton 2010, 69.

117. Richter 2013, 28, 40–2.

118. Elliott, Gerber, and Sinke 2006, 9–10.

119. Sierra 2009, 139.

120. Irishacw 2015; Markelis 2006, 115.

121. Gerber 2006b, 342n13.

122. Marlborough Press 1873, cited in Te Ara.

123. Serra 2009, 138.

124. Cameron, Haines, and Maude 2000, xv–xl.

125. Harper 2010, 1–21; University of Waterloo 2002.

126. Cameron, Haines, and Maude 2000, xl.

127. Jones 2006; Jaroszyńska-Kirchmann 2006, 200–20.

128. Gentz 2015, 900–31.

129. Flom 1909, 80–3.

130. Kosak 2000, 34–8.

131. Serra 2009, 137–8.

132. Kamphoefner 2007.

133. Haiming Liu 2005, 11, 79.

134. Miller, Schrier, Boling, and Doyle, eds., 2003, 9.

135. Bonnie McDougall (2015, 547) makes this point in a different context.

136. Blitstein 2015, 331–62; Tsui 2015, 363–97.

137. Richter 2015b, 5–6.
138. Haiming Liu 2005, 136–40.
139. Richter 2015a, 240, 257.
140. Richter 2013, 42.
141. Richter 2015a, 240–5.
142. Serra 2009, 137.

CONCLUSIONS

1. Chen Chunsheng 2000, 59–60.
2. Dai Yifeng 2003, 75–6.
3. On the term "sub-ethnic," see chapter 3.
4. Desai 2009.
5. Eisenstadt and Schluchter 1998; Eisenstadt 2000.
6. Zhang Linyou 2014, 223; Hamashita 2008.
7. Chen Hanchu 2014, 121.
8. Huang Qinghai 2009b, 54–5.

APPENDIX: SELECTED *QIAOPI* AND *HUIPI* LETTERS

Letters 1–10 are *qiaopi* (emigrants sent home from overseas which contained money). Letters 11–13 are *huipi* (letters sent by families at home to emigrants abroad). The titles of the letters are added by the authors of this book for illustrative purposes.

1. Gold Mountain refers to North America.
2. A place in America.
3. Saltwater Port refers to Vancouver; perhaps eye problems can be used as a pretext for excluding a person.
4. A genealogically senior relative or fellow villager.
5. In the Chenghai region, fathers were sometimes addressed as "uncle."
6. The letter writer uses "younger sister" in the original letter, which could also mean "fiancée" or "wife." Judging from the content of this letter, it means "wife" and is translated accordingly.
7. In pre-1949 China, the wife sometimes called herself "concubine."

REFERENCES

Anderson, Benedict R. 2016. *Imagined Communities: Reflections on the Origin and Spread of Nationalism*, revised and extended edition. London: Verso.

Arnold, Rollo. 1981. *The Farthest Promised Land: English Villagers, New Zealand Immigrants of the 1870s*. Wellington: Victoria University Press.

Baker, Christopher. n.d. "Re-distributive Philanthropy and the Chinese Australian Diaspora." https://researchbank.swinburne.edu.au/file/3d8b1223-c10f-429c-9e4e-afdc2c 92362c/1/PDF%20%28Published%20version%29.pdf

Ban Guorui 班国瑞, Liu Hong 刘宏, and Zhang Huimei 张慧梅. 2014. "Hongyan chuanshu qian wanli: Ou Mei Ao Huaqiao yimin yu jiaxiang zhi shuxin wanglai" ("Letters across Ten Thousand *li*: Correspondence between Chinese Migrants in Europe, America, and Australia and Their Home Villages"). In Zhongguo lishi wenxian yanjiu hui, eds., 23–30.

Baran, Madeleine. 2010. "The Immigrant's Story, Told through Letters." Minnesota Public Radio, December 1. http://minnesota.publicradio.org/features/2010/11/immigrant-letters -home/.

Barclay, David E., and Elisabeth Glaser-Schmidt, eds. 1997. *Transatlantic Images and Percep- tions: Germany and America Since 1776*. Cambridge: Cambridge University Press.

Barton, Hildor Arnold. 2007. *The Old Country and the New: Essays on Swedes and America*. Carbondale: Southern Illinois University Press.

Batto, Patricia R. S. 2006. "The *Diaolou* of Kaiping (1842-1937): Buildings for Dangerous Times." *China Perspectives* 66:2–17.

Benton, Gregor. 1992. *Mountain Fires: The Chinese Communists' Three-Year War in South China, 1934–1938*. Berkeley: California University Press.

Benton, Gregor, and E. T. Gomez. 2008. *Chinese in Britain, 1800–2000: Economy, Transna- tionalism, Identity*. Basingstoke: Palgrave.

Benton, Gregor, and Edmund Terence Gomez, eds. 2015. *Belonging to the Nation: Genera- tional Change, Identity and the Chinese Diaspora*. London: Routledge.

Benton, Gregor, Hong Liu, and Huimei Zhang, eds. 2018. *The Qiaopi Trade and Transnational Networks in the Chinese Diaspora*. London: Routledge.

Bielenberg, Andy, ed. 2000. *The Irish Diaspora*. Harlow: Longman.

Blakeslee, George H., ed. 1910. *China and the Far East, Clark University Lectures*. New York: Thomas Y. Crowell.

Blegen, Theodore C., ed. 1955. *Land of Their Choice: The Immigrants Write Home*. Minneapolis: University of Minnesota Press.

Blitstein, Pablo Ariel. 2015. "Liu Xie's Institutional Mind: Letters, Administrative Documents, and Political Imagination in Fifth- and Sixth-Century China." In Richter, ed., 2015, 331–62.

Brinks, Herbert J. 1995. *Dutch American Voices: Letters from the United States, 1850–1930*. Ithaca, NY: Cornell University Press.

Bueltmann, Tanja. 2011. *Scottish Ethnicity and the Making of New Zealand Society, 1850–1930*. Edinburgh: Scottish Historical Review Monograph Series, no. 19.

Cai Huanqin 蔡焕钦. 2009. "Haiwai chizi de sangzi qinghuai" ("Feelings of Love for One's Native Place among People Overseas"). In Chen Xiaogang, ed., 2009, 142–8.

———. 2014. "Jiefang hou youzheng bumen dui qiaopi ye de guanli" ("The Postal Department's Administration of the *Qiaopi* Trade after Liberation"). In Zhongguo lishi wenxian yanjiu hui, eds., 176–83.

Cai Jinhe 蔡金河 and Xu Guanghua 许光华. 2014. "Shilun Taiguo Huawen bao dui Taiguo qiaopi ye de gongxian" ("On the Contribution of Thailand's Chinese-Language Press to Thailand's *Qiaopi* Trade"). In Zhongguo lishi wenxian yanjiu hui, eds., 365–70.

Cai Shaoming 蔡少明. 2008. "Taiguo qiaopi ju yi ju weituo jidi de qiaopi" ("The *Qiaopi* Delivered by *Qiaopi* Offices on Behalf of Other Offices"). In Wang Weizhong, ed., 478–86.

Cameron, Wendy, Sheila Haines, and Mary Maude. 2000. "Introduction." In *English Immigrant Voices: Labourers' Letters from Upper Canada in the 1830s*, edited by Wendy Cameron, Sheila Haines, and Mary Maude. Montreal: McGill-Queen's University Press.

Cancian, Sonia. 2010. *Families, Lovers, and Their Letters: Italian Postwar Migration to Canada*. Winnipeg: University of Manitoba Press.

Candela, Ana Maria. 2013. "*Qiaoxiang* on the Silk Road." *Critical Asian Studies* 45 (3): 431–58.

Cassel, Susie Lan, ed. 2002. *The Chinese in America: A History from Gold Mountain to the New Millennium*. Lanham, MD: Rowman and Littlefield.

Chan, H. D. 2007. "*Qiaoxiang* and the Diversity of Chinese Settlements in Australia and New Zealand." In Tan Chee Beng, ed., 153–71.

Chan, Kwok Bun. 1997. "A Family Affair: Migration, Dispersal, and the Emigrant Identity of the Chinese Cosmopolitan." *Diaspora* 6 (2): 195–214.

Chan, Shelley. 2015. "The Case for Diaspora: A Temporal Approach to the Chinese Experience." *Journal of Asian Studies* 74 (1): 107–28.

Chang Zengshu 常增书. 2008. "Aozhou taojin Huagong de 'yinxin'" ("The Australian Gold-miners' 'Silver Letters'"). In Wang Weizhong, ed., 455–60.

———. 2010. "Qiaopi shi guojia ji wenxian shiliao" ("*Qiaopi* Are Historical Materials at State Level"). In Wang Weizhong, ed., 66–7.

Chang, Iris. 2004. *The Chinese in America: A Narrative History*. London: Penguin.

Chaoshan lishi wenhua yanjiu zhongxin 潮汕历史文化研究中心, eds. 2007. Vol. 1 of *Chaoshan qiaopi jicheng (Collection of Chaoshan* Qiaopi). Nanning: Guangxi shifan daxue chuban she.

———, eds. 2011. Vol. 2 of *Chaoshan qiaopi jicheng (Collection of Chaoshan* Qiaopi). Nanning: Guangxi shifan daxue chuban she.

Chaoshan lishi wenhua yanjiu zhongxin, qiaopi dang'an guan 潮汕历史文化研究中心、侨批档案馆, eds. 2017. *Guangcang wanQing qiaopi xuandu (Selected* Qiaopi *of the Late Qing Dynasty)*. Guangzhou: Ji'nan daxue chuban she.

Char, Tin-Yuke, ed. 1975. *The Sandalwood Mountains: Readings and Stories of the Early Chinese in Hawaii.* Honolulu: The University Press of Hawaii.

Chatterjee, Partha. 1993. *The Nation and Its Fragments: Colonial and Postcolonial Histories.* Princeton: Princeton University Press.

Chen Chuangyi 陈创义. 2004. "Qiaopi: Fengge dute de qunti shuxin" ("*Qiaopi*: Collective Letters with a Special Character"). In Wang Weizhong, ed., 303–6.

Chen Chucai 陈楚材 and Chen Xinyuan 陈新缘. 2009. "Shanghai Fujian bang yu Minnan qiaopi guanxi shiduo ji pouxi" ("Putting in Order and Analyzing the Relationship between the Shanghai Fujian *Bang* and Southern Fujian's *Qiaopi*"). In Chen Xiaogang, ed., 159–69.

Chen Chunsheng 陈春声. 2000. "Jindai Huaqiao huikuan yu qiaopi ye de jingying: Yi Chaoshan diqu de yanjiu wei zhongxin" ("Modern Overseas-Chinese Remittances and the Administration of the *Qiaopi* Trade: With a Focus on Research on the Chaoshan Region"). *Zhongguo shehui jingji shi yanjiu* 4:57–66.

———. 2004. "Lishi de neizai mailuo yu quyu shehui jingji shi yanjiu" ("Studies on the Internal Historical Context and Regional Social and Economic History"). *Shixue yuekan* 8:8–9.

———. 2005. "Haiwai yimin yu difang shehui de zhuanxing: Lun Qingmo Chaozhou shehui xiang 'qiaoxiang' de zhuanbian" ("Diasporic and Local Social Transformations: Transformations in the Late-Qing Chaozhou *Qiaoxiang*"). Di san jie renlei xue gaoji luntan ("Third Anthropology Advanced Forum"), October 29.

Chen Haizhong 陈海忠. 2013. "Lishi jiyi zhong de Chaoshan qiaopi yu xiangcun shehui" ("Chaoshan *Qiaopi* and Village Society in Historical Memory"). In Zhongguo qiaopi shijie jiyi gongcheng guoji yantao hui zuwei hui, eds., 296–307.

Chen Hanchu 陈汉初. 2010. "Chaoshan qiaopi de dang'an wenxian jiazhi" ("The Documentary Value of the Chaoshan *Qiaopi* Archive"). In Wang Weizhong, ed., 82–93.

———. 2014. "Qiaopi toudi: Dute de 'haishang sichou zhi lu'" ("*Qiaopi* Delivery: A Unique 'Maritime Silk Road'"). In Zhongguo lishi wenxian yanjiu hui, eds., 109–22.

Chen Hua 陈骅. 2010. "Dui qiaopi yanjiu sheji de jige wenti de taolun" ("A Discussion of Some Questions in the Design of *Qiaopi* Research"). In Wang Weizhong, ed., 190_8.

Chen Jiashun陈嘉顺.2014. "Yishu shi shiye xia de Chaoshan qiaopi shufa" ("The Calligraphy of Chaoshan *Qiaopi* from the Angle of Art History"). In Zhongguo lishi wenxian yanjiu hui, eds., 323–8.

Chen, Joyce. 2011. "Chinese Immigration to the United States: History, Selectivity and Human Capital." Working paper, Ohio State University.

Chen Lie 陈列. 2008. "Guanyu Chaoshan qiaopi wenhua ruogan wentide qiantan" ("Some Observations on Some Questions Concerning Chaoshan *Qiaopi* Culture"). In Wang Weizhong, ed., 225–36.

Chen Liyuan 陈丽园. 2003. "Jindai haiwai Huaren de kuaguo zhuyi yanjiu" ("Research into Transnationalism among Today's Overseas Ethnic Chinese"). In Li Zhixian, ed., 85–101.

———. 2008. "Qiaopi jingying wangluo de zuzhi xingtai yanjiu" ("Research into the Organizational Form of the Management of the *Qiaopi* Network"). In Wang Weizhong, ed., 185–94.

———. 2010. "Qiaopi yu kuaguo Huaren shehui de jiangou" ("*Qiaopi* and the Construction of Transnational Ethnic-Chinese Society"). In Wang Weizhong, ed., 164–80.

Chen Shengsheng 陈胜生. 2013. "Cong kangzhan houqi de 'Dongxing huilu' shixi qiaopi de shijie yiyi" ("Analyzing the World Significance of *Qiaopi* on the Basis of the 'Dongxing Remittance Route' of the Later Period of the War of Resistance"). In Zhongguo qiaopi shijie jiyi gongcheng guoji yantao hui zuwei hui, eds., 219–40.

———. 2014. "Chaoshan qiaopi shenyi shimo" ("The Whole Story of the Chaoshan *Qiaopi* Application"). In Zhongguo lishi wenxian yanjiu hui, eds., 371–8.

Chen, Shuhua. 2017. "Cosmopolitan Imagination: A Methodological Quest for *Qiaopi* Archival Research." *Yearbook in Cosmopolitan Studies* 3. https://ojs.st-andrews.ac.uk /index.php/ycs/article/view/1385.

Chen Shuisheng 陈水生. 2014. "Qiaopi (yinxin) yanjiu wenxian jiliang fenxi" ("A Bibliometric Analysis of Research Literature on *Qiaopi* [*Yinxin*]"). *Wuyi daxue xuebao (kexue xuebao)* 16 (2): 6–10.

Chen, Ta. 1940. *Emigrant Communities in South China: A Study of Overseas Migration and Its Influence on Standards of Living and Social Change.* English version edited by Bruno Lasker. New York: Institute of Pacific Relations.

Chen Xiaogang 陈小钢, ed. 2009. *Huiwang Minnan qiaopi: Shoujie Minnan qiaopi yantao hui lunwen ji* (*Looking Back on Minnan Qiaopi: Collection of Papers of the First Minnan Qiaopi Conference*). Quanzhou: Huayi chuban she.

Chen Xiaojie 陈晓杰 et al. 2008. "Fengge dute de Chaoshan qiaopi" ("The Special Style of Chaoshan *Qiaopi*"). In Wang Weizhong, ed., 442–9.

Chen Xinyuan 陈新缘. 2009. "Qiantan Quanzhou qiaopi ye yu Zhongguo yinhang Quanzhou zhihang" ("Some Remarks on Quanzhou's *Qiaopi* Trade and the Bank of China's Quanzhou Branch"). In Chen Xiaogang, ed., 112–7.

Chen Xuanzhu 陈璇珠. 2008. "Qiaopi fengshang de 'chubeijuan'" ("'Reserve Tickets' on *Qiaopi* Envelopes"). In Wang Weizhong, ed., 487–91.

Chen Xunxian 陈训先. 2004. "Shilun Qing dai Chao bang qiaopi ye dui wo guo yuanshi jinrong shichang de cujin yu gongxian" ("On the Chao Gang's Acceleration of and Contribution to Our Country's Primitive Financial Market in the Qing Dynasty"). In Wang Weizhong, ed., 187–92.

———. 2006. "Yifen Huaqiao kangzhan zhongyao wenxian de faxian yu yitiao 'koupi' lishi ziliao de gouchen" ("The Discovery of an Important Document from an Overseas Chinese during the War of Resistance and the Evocation of a *Koupi* Historical Document"). In Hong Lin and Li Daogang, eds., 93–6.

———. 2008. "Qiaopi ye yu Chao shang wenhua yuan" ("The *Qiaopi* Trade and the Origins of Chao Merchant Culture"). In Wang Weizhong, ed., 167–71.

———. 2010. "Lun 'yinxin hefeng'" ("On 'Silver and Letter in one Envelope'"). In Wang Weizhong, ed., 181–9.

Chen Yingxun 陈瑛珣. 2010. "Guangdong qiaopi shou, ji xinhuobi zhonglei de diyu shehui fenxi" ("A Social Analysis of the Guangdong *Qiaopi*'s Collecting and Delivering of Letters, Goods, and Currency"). In Wang Weizhong, ed., 134–50.

Chen Youyi 陈友义 and Xue Can 薛灿. 2010. "Shilun Chaoshan qiaopi de qingshao nian qinggan jiaoyu jiazhi" ("On the Value of Chaoshan *Qiaopi* for the Emotional Education of Young People"). In Wang Weizhong, ed., 353–64.

Chen, Yong. 2000. *Chinese San Francisco, 1850–1943: A Trans-Pacific Community*. Stanford, CA: Stanford University Press.

Chen, Zhongping. 2011. *Modern China's Network Revolution: Chambers of Commerce and Sociopolitical Change in the Early Twentieth Century*. Stanford, CA: Stanford University Press.

Cheng, Oi Man. 2012. "Epistolary Guidebooks for Women in Early Twentieth Century China and the Shaping of Modern Chinese Women's National Consciousness." *New Zealand Journal of Asian Studies* 14 (2): 105–20.

Cheok, Cheong Kee, Lee Kam Hing, and Poh Ping Lee. 2013. "Chinese Overseas Remittances to China: The Perspective from Southeast Asia." *Journal of Contemporary Asia* 43 (1): 75–101.

City of Vancouver Archives. n.d. "Older Letters in Chinese." Reference code AM1108-S2-3.

Cochran, Sherman. 2006. *Chinese Medicine Men: Consumer Culture in China and Southeast Asia*. Cambridge: Harvard University Press.

———. 2000. *Encountering Chinese Networks: Western, Japanese, and Chinese Corporations in China, 1880–1937*. Berkeley: University of California Press.

Conway, Alan, ed. 1961. *The Welsh in America: Letters from the Immigrants*. St. Paul, MN: University of Minnesota Press.

Cooke Johnson, Linda. 1993. "Shanghai: An Emerging Jiangnan Port, 1683–1840." In *Cities of Jiangnan in Late Imperial China*, edited by Linda Cooke Johnson, 151–80. Albany: State University of New York Press.

Coons, Arthur Gardiner. 1930. *The Foreign Public Debt of China*. Philadelphia: University of Pennsylvania Press.

Cotreau, James D. 1975. *The Historical Development of the Universal Postal Union and the Question of Membership*. PhD dissertation. University of Fribourg, Fribourg, Switzerland. Boston: n.p.

Cui Pi 崔丕 and Yao Yumin 姚玉民, trans. 2011. Vol. 1 of *Riben dui Nanyang Huaqiao diaocha ziliao xuanbian (1925–1945)* (*Japanese survey materials on overseas Chinese in Southeast Asia, 1925–1945*). Guangzhou: Guangdong gaodeng jiaoyu chuban she.

Dai Yifeng 戴一峰. 2003. "Wangluo hua qiye yu qianru xing: Jindai qiaopi ju de zhidu jiangou (1850s–1940s)" ("Networked Enterprise and Embeddedness: The Systemic Construction of the Modern Remittance Office [1850s–1940s]"). *Zhongguo shehui jingji shi yanjiu* 1:70–8.

Debouzy, Marianne. 1992. *In the Shadow of the Statue of Liberty: Immigrants, Workers, and Citizens in the American Republic, 1880–1920*. Urbana: University of Illinois Press.

Deeney, John. 2002. "A Neglected Minority in a Neglected Field: The Emerging Role of Chinese American Philanthropy in U.S.-Chinese Relations." In *The Expanding Roles of Chinese Americans in U.S.-Chinese Relations*, edited by Peter H. Koehen and Xiao-Huan Yin. Armonk, NY: M. E. Sharpe.

DeHaan, Kathleen. 2001. "Wooden Shoes and Mantle Clocks: Letter Writing as a Rhetorical Forum for the Transforming Immigrant Identity." In Laura Gray-Rosendale and Sibylle Gruber, eds., 53–68.

Deng Dahong 邓达宏. 2009. "Minnan qiaopi: Zhonghua ru wenhua suoying" ("Minnan Qiaopi: The Epitome of China's Confucian Culture"). In Chen Xiaogang, ed., 45–9.

———. 2013a. "Guoji yimin shuxin yu Minyue qiaoxiang jiaoyu tanlüe" ("International Emigrants' Letters and Education in the Fujian and Guangdong Emigrant Regions"). In Guangzhou "Guangdong Huaqiao shi" et al., eds., 338–51.

———. 2013b. "Qiaopi yu Minyue qiaoxiang jiaoyu tanlüe" ("Qiaopi and Education in the Fujian and Guangdong Emigrant Regions"). Dongnan xueshu 6:291–5.

———. 2013c. "Fujian qiaopi duoyuan wenhua jiazhi tanlüe" ("Explorations into the Value of the Multivariant Culture of Fujian's Qiaopi"). In Zhongguo qiaopi shijie jiyi gongcheng guoji yantao hui zuwei hui, eds., 85–94.

———. 2014. "Lüelun guoji yimin shuxin dui qiaoxiang jiaoyu de yingxiang" ("On the Influence of International Migrants' Letters on Qiaxiang Education"). In Zhongguo lishi wenxian yanjiu hui, eds., 99–108.

Deng Rui 邓锐. 2004. "Cong Meizhou shi qiaohui de fazhan guocheng kan qiaopi ju xingshuai" ("Looking at the Rise and Fall of Qiaopi Offices from the Point of View of the Development of Overseas Remittances in Meizhou"). In Wang Weizhong, ed., 57–64.

———. 2008. "Shixi qiaopi ye yu Meizhou jinrong ye de guanxi" ("Preliminary Investigation of the Relationship between the Qiaopi Trade and Meizhou's Financial Industry"). In Wang Weizhong, ed., 84–9.

———. 2010. "Qiantan qiaopi de zhongyao zuoyong ji kaifa liyong" ("On the Important Role and Uses of Qiaopi"). In Wang Weizhong, ed., 103–17.

Desai, Radhika. 2009. "The Inadvertence of Benedict Anderson: Engaging Imagined Communities." The Asia-Pacific Journal 7 (March 16).

Du Shimin 杜式敏. 2004. "Chaoshan qiaopi de funü guan chutan" ("On the View of Women in Chaoshan Qiaopi"). In Wang Weizhong, ed., 286–93.

Dunn, Kathleen. 2004. "Diaspora Giving and the Future of Philanthropy." Boston: The Philanthropic Initiative, May 16.

Duara, Prasenjit. 1997. "Transnationalism and the Predicament of Sovereignty: China, 1900–1945." American Historical Review 102 (4): 1030–51.

"Earliest Remittance Centres: Letters with Money, The." 2013. Bukit Brown Cemetery blog. http://blog.bukitbrown.org/post/57508567506/the-earliest-remittance-centres-letters-with-money.

Efford, Alison Clark. 2013. German Immigrants, Race, and Citizenship in the Civil War Era. New York: Cambridge University Press.

Eisenstadt, Shmuel N., and Wolfgang Schluchter. 1998. "Introduction: Paths to Early Modernities—A Comparative View." Daedalus 127 (3): 1–18.

———. 2000. "Multiple Modernities." Daedalus 129 (1): 1–29.

El Qorchi, Mohammed, Samuel Munzele Maimbo, and John F. Wilson. 2003. Informal Funds Transfer Systems: An Analysis of the Informal Hawala System. Occasional Paper no. 222. Washington, DC: International Monetary Fund.

Elliott, Bruce S. 2017. "Immigrant Diaries and Memoirs." Library and Archives Canada. https://www.collectionscanada.gc.ca/immigrants/021017-1800-e.html.

Elliott, Bruce S., David A. Gerber, and Suzanne M. Sinke. 2006. "Introduction." In Elliott, Gerber, and Sinke, eds., 1–25.

———, eds. 2006. *Letters Across Borders: The Epistolary Practices of International Migrants.* Houndmills: Palgrave.

Ernst, Robert. 1994. *Immigrant Life in New York City, 1825–1863.* Syracuse, NY: Syracuse University Press.

Eisenstadt, Shmuel N. 2000. "Multiple Modernities." *Daedalus* 129 (1): 1–29.

Faure, David. 2006. *China and Capitalism: A History of Business Enterprise in Modern China.* Hong Kong: Hong Kong University Press.

———. 2007. *Emperor and Ancestor: State and Lineage in South China.* Stanford, CA: Stanford University Press.

Faure, David, and Helen Siu, eds. 1995. *Down to Earth: The Territorial Bond in South China.* Stanford, CA: Stanford University Press.

Fei, Xiaotong. 1992. *From the Soil, the Foundation of Chinese Society.* Translated by Gary Hamilton and Zheng Wang. Berkeley: University of California Press.

Ferdinand, P. 2016. "Westward Ho—The China Dream and 'One Belt, One Road': Chinese Foreign Policy under Xi Jinping." *International Affairs* 92 (4): 941–57.

Fitzgerald, John. 2007. *Big White Lie: Chinese Australians in White Australia.* Sydney: University of New South Wales.

Fitzgerald, Shirley. 1996. *Red Tape, Gold Scissors.* Sydney: State Library of New South Wales.

Fitzpatrick, David. 1994. *Oceans of Consolation: Personal Accounts of Irish Migration to Australia.* Ithaca, NY: Cornell University Press.

———. 2006. "Irish Emigration and the Art of Letter-Writing." In Elliott, Gerber, and Sinke, eds., 2006, 97–106.

Flom, George T. 1909. *A History of Norwegian Immigration to the United States.* Iowa City: privately printed.

Freedman, Maurice. 1967. "Ancestor Worship: Two Facets of the Chinese Case." In *Social Organization and Peasant Societies: Festschrift in Honor of Raymond Firth*, edited by Maurice Freedman, 85–104. London: Frank Cass.

Frishkopf, Michael. 2003. "Spiritual Kinship and Globalization." *Religious Studies and Theology* 22 (1).

Fujian sheng dang'an guan 福建省档案馆, eds. 1990. *Fujian Huaqiao dang'an shiliao* (*Fujian Archival Materials in Relation to Overseas Chinese*). Beijing: Dang'an chuban she.

———, eds. 2013 *Bainian kuaguo liangdi shu* (*Hundred Years of Letters between Two Transnational Places*). Xiamen: Lujiang chuban she.

Fukuda, Shozo. 1995. *With Sweat and Abacus: Economic Roles of Southeast Asian Chinese on the Eve of World War II.* Translated by Les Oates. Edited by George Hicks. Singapore: Select Books.

Gabaccia, Donna R., and Mary Jo Maynes, eds. 2013. *Gender History Across Epistemologies.* Chichester: Wiley-Blackwell.

Gaberman, Barry D. 2004. "Preface." In Geithner, Johnson, and Chen, eds., vii–viii.

Ganzevoort, Herman, trans. and ed. 1999. *The Last illusion: Letters from Dutch Immigrants in the "Land of Opportunity," 1924–1930.* Calgary: University of Calgary Press.

Geithner, Peter E., Paula D. Johnson, and Lincoln C. Chen, eds. 2004. *Diaspora Philan-thropy and Equitable Development in China and India.* Cambridge, MA: Global Equity Initiative, Harvard University.

Gentz, Natascha. 2015. "Opinions Going Public: Letters to the Editors in China's Earliest Modern Newspapers." In Richter, ed., 900–31.

Gerber, David A. 2006a. "Epistolary Masquerades: Acts of Deceiving and Withholding in Immigrant Letters." In Elliott, Gerber, and Sinke, eds., 141–57.

———. 2006b. *Authors of Their Lives: The Personal Correspondence of British Immigrants to North America in the Nineteenth Century.* New York: New York University Press.

———. 2013. "Exploring the Mental Lives of Immigrant Letter Writers: Nostalgia and Adjustment to Changed Circumstances." In Guangzhou "Guangdong Huaqiao shi" et al., eds., 94–112.

Godley, Michael. 2002. *The Mandarin-Capitalists from Nanyang: Overseas Chinese Enter-prise in the Modernization of China, 1893–1911.* Cambridge: Cambridge University Press.

Goldman, Corrie. 2012. "Stanford Scholars Search for Documents from the Chinese Work-ers Who Built the U.S. Transcontinental Railroad." *Stanford Report,* September 21.

Gomez, Edmund Terence, and Gregor Benton. 2004. "Introduction: De-essentializing Cap-italism: Chinese Enterprise, Transnationalism, and Identity." In *Chinese Enterprise, Transnationalism, and Identity,* edited by Edmund Terence Gomez and Michael Hsiao, 1–19. London: RoutledgeCurzon.

Grafton, Anthony, Glenn W. Most, and Salvatore Settis. 2010. *The Classical Tradition.* Cam-bridge: Harvard University Press.

Gray-Rosendale, Laura, and Sibylle Gruber, eds. 2001. *Alternative Rhetorics: Challenges to the Rhetorical Tradition.* Albany: State University of New York Press.

Greif, Avner, and Guido Tabellini. 2012. "The Clan and the City: Sustaining Cooperation in China and Europe." Stanford University and Bocconi University. http://projects.iq.harvard.edu/files/pegroup/files/greif_tabellini.pdf.

Gu Zi 谷子. 2006. "Youliang Zhongguo chuantong wenhua yunyu ducheng shouxin qiaopi ye" ("China's Excellent Cultural Traditions Breed a Sincere Trust in the *Qiaopi* Trade"). In Hong Lin and Li Daogang, eds., 123–9.

Guangzhou "Guangdong Huaqiao shi" bianzuan weiyuan hui 广州《广东华侨史》编纂委员会 et al., eds. 2013. *"Bijiao, jiejing yu qianzhan: Guoji yimin shuxin yanjiu" guoji xueshu huiyi (Comparison, Exchange, and New Perspectives: International Symposium on International Migrants' Letters).* Jiangmen: n.p.

Guest, Kenneth J. 2003. *God in Chinatown: Religion and Survival in New York's Evolving Immigrant Community.* New York: New York University Press.

Gulshan, S. S., and G. K. Kapoor. 2003. *Business Law, Including Company Law.* New Delhi: New Age International.

Gunderson, Steve. 2006. Interview. *Philanthropy* (May/June). http://www.philanthropyroundtable.org/topic/excellence_in_philanthropy/steve_gunderson.

Guo Boling 郭伯龄. 2009. "Tianyi piguan de lishi fuchen" ("Meanderings through the His-tory of the Tianyi Remittance Firm"). In Chen Xiaogang, ed., 123–31.

———. 2014. "Tianyi qiaopi ju shi daobi haishi guanbi" ("Did the Tianyi Remittance Company go Bankrupt or Close Down"). In Zhongguo lishi wenxian yanjiu hui, eds., 157–60.

Guo Cunxiao 郭存孝. 2013. "Aodaliya de qiaopi dang'an yu wenwu chutan" ("Preliminary Research into Australia's *Qiaopi* Archives and Artifacts"). In Guangzhou "Guangdong Huaqiao shi" et al., eds., 294–306.

Guo Mafeng 郭马风. 2004. "He wei pi?" ("What is a *pi*?"). In Wang Weizhong, ed., 215–8.

Hamashita, Takeshi. 2001. "Overseas Chinese Financial Networks and Korea." In *Commercial Networks in Modern Asia*, edited by S. Sugiyama and Linda Grove, 55–70. Richmond: Curzon.

———. 2008. *China, East Asia and the Global Economy: Regional and Historical Perspectives*. London: Routledge.

———. 2013. *Kakyokajin to choukamou: yimin-koueki-soukin nettwoaku no kouzou to tenka* (*Huaqiao, Ethnic Chinese, and Chinese Networks: Migration, Trade, and the Structure and Development of the Remittance Network*). Tokyo: Iwanami Shoten.

Harper, Marjory. 2005. *Emigrant Homecomings: The Return Movements of Emigrants, 1600–2000*. Manchester: Manchester University Press.

———. 2010. "Opportunity and Exile: Snapshots of Scottish Emigration to Australia." *Australian Studies* 2 (2): 1–21.

Harris, Lane Jeremy. 2012. "The Post Office and State Formation in Modern China, 1896–1949." PhD dissertation, University of Illinois at Urbana-Champaign.

———. 2013. "The 1876 Post Office Riot in Singapore." *The Newsletter* (IIAS) 63.

———. 2015. "Overseas Chinese Remittance Firms: The Limits of State Sovereignty, and Transnational Capitalism in East and Southeast Asia, 1850s–1930s." *Journal of Asian Studies* 74 (1): 129–51.

Harris, Sharon M., and Gaul Theresa Strouth, eds. 2009. *Letters and Cultural Transformations in the United States, 1760–1860*. Farnham: Ashgate.

Hegel, G. W. F. 1991 [1820]. *Elements of the Philosophy of Right*. Translated by H. B. Nisbet. Edited by Allen Wood. Cambridge: Cambridge University Press.

Helbich, Wolfgang. 1997. "Different, but Not Out of This World: German Images of the United States between Two Wars, 1871–1914." In Barclay and Glaser-Schmidt, eds., 109–30.

Helbich, Wolfgang, and Walter D. Kamphoefner. 2006. "How Representative Are Emigrant Letters? An Exploration of the German Case." In Elliott, Gerber, and Sinke, eds., 29–55.

Henkin, David M. 2006. *The Postal Age: The Emergence of Modern Communications in Nineteenth-Century America*. Chicago: University of Chicago Press.

Hicks, George, ed. 1993. *Overseas Chinese Remittances from Southeast Asia, 1910–1940*. Singapore: Select Books.

Hisasue, Ryoichi. n.d. "Chinese Banking Business in Singapore: Background and Development in the First Half of the Twentieth Century." Working paper.

Hong Lin 洪林. 2004. "Shilun heping hou (1945–1955) Taiguo qiaopi shi yanbian" ("On the History of the Evolution of Thailand's *Qiaopi* Trade after the Peace [1945–1955]"). In Wang Weizhong, ed., 22–30.

———. 2006a. "Jianshu Chaoshan lunxian qianhou yu Xianluo qiaopi ye" ("On Chaoshan before and after Its Fall [to Japan] and the Siam *Qiaopi* Trade"). In Hong Lin and Li Daogang, eds., 73–7.

———. 2006b. "Taiguo qiaopi yu yinxin ju chuyi" ("A Modest Proposal Regarding Thailand's *Qiaopi* and Remittance-Letter Offices"). In Hong Lin and Li Daogang, eds., 23–38.

———. 2006c. "Xianluo Huaqiao yinxinju gonghui" ("Siam's Overseas-Chinese Remittance Trade's General Association"). In Hong Lin and Li Daogang, eds., 221–6.

———. 2010. "Cong jiapi kan qiaopi ji qi beijing" ("Looking at *Qiaopi* and Their Background from the Angle of Family Letters"). In Wang Weizhong, ed., 118–27.

Hong Lin 洪林 and Li Daogang 黎道纲, eds. 2006. *Taiguo qiaopi wenhua* (*Thailand's Qiaopi Culture*). Taizhong xuehui congshu.

Honig, Emily. 1992. *Creating Chinese Ethnicity: Subei People in Shanghai, 1850–1980*. New Haven: Yale University Press.

Hooper, Kate, and Jean Batalova. 2015. "Chinese Immigrants in the United States." Migration Policy Institute, January 28.

Hou Weixiong 侯伟雄. 2009. "Gulangyu yu Minnan qiaopi ye yizhi" ("Gulangyu and the Site of the Minnan *Qiaopi* Trade"). In Chen Xiaogang, ed., 136–41.

Hsu, Madeline Y. 2000a. "Migration and Native Place: *Qiaokan* and the Imagined Community of Taishan County, Guangdong, 1893–1993." *Journal of Asian Studies* 59 (2): 307–31.

———. 2000b. *Dreaming of Gold, Dreaming of Home: Transnationalism and Migration between the United States and South China, 1882–1943*. Stanford, CA: Stanford University Press.

Hu, S. and S. Chen. 2013. "The Co-evolution between Remittance Business for Overseas Chinese and Institutions: The Case of Chaoshan Region during 1860–1949." *Frontiers of Business Research in China* 7 (1): 138–64.

Hu, Shao-Dong, and Si-Yan Chen. 2015. "Cultural Beliefs, Agency Relationship, and Network Governance: Study on the Teochew Remittance Network." *Chinese Management Studies* 9 (2): 176–96.

Huang, Annian. 2014. "Emphasis on Overseas Chinese News Research." Huang Annian Science Blog. http://blog.sciencenet.cn/blog-415-788201.html.

Huang, Cen, and Michael R. Godley. 1999. "A Note on the Study of *Qiaoxiang* Ties." In *Qiaoxiang Ties: Interdisciplinary Approaches to "Cultural Capitalism" in South China*, edited by Leo Douw, Cen Huang, and Michael R. Godley, 306–38. London: Kegan Paul.

Huang Jiaxiang 黄家祥. 2008. "Zhaoan qiaopi ye chutan" ("Preliminary Investigations into the Zhaoan *Qiaopi* Trade"). In Wang Weizhong, ed., 337–44.

———. 2010 "Zhaoan qiaopi ye liubian" ("Flow and Change in the Zhaoan *Qiaopi* Trade"). In Wang Weizhong, ed., 502–10.

Huang Qinghai 黄清海. 2009a. "Minnan qiaopi: Qiaoyuan guanxi yu qiaoxiang jingji" ("Minnan *Qiaopi*: Diasporic Relations and the *Qiaoxiang* Economy"). In Chen Xiaogang, ed., 59–66.

———. 2009b. "Cong Quanzhou qiaoxiang jingji fazhan guiji kan Minnan qiaopi baohu de yiyi" ("Looking at the Meaning of the Preservation of *Qiaopi* from the Point of View of the Trajectory of the Development of the Southern Fujianese Economy"). *Haiwai chuanzhen* 2:53–55.

———. 2015. *Kangzhan jiashu* (*Overseas Chinese People's Home Letters during World War II*). Fuzhou: Haixia chuban faxing jituan lujiang chuban she.

———. 2016a. *Feihua Huang Kaiwu qiaopi: Shijie jiyi yichan (1907–1922)* (*Memory of the World Heritage: The Philippines Chinese Huang Kaiwu and His Emigrant Mail [1907–1922]*). Fuzhou: Haixia chuban faxing jituan LuJiang chuban she.

———. 2016b. *Haiyang yimin, maoyi yu jingrong wangluo: Yi qiaopi ye wei zhongxin (Maritime Migration, Trade and Financial Network: A Case Study of* Qiaopi). Beijing: Shehui kexue wenxian chuban she.

Huang Qinghai 黄清海 and Liu Bozi 刘伯孳. 2010. "Qiantan Xinjiapo qiaopi zhongxin" ("On the Singapore *Qiaopi* Center"). In Wang Weizhong, ed., 392–401.

Huang Shaoxiong 黄少雄. 2004. "Chao ji qiaopi lishi tan yuan" ("Exploring the Origins of Chao *Qiaopi* History"). In Wang Weizhong, ed., 107–10.

———. 2010. "Qiaopi: Qiaoxiang renmin de ming genzi" ("*Qiaopi*: The Lifelines of the People in the *Qiaoxiang*"). In Wang Weizhong, ed., 487–91.

Huang Ting 黄挺. 2008. "'Gongan bu' suo jian zaoqi qiaopi ye yunying de yixie wenti" ("Some Questions on the Operations of the *Qiaopi* Trade in the Early Period Encountered in the 'Public Ledgers'"). In Wang Weizhong, ed., 208–17.

Huang Zijian 黄子坚. 2013. "Malaixiya qiaopi: Shehui shi ji qiaohui shi shiliao" ("Malaysian *Qi*: Historical Materials for Social History and Remittance History"). In Zhongguo qiaopi shijie jiyi gongcheng guoji yantao hui zuwei hui, eds., 131–41.

Irishacw. 2015. "Analysing 19th Century Emigration, a Case Study: Dissecting One Irishman's Letter Home." Damian Sheils blog. http://irishamericancivilwar.com/2015/12/20/analysing-19th-century-emigration-a-case-study-dissecting-one-irishmans-letter-home/.

Jao Tsung-i 饶宗颐, ed. 1965. *Chaozhou zhi huibian (Chaozhou Gazetteer Compilation)*. Hong Kong: Longmen shudian.

Jaroszyńska-Kirchmann, Anna D. 2006. "As If at a Public Meeting: Polish American Readers, Writers, and Editors of *Ameryka-Echo*, 1922–1969." In Elliott, Gerber, and Sinke, eds., 200–20.

Jia Junying 贾俊英. 2012. "Qiaopi shi yanjiu: Yi Tianyi ju wei gean de kaocha" ("Research into the History of *Qiaopi*: An Investigation Using the Tianyi Office as a Case Study"). MA thesis, Huaqiao University.

———. 2014. "Jindai Minnan qiaopi ju xinyong de shanbian: Yi Tianyi ju wei gean de kaocha" ("The Evolution of Trust in Modern *Qiaopi* Shops in Southern Fujian: Using Tianyi as a Case Study"). In Zhongguo lishi wenxian yanjiu hui, eds., 138–56.

———. n.d. "Jindai Minnan qiaopi ju xinyong de shanbian: Yi Tianyi ju wei gean de kaocha" ("The Evolution of Trust in Modern Southern Fujian's *Qiaopi* Offices: An Investigation Using the Tianyi Office as a Case-Study"). Working paper.

Jiang Bowei 江柏炜 and Cai Mingsong 蔡明松. 2008. "Jinmen minxinju (piju) jingying moshi zhi tantao" ("Discussion of the Operational Model of the Jinmen Remittance Shop [*Piju*]"). In Wang Weizhong, ed., 264–79.

Jiang Guohua 蒋国华. 2009. "Qiaopi ye wei guojia waihui shouru zuochu zhongyao gongxian" ("The *Qiaopi* Trade's Important Contribution to National Foreign-Currency Income"). In Chen Xiaogang, ed., 56–8.

Jiang Ning 江宁. 2008. "Qiaopi yu kuaguo jinrong de hudong" ("The Interaction between *Qiaopi* and International Finance"). In Wang Weizhong, ed., 95–110.

———. 2010. "Bu tong zhengzhi tongzhi xia de qiaopi ju" ("Remittance Offices under Two Different Political Control Systems"). In Wang Weizhong, ed., 328–36.

Jiao Jianhua 焦建华. 2005. "Zhidu chuangxin yu wenhua chuantong: Shixi jindai pixinju de jingying zhidu" ("System Creation and Cultural Tradition: Analyzing the Management

System of the Modern Remittance Company"). *Zhongguo shehui jingji shi yanjiu* 2:64–70.

———. 2006. "Jin bainian lai Zhongguo qiaopi ye yanjiu zongshu" ("Summary of Research on China's *Qiaopi* over the Last Century and More"). *Huaqiao Huaren lishi yanjiu* 2:49–58.

———. 2007. "Jingzheng yu longduan: Jindai Zhongguo youzheng ye yanjiu" ("Competition and Monopoly: Studies in Modern China's Postal Industry"). *Xueshu yuekan* 39 (1): 142–7.

———. 2010. "Zhongguo jindai de longduan yu 'guizhi'" ("China's Modern Monopoly and 'Regularization'"). In Wang Weizhong, ed., 311–27.

———. 2013. "Qudi yu cunliu: Shilun Nanjing guomin zhengfu qiaopi ye zhengce de chubu queli" ("Banning and Retaining: Investigating the Nanjing Republican Government's Policy toward the *Qiaopi* Trade"). In Zhongguo qiaopi shijie jiyi gongcheng guoji yantao hui zuwei hui, eds., 319–25.

Jiao Jianhua 焦建华 and Xu Cuihong 徐翠红. 2004. "Jindai pixin ju tese tanyuan" ("Origins of the Special Features of Modern Remittance Offices"). In Wang Weizhong, ed., 164–73.

Jin Wenjian 金文坚. 2014. "Rang qiaopi ziliao zai shuzi hua shijie shixian zhenzheng de tuanju" ("Let *Qiaopi* Materials Realize True Unity in a Digitalized World"). In Zhongguo lishi wenxian yanjiu hui, eds., 245–52.

John, Richard R. 1995. *Spreading the News: The American Postal System from Franklin to Morse*. Cambridge: Harvard University Press.

Johnson, Paula Doherty. 2007. *Diaspora Philanthropy: Influences, Initiatives, and Issues*. Boston and Cambridge: The Philanthropic Initiative, Inc. and the Global Equity Initiative, Harvard University.

Jones, Bill. 2005. "Writing Back: Welsh Emigrants and their Correspondence in the Nineteenth Century." *North American Journal of Welsh Studies* 5 (1): 23–46.

Jones, William D. 2006. "'Going into Print': Published Immigrant Letters, Webs of Personal Relations, and Emergence of the Welsh Public Sphere." In Elliott, Gerber, and Sinke, eds., 175–99.

Jost, Patrick M., and Harjit Singh Sandhu. n.d. *The Hawala Alternative Remittance System and Its Role in Money Laundering*. Prepared by the Financial Crimes Enforcement Network in cooperation with Interpol/FOPAC.

Kamphoefner, Walter D. 2007. "The Uses of Immigrant Letters." *Bulletin of the German Historical Institute* 41:137–40.

Kamphoefner, Walter D., and Wolfgang Johannes Helbich, eds.. 2006. *Germans in the Civil War: The Letters They Wrote Home*. Chapel Hill: University of North Carolina Press.

Kaiping huaqiao yuekan she 开平华侨杂志社. 1940. Kaiping Huaqiao yuekan (*Kaiping Overseas Chinese Monthly*). http://mylib.nlc.cn/web/guest/minguoqikan.

Kang Yefeng 康业丰. 2014. "Ying kua diqu, kua guodu yanjiu qiaopi wenhua" ("Studying *Qiaopi* Culture from the Point of View of Transregionalism and Transnationalism"). In Zhongguo lishi wenxian yanjiu hui, eds., 261–6.

Kapur, Devesh, Ajay S. Mehta, and R. Moon Dutt. 2004. "Indian Diapora Philanthropy." In Geithner, Johnson, and Chen, eds., 177–213.

Ke Mulin (Kua Bak Lim) 柯木林. 1991. "Chengyi Maxi xiang Lin shi zupu de faxian ji qi shiliao jiazhi" ("The Discovery of the Lin Lineage Genealogy of Chengyi's Maxi Village and its Historical Value"). *Nanyang wenti yanjiu* 1:70–6.

———. 2008. "Xinjiapo minxinye lingxiu Lin Shuyan" ("The Singapore Remittance Trade Leader Lin Shuyan"). In Wang Weizhong, ed., 470–7.

———. 2013. "'Yun zhong shui ji jin shu lai' Qiaopi cong jiashu dao wenhua yichan" ("'Who in the Clouds Will Send a Letter?' Qiaopi from Family Letter to Cultural Heritage"). *Minshang wenhua yanjiu* 7 (1): 56–9.

Kirby, William. 1984. *Germany and Republican China*. Stanford, CA: Stanford University Press.

Kollewe, Julia. 2010. "Stanley Gibbons To Put Stamp on China." *The Guardian*, March 26.

Kosak, Hadassa. 2000. *Cultures of Opposition: Jewish Immigrant Workers, New York City, 1881–1905*. Albany: State University of New York Press.

Kraus, Richard Curt. 1991. *Brushes with Power: Modern Politics and the Chinese Art of Calligraphy*. Berkeley: University of California Press.

Kuhn, Philip A. 2008. *Chinese among Others: Migration in Modern Times*. Lanham: Roman and Littlefield.

Lai Chi Kong 黎志刚 and Tzu-Hsien (Chris) Yuan 袁子贤. 2013. "Difang wenxian yu Huaqiao shi yanjiu: Cong difang shiliao kan Wuyi diqu de 'qiaoxiang wenhua'" ("Historical Documents and Wuyi *Qiaoxiang* Culture"). *Chinese Southern Diaspora Studies* 6:155–64.

Lake, Marilyn, and Ann Curthoys. 2013. *Connected Worlds: History in Transnational Perspective*. Canbera: ANU Press.

Lary, Diana. 2010. *The Chinese People at War: Human Suffering and Social Transformation, 1937–1945*. Cambridge: Cambridge University Press.

Lee, Catherine. 2013. *Fictive Kin: Family Reunification and the Meaning of Race and Nation in American Immigration*. New York: Russell Sage Foundation.

Lee, Shelley Sang-Hee. 2014. *A New History of Asian America*. Abingdon: Routledge.

Lemiski, Karen. 2006. "The Ukrainian Government-in-Exile's Postal Network and the Construction of National Identity." In Elliott, Gerber, and Sinke, eds., 248–68.

Lévi-Strauss, Claude. 1963. *Structural Anthropology*. New York: Basic Books.

Li Boda 李柏达. 2013. "Guba Huaqiao shuxin yu qiaohui" ("Cuba's Overseas-Chinese Letters and Remittances"). In Guangzhou "Guangdong Huaqiao shi" et al., eds., 227–38.

Li Daogang 黎道纲. 2006a. "Shantou lunxian zhi Ri jun ru Xian shiqi Manggu qiaopi jie de jingying zhuangkuang" ("The Management of the *Qiaopi* World in Bangkok between the Fall of Shantou and the Japanese Invasion of Siam"). In Hong Lin and Li Daogang, eds., 105–22.

———. 2006b. "Taiguo qiaopi yanjiu de ruogan wenti" ("Some Questions Regarding the Study of Thailand's *Qiaopi*"). In Hong Lin and Li Daogang, eds., 57–60.

———. 2008. "Taiguo quanqiao xing yinxinju zuzhi de chengli" ("The Establishment of the All-Thai Overseas-Chinese Remittance Office"). In Wang Weizhong, ed., 172–84.

———. 2010. "Wushi niandai chu Taiguo qiaopi pin xian kunjing yuanyou" ("The Reason Thailand's *Qiaopi* Frequently Fell into Difficulties in the Early 1950s"). In Wang Weizhong, ed., 128–33.

Li, Minghuan. 2010. *'We Need Two Worlds': Chinese Immigrant Associations in a Western Society*. Amsterdam: Amsterdam University Press.

Li, Peter S. 1988. *The Chinese in Canada*. Toronto: Oxford University Press.

Li, Peter and Eva Li. 2013. "The Chinese Overseas Population." In Tan Chee-Beng, ed., 15–28.

Li Wenhai 李文海, ed. 2009. *Minguo shiqi shehui diaocha congbian, er bian, Huaqiao juan* (*Collection of Social Investigations from the Republican Period, Overseas Chinese Volume*), Fuzhou: Fujian jiaoyu chuban she.

Li Xiaoyan 李小燕. 2004. "Kejia diqu de shuike yu qiaopi ju" ("*Shuike* and *Qiaopi* Offices in Hakka Regions"). In Wang Weizhong, ed., 51–6.

———. 2008. "Qiaopi yu Chao Mei qiaoxiang diqu renmin shenghuo fangshi de bianqian" ("*Qiaopi* and Changes in Life-style of the People in the Chao and Mei Areas"). In Wang Weizhong, ed., 287–95.

Li Zhixian (Lee Chee Hiang) 李志贤, ed. 2003. *Haiwai Chao ren de yimin jingyan* (*The Emigration Experience of Chao Overseas*). Singapore: Xinjiapo Chaozhou bayi huiguan.

———. 2013. "Gongtong jiyi, kuayu wangluo: Ershi shiji Xinjiapo Chao ren qiaopi ju de tese" ("Shared Memories, Supra-regional Networks: Special Characteristics of Singapore Chao People's *Qiaopi* Offices"). In Zhongguo qiaopi shijie jiyi gongcheng guoji yantao hui zuwei hui, eds., 247–61.

———. 2014. "Shijiu zhi ershi shiji qijian Xinjiapo ge bang minxin ju de yingyun yu tongye zuzhi" ("The Operation and Professional Organization of the Remittance Houses of the Various *Bang* in Singapore from the Nineteenth to the Twentieth Century"). In Zhongguo lishi wenxian yanjiu hui, eds., 1–15.

Liao Yun 廖耘 and Wu Erchi 吴二持. 2010. "Qiaopi yu Zhongguo chuantong de daode guannian" ("*Qiaopi* and China's Traditional Values"). In Wang Weizhong, ed., 259–70.

Lin Jiajing 林家劲, et al. 1999. *Jindai Guangdong qiaohui yanjiu* (*A Study of Qiaohui in Guangdong in Modern Times*). Guangzhou: Zhongshan daxue chuban she.

Lin Jinzhi 林金枝. 1983. *Jindai Huaqiao touzhi guonei qiyueshi yanjiu* (*A Study of Overseas Chinese Investment in China's Domestic Enterprises*). Fuzhou: Fujian renmin chuban she.

Lin Jinzhi 林金枝 and Zhuang Weiji 庄为矶. 1985. *Jindai huaqiao touzhi guonei qiyueshi ziliao: Fujian juan* (*A Collection of Materials on Overseas Chinese Investment in China's Domestic Enterprises: Fujian*). Fuzhou: Fujian renmin chuban she.

———. 1989. *Jindai huaqiao touzhi guonei qiyueshi ziliao: Guangdong juan* (*A Collection of Materials on Overseas Chinese Investment in China's Domestic Enterprises: Guangdong*). Fuzhou: Fujian renmin chuban she.

Lin Nanzhong 林南中. 2010. "Minnan 'fanpi' yu 'fanyin'" ("'Foreign *Pi*' and 'Foreign Silver' in Southern Fujian"). In Wang Weizhong, ed., 492–501.

———. 2014. "'Fanpi' 'fanyin'" ("'Foreign *Pi*' and 'Foreign Silver'"). In Zhongguo lishi wenxian yanjiu hui, eds., 216–22.

Lin Qingxi 林庆熙. 2010. "Chaoshan qiaopi zai renshi" ("Once Again Recognizing Chaoshan *Qiaopi*"). In Wang Weizhong, ed., 207–17.

Lin Sha 林沙. 2008. "Xiamen qiaopi ye de chansheng he fazhan" ("The Origins and Development of the Xiamen *Qiaopi* Trade"). In Wang Weizhong, ed., 354–7.

Lin Tengyun 林腾云. 2008. "Cong qiaopi he piju shouju tan Meizhou Huaqiao yu Shantou bang de guanxi" ("Talking about the Relationship between the Meizhou Overseas Chinese and Shantou on the Basis of *Qiaopi* and *Piju* Receipts"). In Wang Weizhong, ed., 411–6.

Liu Bozi 刘伯孳. 2009. "Ershi shiji shangban ye Feilübin Huaqiao yu qiaopi ye de fazhan" ("The Development of the *Qiaopi* Trade in the First Half of the Twentieth Century in the Philippines"). In Chen Xiaogang, ed., 75–86.

———. 2010. "Ershi shiji shangban ye Feilübin Huaqiao yu qiaopi ye de fazhan" ("The Development of the *Qiaopi* Trade in the First Half of the Twentieth Century in the Philippines"). In Wang Weizhong, ed., 278–91.

———. 2014. "Huaqiao yinhang de qiaopi yewu jingying" ("The Overseas Chinese Banks' Management of the *Qiaopi* Business"). In Zhongguo lishi wenxian yanjiu hui, eds., 228–36.

Liu, Haiming. 2002. "The Social Origins of Early Chinese Immigrants: A Revisionist Perspective." In Cassel, ed., 21–36.

———. 2005. *Transnational History of a Chinese Family: Immigrant Letters, Family Business, and Reverse Migration.* Piscataway, NJ: Rutgers University Press.

Liu, Hong. 1999. "Organized Chinese Transnationalism and the Institutionalization of Business Networks: Singapore Chinese Chamber of Commerce and Industry as a Case Analysis." *Tonan Ajia Kenkyu (Southeast Asian Studies)* 37(3): 391–416.

———. 2006. "Introduction: Toward a Multi-dimensional Exploration of the Chinese Overseas." In Vol. 1 of *The Chinese Overseas*, edited by Hong Liu, 1–30. London: Routledge.

———. 2011. "An Emerging China and Diasporic Chinese: Historicity, the State, and International Relations." *Journal of Contemporary China* 20 (71): 856–76.

———. 2012. "Beyond a Revisionist Turn: Networks, State, and the Changing Dynamics of Diasporic Chinese Entrepreneurship." *China: An International Journal* 10 (3): 20–41.

Liu, Hong, and Els van Dongen. 2013. "The Chinese Overseas." *Oxford Bibliographies.* DOI: 10.1093/OBO/9780199920082-0070. http://www.oxfordbibliographies.com/view/docu ment/obo-9780199920082/obo-9780199920082-0070.xml?rskey=yaZ8EQ&result=1&q =Chinese+diaspora#firstMatch.

Liu, Hong, and Gregor Benton. 2016. "The *Qiaopi* Trade and Its Role in Modern China and the Chinese Diaspora: Toward an Alternative Explanation of 'Transnational Capitalism.'" *Journal of Asian Studies* 75 (3): 575–94.

Liu, Hong, and S. K. Wong. 2004. *Singapore Chinese Society in Transition: Business, Politics and Socio-economic Change, 1945–1965.* New York: Peter Lang Publishing.

Liu Jin 刘进. 2007. "Minguo shiqi Wuyi qiaokan zhong de yinxin guanggao" ("Remittance Advertisements in Wuyi *Qiaokan* in the Republican Period"). *Wuyi daxue xuebao* 9 (1): 33–7.

———. 2008. "Xunchengma chutan" ("Preliminary Exploration of *Xunchengma*"). In Wang Weizhong, ed., 69–83.

———. 2009. *Wuyi yinxin (Wuyi Silver and Letters).* Guangzhou: Guangdong renmin chuban she.

———. 2010. "Zai qing yu li zhi jian" ("Between Affection and Interest"). In Wang Weizhong, ed., 300–10.

———. 2013a. "Jiazu shuxin yu Huanan qiaoxiang de guoji yimin" ("Family Letters and South China's International Migration"). In Zhongguo qiaopi shijie jiyi gongcheng guoji yantao hui zuwei hui, eds., 143–50.

———. 2013b. "Minguo shiqi beiMei Huaqiao yu Huanan xiangcun shehui zhuanxing" ("Overseas Chinese in North America and Social Transformation in the South China Villages"). In Guangzhou "Guangdong Huaqiao shi" et al., eds., 319–37.

———. 2015. "Rao Zhongyi xiansheng dui hongyan qiaopi jiazhi de gongxian" ("The Contribution of Jao Tsung-i to Promoting and Developing the Value of *Qiaopi*"). *Bagui Qiaokan* 4:11–6.

Liu Youyuan 刘猷远. 2008. "Qianxi qiaopi yu jinrong" ("Some Observations of *Qiaopi* and Finance"). In Wang Weizhong, ed., 52–6.

Lu Xiaoxia 路晓霞. 2014. "Chaoshan qiaopi shangye xinyu ji qi dangdai qishi" ("The Chaoshan *Qiaopi* Trade's Reputation and Its Contemporary Inspiration"). In Zhongguo lishi wenxian yanjiu hui, eds, 267–72.

Lu Yongguang 卢永光. 2006. "Wo kao qiaopi zhangda" ("I Grew Up on *Qiaopi*"). In Hong Lin and Li Daogang, eds., 155–7.

Luo Daquan 罗达全, Zhang Xiuming 张秀明, and Liu Jin 刘进. 2016. Vols. 1 and 2 of *Qiaoxiang wenshu kangzhan shiliao xuanbian (Wuyi qiaoxiang juan)* (*Selected World War II Materials in Overseas Chinese's Hometowns in Wuyi*). Guangzhou: Guangdong renmin chuban she.

Luo Dunjin 罗敦锦. 2008. "Cong qiaopi kan kejia ren dui zinü houdai jiaoyu de zhongshi chengdu" ("Considering the Extent of Attention Paid by Hakkas to the Education of the Next Generation of Girls on the Basis of *Qiaopi*"). In Wang Weizhong, ed., 425–8.

Luo Peiheng 罗培衡 and Zhan Guoshuang 詹国双. 2008 "Fengshun qiaopi ye shulüe" ("Brief Description of the Fengshun *Qiaopi* Trade"). In Wang Weizhong, ed., 345–53.

Luo Zeyang 罗则扬. 2004. "Qiaopi wenhua yu haiyang wenhua" ("*Qiaopi* Culture and Oceanic Culture"). In Wang Weizhong, ed., 208–14.

———. 2008. "Lüelun qiaopi geyin" ("On *Qiaopi* Songs"). In Wang Weizhong, ed., 429–37.

———. 2010. "Dixia dang can yu qiaopi (hui) shiye de lishi yuanyou" ("The Reasons in History Why the Underground Communist Party Joined in the *Qiaopi* [and Remittance] Trade"). In Wang Weizhong, ed., 518–22.

Lyons, Martyn. 2007. "'Ordinary Writings' or How the 'Illiterate' Speak to Historians." In *Ordinary Writings, Personal Narratives: Writing Practices in 19th and early 20th-Century Europe*, edited by Martyn Lyons, 13–32. Berne: Peter Lang.

———. 2012. *The Writing Culture of Ordinary People in Europe, c. 1860–1920*. Cambridge: Cambridge University Press.

Ma Chujian 马楚坚. 2003. "Chao bang pixin ju zhi chuangsheng ji qi gongneng de tansuo" ("Research into the Creation of the Chao Gang Remittance Office and Its Functions"). In Li Zhixian, ed., 55–84.

———. 2008. "Chao bang pixin ju yu qiaohui liutong zhi fazhan chutan" ("Preliminary Investigation of the Chao *Bang* Remittance Offices and the Development of the Circulation of Overseas Remittances"). In Wang Weizhong, ed., 19–40.

———. 2010. "Wenwu yu qiaopi wenhua xueshu yanjiu zhi fazhan wei 'qiaopi xue' yi" ("The Development of the Study of Artifacts and *Qiaopi* Culture for the Purposes of 'Qiaopi* Studies'"). In Wang Weizhong, ed., 21–32.

Ma Mingda 马明达 and Huang Zechun 黄泽纯. 2004. "Chaoshan qiaopi ju de jingying wangluo" ("The Economic Network of the Chaoshan Remittance Offices"). *Ji'nan daxue bao (renwen kexue yu shehui kexue ban)* 1:123–7.

Ma Zhenhui 马祯辉. 2008. "Qiantan qiaopi yu jinrong de guanxi" ("Observations on the Relationship between *Qiaopi* and Finance"). In Wang Weizhong, ed., 90–4.

Maclachen, Patricia L. 2011. *The People's Post Office: The History and Politics of the Japanese Postal System, 1871–2010*. Cambridge: Harvard University Asia Center.

Mai Guopei 麦国培. 2004. "Siyi qiaopi yu Chaoshan qiaopi zhi bijiao" ("A Comparison of Siyi *Qiaopi* and Chaoshan *Qiaopi*"). In Wang Weizhong, ed., 241–4.

Markelis, Daiva. 2006. "'Every Person Likes a Letter': The Importance of Correspondence in Lithuanian Immigrant Life." In Elliott, Gerber, and Sinke, eds., 107–23.

Marchetti, G. 2006. *From Tian'anmen to Times Square: Transnational China and the Chinese Diaspora on Global Screens, 1989–1997*. Philadelphia: Temple University Press.

Martin, Marina. 2009. "*Hundi/Hawala*: The Problem of Definition." *Modern Asian Studies* 43 (4): 909–37.

Masdeu Torruella, Irene. 2014. "Mobilities and Embodied Transnational Practices: An Ethnography of Return(s) and Other Intersections Between China and Spain." PhD dissertation, Universitat Autònoma de Barcelona.

McDermott, Joseph P. 2013. *The Making of a New Rural Order in South China*. Vol. 1 of *Village, Land, and Lineage in Huizhou, 900–1600*. Cambridge: Cambridge University Press.

McDougall, Bonnie. 2015. "Infinite Variations of Writing and Desire: Love Letters in China and Europe." In Richter, ed., 546–81.

McKeown, Adam. 1999. "Conceptualizing Chinese Diasporas, 1842 to 1949." *Journal of Asian Studies* 58 (2): 306–37.

———. 2002. *Chinese Migrant Networks and Cultural Change: Peru, Chicago, and Hawaii 1900–1936*. Chicago: University of Chicago Press.

———. 2010. "Chinese Emigration in Global Context, 1850–1940." *Journal of Global History* 5 (1): 95–124.

McNair, Amy. 2015. "Letters as Calligraphy Exemplars: The Long and Eventful Life of Yan Zhengqing's (709–785) Imperial Commissioner Liu Letter." In Richter, ed., 53–96.

Mei Weiqiang 梅伟强 and Guan Zefeng 关泽峰. 2010. *Guangdong Taishan Huaqiao shi* (*Overseas Chinese History in Taishan, Guangdong*). Beijing: Zhongguo Huaqiao chuban she.

Mei Weiqiang 梅伟强 and Mei Xue 梅雪. 2007. "*Jiti jiashu*" *lian Wuzhou-Wuyi qiaokan xiangxun yanjiu (1978–2005)* ("*Collective Family Letters*" *Connecting the World: A Study of Wuyi* Qiaokan *and Village Newsletters [1978–2005]*). Hong Kong: Xianggang shehui kexue chuban she.

Menkhoff, Thomas, and Hoon Chang-yau. 2010. "Chinese Philanthropy in Asia between Continuity and Change." *Journal of Asian Business* 24 (1–2): 1–12.

Meskill, Johanna M. 1970. "The Chinese Genealogy as a Research Source." In *Family and Kinship in Chinese Society*, edited by Ai-li S. Chin and Maurice Freedman, 139–64. Stanford, CA: Stanford University Press.

Middleton, Sue. 2010. "The Seven Servants of Ham: Labourers' Letters from Wellington in the *New Zealand Journal*, 1840–45." *New Zealand Journal of History* 44 (1): 54–75.

Miller, Kerby A., Arnold Schrier, Bruce D. Boling, and David N. Doyle, eds. 2003. *Irish Immigrants in the Land of Canaan: Letters and Memoirs from Colonial and Revolutionary America, 1675–1815*. New York: Oxford University Press.

Milne, Esther. 2012. *Letters, Postcards, Email: Technologies of Presence*. Abingdon: Routledge.

Mo Zhen 莫震, ed. 2013. *Haibang chengfu: Guangdong qiaopi dang'an* (*Fragrance from Abroad: Guangdong's Qiaopi Archive*). Guangzhou: Lingnan meishu chuban she.

Morse, H. B. 1904. *An Inquiry into the Commercial Liabilities and Assets of China in International Trade*. Shanghai: Chinese Maritime Customs.

Moreton, Emma. 2013. "Profiling the Female Immigrant: A Method of Linguistic Enquiry for Examining Correspondence Collections." In Gabaccia and Maynes, eds., 97–126.

Nadel, George. 1953. "Letters from German Immigrants in New South Wales." *Royal Australian Historical Society Journal* 39 (5): 257–8.

Newland, Kathleen, Aaron Terrazas, and Roberto Munster. 2010. *Diaspora Philanthropy: Private Giving and Public Policy*. Washington, DC: Migration Policy Institute.

Ng, Wing Chung. 1999. *The Chinese in Vancouver, 1845–80: The Pursuit of Identity and Power*. Vancouver: University of British Columbia Press.

Ong, Aihwa and Donald Nonini, eds. 2003. *Ungrounded Empires: The Cultural Politics of Modern Chinese Transnationalism*. London: Routledge.

Olson, James Stuart. 1998. *An Ethnohistorical Dictionary of China*. Westport, CT: Greenwood Press.

Oyen, Meredith Leigh. 2007. "Allies, Enemies and Aliens: Migration and U.S.-Chinese Relations, 1940–1965." 2 vols. PhD dissertation, Georgetown University.

Pan Meizhu 潘美珠 (Joanne Poon). n.d. "Huagong shuxin" ("Chinese Laborers' Letters"). Unpublished manuscript.

Pan, Yuling, and Daniel Z. Kádár. 2011. *Politeness in Historical and Contemporary Chinese*. London: Continuum.

Pei Yan 裴艳. 2013. "Qiaopi beijing xia de Zhongshan yimin yu jinrong wangluo" ("Zhongshan Migrants and Financial Networks against the Background of *Qiaopi*"). *Bagui qiaokan* 3:45–50.

Perkins, Dwight, ed. 1975. *China's Modern Economy in Historical Perspective*. Stanford, CA: Stanford University Press.

Peterson, Glen. 2005. "Overseas Chinese and Merchant Philanthropy in China: From Culturalism to Nationalism." *Journal of Chinese Overseas* 1 (1): 87–109.

———. 2012. *Overseas Chinese in the People's Republic of China*. Abingdon: Routledge.

Pietropaolo, Vincenzo. 2002. *Not Paved with Gold: A Selection of Photographs: Toronto's Italian-Canadian Community in the 1970s*. Endwell, NY: American Italian Museum.

Pooley, Colin G., and Ian D. White, eds. 1991. *Migrants, Emigrants and Immigrants: A Social History of Migration*. London: Routledge.

Porter, Robin. 1993. *Industrial Reformers in Republican China*. Armonk, NY: M. E. Sharpe.

Portes, Alejandro, Luis E. Guarnizo, and Patricia Landolt. 1999. "The Study of Transnationalism: Pitfalls and Promise of an Emergent Research Field." *Ethnic and Racial Studies* 22:217–37.

Rana, Pradumna B., and Wai-Mun Chia. 2014. "The Revival of the Silk Roads (Land Connectivity) in Asia." Singapore: RSIS Working Paper No. 274.

Rao Min 饶敏. 2010. "Chaoshan qiaopi yanjiu, xunzhao ta xiang de jiyi" ("Research into Chaoshan *Qiaopi*, Memories of Seeking other Shores"). In Wang Weizhong, ed., 481–6.

Remer, Carl F. 1926. *The Foreign Trade of China*. Shanghai: The Commercial Press.

———. 1933. *Foreign Investments in China*. New York: Macmillan.

Ren Guixiang 任贵祥. 1989. *Huaqiao di er ci aiguo gaochao (The Second High Tide of Patriotism among Overseas Chinese)*. Beijing: Zhonggong dangshi ziliao chuban she.

Reynolds, Kathrine M. 2009. *The Frauenstein Letters: Aspects of Nineteenth Century Emigration from the Duchy of Nassau to Australia*. Berne: Peter Lang.

Richards, Eric. 1991. "Voices of British and Irish Migrants in Nineteenth-Century Australia." In Pooley and White, eds., 19–41.

———. 2005. "Running Home from Australia: Intercontinental Mobility and Migrant Expectations." In Harper, ed., 77–104.

———. 2006a. "Australian Colonial Mentalities in Emigrant Letters." Paper presented at the biennial conference of the British Australian Studies Association, University of Exeter, September 7.

———. 2006b. "The Limits of the Australian Emigrant Letter." In Elliott, Gerber, and Suzanne Sinke, eds., 56–74.

———. 2013. "Australian Colonial Mentalities in Emigrant Letters." In Guangzhou "Guangdong Huaqiao shi" et al., eds., 72–93.

Richter, Antje. 2013. *Letters and Epistolary Culture in Early Medieval China*. Seattle: University of Washington Press.

———. 2015a. "Between Letter and Testament: Letters of Familial Admonition in Han and Six Dynasties China." In Richter, ed., 239–75.

———. 2015b. "Introduction: The Study of Chinese Letters and Epistolary Culture." In Richter, ed., 1–14.

———, ed. 2015. *A History of Chinese Letters and Epistolary Culture*. Leiden: Brill.

Romani, Gabriella. 2013. *Postal Culture: Reading and Writing Letters in Post-unification Italy*. Toronto: University of Toronto Press.

Rong Xinjiang. 2013. *Eighteen Lectures on Dunhuang*. Leiden: Brill.

Santasombat, Yos, ed. 2015. *Impact of China's Rise on the Mekong Region*. New York: Palgrave Macmillan.

Schrier, Arnold. 1958. *Ireland and the American Immigration, 1850–1900*. Minneapolis: University of Minnesota Press.

See, C. S. 1919. *The Foreign Trade of China*. New York: Longmans, Green, and Co.

Serra, Ilaria. 2009. *The Imagined Immigrant: Images of Italian Emigration to the United States Between 1890 and 1924*. Madison, NJ: Fairleigh Dickinson University Press.

Shantou shi renmin zhengfu qiaowu bangong shi, eds. 2004 [1990]. *Shantou Huaqiao zhi (chugao)* 汕头华侨志 (初稿) ("Shantou Overseas Chinese Gazetteer [first draft]"). In Yang Qunxi, ed., 131–7.

Shantou University website. http://www.wxy.stu.edu.cn/Eng/Intro/index.aspx?fkID=6.

Shen Dunwu 沈敦武. 2014. "Qiantan kangRi zhanzheng shiqi jing youzheng zhuanyun de qiaopi" ("A Short Discussion of the Conveying of *Qiaopi* by the Postal Service during the Anti-Japanese War"). In Zhongguo lishi wenxian yanjiu hui, eds., 237–41.

Shen Huifen. 2012. *China's Left-Behind Wives: Families of Migrants from Fujian to Southeast Asia, 1930s–1950s*. Singapore: National University of Singapore Press.

Shen Jianhua 沈建华. 2014 "Tansuo Liaoguo pixin ju de jingying fangshi" ("Investigating the Management Methods of Laos' Remittance Office"). In Zhongguo lishi wenxian yanjiu hui, eds., 162–7.

Shi Jianping 石坚平. 2013. "Siyi yinxin zhong de xiangzu niudai yu haiwai yimin wangluo" ("The tie of Consanguinity in Siyi's Remittance Letters and Overseas Emigrants' Networks"). In Guangzhou "Guangdong Huaqiao shi" et al., eds., 307–18.

Shiroyama, Tomoko. 2008. *China During the Great Depression: Market, State, and the World Economy, 1929–1937*. Cambridge: Harvard University Asia Center.

———. Forthcoming. "Structures and Dynamics of Overseas Chinese Remittances in the Mid Twentieth Century." In *Chinese and Indian Merchants in Modern Asia Networking Businesses and Formation of Regional Economy*, edited by Chi-Cheung Choi, Takashi Oishi, and Tomoko Shiroyama. Leiden and Boston: Brill.

Sidel, Mark. 2004. "Diaspora Philanthropy to India: A Perspective from the United States." In Geithner, Johnson, and Chen, eds., 215–57.

Singapore Chaozhou Bayi Association (Singapore Teochew Poit Ip Huay Kuan). 1922–1939. Minutes of Executive Meetings. Singapore: Singapore Teochew Poit Ip Huay Kuan.

Sinn, Elizabeth. 2013. *Pacific Crossing: California Gold, Chinese Migration, and the Making of Hong Kong*. Hong Kong: Hong Kong University Press.

Siu, Paul C. P. 1987. *The Chinese Laundryman: A Study in Social Isolation*. Edited by John Kuo Wei Tchen. New York: New York University Press.

Smith, J. F. H. 1987. "Benevolent Societies: The Reshaping of Charity during the Late Ming and Early Ch'ing." *Journal of Asian Studies* 46 (2): 309–37.

Stanley, Liz. 2004. "The Epistolarium: On Theorizing Letters and Correspondences." *Auto/Biography* 12:201–35.

Stellingwerff, Jan. 1975. *Amsterdamse Emigranten: Onbekende brieven uit de prairie van Iowa 1846–1873*. Amsterdam: Buijten en Schipperheijn.

Stott, Richard Briggs. 1990. *Workers in the Metropolis: Class, Ethnicity, and Youth in Antebellum New York City*. Ithaca: Cornell University Press.

Su Wenjing 苏文菁, ed. 2013. *Minshang fazhan shi zong lun juan (jindai bufen)* (*Collection on the Development of Fujian Merchants [Modern Section]*). Xiamen: Xiamen daxue chuban she.

Su Wenjing 苏文菁 and Huang Qinghai 黄清海. 2013a. "Minshang yu qiaopi ye" ("Fujian Merchants and the *Qiaopi* Trade"). *Minshang wenhua yanjiu* 7 (1): 18–32.

———. 2013b. "Quanqiu hua shiye xia de qiaopi ye: Jian lun qiaopi wenhua de haiyang wenming shuxing" ("On the *Qiaopi* Trade in the Perspective of Globalization: Also on the Oceanic Civilizational Quality of *Qiaopi* Culture"). *Minshang wenhua yanjiu* 7 (1): 33–47. Summers, T. 2016. "China's 'New Silk Roads': Sub-national Regions and Networks of Global Political Economy." *Third World Quarterly* 37 (9): 1628–43.

Sung, B. L. 1967. *The Story of the Chinese in America*. New York: Collier Books.

Tan Chee Beng, ed. 2007. *Chinese Transnational Networks*. London: Routledge.

———. 2012. "*Shantang*: Charitable Temples in China, Singapore, and Malaysia." *Asian Ethnology* 71 (1): 75–107.

———, ed. 2013. *Routledge Handbook of the Chinese Diaspora*. London: Routledge.

Tang Cunfang 唐存放. 2008. "Modai qiaopi, zouru lishi" ("*Qiaopi* in the Final Stages, Entering History"). In Wang Weizhong, ed., 323–30.

Tavuchis, Nicholas. 1963. *Pastors and Immigrants: The Role of a Religious Elite in the Absorption of Norwegian Immigrants*. The Hague: Martinus Nijhoff.

Te Ara—The Encyclopedia of New Zealand. "Letters from Happy English Immigrants." http://www.teara.govt.nz/en/document/2060/letters-from-happy-english-immigrants.

Thomas, William I., and Znaniecki Florian. 1958. *The Polish Peasant in Europe and America*. 2nd ed. 2 vols. New York: Dover.

Thunø, Mette, ed., 2007. *Beyond Chinatown: New Chinese Migration and the Global Expansion of China*. Copenhagen: Nordic Institute of Asian Studies.

Tianmen ren lüju haiwai shi bianzuan weiyuan hui 天门人旅居海外史 编纂委员会, eds. 2001. *Tianmen ren lüju haiwai shi* (*A History of Tianmenese Residing Overseas*). Tianmen: Hubei sheng xinHua yinwu youxian gongsi.

Trasciatti, Mary Anne. 2009. "Letter Writing in an Italian Immigrant Community: A Transatlantic Tradition." *Rhetoric Society Quarterly* 39 (1): 73–94.

Truzzi, Oswaldo, and Matos Maria Izilda. 2015. "Saudades: Sensibilities in Letters from Portuguese E/immigrants (Portugal-Brazil 1890–1930)." *Revista Brasileira de História* 35(70).

Tsai, Kellee Sing. 2010. "Friends, Family or Foreigners? The Political Economy of Diasporic FDI and Remittances in China and India." *China Report* 46 (4): 387–429.

Tsui, Lik Hang. 2015. "Bureaucratic Influences on Letters in Middle Period China: Observations from Manuscript Letter and Literati Discourse." In Richter, ed., 363–97.

University of Waterloo. 2002. "Letters Collected by the Canada Company to Encourage Emigration, 1842." https://personal.uwaterloo.ca/marj/genealogy/letters/1842letters.html.

Ureland, P. Sture, and Iain Clarkson, eds. 1993. *Language Contact across the North Atlantic*. Tübingen: Max Niemeyer Verlag.

Vargas, Miguel Angel. 2006. "Epistolary Communication between Migrant Workers and Their Families." In Elliott, Gerber, and Sinke, eds., 124–38.

Vertovec, Steven. 2004. "Migrant Transnationalism and Modes of Transformation." *International Migration Review* 38:970–1001.

Wagel, S. R. 1914. "Finance in China." *North China Daily News and Herald* (Shanghai).

Walden, Sue. 1995. "The Tin Fields of Northeast Tasmania: A Regional Variation?" In *Histories of the Chinese in Australasia and the South Pacific*, edited by Paul Macgregor, 177–90. Melbourne: Museum of Chinese Australian History.

Wan Dongqing 万冬青. 2009. "Qingmo Quanzhou pixinju ji qiaopi" ("Remittance Offices and *Qiaopi* in Quanzhou in the Late Qing"). In Chen Xiaogang, ed., 88–94.

——. 2010. "Touguo Minyue bianqu qiaopi kan qiaoxiang chuantong wenhua" ("Looking at the Traditional Culture of the *Qiaoxiang* from the Angle of the Fujian-Guangdong *Qiaopi*"). In Wang Weizhong, ed., 292–310.

Wang, Di. 2008. *The Teahouse: Small Business, Everyday Culture, and Public Politics in Chengdu, 1900–1950*, Stanford, CA: Stanford University Press.

Wang Dongxu 王东旭. 2009. "Fujian qiaopi si da diyu xi chutan" ("Preliminary Investigation into the System of Four Big Areas of *Qiaopi* in Fujian"). In Chen Xiaogang, ed., 103–7.

Wang Fubing 王付兵. 2013. "Qiaopi dang'an wenxian de jiazhi" ("The Documentary Value of the *Qiaopi* Archives"). *Dongnan Ya zongheng* 7:58–62.

Wang, Gungwu. 2000. *The Chinese Overseas: From Earth-Bound China to the Quest for Autonomy*. Cambridge: Harvard University Press.

Wang Hanwu 王汉武. 2010. "Qiaopi wenhua shengtai yishi chutan" ("Explorations in the Ecological Consciousness of *Qiaopi* Culture"). In Wang Weizhong, ed., 236–48.

Wang Linqian 王琳乾. 2008. "Qiantan jiefang hou Chaoshan de huobi liutong yu qiaopi ye huodong he qiaohui wuzi gongying" ("On the Circulation of Money in Post-liberation Chaoshan and the Activities of the *Qiaopi* Trade, Together with Materials Provided by Remittances"). In Wang Weizhong, ed., 461–9.

Wang, Shuo. 2006. "The 'New Social History' in China: The Development of Women's History." *The History Teacher* 39 (3): 315–23.

Wang Weizhong 王炜中, ed. 2004. *Shou jie qiaopi wenhua yanjiu hui lunwen ji* (*The First Research Symposium on Qiaopi Culture*). Shantou: Chaoshan lishi wenhua yanjiu zhongxin.

———. 2006. "Taiguo qiaopi yu Chaoshan qiaoxiang de miqie guanxi" ("The Close Relationship between Thailand's *Qiaopi* and Chaoshan's *Qiaoxiang*"). In Hong Lin and Li Daogang, eds., 61–72.

———. 2007. *Chaoshan qiaopi* (*Chaoshan Qiaopi*). Guangzhou: Guangdong Renmin chuban she.

———. 2008. "Chaoshan qiaopi yuan heri yu Huizhou qiyue pimei??" ("The *qiaopi* origins rival those of the Huizhou contracts"), in Wang Weizhong, ed., 2008, pp. 195-207.

———, ed. 2008. *Di erjie qiaopi wenhua yantao hui lunwen xuan* (*Selection of Papers from the Second Qiaopi Culture Symposium*). Gongyuan chuban youxian gongsi.

———. 2009. "Chuxi Chaoshan qiaopi de chuantong wenhua de jiyin" ("Preliminary Research into the Genes of Chaoshan's Traditional *Qiaopi* Culture"). In Chen Xiaogang, ed., 50–5.

———, ed. 2010. *Di san jie qiaopi wenhua yantao hui lunwen xuan* (*Third Symposium on Research into Qiaopi Culture*). Hong Kong: Tianma chuban youxian gongsi.

———. 2010a. "Qiaopi wenxian de zhengji yu zhengli" ("The Collecting and Putting in Order of *Qiaopi* Documents"). In Wang Weizhong, ed., 43–53.

———. 2010b. "Wei tigao qiaopi wenhua yanjiu shuiping er bu xie nuli" ("Let's Not Slacken in Our Efforts to Raise the Level of *Qiaopi* Cultural Studies"). In Wang Weizhong, ed., i-vi.

———. 2013. "Qiaopi ju: Zhongguo jinru guoji jinrong shichang de xianxing zhe" ("*Qiaopi* Offices: China's Forerunners in Entering the International Financial Market"). In Zhongguo qiaopi shijie jiyi gongcheng guoji yantao hui zuwei hui, eds., 285-95.

Wang, Xinyang. 2001. *Surviving the City: The Chinese Immigrants Experience in New York City, 1890–1970*. Lanham: Roman and Littlefield.

Wang Zhuchun 王朱唇. 2004. "Kua dai qiaopi yanjiu de fangfa" ("How to Divide *Qiaopi* Studies into Periods"). In Wang Weizhong, ed., 151–7.

———. 2008. "Qiaopi de jinrong yunzuo" ("*Qiaopi* Financial Operations"). In Wang Weizhong, ed., 11–9.

Waters, Johanna. 2005. "Transnational Family Strategies and Education in the Contemporary Chinese Diaspora." *Global Networks* 4 (4): 359–77.

Williams, Michael. 1999a. "Brief Sojourn in Your Native Land: Sydney Links with South China." *Queensland Review* 6 (2): 11–23.

———. 1999b. "Chinese Settlement in NSW: A Thematic History." A Report for the NSW Heritage Office in NSW. http://www.environment.nsw.gov.au/resources/heritagebranch/heritage/chinesehistory.pdf.

———. 2003. "In the Tang Mountains We Have a Big House." *East Asian History* 25-6:85–112.

———. 2004. "Hong Kong and the Pearl River Delta *Qiaoxiang*." *Modern Asian Studies* 38 (2): 257–82.

Wong, Siu-lun. 1985. "The Chinese Family Firm: A Model." *British Journal of Sociology* 36 (1): 58–72.

Wright, Suzanne E. 2015. "Chinese Decorated Letter Papers." In Richter, ed., 97–134.

Wu Baoguo 吴宝国. 2008. "Qiaopi yu qianzhuang ji jinpu yinlou" ("*Qiaopi* and Money Shops and Silver Shops"). In Wang Weizhong, ed., 62–8.

———. 2014. "Qiaopi yu youzheng" ("*Qiaopi* and the Postal Service"). In Zhongguo lishi wenxian yanjiu hui, eds., 199–203.

Wu Hongli 吴鸿丽. 2008. "Chuxi Minnan qiaopi wenhua" ("Preliminary Investigation of Southern Fujian's *Qiaopi* Culture"). In Wang Weizhong, ed., 358–69.

Wu Kuixin 吴奎信. 2004. "Qiaopi chuandi guandao de gengzu yu shutong" ("The Blocking and Dredging of the Channels through Which *Qiaopi* Were Delivered"). In Wang Weizhong, ed., 200–7.

Wu Rongqing 吴榕青, Li Lipeng 李利鹏, and Wang Lisha 王丽莎. 2014. "Chaoan xian Dongfeng Zhang Jieqian jiazu de qiaopi yu koushu shi yanjiu (1906–1986 nian)" ("The *Qiaopi* of the Family of Zhang Jieqian in Dongfeng in Chaoan County and Oral-History Research [1906–1986]"). In Zhongguo lishi wenxian yanjiu hui, eds., 338–52.

Wu Yixiang 吴以湘, ed. 1949. Vol. 2, no. 2, of *Chaozhou xiangxun* ("Chaozhou Village Bulletins"), March 1. Singapore: Chaozhou xiangxun she.

Xia Shuiping 夏水平 and Fang Xuejia 房学嘉. 2004. "Meizhou keshu diqude shuike ye shulüe" ("Discussion of the *Shuike* Trade in the Hakka Region of Meizhou"). In Wang Weizhong, ed., 179–86.

Xia Yuanming 夏远鸣. 2008. "Meizhou keshu diqu de shuike yu qiaopi ye shulüe" ("Short Account of the *Shuike* in the Meizhou Hakka Region"). In Wang Weizhong, ed., 370–90.

Xiamen wenshi ziliao 厦门文史资料 ("Xiamen documentary materials"). 2004 [1983]. No. 5 (December). In Yang Qunxi, ed., 423–40.

Xiao Wenping 肖文评. 2004. "Kejia shancun de shuike, qiaopi, yu qiaoxiang shehui" ("*Shuike*, *Qiaopi*, and *Qiaoxiang* Society in the Hakka Mountain Villages"). In Wang Weizhong, ed., 253–63.

Xiao Wenping 肖文评, Tian Lu 田璐, and Xu Ying 许颖. 2014. "Cong qiaopi kan minguo shiqi Meizhou qiaoxiang yu Yinni diqu jindai jiaoyu de fazhan" ("Looking at the Development of Modern Education in the Meizhou *Qiaoxiang* and the Indonesian Region in the Republican Period from the Point of View of *Qiaopi*"). In Zhongguo lishi wenxian yanjiu hui, eds., 31–45.

Xie Jiaolan 谢娇兰. 2014. "Lunshu qiaopi dui tuidong Chaoshan jingji, wenhua fazhan de yiyi" ("On the Significance of *Qiaopi* for Promoting the Development of Chaoshan Economy and Culture"). In Zhongguo lishi wenxian yanjiu hui, eds., 273–4.

Xinjiapo Shunde Tongxiang Hui 新加坡顺德同乡会, eds. 1948. *Shunde qiaokan*. No. 2 (August). Singapore: Shunde qiaokan she.

Xu Guanghua 徐光华 and Cai Jinhe 蔡金河. 2010. "Lüelun qiaopi dui koutou minsu wenhua de yingxiang" ("On the Influence of *Qiaopi* on Oral Popular Culture"). In Wang Weizhong, ed., 229–35.

Xu Hanjun 许汉钧. 2006. "Tan xiri pilu gaikuang" ("On *Pi* Routes in Former Days"). In Hong Lin and Li Daogang, eds., 97–9.

Xu Jianping 许建平. 2010. "Ying yi lishi wenxian xue lai jiaqiang qiaopi de shouji yu yanjiu" ("We Should Strengthen the Collecting and Study of *Qiaopi* Using Historical Philology"). In Wang Weizhong, ed., 54–65.

Xu Yun 徐云. 2012. "Huaqiao Huaren minjian wenxian duochong jiazhi chutang" ("A Preliminary Study on Varied Values of Non-governmental Overseas and Ethnic Chinese Documents"). *Huaqiao Huaren Lishiyanjiu* 3:12–22.

Yamagishi Takeshi 山岸猛. 2013. *Qiaohui: Xiangdai zhongguo jingji fenxi (Overseas Chinese Remittance: An Analysis of Modern Chinese Economy)*. Translated by Liu Xiaomin 刘晓民. Xiamen: Xiamen daxue chuban she.

Yan Xing 晏星, ed. 1994. *Zhong Hua youzheng fazhan shi (A History of the Development of the Chinese Post Office)*. Taibei: Taiwan shangwu yinshu guan.

Yang, Dean. 2011. "Migrant Remittances." *Journal of Economic Perspectives* 25 (3): 129–51.

Yang, Guobin. 2003. "The Internet and the Rise of a Transnational Chinese Cultural Sphere." *Media, Culture & Society* 25 (4): 469–90.

Yang Jian 杨剑. 2014. "Shixi Chaoshan qiaopi duandai de yiyi ji fangfa" ("Preliminary Analysis of the Meaning and Methodology of the Periodization of Chaoshan's *Qiaopi*"). In Zhongguo lishi wenxian yanjiu hui, eds., 253–60.

Yang Jiancheng 杨建成, ed. 1983. *Sanshi niandai Nanyang Huaqiao qiaohui touzi baogao shu (Report on Investment and Remittances from Overseas Chinese in Southeast Asia in the 1930s)*. Taibei: Zhonghua xueshu yuan nanyang yanjiu suo.

Yang, Mei-hui Mayfair. 1999. "Introduction." *Spaces of Their Own: Women's Public Sphere in Transnational China*, edited by Mei-hui Mayfair Yang, 1–31. Minneapolis: University of Minnesota Press.

Yang Qunxi 杨群熙, ed. 2004. *Chaoshan diqu qiaopi ye ziliao (Materials Concerning the Qiaopi Trade in the Chaoshan Region)*. Shantou: Shantou shi tushu guan.

———. 2004. "Shilun Chao bang qiaopi ju jingying de tedian" ("On the Special Features of the Management of the Chao Gang's Remittance Offices"). In Wang Weizhong, ed., 193–9.

———. 2010. "Jindai Chaoshan qiaopi wuxiang zhongyao jingji jiazhi" ("Five Important Economic Values of Modern Chaoshan *Qiaopi*"). In Wang Weizhong, ed., 94–102.

Yang Ximing 杨锡铭. 2008. "Qiaopi ye de xing shuai yu haiwai Chao ren rentong de bianhua qian shuo" ("The Rise and Fall of the *Qiaopi* Trade and Changes in Overseas Chao People's Identity"). In Wang Weizhong, ed., 279–86.

Yao Ting 姚婷. 2011. "Qiaokan zhong de qiaoxiang shehui yu 'qiao' 'xiang' wangluo—jiyu 1949 nian qian *Xinning zazhi* 'guanggao' lanmu de fenxi" ("*Qiaoxiang* Society and '*Qiao*' and '*Xiang*' Networks in *Qiaokan*—Based on an Analysis of the Advertisement Columns in *Xinning zazhi* before 1949"). *Huaqiao Huaren lishi yanjiu* 4:21–30.

Yao Ting 姚婷 and Mei Weiqiang 梅伟强. 2009. *Bainian qiaokan: "Xinning zazhi" lishi wenhua lun (One Hundred Years of Qiaokan: Xinning Zazhi and Historical Culture)*. Beijing: Zhongguo Huaqiao chuban she.

Ye Fangrong 叶芳蓉 and Yang Huichang 扬惠嫦. 2013. "Shou zang jie de xin gui: Qiaopi" ("A New Treasure of the Archive World: *Qiaopi*"). *Yuan* 2:7–9.

Yee, Paul. 2005. *Chinatown: An Illustrated History of the Chinese Communities of Victoria, Vancouver*. Calgary, Winnipeg, Toronto, Ottawa, Montreal, and Halifax: James Lorimer.

Yen, Ching-hwang. 2013. "Chinese Coolie Emigration." In Chee Beng Tan, ed., 73–88.

Yi Jian 蚁健. 2010. "Xianggang zai qiaopi ye zhong de diwei yu zuoyong" ("The Position and Role of Hong Kong in the *Qiaopi* Trade"). In Wang Weizhong, ed., 381–4.

Yin, Xiao-huang, and Zhiyong Lan. 2004. "Why Do They Give? Chinese American Transnational Philanthropy since the 1970s." In Geithner, Johnson, and Chen, eds., 79–127.

Yong, Ching-Fatt. 2013. *Tan Kah-Kee: The Making of an Overseas Chinese Legend.* Rev. ed. Singapore: World Scientific.

Young, John. 1966. *The Research Activities of the South Manchurian Railway Company, 1907–1945: A History and Bibliography.* New York: Columbia University Press.

Young, Nick, and June Shih. 2004. "Philanthropic Links between the Chinese Diaspora and the People's Republic of China." In Geithner, Johnson, and Chen, eds., 129–75.

Yow, Cheun Hoe. 2013. *Guangdong and Chinese Diaspora: The Changing Landscape of Qiaoxiang.* London: Routledge.

Yuan Ding 袁丁, Chen Liyuan 陈丽园, and Zhong Yunrong 钟运荣. 2014. *Minguo zhengfu dui qiaohui de guanzhi* (*The Republican Government's Control of Remittances*). Guangzhou: Guangdong renmin chuban she.

Yuan Shingyen 袁兴言. 2011. "You yimin juluo dao kuahai zongzhu shehui: 1949nian yiqian de Jinmen Zhushan qiaoxiang" ("From a Migrant Village to a Trans-oceanic Lineage Society: The Zhushan *Qiaoxiang* in Quemoy before 1949"). PhD dissertation, National Taiwan University.

Yuan Shingyen 袁兴言 and Wu Dijia 邬迪嘉. 2012. "Qiaoxiang de jingji huodong yu kongjian yingzao: Yi 1928–1937 nianjian Jinmen Zhushan 'Xianying' qiaokan wei li" ("*Qiaoxiang* Economic Activity and the Creation of Space: The Example of the *Qiaokan Xianying* from Zhushan in Jinmen"). *Guoli Taiwan daxue jianzhu yu chengxiang yanjiu xuebao* 19:65–100.

Zeng Xubo 曾旭波. 2004. "Lüetan anpi de chansheng ji caozuo de fangfa" ("On the Birth and Way of Operating Secret *Pi*"). In Wang Weizhong, ed., 219–31.

———. 2008. "Huaqiao yinhang Xiamen fenhang 1930 niandai qiaohui ye yushi" ("Reflections of Overseas Remittances through the Xiamen Branch of the Overseas-Chinese Bank in the 1930s"). In Wang Weizhong, ed., 152–66.

———. 2010. "Dongnan Ya Chao bang pixin ju de jingying fangshi" ("Southeast Asian Chao People's Way of Managing Remittance Offices"). In Wang Weizhong, ed., 417–27.

———. 2014. "Shilun qiaopi dingyi de jieding" ("On Demarking the Definition of *Qiaopi*"). In Zhongguo lishi wenxian yanjiu hui, eds., 168–75.

Zhang Guoxiong 张国雄. 2010. "Guangdong qiaopi de yichan jiazhi" ("The Heritage Value of Guangdong *Qiaopi*"). In Wang Weizhong, ed., 68–81.

———. 2014. "Qiaoxiang wenhua yanjiu zhilu" ("Paths of *Qiaoxiang* Culture Studies"). In *Zhongguo Qiaoxiang Yanjiu* 1:1–12. Beijing: Zhongguo Huaqiao chuban she.

Zhang Guoxiong 张国雄 and Zhao Hongying 赵红英. 2013. "Qiaopi wenhua de yichan jiazhi" ("The Heritage Value of *Qiaopi* Culture"). In Zhongguo qiaopi shijie jiyi gongcheng guoji yantao hui zuwei hui, eds., 1–11.

Zhang Huimei 张慧梅. 2004. "Zhanzheng zhuangtai xia zhi jinrong yu chuantong renwen wangluo: 1939–1945 nian Chaoshan yu dongnan Ya jian qiaohui liutong yanjiu" ("Finance and Traditional Human Networks in a War Situation: Studying the Circulation of Remittances between Chaoshan and Southeast Asia, 1939–1945"). In *Chaoxue yanjiu* 10, edited by Chaoshan lishi wenhua yanjiu zhongxin, 157–92. Guangzhou: Huacheng chuban she.

Zhang Linyou 张林友. 2014. "Qiaopi dang'an yu Minyue jindai jinrong shi yanjiu: Jiyu shiliao bijiao de fenxi kuangjia" ("Research on the *Qiaopi* Archives and the Modern Financial History of Fujian and Guangdong: An Analytical Framework on the Basis of a Comparison of Historical Materials"). In Zhongguo lishi wenxian yanjiu hui, eds., 223–7.

Zhang Meisheng 张美生. 2014. "Shilun 'qiaopi dang'an' de baohu yu yanjiu" ("On Preserving and Studying the '*Qiaopi* Archive'"). In Zhongguo lishi wenxian yanjiu hui, eds., 292–5.

Zhang Mingshan 张明汕. 2006. "Qiaopi ye zhe jianfu lishi shiming" ("*Qiaopi* Traders Shoulder a Historical Responsibility"). In Hong Lin and Li Daogang, eds., 101–4.

Zhang Shuoren 张朔人. 2013. "Minguo shiqi Hainan qiaohui wenti shulun" ("On Some Questions Regarding Hainan Overseas Remittances in the Republican Period"). In *Hainan yimin lunwenji (Collection of Essays on Hainan Emigration)*, edited by Hainan wenhua yanjiu zhongxin. Singapore: Xinjiapo Hainan wenhua zhongxin.

Zhang Xing 张行. 2013. "Kangzhan shiqi de Minyue qiaopi ye yanjiu" ("Researching the Fujian-Guangdong *Qiaopi* Trade in the Period of the War of Resistance"). In Zhongguo qiaopi shijie jiyi gongcheng guoji yantao hui zuwei hui, eds., 326–37.

Zheng, Songhui. 2008. "Developing Oral History in Chinese Libraries." *Journal of Academic Librarianship* 34 (1): 74–8.

Zheng Yisheng 郑一省. 2013. "Guangxi Rongxian qiaohui zhuang de jingying moshi ji wangluo chutan" ("Exploring the Management Model of Remittance Shops in Guangxi's Rongxian and Networks"). In Zhongguo qiaopi shijie jiyi gongcheng guoji yantao hui zuwei hui, eds., 308–18.

Zheng Youguo 郑有国. 2013. "Heigeer 'haiyang wenhua' chanshi" ("Expounding Hegel's Notion of 'Oceanic Culture'"). *Minshang wenhua yanjiu (Studies on Southern Fujian's Entrepreneurial Culture)* 7 (1): 60–9.

Zhongguo lishi wenxian yanjiu hui, Shantou shi Chaoshan lishi wenhua yanjiu zhongxin 中国历史文献研究会，汕头市潮汕历史文化研究中心, eds. 2014. *Shijie jiyi yichan: Qiaopi dang'an yanjiu hui lunwen ji (World Memory Heritage: Collection of Papers from the Qiaopi Archive Symposium)*. Shantou: n.p.

Zhongguo qiaopi shijie jiyi gongcheng guoji yantao hui zuwei hui 中国侨批世界记忆工程国际研讨会组委会, eds. 2013. *Lunwen ji (Conference Papers Collection)*. Beijing: n.p.

Zou Jinsheng 邹金盛. 2010. "Chenghai ren kaishe de qiaopi ju" ("The *Qiaopi* Offices Opened by Chenghai People"). In Wang Weizhong, ed., 402–12.

Zhou, Min. 1992. *Chinatown: The Socioeconomic Potential of an Urban Enclave*. Philadelphia: Temple University Press.

———. 2009. *Contemporary Chinese America: Immigration, Ethnicity, and Community Transformation*. Philadelphia: Temple University Press.

Zhou, Min, and Li Xiangyi. 2016. "Remittances for Collective Consumption and Social Status Compensation: Variations on Transnational Practices among Chinese International Migrants." *International Migration Review* (April). doi:10.1111/imre.12268.

Zou Qiudong 邹求栋 and Su Tonghai 苏通海. 2009. "Shuo 'huipi'" ("About '*Huipi*'"). In Chen Xiaogang, ed., 70–4.

Zurndorfer, Harriet Thelma. 1995. *Chinese Bibliography: A Research Guide to Reference Works about China Past and Present*. Amsterdam: Brill.

INDEX

admonition, letters of, 172–74
agents, independent *(lianhao),* 49
Alfred Holt & Co., 35
America letters, 171–72
Americas: Chinese "native" banks, 104; migrant mobility in, 92; *shuike* (couriers), 34, 94. *See also* Canada; North America; United States
Amoy University, 137
Anderson, Benedict, 71, 72, 77, 179
anpi (secret *pi*), 16
anti-Japanese movement, 11
Anxi, 138
archives, of *qiaopi,* 19–21, 24–25; decoding *qiaopi,* methodology for, 27–32; digitization of, 28–29, 32; *qiaopi* scholarship since 2013, 25–27
arrival narratives, 168
Australia: banking system, 87; Guangfu *qiaopi,* geographic differences, 92–94; postal system, 87; *qiaopi,* geographic differences, 86–87, 108, 220n4

baixin (letter without money), 7. *See also* letters *(pixin)*
Baker, Christopher, 131
balance of payments, 105–9, 106*tab*
bang (dialect groups), 8, 61, 64
banghao (shipment number), 8

Bangkok, 56*map,* 83*map*; banking system, 104; *piju,* institutionalization of trade, 40, 82; postwar years (1945-1949), 123; Sino-Japanese War (1937-45), 116
banking system: Australia *qiaopi,* geographic differences, 93; Bank of China, efforts to control *qiaopi* trade, 89–90, 91, 96–97, 101–2; Bank of China, founding of, 96–97; clan banks, Australia, 92–93; collaborations with *piju,* 102–4; evolution of, *qiaopi* and, 95–104, 177; foreign banks in China, 96; in Hakka counties, 85; history of, 7; in Hong Kong, 107–8; interest paid on *piju* accounts, 102; international finance system, evolution of, 103; modernization of China, 180; North America and Australia *qiaopi* trade, 86–87; overseas banks, *qiaopi* trade and, 96; *piaohao* banks, 107; *piju,* institutionalization of trade, 43–46; *piju,* operational model, 48–52; postwar years (1945-1949), 118–24; *qiaopi* business model, evolution of, 67–70; during Sino-Japanese War (1937-45), 111–14, 116–17, 118; stores as banks, 41; *taobi* (financial evasion), 90–91; Tianyi, history of, 54–58, 56*map*; Wing On Bank, 93
Bank of China: Communists, *qiaopi* and, 126, 127, 128–29; efforts to control *qiaopi* trade, 89–90, 91, 96–97, 101–2; founding of, 96–97; postwar years (1945-1949), 118, 119–22; *qiaopi*

Bank of China *(continued)*
business model, evolution of, 70; Sino-Japanese War (1937–45), 110, 111; Wuyi,
qiaopi trade in, 87–88, 89
baojia system, 60
Batavia (Jakarta): *hantar* system, 67–68;
network-based associations, 62; religious
charity, 144; *shuike* (couriers), 35, 36, 39
Beijing: charitable associations, 143; modernization of China, 180; regulation and control of
qiaopi trade, 63, 79, 101, 148
Beijing Convention (1860), 6, 40
Beiyang government: efforts to control *qiaopi*,
96; regulation and control of *qiaopi* trade, 101
bianhao (serial number), 8, 12
boardinghouses, 41–42, 96
book-keeping barter, 103
bowing letters, 165
bridges, *qiaopi* charity and, 140–41
Buddha-face silver, 148
Buddhism, charitable giving, 143–46
Burma, 111
business investment, *qiaopi* uses, 135
business model, *qiaopi* trade, 66–70. *See also*
trade networks
Business Revitalization campaign, 11

Cai Quan, 136
calligraphy, 10, 158–59
Cambodia, 83*map*; network-based associations,
61; Sino-Japanese War (1937–45), 116
Canada: Communists, *qiaopi* and, 128; education, schools movement, 138; European
migrants, 170; mobility of Chinese migrants,
11, 92; Wuyi *qiaopi*, geographic differences,
86–92. *See also* North America
canceling the number *(xiaohao)*, 8
capitalism. *See* Chinese capitalism, *qiaopi* trade
as form of
Center for the Study of Chaoshan History and
Culture, 23
chains *(lianhao)* of independent agents, 49
chaitou (boss, messenger boss), 59
Chaoshan: Center for the Study of Chaoshan
History and Culture, 23; *Collections of
Chaoshan Qiaopi* (2015), 25; Communists,
qiaopi and, 128; companies that ran *qiaopi*
trade, 17; dates, decoding *qiaopi*, 28; education, schools movement, 137; famine in, 116;
maritime (oceanic) culture, 80; natural disasters, charitable giving for, 141; network-based
associations, 62; *pi*, meaning of, 15, 16; *piju*,

institutionalization of trade, 40; *piju*, role in
economy, 50–51; postwar years (1945-1949),
119, 120, 122; *qiaopi*, geographic differences,
178; *qiaopi* archives, 23, 24, 25; remittance
trade data collection, 24; *shuike* (couriers),
35; Sino-Japanese War (1937–45), 115, 116;
Zeng Yangmei, 140
Chaoyang, 110
Chaozhou: *bang* (dialect groups), 61; natural disasters, charitable giving for, 141–42; *qiaopi*,
China's economy and, 107
Chaozhou-Meixian Committee, 125
Chaozhou zhi (Chaozhou gazetteer), 24, 75
chapbook, 155
charitable giving: charity, definitions of, 131,
132–33; donations from *qiaopi* managers and
shop owners, 237n19; family and kinship
definitions, 236–37n10; historical and insti-
tutional perspective, 148–49; national cause
and the state, 141–43; *qiaopi* and, 130–35;
religious charity and modern philanthropy,
143–46; six main issues of focus, 135; transformations in the *qiaoxiang*, 146–49
Chatterjee, Partha, 72
Chen Chenliu, 40
Chen Chunsheng, 23
Chen Ta, 24
Chenghai, 42, 75, 101, 131, 135, 142
Chen Jiageng, 137
Chen Xunxian, 54
Chen Zhifang, 115–16, 117
Chiang Kai-shek, 107, 141, 180
chidanshui (freshwater eaters), 15
China and Chinese culture, 83*map*; business
culture of diaspora, 66–67; calendar and
festivals, 51; citizenship requirements, 15;
decoding *qiaopi*, methodology for, 27–32;
domestic Overseas Chinese status, 20;
emigration, restrictions on, 24; family and
kinship definitions, 236–37n10; formal and
informal networks, 228–29n11; historical
resources, types of, 30–31, 180–81; kinship institutions, 20, 42; maritime (oceanic) culture,
77–81; mass-based investigation, 21; network-
based associations, 60–65; privacy rights,
29; *qiaokan* (overseas Chinese magazines)
phenomenon, 70–77; *qiaopi* and general
economy, 104–9, 106*tab*; *qiaopi* scholarship
since 2013, 25–27; regard for written word,
20; remittance data, World Bank, 5–6; social
and regional history (before 2013), 21–25;
social structures and document retrieval,

www.ingramcontent.com/pod-product-compliance
Lightning Source LLC
Chambersburg PA
CBHW020504270326
41926CB00008B/740